THE LOCATION OF FOREIGN DIRECT INVESTMENT

The Location of Foreign Direct Investment

Geographic and business approaches

Edited by
MILFORD B. GREEN
The University of Western Ontario

ROD B. MCNAUGHTON
The University of Lethbridge

Avebury
Aldershot · Brookfield USA · Hong Kong · Singapore · Sydney

Published by
Avebury
Ashgate Publishing Ltd
Gower House
Croft Road
Aldershot
Hants GU11 3HR
England

Ashgate Publishing Company
Old Post Road
Brookfield
Vermont 05036
USA
Reprinted 1996
British Library Cataloguing in Publication Data

Location of Foreign Direct Investment:
Geographic and Business Approaches
I. Green, Milford B. II. McNaughton, Rod B.
332.672

ISBN 1 85972 067 6

Library of Congress Catalog Card Number: 95-78421

Printed and bound by Athenaeum Press, Ltd.,
Gateshead, Tyne & Wear.

Contents

Figures and tables

Contributors

Gabriel R. G. Benito, Department of Marketing and Logistics, Norwegian School of Management, N-1300, Sandvika, Norway.

David M. Dahm, Indian and Northern Affairs Canada, Information Quality and Research, Room 1008, 10 Wellington Street, Ottawa, Ontario, Canada, K1A 0H4.

David W. Edgington, Department of Geography, The University of British Columbia, Vancouver, British Columbia, Canada, V6T 1Z2.

Prescott C. Ensign, Department of Administrative Sciences, Graduate School of Management, Kent State University, Kent, Ohio, USA, 44242-0001.

Milford B. Green, Department of Geography, University of Western Ontario, London, Ontario, Canada, N6A 5C2.

Geir Gripsrud, Department of Marketing and Logistics, Norwegian School of Management, N-1300, Sandvika, Norway.

Thomas R. Leinbach, Department of Geography, University of Kentucky, Lexington, Kentucky, USA, 40506-0027.

Peter Liesch, Faculty of Business, University of Southern Queensland, Toowoomba, Queensland, Australia, 4350.

M. Wayne Marr, Department of Finance, Clemson University, Clemson, South Carolina, USA, 29634.

Rod B. McNaughton, Department of Geography, University of Lethbridge, Lethbridge, Alberta, Canada, T1K 3M4.

Stephen Meyer, Department of Geography, The University of Western Ontario, London, Ontario, Canada, N6A 5C2.

Sanjeev Mohta, Department of Finance, Clemson University, Clemson, South Carolina, USA, 29634.

Kee-Bom Nahm, Department of Geography, University of Saskatchewan, Saskatoon, Saskatchewan, Canada, S7N 0W0.

Breandán Ó hUallacháin, Department of Geography, Arizona State University, Tempe, Arizona, USA, 85287.

Mike W. Peng, Department of Management, College of Business Administration, University of Hawai'i at Mānoa, Honolulu, Hawai'i, USA, 96822.

Tao Qu, Department of Geography, The University of Western Ontario, London, Ontario, Canada, N6A 5C2.

Neil Reid, Department of Geography and Planning, The University of Toledo, Toledo, Ohio, USA, 43606.

R. Keith Semple, Department of Geography, University of Saskatchewan, Saskatoon, Saskatchewan, Canada, S7N 0W0.

Andrew Solocha, Department of Marketing, The University of Toledo, Toledo, Ohio, USA, 43606.

Michael J. Spivey, Department of Finance, Clemson University, Clemson, South Carolina, USA, 29634.

Ewan Sutherland, Centre for Informatics, University of Wales, Lampeter, Wales, SA48 7ED.

April Wright, Faculty of Commerce, University of Southern Queensland, Toowoomba, Queensland, Australia, 4350.

Preface

Rod B. McNaughton
Milford B. Green

June 1995

This volume concerns the location of transnational corporations (TNCs) and their foreign direct investments (FDIs). This is an important topic as a major part of worldwide economic activity is organized within TNCs. In its *World Investment Report - 1994*, the United Nations Conference on Trade and Development reported that there are more than 37,000 TNCs. These firms control one third of world output, and one third of world trade. The largest 100 TNCs have $US3.4 trillion in assets, of which approximately $US1.3 trillion is held outside of their home countries. Further, TNCs employ over 73 million people, nearly 10% of worldwide non-agricultural employment.

One of the salient characteristics of the foreign investments made by TNCs is their location. While the phrase 'globalization of economic activity' may give the impression of ubiquitous international flows of investment, FDI has distinct and often concentrated spatial patterns. These are created by the investment decisions of TNCs which react to differences in regional growth rates, labour costs, availability of skilled labour and technology, government regulations, and the incentives offered by locations hoping to attract investment.

The locational aspect of FDI is evident in almost all studies of the behaviour of international firms, their investment decisions, and economic impacts. However, the way in which this variable is manifest, the importance attached to it, and the appropriate scale of analysis varies considerably between researchers and the academic paradigms in which they operate. In one study, location may be represented by the unique combination of characteristics that attract a firm to a particular city or site. In another, the important aspect of a location may simply be its distance from other places - a significant determinant of transportation costs. In yet another study, large regions might be compared to assess the economic impacts of FDI. Indeed, location may not even be defined in the traditional sense of place or physical space, but might be measured on a scale such as the relative cultural proximity between business environments.

One of the more noticeable differences in the treatment of 'location' as a variable is between economic geographers, and researchers in economics or management disciplines. The difference is one of emphasis - for geographers, location is paramount. An economist, for example, might use the concept of transaction costs to explaining why firms enter foreign markets through direct investment. An economic geographer would not be as concerned with the entry mode choice itself, but with how distance reduces the efficiency of monitoring contracts, thus increasing transaction costs, or how an externally controlled direct investment impacts the local economy.

As a practical matter, the level of research interaction between economic geographers and those in economics and management disciplines is unfortunately low. The pattern of research citations between disciplines reveals a 'one-way flap' where theoretical developments in economics and management disciplines are adopted and influence geographic research, but the reverse is seldom the case. Indeed, surprise is often expressed at the extent of FDI research that is undertaken by economic geographers. Similarly, economic geographers sometimes fail to appreciate the extent to which empirical work in economics and management can be 'geographic'.

The goal of this book is to illustrate the variety of ways in which the concept of location is important in the study of FDI. This is not accomplished by a systematic analysis of the concept of 'location' in FDI research. Rather a collection of original research papers is presented which are examples of different approaches to studying the location of FDI. Some of the chapters advance the theory of FDI, some provide empirical tests of existing theories, and others describe patterns of FDI in a particular region, or sector. Contributors come from a variety of disciplinary backgrounds, including: marketing, administrative science, finance, commerce, management, informatics, and economic geography.

The volume contains twelve chapters, the first two of which provide reviews of the extant literature on the location of FDI. In Chapter One Stephen Meyer and Tao Qu review the way in which FDI theories have been interpreted and empirically tested by economic geographers. Their review categorizes the literature into studies of host country, and home country relationships. The importance to the first group of Dunning's eclectic approach, and to the second group of Porter's diamond theory is evident as both explicitly consider the impact of locational characteristics on FDI. The second chapter, authored by Prescott Ensign, describes the variety of explanations for foreign direct investment that have emerged from economics and management disciplines, and relates the potential locational implications of each. While some of these approaches are well known in economic geography, others (such as appropriability theory and strategic management approaches) are less familiar, and provide additional insight on certain locational issues.

The third chapter, by Mike Peng, provides an example of how one of these theories can add to our understanding of the FDI phenomenon. Drawing on the strategic management literature, Peng argues that a third tenet, the option for organizational learning and innovation, should be added to existing theories of FDI which focus on comparative advantage and market imperfections. Peng develops a rationale for the attraction of FDI into high wage countries such as the United States, arguing that the motivation for such investment is access to technological and organizational innovations that offer options for future organizational growth and learning.

The following chapter, by Gabriel Benito and Geir Gripsrud, is an empirical study of FDI which attempts to explain the distance between the home country of an investor company and the location of its foreign investment. Following the internationalization process model, they posit a positive relationship between measures of the distance between home and host countries of an investment, and the levels of international experience, operation specific experience, and resources of the investing company. Their hypotheses are tested for a set of 203 investments made by Norwegian manufacturing firms in 1984. The dependent variable 'distance' is measured three ways: cultural distance, economic distance and physical distance. Interestingly, while the results provide limited support for the internationalization process approach, a strong positive relationship is found between operation specific experience and geographic distance. The authors interpret this as evidence that experience may be a determinant of FDI location decisions.

Chapters Five through Nine provide descriptions of foreign direct investment activities in particular regions or countries. In Chapter Five, Ewan Sutherland presents an historical account of foreign direct investment by electronics firms in Scotland. This chapter illustrates government efforts to actively promote 'place' advantages to foreign investors, and the impacts of foreign direct investment on a peripheral region with a developed economy.

Chapters Six and Seven concern Japanese FDI in North America. David Edgington profiles the investments of Japanese manufacturing firms in the Southern Ontario region. His chapter is based on interviews with executives from 39 Japanese owned firms. He identifies four groups of firms based on their motivation for locating in Ontario, and their view of the North American market under NAFTA. Insight into these different types of firms is provided through representative case studies. Neil Reid, Andrew Solocha and Breandán Ó hUallacháin describe the organizational structure of Japanese firms into *keiretsu*, enterprise groups, and vertical distribution groups. They explain how these relationship structures influence the investment patterns of Japanese automobile assembly and component parts manufacturers in the United States. This investment is dominated by greenfield plants, located in small towns, and concentrated in a few midwestern and upper southern states. The authors argue that this pattern reflects a desire to maintain long term relationships with component parts suppliers, and attempts to locate in areas where they can replicate the employee and labour-management relationships experienced in Japan. This chapter suggests an interesting link between industrial organization and the location of FDI.

In Chapter Eight, Wayne Marr, Sanjeev Mohta and Michael Spivey provide an empirical test of real sector imperfection models of FDI motives. Using a database of US firms that were the targets of foreign takeovers between 1975 and 1987, and comparing them with similar firms that were not taken over, and a group of firms that were taken over by domestic bidders, they asses whether or not imperfections in pre-takeover product and factor markets contribute to foreign acquisition. In comparison to the control groups, firms taken over by foreign bidders are found to be smaller, have a high degree of marketing skills, are in mature low R and D sectors, and have low levels of intangible assets. The authors conclude that these results are consistent with the notion that foreign investors are motivated by real sector imperfections. Thus, foreign takeovers are motivated by the desire to expand quickly in the US market, and to obtain synergistic gains by acquiring targets in which they can make use of their own intangible assets. This chapter illustrates: (1) the link between merger and acquisition theory and FDI theory, and (2) the motives of foreign investors in an advanced economy like the US.

Chapter Nine, written by Thomas Leinbach, describes the liberalization and trade reform efforts of Indonesia, and relates these changes in the business environment to the changing pattern of FDI in that country. This chapter provides insight into the relationships between patterns of trade and FDI, and the effects of FDI on a developing nation.

Chapters Ten and Eleven concern patterns of FDI in the banking industry. These chapters illustrate the patterns of FDI in a service sector that is being rapidly deregulated in many countries. April Wright and Peter Liesch use the case of Australia to illustrate the entrance of foreign banks into a previously protected domestic market. The foreign entrants have not performed as well as their owners had hoped. Almost ten years after being allowed into the market, they are still less profitable than the established domestic banks. The authors interpret this in terms of changes in the locational advantage of Australia that constrain the ability of foreign banks to effectively exploit their ownership and internationalization advantages. In Chapter Eleven, Dahm and Green add to our understanding of transnational banking through an empirical analysis of the branch networks of the world's largest 250 banks. Using multidimensional scaling they produce maps of the leading and emerging financial centres in 1976 and 1986. They attribute the significant growth in branch banking activity during that period to the need for more efficient export of capital to nonsaturated markets abroad.

Finally, in Chapter Twelve, Kee-Bom Nahm and Keith Semple discuss the way in which FDI flows are changing the spatial structure of the quaternary sector. They argue that the cities which house the corporate headquarters of transnational firms are nodal points in world wide control, information, communication, and financial networks. They combine quaternary place theory, which is explicitly spatial, with industrial network theory which is grounded in organizational theory, to form a unique explanation of the consequences of investment patterns on the position of cities in the market for corporate control and economic prominence. Their empirical analyses of TNC headquarters location changes between 1974 and 1991 show a decline in importance of American cities, and a rise in the importance of Japanese centres. By 1991 international control was centred on Tokyo, London, and New York, with a second tier of mid-sized American, European and Asian cities.

While each of the above described chapters is a valuable contribution to the discipline of its author, we ask the reader not to evaluate the volume in disciplinary terms. It is our contention that the value of this volume lies in the juxtaposition of an eclectic mix of approaches, each concerned with the central theme of 'the location of FDI'. We hope that readers who are active in FDI research will find inspiration for cross disciplinary approaches by comparing chapters authored by researchers from different disciplines, in particular, between management disciplines and economic geography.

1 Place-specific determinants of FDI: The geographical perspective

Stephen Meyer and Tao Qu

Introduction

A considerable amount of work has been done in an effort to better understand the spatial distribution, characteristics and effects of foreign direct investment (FDI) as well as on attempting to more completely address the factors that influence the investment decisions of multinational enterprises (MNEs). Most FDI-related studies have used an implicit geographical-slant to what has generally been considered a topic exclusively grounded within the business or economics disciplines. The intent of this chapter is to highlight the contribution of geography to the FDI question by emphasizing the importance of place-specific attributes within the MNE decision's process, discussing the role FDI has in fostering regional development, and providing a literature review of empirical studies of FDI that have used statistical substantiation to confirm observed location patterns.

According to the US Department of Commerce, foreign direct investment is defined as: 'the movement of long-term capital to finance business activities abroad, whereby investors control at least 10% of the enterprise' (Poniachek, 1986, p. 21). Any foreign investment, then, with less than ten per cent controlling interest is generally considered a portfolio investment. Therefore, FDI is distinguished from other types of foreign market penetration by an MNE's intent to control. These controlled investments in foreign destinations take the form of subsidiaries (incorporated subordinate companies) or branch plants (unincorporated extensions of the parent company) and are typically formed through various greenfield, acquisition, merger or joint-venture business constructs.

The rapid growth of all forms of FDI and the expanding role of corporations that service one or more foreign markets in the post World War II era has become increasingly important over time. The average annual growth in the stock of direct investment during the 1970s was around 22 per cent and by 1984 the global book value of direct investment was estimated at $600 billion (Poniachek, 1986, p. 1). Poniachek also found that (nearly three-fourths) of direct investment is in Organization for Economic Cooperation and Development (OECD) countries with the remaining 25 per cent or so being centred in Less Developed Countries (LDCs).

Since the mid-1970s, multinationals have continued to grow in importance. Carnoy (1993, p. 49) found that the sales from the top 50 largest industrial multinationals grew at an average annual rate of 3.5% from 1975 to 1990 ($540 billion in sales to $2.1 trillion, respectively). By comparison,

> ... the US economy grew at a 2.8% rate over the same period, and the economies of the OECD averaged a 2.9% per cent rate of growth. Put a different way, sales of the fifty largest industrial multinationals were 28 per cent of US GNP in 1975 and 39 per cent of US GNP in 1989 (Carnoy, 1993, p. 49).

This trend towards more intense internationalization of investment has been suggested to be a result of two global developments: an increasing need for growth-seeking MNEs to expand markets and a simultaneous rise in national pressures for protectionism in trade (Gordon and Lees, 1986, p. 9). Although much of the theory explaining FDI and the ever-rising prominence of multinational corporations within the global economy still supports these corporate growth and tariff-jumping ideas, other scenarios have emerged as well. At this point, a more comprehensive discussion concerning why firms invest directly in foreign destinations may be of value. Generally, the levels of FDI within specific locations or originating out of a specific location relate to attributes of the host or home country, respectively.

Theories of the MNE and host country relationships

Dunning's 'eclectic' approach to the theory of FDI

Although ideas of market imperfection ideas remain fundamental to foreign investment study, there has been a more recent shift in emphasis away from neoclassical economic FDI theory to specifically understanding the nature of the multinational firm (Calvet, 1981, pp. 43-56). Specifically, FDI was modelled to be a result of an MNE's inherent drive to access and retain knowledge. Yet, the role of location, although often not emphasized, has remained integral within this 'behaviour of the firm' theoretical shift.

In his eclectic approach to the theory of FDI, John Dunning (1977) provided a consolidation of the literature and specified a set of conditions required if a firm is to engage in FDI (see Rugman, Lecraw and Booth, 1985, pp. 117-20). According to Dunning's model, a firm is theoretically unlikely to invest directly in a foreign country if any one of the firm-specific, internalization or country-specific advantages is not intact.

A multinational's firm-specific advantage (FSA), according to Dunning, is largely in the form of intangible assets (such as knowledge or ideas) and are exclusive to the firm possessing them. Such advantages could include: a unique technology (that improves production or distribution), large company size (most multinationals are large and efficient through economies of scale cost savings), or the contributions of a key manager (sometimes a company's true advantage can be traced back to the actions of one extremely dynamic individual). In general terms, a FSA can be thought of as some 'competitive edge' that a would-be direct investor has vis-a-vis other similar firms operating in a given foreign destination. Essentially, it is this firm-specific advantage (in some form or another) that gives multinationals the ability to compete with local firms and therefore the inclination to keep it privately known (through internalization).

Dunning's idea of internalization relates to the multinational's unique ability to insulate its FSA from competitors. This can be achieved through trademarks and patents but is also attainable by, as MNEs are apt in doing, establishing foreign subsidiaries and enclosing the production and/or distribution process (through vertical and/or horizontal integration). Internalization also allows for transfer pricing (or the 'price' that is set on product, capital or royalties interflowing among parent and subsidiary entities within the MNE). Often there is motivation for a given MNE to deflect resources away from, and under-price intermediate products within, countries with high tax rates - even if this does not accurately reflect a given subsidiary's level of performance.

One more point should be made regarding a multinational's assumed need to internalize its competitive advantages. This notion makes the implicit assumption that it is more beneficial for the enterprise possessing these advantages to internalize them through subsidiaries than to sell or lease them to foreign firms (such as through licensing, franchising, technical service agreements or subcontracts). If the dissipation of the FSA is not a major concern, or if (using Vernon's product cycle analogy) the product has become completely standardized, then licensing-type arrangements may be a more desirable choice of action (Vernon, 1966; Rugman, Lecraw and Booth, 1985, pp. 117-18).

Finally, Dunning concluded, once a firm has the ability and inclination to internalize its FSA, it must then decide where geographically it is going set up foreign subsidiaries and consider country-specific advantages (CSAs). Presumably, locations that are most frequently chosen as host sites are those that allow for the most profitable use of a MNE's FSA. A host of factors are assumed to be important for inducing FDI in a host country. As summarized by Dunning (1973, p. 297), factors usually included in survey studies fall into the following categories:

1. Market factors which not only include market size and growth potential, but also include the ability to maintain market share and the promotion of trade between the subsidiary and parent company,

2. Trade barriers,

3. Cost factors which encompass various factors influencing cost of production (such as labour and the achievement of economies of scale), and

4. The investment climate which consists mainly of political stability, general attitude towards FDI, incentives and disincentives of host countries.

As Dunning reports, these survey studies 'stress the host government's attitude to inward foreign investment, political stability, and the prospects of market growth as the most important considerations prompting foreign activities' (1973, p. 295).

In summary, Dunning predicted that if a corporation has a firm-specific advantage, is able to internalize this advantage, and can benefit from specific host country attributes; then FDI will occur.

FDI and host country regional development

Reuber (1973, pp. 73-81) provided an adequate classification scheme that justifies FDI from the perspective of a MNE's relationship with the host nation and its regional economic development potential. He saw a MNE's decision to invest directly as originating out of three control-based motivations: either the investment decision is export-oriented, market development-induced, or government-initiated.

A multinational firm that invests with an export-oriented ploy is typically attempting to secure new sources of inputs. Often these inputs are in the form of raw materials or component parts, but can as well be finished products. Investments such as these are often made in LDCs where cost-savings can be realized through relatively less expensive labour and/or abundant resources. Interestingly, in this scenario, the MNE is often not inclined to service the host country's market at all.

> Generally, such foreign investors are mainly interested in extracting the product in question from the host country and selling (exporting) it through established market channels (Reuber, 1973, p. 73).

Thus, in export-oriented FDI, the firm's over-riding motivation for making the investment decision is to protect or improve its competitive position through more cost-effective vertical integration.

In contrast, the distinguishing feature of the market development-type of investment is to unambiguously cater to the host market (or to horizontally integrate its operations). As a result, host-specific considerations (such as the size of the local market and its long-run potential, local production costs, tariffs and trade controls, taxes, subsidies, and so forth) become vital issues for the MNE. Essentially, FDI takes place to develop (or to compete within) the foreign market often through the implementation of a new technology. Because of this and the fact that profit is not usually realized in the short-term of this long process of market development, this type of investment is often cited as the 'healthiest' form of FDI because of the MNE's inclination for a more long-term relationship with the host country.

The third classification of FDI as identified by Reuber is government-initiated investment where the MNE is enticed into the host nation via some type of government subsidy. Clearly, this is a regional development strategy closely akin to the growth-pole analogy and is meant to increase employment opportunities, add to domestic output, and stimulate the economy through linkages to other sectors and activities (Reuber, 1973, p. 78).

In efforts to improve the national level of well-being, it has often been the case that governments of LDCs have pursued a policy of encouraging external investment - even if it has meant forgoing some control over the domestic economy. The use of industrial incentives aimed at foreign investors has not been limited to just LDCs. Many state governments in the US have been highly competitive in their pursuit of foreign capital and, as such, have offered extensive business incentive packages (such as tax grants and soft loans) (Price Waterhouse, 1993).

Local linkages and technology transfer

To summarize, the positive direct impacts of FDI on a host economy are distributed mainly through three channels (Reuber, 1973). The first is via tax payments from FDI to the host government. The second is through the outlays of foreign affiliates on the host economy which directly increase the income of local factors of production. The third is via increased output, exports, and employment. The indirect impacts which are experienced by society as a whole are of great variety, such as the transfer of technology and the various spill-over effects caused by the presence of foreign investment through their linkages with the local economy (Reuber, 1973; Lall, 1978; Caves, 1974).

Although it is hard to measure, the level of integration foreign subsidiaries have within the local economy is usually used to assess the impact of FDI. It is logical to believe that a local economy will benefit more if foreign firms create extensive backward and forward linkages with local firms. It may be that foreign affiliates on average display a lower level of integration with the local economy than domestically-owned firms do, but many other factors affect the extent of local linkages beyond the 'nationality' of the business.

It is difficult to draw simple conclusions about the linkage impact of FDI on a host economy, especially when different case studies are involved (Schive and Majumdar, 1990; Stewart, 1976). On one hand, the extent of local linkages depends on the characteristics of the actual direct investment; such as its ownership characteristics, type of investment, technological structure, product type and diversity, and method of entry (Reuber, 1973; Lall, 1978; Ó hUallacháin, 1984). On the other hand, the extent of linkage creation also depends on the characteristics of the local economy. As such, a country's stage of industrial development, technological capabilities, industrial policies and regulatory framework for FDI all contribute to the linkage behaviour of foreign affiliates within the economy (Lall, 1978, p. 223).

Given the important role that many MNEs play in fostering both innovation and the application of advanced industrial technologies and the increasing importance of technology in economic development, the transfer of technology has been considered the crux of FDI-host country relationships (Quinn, 1969; Johnson, 1970). This issue has also sparked much controversy. It has been alleged that MNEs are either unduly restrictive in the transmission of modern technologies, or responsible for transferring inappropriate technologies into developing countries. Part of the reason for this controversy has to do with the complexity of technology transfer which is considered to be 'a bundle of information, rights, and services' (Contractor, 1981, p.115).

Yet, even if MNEs are willing to render their technology, the effective transfer is still largely conditional on the following four circumstances inherent to a given host country's economy (Baranson, 1970; Contractor, 1981). First, the most appropriate technology (if it involves a means of labour-saving) depends on the degree of substitutability between capital and labour within the production process. Second, the appropriateness of a technology not only depends on the condition of production factors in a host country, but it also rests on the location's market potential. Essentially, a host country with a large market is more likely to successfully adopt an advanced technology. Third, the existing technological structure of the host economy is another critical component that can affect its capability to absorb the imported technology. Fourth, under certain circumstances, government intervention may also be crucial in the successful transfer of technology. Local government can not only motivate and directly assist a local firm in the assimilation of a major technology, but can also help upgrade its related suppliers to competitive levels (Li and Qu, 1989).

Therefore, because of these location-specific attributes of the host country that can affect its ability to assimilate a new technology and to develop extensive local linkages, the benefits of FDI will vary spatially. In particular, there has been considerable controversy about the extent to which developing countries benefit from FDI. Some of the common negative externalities that can arise through FDI includes the following:

1. the development of a foreign enclave within the host countries with little or no economic contact with the local economy,
2. the failure to adequately develop domestic research and to fully adapt imported technology to local conditions, and
3. the inadequate efforts made to train and develop local managerial and technical talents (Reuber, 1973, p.20)

Also, from a national perspective, concern has been voiced by many host governments regarding the potential link between FDI and balance of payment problems (Vernon and Wells, 1991, p. 98) and with national sovereignty and control issues (Johnson, 1970, p. 460).

Location determinants of FDI: host country empirical studies

Empirical studies that have attempted to apply some of the theoretical arguments inherent to the FDI situation have overwhelmingly concentrated on determining the place-specific conditions necessary for inducing FDI inflow. Some researchers have then gone on to empirically assess how successful FDI has been in developing (or becoming integrated within) a given host country's/region's economy. Common to this type of research has been the collection of actual records of FDI in which locations, industry type, mode of entry, and value of investment estimates have (where possible) been noted and spatial trends assessed. This type of geographical research is, however, quite distinct from the questionnaire-driven survey studies which have encompassed much of the FDI literature in business publications.

The studies presented below, although still addressing the question of why international production tends to be strong in some locations rather than others, feature a more substantiated approach to the FDI question for the following reasons. First, these empirical studies are based on actual observation of realized FDI inflow, rather than on the perception's of MNEs' CEOs, and therefore the conclusions drawn concerning host country attractions are considerably more objective. Second, the factors addressed in these studies include a comparatively broader range of criteria as often social, economic and political place-specific conditions are tested with FDI levels. Third, the conclusions derived from these studies have been inferred through statistical substantiation and therefore are more convincing than small sample-sized, descriptive summaries.

Conveniently, these studies can be further classified by scale of spatial assessment: at either the national or the subnational level. In either case, the literature presented is not exhaustive; but the studies discussed are, however, believed to be representative of the FDI literature universe that considers FDI from a more geographical perspective.

The spatial distribution of FDI within a national context

Scaperlanda and Mauer's study (1969) was among the first to divert attention away from descriptive analysis toward statistically testing the importance of determinants of FDI inflow. Three important hypotheses were evaluated as possible determinants of FDI inflow: market size, economic growth, and tariff discrimination. By testing US direct investment in the EEC during the period of 1952-1966 against these three variables, only market size was found to be statistically significant.

Korbin's study (1976) was more comprehensive in terms of the variables considered, as the inclusion of social and political criteria was made along with economic determinants. With the use of factor analysis, the major factors for assessment were denoted as: social/economic development (including infrastructure, basic economic variables, and social variables), market size, market growth, and three political environment factors (completed with measures of rebellion, instability, and subversion). By regressing US manufacturing investment (as of year end 1967) on the six factor groups, market size was found to be the overriding determinant. Social/economic development and market growth were also statistically significant factors. Interestingly, all three political factor groups could not be significantly linked with US manufacturing levels; as some even had negative coefficients.

A more recent statistical study by Koechlin (1992) uncovered some of the location-specific determinants of American outward direct investment. US direct investment in manufacturing between 1966 and 1985 was employed as the independent variable, and it was tested against various country-related independent variables. In all, Koechlin constructed three regression models. Two of the models tested only economic criteria (the 'cost' and 'demand' models), and one a 'hybrid economic' model which included not only demand and cost factors, but also included social and political variables. Thus, this hybrid model included measures of a host country's political stability, overall attitude toward foreign investment, dependence and political ties with the US, and dominant language. This study was able to establish that economic criteria alone can not fully explain direct investment patterns as the hybrid model was the best in explaining the distribution of US FDI among countries.

While the above three studies were able to illustrate some likely place-specific determinants of FDI that originates from developed countries, Yeon's findings (1992) revealed some distinct conclusions from the perspective of newly industrialized countries (NICs). For instance, FDI from South Korea (a NIC) to developed countries seemed to be motivated by the desire to overcome non-tariff trade barriers. Direct investment that went to LDCs, on the other hand, appeared to be driven mainly by cheap labour and other comparative cost advantages that can often be experienced in developing nations.

Schneider and Frey (1985) also found that a model using both political and economic information tends to explain the distribution of FDI among countries most adequately (as was the case with Koechlin's assessment). Yet, unique to this study was the discovery that the amount of bilateral aid from Western countries to LDCs was found to have the strongest effect (among other political factors) in stimulating direct investment. Conversely, aid from communist countries had significantly dampened the amount of direct investment from Western nations.

Instead of using regression analysis like most studies mentioned above, Root and Ahmed's study (1979) employed a discriminant analysis to identify some location-specific attractions of FDI. Each of the 70 sampled countries were classified as either unattractive, attractive, or highly attractive in terms of their annual per capita inflow of FDI over the period of 1966-70. Of the 37 different economic, social and political factors, only six emerged as essential discriminators: per capita GDP, GDP growth rate, economic integration, extent of urbanization, commerce, transport and communication, and regular executive transfers (which emerged only for the period of 1956-1967). The only political factor (regular executive transfer) failed to distinguish among the three country groups during 1960-1970 because, it was argued, foreign investors view political stability from a longer term perspective.

Unlike most others, Lim's (1983) study paid more attention to the impact of fiscal incentives on the distribution of FDI in less developed countries. The hypothesis that greater generosity of fiscal incentives attracts more FDI was rejected as a result of statistical testing. This finding confirms the work of Reuber (1973) concerning the impact of incentives on FDI inflow. It seems clear that while incentives in developing countries have become increasingly more generous (as countries compete for foreign capital), the overall impact of incentives on FDI is minimal. Nevertheless, there is evidence that fiscal incentives may still be important to small firms.

The fact that developing countries still use incentives extensively even though there is some evidence of their ineffectiveness in attracting FDI presents an apparent paradox (Lim, 1983, p. 210). It is possible that developing countries must compete with each other and/or must compensate for their lack of resources and other endowments that induce the inflow of FDI. Another explanation is offered by Argrwal (1980) who argues that the effect of incentives may be eliminated by various regulatory disincentives such as restrictions on ownership and inter-firm exports.

The spatial distribution of FDI within a subnational context: US and UK examples

While a substantial body of research has been devoted to identifying and explaining the international flow of capital investment, attention on the locational aspects of FDI at a subnational level is a relatively more recent academic endeavour. Therefore, the body of literature generated is smaller, yet not lacking in important findings. Common to most empirical studies that have considered the regional distribution of FDI within the United States and United Kingdom has been the use of an aggregated data-base built from government sources. The actual regional variables tested, however, have varied from one study to another.

With respect to the American situation, McConnell (1980; 1983) was one of the first to deal with the spatial distribution of FDI at the subnational level. The oligopolistic-reaction model of foreign investment (see Knickenbocker, 1973) stipulates that firms tend to follow the leaders in their respective industries to minimize risk and to maintain the momentum established by the leaders. The hypothesis put forth by McConnell (1980) was based on this model and assumed that the location behaviour of foreign affiliates 'should be strongly influenced by the locational force and industrial pattern that are already prevailing in the country' (p. 263).

However, this hypothesis could not be confirmed through empirical testing. By using 1974-78 data, evidence suggested that there were distinct dissimilarities between foreign and domestic firms operating in the United States. The spatial pattern of FDI seemed to be well explained by traditional predictors of industrial location such as agglomeration economies, urban density, and 'economic shadow' effect (see Ray, 1971). Conversely, the presumed adverse effects of high union membership, high wages, population decline, and the absence of local incentives (important factors in inciting the regional shift in American-owned manufacturing) were not statistically relevant for FDI. McConnell concluded that FDI in the US, although starting to disperse away from the industrial heartland, still lagged behind the regional shift of American industry in general. McConnell (1983) further examined the geographical dispersion of FDI at the sub-state level and found that it is closely associated with population size and the number of R&D private corporations.

Bagchi-sen and Wheeler (1989) developed a spatial and temporal model of FDI in the United States. Based on the premise that there are many location advantages associated with the American economy available to foreign firms (such as large and growing local and regional markets, availability of skilled labour, and necessary technology), independent variables measuring these attributes were tested against the inflow of FDI into metropolitan areas. Not only was it established that metropolitan growth characteristics were most important in determining the accumulation of FDI in metropolitan regions (FDI had shown a bias toward metropolitan areas), but the authors also demonstrated that spatial patterns of FDI were not constant over time. As McConnell had hypothesized earlier but could not fully confirm, it was found that FDI had followed the shifts inherent to the entire US economy. Namely, that FDI had displayed some dispersion from North-Eastern locations to the major growth centres in the South and that the activities of foreign investors had shifted to some degree away from manufacturing towards services.

Glickman and Woodward (1988) disputed the argument that domestic investment should follow foreign investment or vice versa (McConnell, 1980 and 1983; Ó hUallacháin, 1985) and concluded that foreign and domestic investment location determinants have become similar. Their study confirmed that indeed the agglomeration effect, labour climate, transportation infrastructure and urbanization are important variables in explaining the spatial distribution of industry (including that which is foreign-owned), but also found that changes in regional energy costs were 'a central factor in recent shifts of manufacturing capital to the South and West' (p. 149).

Another recent study that updates the growing knowledge pool concerning the spatial pattern of FDI in the US was provided by Coughlin, Terza and Arromdee (1991). These authors were able to confirm the strong association of existing manufacturing activity density, population, extensive infrastructures and promotional expenditure with FDI inflow. Also, it was detected that other factors such as taxes and labour cost also influence the location of FDI within the United States. Many of these factors were either not included in earlier studies or deemed statistically insignificant. One should note that the statistical insignificance of these factors within McConnell's research was the main reason for his conclusion that there was dissimilarity between the location behaviour of foreign affiliates and domestic firms in the United States. Overall, the Coughlin, Terza and Arromdee assessment provided more evidence in support of the notion that the location behaviour of foreign firms and domestic firms has converged over time.

Unlike their US counterpart, studies in the UK have tended to put more emphasis on the overall spatial patterns of FDI without revealing the major underlying locational factors (Dicken and Lloyd, 1976; McDermott, 1977; Watts, 1979, 1980a, 1980b; Law, 1980). Nevertheless, the conclusions from these studies display more consistency than the studies in the United States. Before 1950, FDI was heavily concentrated in the South-Eastern industrial core of the British economy. However, a continuing shift away from the core was discernible by the late 1960s and early 1970s. Because of this process, FDI in the UK was most pronounced in the South-East and in the government-assisted regions, leaving the intermediate regions comparatively underrepresented.

This spatial pattern of FDI seems to indicate that the location behaviour of British firms differs from that exhibited by foreign firms - foreign firms have shown a distinct bias in favour of less developed regions. As suggested by Law (1980), one of the reasons for the different location behaviour may be that foreign firms are generally more sensitive to the incentives available in the peripheral areas.

Although some interesting spatial trends can be noted for foreign firms collectively, variations in the location behaviour of FDI from differing source countries are detectible. As Watts (1979, 1980a, 1980b) explained, there are distinct differences between US-based FDI and direct investment from the EEC. While FDI from the US has largely followed the overall pattern of FDI in the UK, FDI from the EEC was found to be very localized with significant concentrations found in the non-assisted South-East. In other words, regional development policies, aimed at assisting slow-growth regions, seemed to have little impact on influencing the location behaviour of EEC firms. Blackborn's study (1972) on the location of foreign-owned manufacturing plants in Ireland also suggests that location preferences of FDI will vary depending on the nationality of the home country.

Rather than identifying the spatial pattern of FDI in the UK, Hill and Munday (1992) attempted to uncover the underlying factors that have created the noted distribution. The effectiveness of regional infrastructure (which is treated as a surrogate for market access) and financial incentives were found to be important factors in forming the regional distribution of new FDI projects. Considering the more recent data used in this study (1980s), it may be concluded that the general shift identified by previous studies is part of an ongoing process. The agent for this continued shift seems to be new FDI which is directed toward peripheral regions.

Theories of FDI and home country conditions

In general, much of the FDI/MNE theory and empirical analysis that has emerged in the literature has emphasized the relationship between the host country and the MNE. Or in other words, the various 'pull' factors associated with direct investment and the subsequent host country benefits and losses. Studies that have considered the 'push' criteria associated with direct investment have generally concentrated on uncovering the business environment 'negatives' of the home country and identifying the conditions that force domestic companies to look elsewhere for investment opportunities. However, home country conditions need not always be viewed as negatively associated with outward direct investment.

In what has become a revelation of sorts within recent FDI theory relates to Michael Porter's 'diamond theory' (as described in the 1990 book *The Competitive Advantage of Nations*) and its almost exclusive reliance on home country conditions in assessing outward trade and direct investment levels. In overall terms, Porter's study was one that attempted to understand the factors that explain why certain countries became world leaders in certain activities. Specifically, he tried to rationalize various national success stories such as: the Americans in commercial aircraft and motion pictures, the Japanese in semiconductors and VCRs, the Germans in high performance automobiles and chemicals, the Swiss in banking and pharmaceuticals, the Italians in footwear and textiles, and so on (Porter, 1990, p. 27).

Porter's sample of countries was ten in number (Denmark, Germany, Italy, Japan, Korea, Singapore, Sweden, Switzerland, the United Kingdom and the United States) and he estimated each country's international competitive advantage in various activities by either:

> … the presence of substantial and sustained exports to a wide array of other nations and/or significant outbound foreign investment based on skill and assets created in the home country… (Porter, 1990, p. 25).

Porter was most concerned with understanding how countries gain and sustain competitive advantages in sophisticated industries because, as he assumed, these are most vital in encouraging high productivity (and therefore higher levels of wealth and living standards) in the home nation.

With respect to FDI, Porter considered outward direct investment to be generally a positive contributor to a home country's level of competitiveness (and conversely, inward FDI as largely detrimental) and that firms that have flourished in the global market are those that have successfully extended their home-based advantages abroad. He agreed that the benefit accruing from a firm's proper selection of host location is important to international success but that home-based advantages are usually more significant (Porter, 1990, p. 61).

According to Porter, the characteristics of a country (that will either promote or impede a nation's progress towards international success in a particular industry) can be summarized by the following interdependent 'diamond' parameters.

1. Factor conditions - the nation's position in factors of production, such as skilled labour or infrastructure, necessary to compete in a given industry.
2. Demand conditions - the nature of home demand for the industry's product or service.
3. Related and supporting industries - the presence or absence in the nation of supplier industries and related industries that are internationally competitive.
4. Firm strategy, structure and rivalry - the conditions in the nation governing how companies are created, organized and managed, and the nature of domestic rivalry (Porter, 1990, p. 71).

Porter completed his theory with the addition of two exogenous variables that will inevitably affect the diamond: the role of government and chance. He described chance events as developments outside the firm's control (such technological breakthroughs, wars, or major shifts in foreign market demand). Also modelled as exogenous to the diamond is the prevailing political climate. It was argued that specific government policies can greatly improve or inhibit the national advantage as well. Thus, locations where the 'national diamond' is most favourable will foster companies that are most likely to prosper within international competition.

Ultimately, Porter claimed that countries can be classified along a continuum of national competitiveness where progression through the first three stages (factor-driven, investment-driven, and innovation-driven) is associated with rising national competitiveness and, therefore enhanced prosperity. Whereas, the final stage (wealth-driven) is one where competitiveness eventually declines (pp. 546-560).

The criticisms levied against Porter's work have not so much been concerned with his results (which, by-in-large, have not been reported here), but with some of the assumptions made within his theory. Rugman and Waverman (1991), writing from a Canadian perspective, have taken issue with the 'diamond theory' in, particularly, two fundamental ways. First, these authors have argued, that the shape of the host country's diamond is also important to the MNE when making direct investment decisions. This seems especially significant in the case of a multinational that has over 90 per cent of its activities centred outside the home country (as happens with some of Canada's larger multinationals) (Rugman and Waverman, 1991, p. 65). Porter's theory, which is highly reliant on home country conditions, surely could not fully explain the investment decisions of this type of MNE.

Second, it is argued by Rugman and Waverman that Porter has a flawed understanding of the nature of two-way FDI particularly with respect to the benefits the host country receives through technology and capital transfer.

> In the Canadian context, foreign capital and technology have added enormously to Canada's assets. Fully 70 per cent of Canadian trade is done by 50 multinationals, and half of these are foreign-owned (p. 64).

Thus, because of these inherent flaws (and due to an incomplete understanding of the performance of multinationals in Canada) Rugman and Waverman were unwilling to support Porter's view that Canada is a nation stagnating on the first stage of international competitiveness (because of a presumed over-reliance on resource activities).

Conclusions

There have been many models put forth attempting to explain FDI and/or the actions of MNEs but the theories that continue to be most accepted still have this central idea of firm-specific advantage as it applies to the internalization of knowledge. In turn, most empirical researchers have attempted to ascertain what location-specific criteria will influence a MNE's location preference. Or in other words, how does geography influence the use of the FSA and, furthermore, how does the use of the FSA affect a given location. A comparable empirical assessment of home-country conditions and their affect on outward direct investment has not, beyond Porter's assessment, been fully developed.

2 An examination of foreign direct investment theories and the multinational firm: A business/ economics perspective

Prescott C. Ensign

Introduction

Foreign direct investment (FDI) is part of a firm's strategy to grow or expand on a global scale. Global strategy is a direct response to changes that occur in a firm, industry, or national environment. It is viewed as how a firm responds to opportunities and threats in its environment. A firm's strategic decisions and actions result in the deployment of tangible resources (physical assets, human and monetary capital, etc.) and intangible resources (information based assets, skills/know-how, etc.) to achieve competitive advantage.

From a management perspective, FDI must be understood as part of a dynamic strategy process. It is dynamic because strategy develops over a period of time in response to changes (often major changes) in the environment. How a firm chooses to grow internationally - part of a process to achieve competitive advantage - must be viewed from a short- and long-term perspective. Porter (1991) suggests that these choices can be described as cross-sectional and longitudinal research problems. Kogut (1983) suggests that FDI must be understood as a sequential process. Any explanation of FDI must include the initial decision to invest as well as subsequent investment decisions in the form of new capital flows and/or reinvested earnings. Understanding direct investment as part of a dynamic strategy process has important implications for theoretical and empirical research efforts.

Foreign direct investment must also be understood in context. In the past most explanations of FDI focused on the firm, industry and/or host country context. Research often neglected to examine direct investment from a home country perspective. Based on his own research, Porter (1990) concludes that successful firms tend to be geographically concentrated by nation as well as within a nation. There are home country-specific advantages that determine a firm's international growth. These advantages are described in a 'diamond' as 'determinants of national competitive advantage'. In the future, research work on FDI may need to consider the home country context more explicitly.

From a strategic standpoint, foreign direct investment is unlikely to occur unless there is some perceived advantage or disadvantage. These advantages and disadvantages are often described in the literature as firm-specific, industry-specific, and country-specific factors. Boddewyn (1985) calls these factors the *conditions* that explain FDI. One or more of these conditions is necessary but not sufficient for a decision to be made or an investment to succeed. *Motivations* and *precipitating circumstances* are also part of this decision process.

Attempts to explain the reasons why firms undertake direct investment abroad are described as theories of FDI. A theory of FDI must explain the mode of foreign involvement. Why does a firm undertake direct investment? Why is it FDI rather than some other mode of foreign participation? A theory must also explain *location*. Why does FDI occur in a particular geographic location? In this chapter it is suggested that most theories or explanations of FDI are based on: market/industrial organization theory; theory of the firm/growth of the firm; finance/investment theory; international trade theory; location theory; transaction cost theory; dynamic theory of strategy; and theory of international business. This review is provided as a framework for understanding the strategic decisions that result in foreign direct investment.

Explanations of foreign direct investment

Market/industrial organization theory

From the perspective of neoclassical economics - where markets operate efficiently, no barriers to trade or competition exist, information is costless, and there are external economies of production or marketing - exporting would be the mode of choice for foreign involvement. Such a perspective, however, does not provide a complete explanation for why a firm chooses export, license, joint alliance or direct investment. Any explanation for choice of mode must be based on departures from a traditional economic model.

Until the 1960s the primary explanation for the international movement of capital focused on portfolio theory which suggests that capital moves in response to changes in interest rate differentials. There was no role for the multinational enterprise and no separate explanation for foreign direct investment. Some scholars were interested in where capital moved but there was little interest in why capital moved or why a firm chose direct investment as the mode of foreign involvement. A major change in thinking occurred with the work of Stephen Hymer. His dissertation, completed in 1960 (published posthumously in 1976), provides an explanation for FDI based on industrial organization theory. These ideas are described as the oligopoly theory or industrial organization theory of foreign direct investment.

From a conceptual standpoint, Hymer's work (1976) changed the explanation of direct investment from traditional trade and finance theory to an analysis of the firm (multinational enterprise) and the market (imperfections). Foreign direct investment not only involves the long term flow of assets but control over these assets. The firm can maintain control over capital by engaging in production activities abroad. Hymer's explanation was that oligopolistic market structures provide the conditions for foreign expansion. Firms which dominate their domestic markets have ownership-specific advantages. These advantages are important because they involve assets that are unique to the firm, can be transferred at a relatively low cost within the firm and cannot be easily acquired by other domestic or foreign companies. A firm that possesses monopoly power at home can use these advantages abroad by internalizing the barriers to entry which exist for other firms.

Hymer's approach focused on the firm (it must possess an advantage over firms in the foreign market) and the market (the sale of this advantage must be imperfect). The multinational enterprise (MNE) is the result of market imperfections. The MNE has the ability to use international operations to separate markets and remove competition. Kindleberger (1969) shared Hymer's ideas that market imperfections can explain FDI. His explanation of FDI is based on imperfections in goods markets, imperfections in factor markets, scale economies, and government-imposed disruptions.

Calvet (1981, p. 44) suggests four classes of imperfections which correspond to 'the chronological order in which new explanations' of FDI have occurred. In the first, conditions that provide incentives for FDI in a particular country are described as market disequilibrium imperfections. These imperfections are generally related to factor markets (labor costs, capital markets, technology markets) or foreign exchange markets (currency changes/overvaluation). If conditions change and equilibrium is established between segmented markets (rates of return are equalized among countries), FDI will no longer be the mode of choice.

The second type of imperfection is described as government-imposed distortions. FDI may occur in a particular geographic location because the policies of host and home governments act as incentives to invest (e.g., differences in tax structure, quotas, tariffs, price controls, etc.). A number of scholars have examined the effect of political (non-market) variables on market imperfections and FDI. This has generally focused on examining the effects of government policies on market imperfections and FDI. Brewer (1993) extends this work by examining government policy variables as causal factors and market imperfection variables as intervening factors. Taking an opposite view, Boddewyn (1988) examines the effects of a firm's political behavior on market imperfections and the political environment. He suggests that the MNE should be viewed as a political actor because it can actively 'influence' (as well as 'respond to') a particular political environment.

The third is described as market structure imperfections. The oligopolistic approach to FDI suggested by Hymer (1976) and Kindleberger (1969) is based on market structure imperfections. A number of other scholars based their work on the oligopolistic feature of direct investment. Caves (1971) emphasized that a firm's control over knowledge can result in the production of a differentiated product. Knickerbocker's (1973) follow-the-leader theory emphasized that the investment decisions of one firm may be followed by other firms in the industry. Vernon's (1966) product cycle theory helped to explain the shift from exporting to foreign production.

Although theories that focus on market structure imperfections explain ownership-specific advantages, they do not provide a complete explanation of FDI. In general they do not adequately account for industry patterns or choice of location, e.g. the location of low skill, labor intensive production processes in low income countries (Mexico, Southeast Asia, etc.), the production or assembly of components in a vertically integrated MNE, or the patterns of direct investment that developed in the 1970s (e.g. the foreign expansion of European and Japanese multinationals).

The fourth class suggested by Calvet (1981) is market failure imperfections. This includes theories based on departures from the model of perfect markets, i.e., assumptions about production techniques and commodity properties. Problems with the market failure imperfections approach became clear with the work of Johnson (1970). His ideas on the welfare implications of transferring knowledge internationally placed the issue of FDI at a different level of investigation.

Theory of the firm/growth of the firm

During the 1970s, explanations of FDI focused primarily on the firm. The emphasis shifted from a focus on theoretical explanations of FDI to an understanding of the MNE. The emphasis shifted from the act of investing to the organization making the investment. Research centered on finding an explanation for FDI by developing a theory of the multinational enterprise. The major approaches that contributed to this change are: internalization theory, appropriability theory, eclectic theory/paradigm, and diversification theory.

Internationalization theory Although Hymer's work suggests why a firm would internalize a market, the work of Buckley and Casson (1976), Dunning (1977), Rugman (1981) and others placed internalization theory in the forefront of theoretical work on FDI. Although the concept of internalization was originally used to explain the growth of the multi-plant indigenous firm, it is equally valid for the MNE. Internalization theory centers on the fact that an MNE carries out many activities that are interdependent and related through flows of intermediate products (mostly in the form of knowledge and expertise). Since markets for intermediate products are difficult to organize, these transactions can be handled more efficiently within the firm by an internal hierarchy rather than by an external market. The creation of internal markets brings these activities under the direct ownership and control of the firm.

Market imperfections make it less costly for firms to undertake certain activities and transactions within their own organization. Market imperfections that result in internalization are generally related to costs or benefits associated with: uncertainties in external market transactions and costs (finding suppliers, negotiating/monitoring contracts, uncertainty over future prices, etc.); imperfections in markets for knowledge and information (when a seller needs to protect the quality of his product, undertake local production in a developing country, etc.); the size of the firm itself (when a firm chooses to engage in oligopolistic business practices or control market outlets, supplies and conditions of sale); and government policies/intervention.

The internalization of markets across national borders results in the MNE. International production is not just the transfer of capital but the extension of managerial control over foreign subsidiaries. Management replaces the market in allocating resources. The primary incentives to internalize activities are to avoid the disadvantages (or capitalize on the advantages) of imperfections in external mechanisms of resource allocation (Dunning, 1977). From a strategic standpoint, firms must possess superior resources (as in Hymer's argument) but they must also have the motivation and ability to profit from possession of these advantages.

Appropriability theory Appropriability theory (Magee, 1976 and 1977) is similar to internalization theory. Appropriability refers to the desire to keep (retain for itself) the ideas that originate within the firm. Such ideas are often based on a firm's unique information and technology. The result is that appropriability becomes particularly important in industries where new product development takes place on a continuing basis. Firms in such industries must invest in five types of information: product creation, product development, production functions, market creation, and appropriability itself. The more uncertain the appropriability of the returns on its information-based assets the more likely it is that the firm will choose direct investment.

This theory goes beyond the internalization theory by introducing two variables which affect appropriability: the efficiency of a nation's legal system to preserve appropriability (which can vary with different types of information) and the changes that take place in industry structure (every industry goes through a technology cycle similar to that of Vernon's product cycle). Some MNEs are motivated to generate technologically sophisticated information because it is less likely to be imitated and can be transferred efficiently within the firm. Appropriability provides an incentive to choose direct investment as the mode of choice. It may also explain the propensity for takeover activity, e.g., to eliminate competitors or slow the depreciation of information. Appropriability theory supports the monopolistic view in the oligopoly theory and the efficiency argument for intra-firm transfers in the internalization theory.

Eclectic theory As theoretical work progressed, scholars questioned whether a single theory can explain all patterns and aspects of foreign direct investment. This was especially evident with an emphasis on understanding the firm as a multinational enterprise. The eclectic theory/paradigm (Dunning, 1977) is an attempt to bring together a number of ideas into an integrated approach. It includes the concepts of location-specific endowments of countries, ownership-specific endowments of enterprises and a firm's ability to internalize markets to its advantage. Dunning's central hypothesis was that a firm will engage in foreign direct investment or licensing rather than serve foreign markets through exports if it possesses ownership specific advantages. If there are some location specific factors, a firm will prefer foreign direct investment to licensing.

Dunning's eclectic theory became the focus of an ongoing debate over what factors constitute a general or integrated theory of FDI. At the center of this debate is the issue of advantages. Buckley (1988) suggests it is 'double counting' to use both ownership and internalization advantages. If internalization is viewed dynamically - and as it was originally used (to develop a model of the growth of the firm) - there is no reason to include ownership advantages. The very act of internalizing a market (as a strategic move, to increase profit, etc.) gives the firm an advantage (and disadvantages other firms). The view taken by 'internalization scholars' is that the theory of internalization already provides a complete explanation of FDI.

Although the theory of the multinational enterprise is generally based on internalization theory, location theory and competitive dynamics, Buckley (1990) indicates there are still a number of problems. First, the key relationships between internalization and market structure and between internalization and competitive advantage must be specified. Second, the central axioms of the internalization theory - that firms choose the least cost location for each activity they perform and that firms grow by internalizing markets up to the point where the benefits are outweighed by the costs - are not independent since the internalization of markets can interact with least cost location (e.g. transfer pricing can bias location choice because of low taxes, etc.).

In Buckley's (1988) view, internalization theory can provide an explanation of foreign direct investment if restrictions are imposed on the theory. Testing cannot be done at a general level. Research must be undertaken at the level of special theories that can be tested by using real firms in a particular industry serving an existing market. The concept of least cost location, for example, can be understood by examining specific economic activities (input availability and cost), the relative requirements for tradeable/nontradeable goods, the location of final markets, transportation costs, other activities in the firm, communication costs, competitor's strategic moves and government policies. The concept that imperfect markets will be internalized until benefits are equal to costs must be restricted by 'carefully defining costs and benefits in relation to particular markets at specific points of time and across limited economic space' (Buckley, 1988, p. 182).

Diversification theory Diversification theory has also been used to explain FDI and growth of the multinational firm. Diversification - a well-documented strategy for expansion of a firm - must be understood as a number of different types of strategies. Diversification relates directly to a firm's operations. It can refer to changes in products, markets or functions. It can take place internally or externally and horizontally or vertically. It can involve related or unrelated changes. Diversification can result from external or internal pressures. A firm's decision to expand globally must be viewed as short and long-term protection against competitors moves, declining domestic market share, or industry changes. When diversification theory is used to explain FDI, these explanations are often based on finance/investment theory.

Finance/investment theory

Scholars in finance and management recognize that FDI is a unique investment decision. Finance/investment theories of FDI tend to account for the fact that: firms seek new markets abroad to diversify their portfolio of sales and reduce risk; foreign firms capitalize host country earnings differently; and market imperfections may lead to FDI (Grosse, 1981).

From a finance perspective, diversification theory suggests that firms choose FDI (choose to produce and sell in a number of different national markets) to reduce the risk or variance of their expected returns. The reasoning is that markets in different countries will experience economic fluctuations at different times. Finance theory also suggests that foreign firms capitalize their earnings differently.

Theoretical work on FDI is also related to capital market imperfections. For example, an undervalued exchange rate which allows production costs in one country to remain below those of other countries may attract direct investment. Another view is that long-term investment in developing countries will be direct investment when little or no knowledge exists about the securities market. From a risk standpoint, the best option may be to retain control of host-country assets through direct investment (Boddewyn, 1985).

Although it is generally assumed that financial markets are efficient, studies have shown that financial market imperfections can provide a number of advantages. From an investment standpoint, direct investment may be chosen because a firm can internalize financial transactions. Lessard (1979) - in a review of the internal financial transfers within MNEs - pointed to sources of gains stemming from exchange control arbitrage, credit market arbitrage, and equity market arbitrage.

International trade theory

International trade theory has been expanded to provide an explanation of direct investment. This can be conceptualized in two ways. In the first, the ideas contained in the product cycle theory are used to describe the process of moving from export to direct investment. The role of firm-specific technology and marketing are used to describe the stages of foreign involvement in different products and into different countries.

In the second, a comparative cost view is used to describe the choice between trade and direct investment. It emphasizes the supply side and the relative abundance of production factors in each country. Comparative cost models help explain:

1 the relationship between trade and direct investment;

2 the phenomenon of offshore assembly; and

3 the expected impact of government policies (tariffs, penalties, etc.) on the flow of FDI.

The comparative cost view provides evidence for why FDI replaces exports. Capital flows and final-product flows can be substitutes for achieving factor price equalization. If constraints are imposed on trade flows or capital flows, the flow of the substitute (FDI) will increase.

Japanese theory

The *Japanese theory* suggested by Kojima (1976) provides another way to view the relationship between trade and FDI. It is described as being trade-oriented rather than trade destroying (oligopolistic/anti-trade). He argues that exports should take place from locations of comparative cost advantage. Direct investment should take place when foreign skills or capital can be combined with host country factors to achieve least-cost production. FDI should occur when a country's comparative advantage in some product is eroded or when comparative disadvantage exists. FDI can move factors (technology, management skills, movable capital) to foreign locations where total production costs would be lowest for any given product. Instead of replacing exports, this theory suggests that FDI can generate new exports. Sales can be made in the host country, to third countries, or even to the home country.

Bhagwati (1991 and 1992) suggests an explanation described as the *quid pro quo theory* of FDI. *Quid pro quo* (something for something) helps to explain the large inflow of Japanese direct investment to the United States in the 1980s. It introduces a political element into 'the conventional political-free approaches to the theory of DFI' (Bhagwati, 1992, p. 189). Direct investment is made in anticipation of trade protection and/or to reduce the possibility of trade restrictions being invoked at a later time (e.g., to defuse its threat). It is based on the notion that actions taken in one period are made to protect the profitability and investment in the next period. A firm (or government) may invest directly in a market that is currently being served by exports. FDI is designed to maintain market access (at the firm level) or buy goodwill (at the government level).

Location theory

As Grosse states (1981, p. 16), 'One could argue that trade theory and location theory approach the same phenomenon from opposite extremes ... .' Trade theory emphasizes the demand side of the market. Location theory often emphasizes the supply side of the market including cost conditions as well as the availability of natural resources. In the past location theory has been used to explain centralized production for local consumption.

In general, location theory provides two explanations for FDI in manufacturing. The first emphasizes that production generally moves from decentralization to centralization or agglomeration as market imperfections arise. The overall benefits of centralization are available to both foreign and domestic firms and different kinds of agglomeration economies can help a firm reduce production costs in a particular location. These are:

1 economies of scale in production (reduce costs at that facility);

2 localization economies (all firms in a single industry at that location can reduce costs because of shared production factors); and

3 urbanization economies (all industries at a single location) can raise demand for the outputs in that industry.

The first - economies of scale in production - may explain why a foreign firm chooses to centralize production at a particular location and sell from there to other locations. The latter two provide an explanation for follow-the-leader behavior and oligopolistic tendencies/reactions.

Second, location theory places an emphasis on the availability of natural resources. Location theory suggests that economic activity often focuses on centers of population and sites of natural resources. Again, these benefits are available to both domestic and foreign investors. Location theory, however, may explain the various stages of the production process with differences by industry and therefore differences in foreign investment. It can explain the concept of stratifying the production process to achieve least-cost delivered output.

Transaction cost theory

As indicated earlier, the primary emphasis in theoretical work should be on why a firm chooses FDI over other modes of serving a particular foreign market. As Calvet (1981, p. 54) suggests, industrial organization theory, location theory and property rights theory all have 'something to contribute to an explanation of why firms decide to transact with foreign countries.' But, as he adds, something must still be added to these ideas to account for the choice of transaction mode. A markets and hierarchies theory (Calvet, 1981) is needed to account for the choice between an external market and an internal hierarchy. Other theories assume there is no choice (market imperfections determine FDI). Most theories take for granted that markets are prevented from functioning efficiently (e.g., by monopolistic power). It is assumed that the domestic configuration of market power determines the international mode of transacting and that industrial organization theory provides an explanation for the international differentiation and internal integration of a firm's activities.

A markets and hierarchies theory is based on the view that the choice of mode to transact internationally is part of a complex decision making process. As Calvet (1981) states, it is not obvious *a priori* which mode of transacting will be used without specifying the nature of the transaction and the environment (location) in which it will take place. Some transactions are handled best by markets, others by hierarchies. This is not to deny the fact that firms can create market imperfections but suggests that the limitations of the market are what explain the emergence of multinational hierarchies. What is important is that these limitations have their roots in organizational factors. 'The markets and hierarchies paradigm suggests that the technological determinism of FDI and MNE theories be replaced by one that is based upon transactional considerations where human and organizational behaviors play a central role' (Calvet, 1981, p. 56).

Dynamic theory of strategy

It is increasingly clear that FDI must be understood in the context of an overall decision making process that is dynamic in nature. When decisions are made, there are a number of interrelationships/interactions that occur. Buckley (1990) suggests that there is an interaction between the internalization of markets and market structure. The process begins with internalization decisions. These decisions have an impact on the number of firms in the industry. Market structure in turn will govern horizontal expansion (e.g., highly concentrated industries will result in greater diversification) and result in imperfections that induce price distortions in multistage processes (providing incentives for forward or backward integration). The process continues with additional internalization decisions that influence market structure further.

There is an interaction process between internalization and competitive advantage also. From an analytical and strategic perspective the concepts of internalization (of markets) and competitive advantage (relative to another firm) are quite different. An understanding of the dynamic nature of these concepts is needed to understand the relationship between these concepts. Although internalization can be used as a competitive weapon (resulting in short-term benefits), internalization generally provides benefits that are long-term in nature. Compared to internalization, competitive advantage (advantage relative to a competitor) is short-term in nature because benefits must be defined over a specific period of time. Competitive advantage is limited by the ability of a competitor to 'catch up' or change how advantage is defined.

In the past, most models of competitive advantage have not accounted for the dynamic nature of strategy. Models usually fail to spell out the advantages that exist in imperfectly competitive markets (the nature of the imperfection is implicit only). Defining imperfections more explicitly will make it easier to see the interaction between internalization and competitive advantage. Although internalization can be used to provide short-term competitive advantages, the 'net wealth' from internalization decisions is determined by the long-run nature of these advantages (or disadvantages). As Buckley (1990, p. 661) states, 'Competitive advantages are a measure of net wealth arising from past entrepreneurial activity and at a point of time are differentially available to individual firms. The key strategy issue is to derive maximum benefit from this net wealth by deploying it effectively.'

From a strategic management perspective, a system theory (Ensign, 1993) provides a way to understand FDI as a dynamic process. It is based on the premise that FDI must be understood as a sequential process because investments occur over a period of time. Initial (entry) decisions are only the first in a series of many investment decisions. Subsequent decisions also contribute to the volume and direction of a firm's direct investments. It is important to understand that all of these decisions are part of a firm's overall strategy to grow/expand on a global scale.

A system theory also provides a way to understand the relationship between internalization, location and competitive dynamics. It is based on the premise that the MNE - with subsidiaries dispersed globally - has advantages because it is a multi-national network. The MNE has opportunities that are not available to a uni-national firm. It has the opportunity to coordinate activities (and maximize profits) on a global scale. Operating as a network, the MNE will base FDI decisions on the strategic relationship between operations in different countries. As Kogut (1983, p.40) states, the MNE is 'a collection of valuable options which permits the discretionary choice of altering real economic activities or financial flows from one country to the next.'

The MNE - because it operates as a multi-national system - has a number of unique advantages. The MNE has the ability to arbitrage institutional restrictions (different tax codes, currencies, legal structures, antitrust legislation, tariffs, financial opportunities and restrictions, risk, etc.). The MNE has the ability to choose whether to exercise an option or not. The value of these options is based on the uncertainty in the firm's institutional environment. The value of the firm is enhanced by the incremental value of these options. The MNE also has the ability to capture externalities (costs or benefits not generally reflected in market prices) in information. For the MNE, these externalities are the very thing that create the imperfections and uncertainties (provide the advantage) in the first place. Another major advantage is that the MNE can gain cost savings (from joint economies, sharing expertise, different location/factor costs, etc.) because it is managed (activities are coordinated) as a multinational network.

Porter (1986) suggests that global strategy is constrained by value chain (the vertical integration imperative), configuration (location costs of interrelated activities internalized within a firm), and coordination issues. It is also clear that strategies will change over time because firms are part of a dynamic or evolutionary environment. The result is a typology of strategies rather than a single global strategy.

Theory of international business

Scholars recognize that foreign direct investment must be understood in the context of an increasingly complex and competitive global/international business environment. FDI must be understood from the perspective that major changes are taking place on a global scale. It is increasingly important to examine political and social - as well as economic factors - since changes in these can have a profound effect on a firm's operations. Research work needs to incorporate internalization ideas into new models of trade, better measures to estimate transaction costs, an examination of costs over time (to predict mode), an understanding of the role of entrepreneurship, etc.

In Buckley's (1990) view, the theory of international business is the basis from which future research and empirical testing should proceed. But, as he suggests, some extensions in the core theory are needed because decisions involving foreign direct investment are not made in a vacuum. Social and political factors can have a profound effect on these decisions. This will require the integration of nontraditional concepts from political science, sociology, geography, etc. It will also require the integration of some areas of research that have become 'disengaged' from the core theory. This may include the integration of trade theory that is more closely related to business strategy/policy ('strategic trade theory') and the integration of economic concepts that can account for dynamic change and disequilibrium states.

Understanding changes taking place in the global/international environment may provide an explanation for changes in net national flows of FDI. Using a macro-based approach can show changes at industry level (the impact of exogenous changes on the structure of an industry) and predict the global configuration/pattern of industries over time. As Buckley (1988) indicates, exogenous changes - social and political conditions, technology, consumer demands, etc. - can have an impact on the division of labor and relative cost conditions. A new division of labor can result in a new (vertically integrated) structure in an industry which results in multi-plant operation and a new configuration of intra-firm trade. Changes in cost conditions can alter the attractiveness of different locations for performing specific activities required in an industry. The final result - a combination of internalization pressures and location costs - is a new configuration of uni-national or multi-national firms in an industry.

If changes are reflected in firm behavior, net flows of foreign direct investment are an indication of specific pressures in a particular industry and global environment. In some industries, a new international division of labor (hierarchy of functions) is emerging. In some, control is shifting from production to distribution and marketing. A solely-owned subsidiary may be replaced by participation in a contract or alliance. Such a change - involving dominance/control over a limited number of core functions - reflects a change in strategy. As Buckley (1988) states, an historical picture of industrial structure is 'industrial archaeology.' Research is needed that is designed to trace actual changes as they occur over a period of time. To understand the dynamic nature of foreign direct investment/international business, research must focus on actual firm behavior as it occurs (real time rather than historical studies) over a period of time (longitudinal rather than cross-sectional studies).

Summary/implications

This review emphasizes that most theories of direct investment identify the factors that Boddewyn (1985) describes as conditions that can explain direct investment. As he states, conditions are necessary but not sufficient for a decision to be made or an investment to succeed. Motivations - generally some perceived profitability - are also necessary for an investment to occur. Motivations can occur directly (based on least-cost opportunities; monopoly rents; etc.) or indirectly (by providing risk reduction or risk diversification). Some aspects of theoretical work on FDI help to explain motivations, e.g., investment or finance theory (minimizing risk), internalization theory (firm growth) or the oligopoly theory (extracting a monopoly rent). Finally, precipitating circumstances - part of the decision making process - may be the specific 'triggers' that result in an investment. These can be described as external (actions of others, changes in factors, moves on the part of competitors, etc.) or internal (decision makers have changed, etc.) circumstances.

From a management perspective, decisions related to foreign direct investment are part of a firm's strategy to grow or expand on a global scale. Decisions related to global strategy - including foreign direct investment - are part of a complex decision-making process. Conditions, motivations and precipitating circumstances (part of the overall strategy process) are involved in this process. The economic analysis of FDI which can be biased toward rationality and rely on broad macro-economic national and industry data needs to be complemented by organization analysis. Research is needed to examine how specific investments are considered, analyzed and decided within the context of real firms by real individuals. As Boddewyn (1985, p. 63) states, 'there are "organization-specific" factors that should be added to the economist's more traditional "company, industry and country" ones, by operationalizing the "internal market" within the firm, left unexplored by them.'

Research must focus more directly on the decisions that result in different types of foreign direct investment. Each type of direct investment - resource-based, trade or import-substituting, export-platform, cost reduction-based, etc. - can have quite different conditions, motivations and precipitating circumstances. This suggests that more differentiated theories are needed that reflect these differences. As Calvet (1981) suggests, the abandonment of a neoclassical framework which assigns an undue advantage to the study of markets will help scholars investigate the factors at the environmental and organizational levels which result in the establishment of markets or hierarchies.

The emphasis in theoretical and empirical work must focus on an analysis of international business and the MNE as a multi-national system/network. Further research is needed that investigates the impact of exogenous factors - particularly the political economy - on decisions related to direct investment. This must include an examination of both home and host country factors as they impact the firm. Any explanation for FDI must account for how changing conditions impact subsequent/sequential direct investments, not just the initial decision to invest.

In the final analysis, theoretical and empirical research must provide a dynamic explanation of foreign direct investment. Using an in-depth examination of firm behavior, it may be possible to determine changes (government policies, transportation, new management, etc.) that act as precipitating circumstances in the decision making process. The dynamic nature of strategy and the predictive power of a theory of FDI require the use of methodologies that examine actual firm behavior over a period of time.

3 Foreign direct investment in the innovation-driven stage: Toward a learning option perspective

Mike W. Peng

[1] As a major strategic decision undertaken by a multinational enterprise (MNE), foreign direct investment (FDI) has been one of the central concerns for scholars in strategic management, international business, international economics, and economic geography for decades (see Bartlett and Ghoshal, 1991 for a review; see also review chapters by Meyer, Qu and Ensign in this book). The changing dynamics of the global economy dictates that MNEs have to adjust their strategy and structure to better fit with the new competitive landscape. In the late twentieth century, increasingly rapid technological innovation and diffusion are fundamentally altering the nature of global competition, strategy and organization. Porter suggested that by this time, most industrial economies in the world have moved from a factor-driven stage to an innovation-driven stage, where firms compete on how to rapidly and profitably innovate (Porter, 1990, p. 554). During such a stage, how do firms make major investment decisions such as FDI when the future environment can only be dimly foreseen?

Building on an earlier paper (Peng, 1994), this chapter develops theory suggesting that FDI can be a powerful vehicle to help firms minimize the risk of being bypassed by competitors and maintain a competitive edge on a worldwide basis during the innovation-driven stage. Existing theories of FDI under the eclectic paradigm rely on two major tenets: comparative advantage and market imperfections (Dunning, 1977, 1980, 1988, 1992; Hymer, 1976). Viewing FDI and trading as substitutes for each other, the notion of comparative advantage is used to explain why initial FDI takes place. Attempting to exploit existing technological advances originated in the home country and take advantage of low cost factors in the host country, MNEs venture abroad. Moreover, the prevailing market imperfect condition in the global economy, notably the inadequate protection of technological know-how and property rights as well as growing protectionist concerns, prompts MNEs to choose FDI over exporting or licensing as the mode of entry (Caves, 1982; Williamson, 1975, 1985). In other words, FDI is used to minimize transaction costs abroad by internalizing the foreign operations (Anderson and Gatignon, 1986; Buckley and Casson, 1976;

Calvet, 1981; Hennart, 1982, 1991; Hill and Kim, 1988; Rugman, 1981; Teece, 1985, 1986a).

In this chapter, we draw from option theory, a recent development in the strategic management literature, to argue that a third major tenet, the option for organizational learning and innovation, should be added to the eclectic paradigm of FDI. Specifically, we contend that in addition to exploiting comparative advantage and overcoming market imperfections, FDI can also be viewed as an option to maintain access to innovations resident in the host country, thus preserving opportunities for future organizational learning and growth (Peng, 1994). Moreover, this rationale for FDI takes on added importance in the late twentieth century in light of the acceleration of technological innovations and intensification of global competition during this innovation-driven stage. In this chapter we advance a set of testable propositions, culminating in a proposed revision of the existing eclectic paradigm that incorporates this learning option perspective.

In the following sections, we first highlight the changing dynamics of country-specific advantages in generating innovations and the importance of organizational learning through FDI for MNEs. Then, we propose a learning option perspective to augment the existing eclectic paradigm on FDI. Finally, implications of this new perspective for FDI researchers and MNE managers are discussed.

FDI and country-specific advantages in innovations

The most fundamental feature that distinguishes international business from domestic business is the national border any transaction must overcome. Despite increased communications, travel and trade between countries that seem to promise an increasingly unified global market (Ohmae, 1985; Levitt, 1983), countries still tend to preserve significant socioeconomic differences (Craig, Douglas and Grein, 1992). As a result, a relatively stable pattern of international competitiveness at the country level has been observed (Cantwell, 1989; Chandler, 1990; Kogut, 1992; Porter, 1990). Despite the catching up processes (Glismann and Horn, 1988), country-specific capabilities are expected to remain stable over a long period of time (Kogut, 1991a).

Recognizing the differences in country-specific advantages, the eclectic paradigm of FDI suggests that FDI is a vehicle to exploit the comparative advantages of the MNE's home and host countries (Dunning, 1988). The home country is used as the base for technological innovations, financial resources, and managerial talents that the MNE rely on when investing abroad. The comparative advantages embodied in host countries typically include lower labor, capital and other factor costs. In this process, the diffusion of technological and organizational innovations is a one-way process that flows from the MNE's home country to various host countries it invests.

However, changing dynamics in international competition during the 'innovation-driven' stage (Porter, 1990) has partially rendered such one-way diffusion of innovations inadequate. Competitive advantages based on low cost labor, access to materials, or abundant capital can erode over time. Instead, 'a company's ability to

Table 3.1
Foreign direct investment: Inflows and outflows of select industrialized countries, 1975-1990

	1975-79	1980-84	1985-89	1990
Total inflows (annual average)	$US33 billion	$US34 billion	$US96 billion	$US156 billion
Country shares				
United States	33%	53%	51%	29%
Great Britain	23%	15%	14%	21%
Germany	7%	2%	2%	2%
France	10%	7%	6%	8%
Canada	2%	1%	1%	5%
Japan	0.5%	0.8%	0.4%	1%
Total outflows (annual average)	$34US billion	$40US billion	$126US billion	$US214 billion
Country shares				
United States	47%	24%	19%	15%
Great Britain	18%	24%	21%	8%
Germany	9%	9%	8%	11%
France	5%	8%	7%	16%
Canada	4%	7%	4%	0.2%
Japan	6%	11%	17%	22%

Source: World Economy Survey, *The Economist*, September 19, 1992, p. 17

innovate is rapidly becoming ***the*** primary source of competitive success' (Bartlett and Ghoshal, 1989, p. 115, *original emphasis*; Kogut and Zander, 1992).

During the innovation-driven stage, the increasingly rapid rate of diffusion of innovations exerts a strong pressure on the MNE to retain competitive vitality through rapid innovation, both technologically and organizationally (Franko, 1989). Such rapidity to imitate and eliminate the opponents' innovation-based competitive advantage has been termed hypercompetition by D'Aveni (1994). In this process, maintaining access to sources of innovation to allow for opportunities in organizational learning becomes of utmost importance. Mansfield (1985) reported that, on the average, information concerning development decisions is generally in the hands of domestic rivals within about 12 to 18 months and information concerning the detailed nature and operation of a new product or process generally leaks out within about a year. Since the subjects of this survey were 100 American firms (Mansfield, 1985), it follows that the speed of similar leakage to foreign competitors might be slower, *if* the foreign competitors have to overcome a great deal of geographic and cultural distances due to their lack of a US presence.

However, foreign rivals of American firms are as interested in obtaining the information concerning innovation and technology as are domestic rivals. One of their solutions to overcome the nationality difference is through FDI, namely US bound investment in this case. For Triad MNEs converging on their economies of scale and changes in levels of technological development over time, they can no longer solely rely on their home countries to generate enough innovations to maintain global competitiveness. Rather, worldwide access to technology and innovation becomes more important (Bartlett and Ghoshal, 1989; Franko, 1989; Kobrin, 1991; Ohmae, 1985). MNEs from the newly developed and developing countries such as Korea (Bettis, Bradley and Hamel, 1992), Indonesia (Lecraw, 1993) and China (Wu, 1993) seem to be in more urgent need to gain access to technological and organizational innovations in host countries (which are typically industrialized countries). As such, the narrow view that host countries can only serve as the receiving end of innovations should be broadened to incorporate a more global view that recognizes the potential contributions host countries may make as a source of innovations.

Such a view echoes the fact that as more and more countries became innovation-driven during the past two decades, the total volume of FDI has increased and the patterns of FDI changed drastically. Table 3.1 documents that among industrial countries, Japan, Germany and France have greatly expanded their share of FDI outflows since the 1970s. On the other hand, after decades of being the main source of FDI, the United States became a net recipient of FDI in the 1980s and such a trend is projected to continue in the 1990s. Therefore, we suggest the following proposition:

Proposition 1. There is a positive relationship between the intensification of innovations and the volume of foreign direct investment.

In sum, while FDI has traditionally been used to exploit comparative advantage and overcome market imperfections such as protectionism, FDI has been increasingly used to tap innovation capabilities abroad during the innovation-driven stage of global competition. Since the MNE's home country can no longer be automatically regarded as the monopolistic center for innovation during this stage, the question now becomes how the MNE can maintain its global competitiveness through worldwide learning. The answer to this important question lies in access to technology and innovations in a variety of host countries, which we now turn to.

FDI as a means for organizational learning

Given the growing importance of worldwide learning and innovation (Argyris and Schon, 1978; Fiol and Lyles, 1985; Levitt and March, 1988), since the 1970s many MNEs have been engaged in the profound process of transforming themselves into learning organizations (Bartlett and Ghoshal, 1989; Ghoshal, 1987; Hamel, 1991; Hamel, Doz and Prahalad, 1989; Hedlund, 1986; Pucik, 1988). Since learning itself can be viewed as 'one of the technologies within which organizations develop competence through use' (Levitt and March, 1988, p. 332; Kogut and Zander, 1992), such learning not only takes place in the MNE's home country but also in many host countries as well (Cheng and Bolon, 1993; Gupta and Govindarajan, 1991; Julian and Keller, 1991). In this process, FDI has been increasingly used as a means to tap innovation capabilities resident in the host country (Cantwell, 1989; Kogut and Chang, 1991). In this section, we consider which industries are more attractive to foreign investors and which countries tend to be more active in innovation-driven FDI?

Which industries are most attractive to innovation-driven FDI?

Among the many industries an industrial economy possesses, internationally competitive industries tend to attract a large share of inbound FDI during the innovation-driven stage. The transformation of the United States from a net investing country to a net recipient of FDI in the 1980s is an especially intriguing illustration of this process. Despite growing international competition since the 1970s, a number of technology-intensive industries in the United States have been able to maintain their global competitiveness due to persistent country-specific advantages in R&D and related organizing principles (Franko, 1989; Kogut, 1991a; Porter, 1990). Such industries include biotechnology, computer, industrial machinery, and aerospace, to name just a few (Shan and Hamilton, 1991; Porter, 1990). MNEs from Europe and Japan have concentrated their US-bound FDI activities on those industries at which the United States is technologically strong. Table 3.2 documents the announced FDI entries from four major investing countries (Japan, Germany, Great Britain, and France) into 20 US manufacturing industries from 1975 to 1990. Not surprisingly, the top three US manufacturing industries which received substantial FDI inflows are electronics and allied products (SIC 36 which includes the computer industry), industrial machinery (SIC 35), and chemicals (SIC 28 which includes the biotechnology industry), respectively. In such cases, Japanese and European FDI to the United States is clearly motivated by a desire to learn from US partners in order to source US technology and innovation, thus presenting an organizational learning rationale.

Of special interest is the rise of Japanese FDI into the United States (Kogut and Chang, 1991; Osborn and Baughn, 1987; Reich and Mankin, 1986). The Japanese have been especially active in US industries such as biotechnology (Saxonhouse, 1986; Shan and Hamilton, 1991), computer and electronics (Prescowitz, 1987), and high-technology-based venture capital investment (Hurry, Miller and Bowman, 1992). It is not hard to imagine, for example, that a Japanese company would take equity

Table 3.2

Frequency of anounced FDI entries from major investing countries into US manufacturing industries, 1975-1990

SIC	Industry	Japan	Great Britain	Germany	France	4-country Total
20	Food and kindred products	101 (#1)	61	18	31	211
21	Tobacco products	0	1 (+1)	0	0	1
22	Textile mill products	24 (#1)	16	17	4	61
23	Apparel and other textile	11 (#1)	8	9	2	30
24	Lumber and wood products	14 (#1)	9	8	0	31
25	Furniture and fixtures	8 (#1)	3	3	5	19
26	Paper and allied products	16	22 (#1)	9	0	47
27	Printing and publishing	16	64 (#1)	26	11	117
28	Chemicals and allied products	117	124	126 (#1)	50	417
29	Petroleum and coal products	2	20 (#1)	5	8	35
30	Rubber and plastic products	40 (#1)	23	19	9	91
31	Leather and allied products	2	6 (#1)	3	4	15
32	Stone, clay, and glass products	31	46 (#1)	31	30	138
33	Primary metal products	95 (#1)	39	9	22	165
34	Fabricated metal products	68 (#1)	38	28	10	144
35	Industrial machinery & equip.	205 (#1)	102	118	33	458
36	Electronics and allied products	253 (#1)	104	71	37	465
37	Transportation equipment	65 (#1)	28	29	19	141
38	Instruments and allied prods.	64 (#1)	56	33	13	166
39	Miscellaneous manufacturing	45 (#1)	25	7	11	88
	TOTAL	1178 (#1)	795	568	299	2840

Sources: *Foreign direct investment in the United States*, US Department of Commerce, Washington, DC, Various years.

stakes in US biotechnology firms in order to gain access to the resident technology.

The increase of inbound FDI into certain US industries is not the only evidence suggesting this learning rationale. Japanese FDI into Europe shows a similar pattern. Yamawaki (1991) provided evidence that the German chemicals industry, which Germany enjoys historical comparative advantage (Chandler, 1990), has been targeted as the most attractive FDI recipient industry, thus reflecting the importance of the pull of resident technologies in the host country .

To summarize:

Proposition 2: There is a positive relationship between the international competitiveness of a nation's particular industry and the amount of inward foreign direct investment this industry receives.

This proposition, of course, needs to be qualified. The occurrence of FDI into a nation's globally competitive industries will only happen when there is a relatively open international trade and investment regime. In cases where the government imposes significant constraints due to protectionist or national sovereignty concerns, foreign investors will not be able to tap into the innovation capabilities resident in the home country's competitive industries. That is why the US defence industry, despite its global competitiveness, has not been a major recipient of FDI. On the other hand, when government regulations are loosened and the country adopts a more open policy toward FDI, then FDI will pour into its competitive industries. The Russian aerospace industry serves as a case in point here. It was only after the breakup of the Soviet Union that FDI from the West start to pour into this internationally competitive industry.

Which countries tend to be more active in innovation-driven FDI?

Most innovations take place through an unfolding chain of relationships - from initial invention through stages of development to final commercialization - connected by a variety of feedback loops (Burgelman and Sayles, 1986; Gerlach, 1994; Kamien and Schwartz, 1982; Kanter, 1983; Kline and Rosenberg, 1986). During the race toward technological advancement in order to disadvantage the competitors, a firm not only needs basic research capabilities, but also a set of complementary assets that will ensure the successful application and commercialization of the initial invention (Teece, 1986b). Moreover, in addition to internally generated innovations, outside sources of innovation may also be critical (March and Simon, 1958; Cohen and Levinthal, 1990; Levitt and March, 1988; Mansfield, 1988; Rogers, 1962; von Hippel, 1988).

In the first systematic empirical investigation of the differences in innovation capabilities between the United States and Japan, Mansfield (1988) conducted a matched sample survey of 200 firms in these two countries. He found that Japanese firms have very great advantages in carrying out innovations based on external technology, which is 'technology developed outside the innovating firm' (p. 1159). Specifically, 'whereas in the United States the commercialization of an innovation based on external technology takes more time and about as much money as the commercialization of one based on internal technology, in Japan it takes about 10 percent less time and over 50 percent less money than the commercialization of an internal-technology-based innovation' (Mansfield, 1988, p. 1162).

Such evidence is consistent with a large body of literature that testifies to the Japanese adeptness at utilizing external technology (e.g. Bettis, et al., 1992; Gerlach, 1994; Hamel, 1991; Hamel et al., 1989; Lynn, 1982). While American firms are stronger at developing basic research, Japanese firms tend to do a better job at commercializing technologies developed externally, thus suggesting that Japanese firms possess a stronger set of complementary assets than their American competitors (Teece, 1986b). In other words, the absorptive capacity (Cohen and Levinthal, 1990) of Japanese firms tends to be better and deeper than American counterparts (Rosenberg and Steinmueller, 1988; Teece, 1986b).

Mansfield (1988: p. 1167) suggested that 'part of their (Japanese) success in this regard hinges on the thoroughness and skill with which they monitor foreign technology and determine which types of external technology to utilize. They invest much more in such monitoring than do American firms.' Building on such observation, we contend that in addition to exploiting comparative advantage and overcoming market imperfection, FDI is increasingly used by the Japanese MNEs to maintain access and monitor foreign technology. To state more formally:

Proposition 3: There is a positive relationship between the strength of complementary assets of MNEs from a particular country and the use of FDI to monitor and source foreign innovations by MNEs from that country.

As noted earlier, during the innovation-driven stage of global competition, we have witnessed the increase of FDI from countries such as Japan to traditional source countries of FDI such as the United States (Table 3.2). At least a partial explanation of such behaviour is the desire to monitor and source innovations originated from the United States, thus allowing for organizational learning opportunities at the investing MNEs. As such, a new perspective on FDI as a means for organizational learning to augment the existing eclectic paradigm seems warranted.

A learning option perspective on FDI

Having suggested that FDI has been increasingly used as a powerful vehicle to gain access to technology and innovation in host countries, it follows that such FDI activities can be viewed as preserving options which may lead toward future opportunities for organizational learning.

The concept of option comes from option theory, a recent development in the strategic management literature (Bowman and Hurry, 1993; Hurry, 1993; Hurry, et al., 1992; Kogut, 1991b). Very briefly, option theory has three key propositions:

1 Following the intuitive notion of keeping options open, the investor makes a small initial investment to buy the option, which gives him/her the right for future investment without being obligated to do so;

2 the typical investor will hold the option until a decision point arrives, and will then decide between striking the option to capture the opportunity (call or option to buy) or abandoning it (put or option to sell); and

3 investments will be made incrementally, from a small amount of initial investment to a full-scale acquisition if a call is exercised (Cox and Rubinstein, 1985).

While the original roots of option theory lie in financial economics, its extension to strategic management, especially to FDI strategy, is highly useful. Given the sequential nature of FDI (Aharoni, 1966; Kogut, 1983), MNEs' investment behaviour follows the incremental approach prescribed by option theory. Typically, a small amount of FDI is initially made in a host country. As the MNE gradually gains market knowledge and operating experience, more investments may be pulled into that country (Davidson, 1980; Johanson and Vahlne, 1977). In terms of the mode of entry, FDI may be first used to acquire a minor equity in a foreign agent, later to establish a joint venture with a foreign partner, and eventually to set up a wholly owned subsidiary abroad (Root, 1987; Hill, Hwang and Kim, 1990; Reid, 1981).

Viewed through such an 'option lens' (Bowman and Hurry, 1993), FDI can be conceptualized as an option to maintain access to technology and innovation in host countries, thus permitting the MNE wider strategic choices for future growth. Given the intensification of global competition during the innovation-driven stage (Franko, 1989; Kobrin, 1991; Mansfield, 1985, 1988; Porter, 1990), today's MNEs simply cannot afford to rely on one country, whether it is the home country or not, to be its sole source of technological and organizational innovations. Instead, MNEs have to maintain access to a wide variety of learning opportunities around the world in order to remain globally competitive. In this process, a few select countries which have been historically renowned as the world's leading innovation centers will be singled out as major FDI targets. As such, it is not surprising that high wage countries such as the United States have attracted an increasing share of global FDI in recent years. Moreover, as described earlier, such investments tend to concentrate in the industries at which the recipient countries have been especially strong, such as the US biotechnology industry (Shan and Hamilton, 1991) and the German chemicals industry (Yamawaki, 1991).

In light of such an option-based perspective on FDI, we suggest the following propositions:

Proposition 4: There is a positive relationship between MNEs holding better developed options through FDI in a variety of host countries and their global innovation capabilities; and

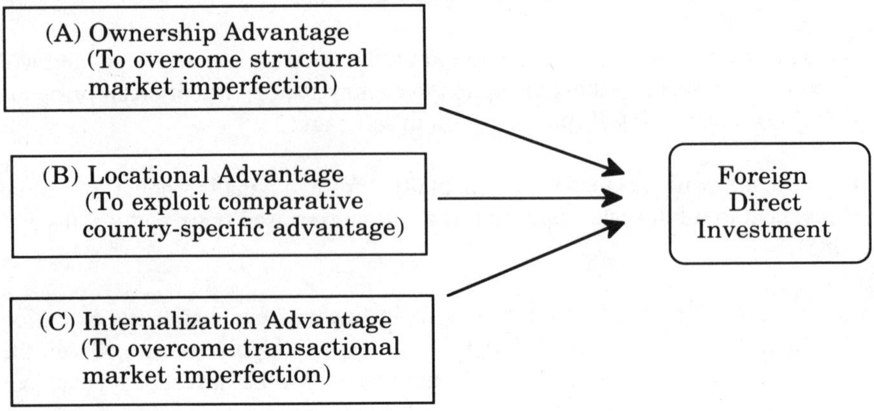

Sources: Dunning (1977, 1980, 1988).

Figure 3.1: The existing eclectic theory of foreign direct investment: The endowment/market failure paradigm

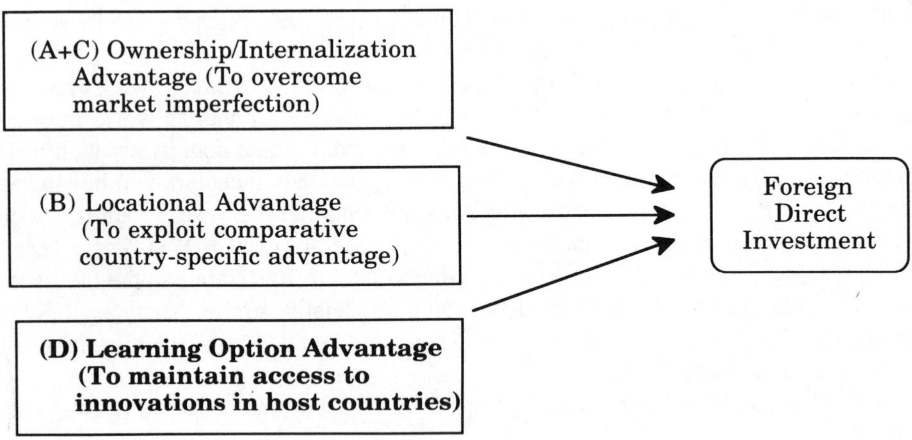

Figure 3.2: The revised eclectic theory of foreign direct investment: incorporating a learning option perspective

Proposition 5: There is a positive relationship between MNEs holding better developed options through FDI in a variety of host countries and the sustainability of their long-run competitive advantage vis-à-vis their competitors holding less well developed FDI options.

Moreover, from a strategy process perspective (Mintzberg, 1990; Mintzberg and Waters, 1985; Van de Ven, 1992), using FDI as options for learning features an incremental process with increasing resource commitments for new markets, businesses, and technologies (Melin, 1992). Facing such an uncertain future, 'organizations are likely to be most effective when they use small investments to develop capabilities; they can build on these investments by linking large investments to deploy those capabilities' (Bowman and Hurry, 1993: p. 768). There is evidence that large investments such as acquisitions often fail in new areas because of lack of appropriate management and production operating skills (Porter, 1987). In contrast, successful MNEs progress from learning investments to full operations in a manner resemble an option chain (Bettis, et al., 1992; Hamel, 1991; Hamel, et al., 1989; Ohmae, 1985; Reich and Mankin, 1986). Therefore,

Proposition 6: There is a positive relationship between the option-based, incremental progression in FDI and the chances of creating and sustaining competitive advantage for MNEs vis-à-vis MNEs that tend to make small, or large, investment decisions.

In sum, an option-based perspective on FDI, termed as the learning option perspective, has emerged. We believe that given the eclectic nature of the existing paradigm, this new perspective can be incorporated. Therefore, in the next section we propose a revision of the existing eclectic paradigm.

Toward a revised eclectic paradigm of FDI

The existing eclectic paradigm, as stated by Dunning (1977, 1980, 1988, 1992), proposes three major drivers for MNEs to undertake FDI (See Figure 3.1):

1 Ownership advantages that arise from the proprietary ownership of specific assets by MNEs vis-à-vis those possessed by other indigenous and competing foreign firms;

2 locational advantages of certain host countries that arise from those countries' factor endowment posture; and

3 internalization advantages that arise from the benefits of being multinational hierarchies through FDI vis-à-vis external market-based transactions (trade and licensing).

We contend that a fourth set of advantages, learning option advantages, should be added to the eclectic paradigm (See Figure 3.2).[2]

Defenders of the existing paradigm may argue that the new perspective we propose is within the domain of locational advantage, since we contend that it is the pull of innovations that attracts a great deal of FDI into certain countries such as the United States. We believe that the learning option perspective is fundamentally different from existing rationales for FDI in following ways. First, conceptually it shifts the source of innovations away from the MNE's home country and focuses on host countries' potenial contribution toward organizational learning, thus presenting a more balanced perspective on the theory of MNE and related FDI strategy. Second, in contrast to the content nature of the existing rationales, the option-based perspective features an incremental investment process, which brings strategy content and strategy process together (Melin, 1992). This contribution echoes strategic management researchers' growing dissatisfaction with the distinction between strategy content and process and their increased interest in combining these two (Mintzberg, 1990; Mintzberg & Waters, 1985; Van de Ven, 1992). Finally, the learning option perspective is consistent with a growing body of conceptual and empirical research on multinational cooperation, strategic alliance and organizational learning in MNEs (e.g., Bartlett and Ghoshal, 1989; Bettis, et al., 1992; Cheng and Bolon, 1993; Contractor and Lorange, 1988; Hamel, 1991; Hamel, et al., 1989; Hladik, 1985; Hurry, et al., 1992; Hurry, 1993; Kogut, 1991b; Kogut and Chang, 1991; Pucik, 1988; Shan and Hamilton, 1991; Yamawaki, 1991). Drawing upon option theory, the learning option perspective synthesizes this body of research into a coherent theoretical contribution that greatly enriches existing theories on FDI.

On the other hand, it must be emphasized that the proposed learning option perspective is meant to augment the rationales for FDI articulated in the eclectic paradigm, but not to replace the existing paradigm. The eclectic paradigm captures the essence of a great deal of FDI behaviour. Certainly a great deal of FDI behaviour can be explained by comparative advantage considerations and market imperfection avoidance. Our contribution lies in our attempt to improve this paradigm by analyzing the unique pattern of FDI into high wage countries such as the United States during the recent, innovation-driven stage of global competition. Our intent has not been to rule out the plausible explanations offered by the existing eclectic paradigm. Rather, through an option lens, we offer some refinement that explains the variance of FDI behaviour on top of that already explained by the existing paradigm.

Conclusions

This paper has argued that given the shifting patterns of FDI during the innovation-driven stage, the existing eclectic paradigm of FDI based on the notion of comparative advantage and transaction cost minimizing needs to be augmented by a new learning option perspective. Developed from option theory, this new perspective on FDI offers compelling explanations of why countries such as the United States famed for their innovation capabilities have been able to attract an increasing share of global FDI in recent years. The rationale behind such FDI lies in the motivation for gaining access to technological and organizational innovations resident in the host country as options for future opportunities for organizational learning and growth. Such rationale takes on added importance in light of the acceleration of innovations and intensification of global competition during the late twentieth century.

Following Dunning's (1988) and Bartlett and Ghoshal's (1991) suggestions that there are close parallels between the main tenets of the eclectic paradigm and that of modern strategic management, the learning option perspective of FDI grows from a recent development in strategy research, option theory. As such, this new perspective offers ample research opportunities for scholars in strategic management and international business, as well as international economics and economic geography, to learn from each other and to jointly advance our knowledge of MNE in general and FDI in particular.

Empirical research is required to resolve all of the critical research questions that have been posed in this paper. For example, integration of the learning option perspective of FDI with established models of acquisitive growth is necessary. At first glance, the learning option perspective seems to be at odds with the acquisitive growth model proposed by Hitt, Hoskisson and Ireland (1990). Hitt and colleagues suggested that acquisitive growth may result in less managerial commitment to innovation in large, diversified firms, thus leading to long-run deterioration of innovation capabilities. In contrast, the learning option perspective contends that an MNE pursuing multiple FDI options reflects the commitment to innovation by corporate management, aiming at improving the global innovation capabilities. It should be noted that the Hitt et al. (1990) model is primarily concerned with domestic diversification using acquisition as a substitute for innovation, while a great deal of FDI during the innovation-driven stage has been motivated by a desire to gain access to technology and innovations resident in the host country. We need future research to see if the model proposed by Hitt and colleagues (1990) or the learning option perspective advanced here will hold with a sample of MNEs pursuing FDI in a variety of host countries.

In their influential book on MNEs, Bartlett and Ghoshal wrote:

> In most industries today, worldwide companies no longer compete primarily with smaller national companies, but with a handful of other giants, comparable in size and geographic diversity. To survive, a company must have achieved global scale, international resource access, and world market position; to emerge as a competitive leader, however, requires much more (1989, p. 115).

For MNE managers aspiring to win the global competitive battle, the new perspective on FDI we have proposed offers a partial solution: much more options for organizational learning and innovation through FDI in a variety of host countries are needed.

Notes

1. A short version of the paper was presented at the Second World IFSAM Conference on Management in Dallas, Texas in August 1994, where comments were sought and incorporated. A two-page summary of that paper (Peng, 1994) was published in the proceedings of the conference entitled *The Best in Management Worldwide*. In addition, I thank Richard Moxon for his valuable comments on an earlier draft of the paper.
2. Figure 3.2 combines ownership advantage and internalization advantage of the existing eclectic paradigm together. We chose to do so not only for graphical simplicity to leave room for the proposed learning option perspective. Conceptually, these two sets of advantages are exploited to overcome structural and transactional market imperfections, respectively (Dunning, 1988). Within the general framework of market failure (Coase, 1937; Williamson, 1975, 1985), the distinction becomes blurred. Indeed, Dunning himself acknowledged that 'the two kinds of imperfection are, of course, interrelated, particularly in a dynamic market situation' (1988, p. 3). While not an emphasis of the present paper, we believe that these two different sets of advantage and market imperfection should be combined as one.

4 The internationalization process approach to the location of foreign direct investments: An empirical analysis

Gabriel R. G. Benito and Geir Gripsrud

Introduction

Foreign direct investment (FDI) serves as an important avenue for company growth, and it plays a significant role in transfers of capital, technology and managerial resources between countries. The immense increase in foreign direct investment during the last decades has therefore attracted the attention of scholars from various fields, in particular business, economics and geography. Location decisions are at the core of FDI as a field of investigation. From the perspective of the investor company, which seeks to maximize the returns from an investment, profit streams may depend on where particular subsidiaries are located. From the perspective of host countries, being able to attract incoming FDI is generally regarded as vital in order to maintain and further develop their economies.

Previous work has analysed the location of FDIs from various perspectives. According to economic theory, decisions about the location of production are predominantly taken on the basis of traditional sources of comparative advantage such as relative wages, market size, and transportation costs (Vernon, 1966; Aliber, 1970; Hirsch, 1976). In addition, impediments to international trade, such as tariffs and nontariff barriers, may also influence the location of production (Clegg, 1992)[1]. A second strand in the literature, rooted in economic geography and dating back to the classic works by Englander (1926) and Palander (1935), focuses on the importance of agglomeration economies in the location of production facilities (Berry, Conkling and Ray, 1993). Agglomeration economies refer to the advantages of co-locating different economic units (Wheeler and Mody, 1992). The attractiveness of an area is increased by factors such as the quality of an infrastructure, the availability of specialized service suppliers and of skilled labour, location related reputational effects, and the development of so-called industrial clusters (Porter, 1990). Once location advantages have been achieved, they tend to be self-perpetuating. The empirical evidence available suggests that both traditional comparative advantage factors, in particular tariff barriers (Culem, 1988), market size and market growth (Kravis and Lipsey, 1982; Culem, 1988; Veugelers, 1991), and agglomeration factors, such as infrastructure quality and the level of the existing stock of FDI in a country (Wheeler and Mody, 1992), have an important impact on international investment location decisions.

However, both economic and geographic approaches to location decisions focus primarily on factors that are external to the individual company (markets for input factors and end-users, macroeconomic and environmental conditions, etc.). As pointed out by Buckley (1987), these approaches tend to neglect how location decisions might be shaped by characteristics of the investor companies and of the individuals actually making the decisions. Buckley (1987, 54) remarks that:

> in the undoubted improvement in the theory of the multinational enterprise, location theory has been curiously stationary. This is partly because theorists believe that there is nothing that has not been said because the rational manager in the individual firm is deemed to be able to calculate location costs, including trade and tariff barriers, and on a comparative cost basis to select the optimal strategy...Crucially, communication costs and cultural values are not fully integrated into the calculus. This lack of interest is unwarranted, and must be rectified through renewed research initiatives.

Buckley's comment may certainly describe the state-of-the-art in economics, but disregards a strong research tradition in international business, the so-called internationalization process model, which, almost exclusively, focuses on precisely internal factors (Vahlne and Nordström, 1993). The internationalization process approach, which builds on the behavioural theory of the firm developed by Cyert and March (1963), has since the pioneering work of Aharoni (1966) constituted the theoretical basis for a large number of studies concerned with various aspects of the internationalization of the firm (e.g., Luostarinen, 1970, 1979; Johanson and Wiedersheim-Paul, 1975; Johanson and Vahlne, 1977).

The aim of the present study is to test some hypotheses on location decisions drawn from the internationalization process framework. The central tenet of this framework is that such decisions should be regarded as a learning process. Decisions at the company level are undertaken by decision makers displaying a high degree of risk aversion. One should, in particular, expect to find a close relationship between factors that increase the perceived level of uncertainty (such as distance), factors that serve to reduce uncertainty (such as experience), and factors that reduce the relative impact of the risk inherent in a project (company resources), in the observed patterns of location choices. The article proceeds as follows; the next section presents a sketch of the internationalization process framework and discusses the central concepts investigated in this study, then follows a description of how the study was conducted, a report of the findings, and finally, there is a concluding discussion of the results and some of their implications.

The process perspective on choice of location

The internationalization of the firm has been described as a process consisting of a series of small steps, whereby firms gradually increase their international involvement (Johanson and Wiedersheim-Paul, 1975; Johanson and Vahlne, 1977; Welch and Luostarinen, 1988). One factor that influences this process is the availability of resources. Welch and Luostarinen (1988, 51) point out that

> The ability to undertake any form of international operations is clearly limited by the means accessible to the firm to carry it out. For smaller firms, given their limitations in many areas, this is an obvious reason why less demanding directions of international development can be undertaken first, with major commitments only occurring well into the longer run.

Another important factor is perceived uncertainty. Decisions about expansion into international operations are for most firms, but particularly for those with limited international experience, characterized by a considerable amount of uncertainty. This uncertainty stems from two sources. The first is a lack of knowledge about the workings of particular foreign markets in terms of customer behaviour, institutional frameworks and so on. The other is lack of knowledge of how to run a given business operation in an unfamiliar context. In both cases, the type of knowledge involved is typically acquired through a process of learning by doing (Carlson, 1975).

The process approach seeks to explain - and predict - two aspects of the internationalization of the firm. The first is the step-by-step fashion by which a firm's engagement in a specific country develops. Although several stages are proposed in the literature, a typical establishment chain could begin with occasional exports, develop into regular exports through agents, followed by setting up sales subsidiaries, and end with fully-owned production facilities abroad. The second aspect is that firms are assumed to successively enter markets at an increasing distance from the home country, not only in terms of physical distance but also in terms of differences in economic development, language, culture, political system, etc. Thus, firms are predicted to start their internationalization by moving into markets they can most easily cope with, entering more distant countries only at a later stage.

The internationalization process model is rooted in a behavioural decision making approach. Luostarinen (1979) discusses in detail the stages in the decision process, building upon Cyert and March (1963), and underlines the importance of lateral rigidity between the stages in the decision process: limited perception of alternatives and selective search leads to confined choice. As more knowledge is acquired, more alternatives will be considered, and foreign direct investment (as well as other modes of foreign operation) will gradually take place in more distant countries. In the following, the choice of location of FDIs is analysed using the core concepts in the internationalization process framework.

Distance

The distance to where a foreign direct investment is made may vary considerably from one case to another. Some production operations are set up in locations near the home country, and sometimes firms choose to establish production subsidiaries in distant locations. What is near and what is distant can, due to the many facets of the concept of distance, be understood in various ways depending on which particular dimension of the concept one is referring to. At least three different dimensions are of relevance here. Firstly, distance can be understood in a physical sense, i.e., it relates to some objective measure of the space between two or more objects. This is usually termed geographical distance. Secondly, distance can refer to differences, or the degree of difference, between entities along some chosen characteristic, such as differences in culture between countries (cultural distance) and in the level of economic development (economic distance). Although the role of economic distance has been highlighted by Teece (1977) and Luostarinen (1979), previous studies have primarily looked at whether geographical distance (Luostarinen, 1979; Kravis and Lipsey, 1982; Terpstra and Yu, 1988; Yu, 1990; Veugelers, 1991), and cultural distance (Johanson and Vahlne, 1975; Luostarinen, 1979; Davidson, 1980; Kravis and Lipsey, 1982; Engwall and Wallenstål, 1988; Veugelers, 1991; Benito and Gripsrud, 1992) have an impact on foreign direct investment behaviour.

Several previous studies suggest that firms tend to start their internationalization by entering countries that are geographically close and that are relatively similar economically and culturally. For example, US firms have usually made their first foreign investments in countries like Canada and the UK (Davidson, 1980), and Finnish firms have tended to go to Sweden when undertaking their first establishment abroad (Luostarinen, 1979). A similar pattern was found for Swedish firms (Johanson and Wiedersheim-Paul, 1975). Several explanations are at hand. First, it has been argued that the development of new products is primarily aimed at customers in the home market (Vernon, 1966). To the extent that a customer base exists in other countries as well, it is likely that the demand for such newly developed products will be found foremost in countries that economically and culturally are fairly similar to the country where the innovation was made (Burenstam-Linder, 1961). Thus, the first foreign markets to be supplied, either by exports or (if export for some reason is not feasible) by local production, are likely to be near ones.

Another explanation is that similarity in culture and economic development makes it easier for a firm to manage a subsidiary abroad. Important components of the FDI package, especially the transfer of technology and managerial competence, are made easier when the countries in question are not too dissimilar (Teece, 1977; Kedia and Bhagat, 1988). Furthermore, closeness may alleviate problems in conducting actual business operations, for example by making it easier to monitor and coordinate production and marketing activities in the various locations. This is of particular importance in the early stages of internationalization when firms often are small and face severe resource constraints.

Finally, countries close to the home country in geographic, economic and/or cultural terms may be the preferred choice as sites for the first investments because the knowledge needed does not differ substantially from the knowledge already acquired. They may therefore be looked upon as the least uncertain locations. However, such perceptions are likely to change as experience is gained. As indicated by Davidson's (1980) study the strong preference for close and/or similar countries weakens as firms acquire experience from operating abroad.

Experience

The decision to undertake a foreign direct investment can be regarded as a strategic decision whereby the firm attempts to achieve the best possible fit between the capabilities of the firm and opportunities and demands in the environment. However, decisions are made by decision makers prone to act cautiously faced with the complexity and the riskiness of such ventures (March and Simon, 1958; Cyert and March, 1963; March, 1978). The environment in which foreign operations are conducted is in principle unknown to the novice international firm (Welch and Luostarinen, 1988). In order to cope with new environments a learning process, whereby knowledge and information are acquired, has to take place. Moreover, the choice of a new environment, that is which country to enter and how, also hinges on past learning. Cyert and March (1963) contend that limited searches are an important characteristic of this process. When confronted with a problem, organizations tend to start their search for solutions among alternatives that are quite close to solutions that have been tried previously. Searches are expanded into unchartered territory only if familiar alternatives do not provide satisfactory solutions. In sum, firms are, from this perspective, assumed to experientially learn which aspects of their environment to focus on, how to operate in that environment, and how to search for solutions to problems that emerge (Björkman, 1990).

Various types of experience might shape the internationalization of the firm. One type of experience relates to the extent to which a company has been exposed to international activities in general. Many - probably most - firms already have some international experience, usually in the form of export activity, when they make their first foreign direct investment. This type of experience can be termed general international experience. By dealing with foreign distributors and/or customers a company acquires knowledge about operating in an international context. Although that knowledge may not always be readily transferable to other settings and other types of operation, it serves to reduce the perceived risk of undertaking international operations beyond those which the company is already familiar with. In addition, such knowledge may facilitate the speed and quality of acquisition of knowledge relating to new international settings and operations. The value of general international experience lies in a higher preparedness for new international ventures: organizational belief and norm systems become less parochial, organization structures change in order to facilitate management of foreign operations, information systems are designed to provide relevant and reliable multi country information, employees are trained to deal with foreign customers, etc. Hence, previous research (Terpstra and Yu, 1988; Yu, 1990) has shown that there is a positive relationship between measures of general international experience - such as the ratio of foreign sales to total sales - and firms' propensity to make a foreign direct investment.

Another type of experience is often termed country-specific experience (Yu, 1990), i.e., the extent to which a firm has conducted business in a given country[2]. Country-specific experience relates to familiarity with the particularities of a given country; e.g., knowledge of the institutional and legal framework, knowledge about customers and market structure, and insight into the *modus operandi* of business conduct. The decision to enter a given country may, due to economies of learning and gradual reduction of perceived uncertainty, therefore reinforce future market presence in that country. For example, Davidson (1980) reports that the presence of an existing subsidiary in a foreign market increases the firm's propensity to make subsequent investments there. Johansen and Wiedersheim-Paul (1975) found that manufacturing operations tend to be located in countries in which the firm already had some presence (usually a sales subsidiary). Finally, the studies of Benito and Gripsrud (1992) and Yu (1990) suggest that experience from neighbouring or culturally similar countries (i.e., transferable country experience) has an impact on the location of subsequent FDIs.

From the perspective of the internationalization process approach, one would expect that hands-on experience from conducting a specific type of activity is a particularly valuable type of experience. Much of the uncertainty surrounding the internationalization of firms relates to the basic unfamiliarity of a nondomestic context, and may be overcome by general international experience. However, specific experience may be an equally important source of knowledge. Thus, even though experience from export activity might contribute in increasing firms' preparedness for other types of international activities, certain aspects of conducting, for example, foreign manufacturing activities are rather unique, and require specific learning. Examples are the organization of the foreign subsidiary, human resource management, and the coordination between the subsidiary and the parent company. Learning about the particularities of managing foreign manufacturing units is easier to do when other sources of uncertainty are kept at a minimum, i.e., in countries that are not too dissimilar and which are easily reached from the home country. This seems to provide a strong rationale for starting the expansion of foreign direct investments in nearby locations. However, although there is empirical evidence to support this line of reasoning (e.g., Johanson and Wiedersheim-Paul, 1975), some recent studies conclude otherwise. For example, in a study of Norwegian FDI in manufacturing Benito and Gripsrud (1992) found no support for the hypothesis that the first FDIs are made in countries that are culturally closer to the home country than later FDIs. Furthermore, the cultural distance to the country where a FDI is made did not increase with the number of FDIs previously undertaken by a given company. One might argue, however, that the number of investments previously undertaken is a somewhat crude proxy for experience, and that the results should therefore be regarded as tentative.

Resources

The impact of company resources on internationalization has been investigated in several studies. Studies of firms' export behaviour indicate that firm size is positively related not only to the propensity to export, but also to the number of export markets served by an individual company (see for example Calof, 1994). Compared to exporting, foreign direct investments usually imply an even more substantial commitment of resources, both managerial and financial, to operations that are considered as risky. Large firms are, due to their larger resource base, often in a better position than smaller firms to make such commitments. Thus, it is not surprising that many studies report that there is a positive relationship between the propensity to make foreign direct investments and the size of the firms (e.g., Caves, 1974; Grubaugh, 1987). Resources are also needed in order to absorb the costs and risk associated with FDI. Clearly, for a given level of resources committed to an operation, the smaller the firm the more vulnerable it is if such ventures turn out to be unsuccessful. Hence, small firms often take a cautious approach to international expansion (Welch and Luostarinen, 1988). Accordingly, since the resource base of the firm is likely to influence the perceived risk of a project, one might expect that the readiness to engage in manufacturing operations in distant locations - which are associated with a higher perceived risk - is dependent on the availability of resources[3].

Hypotheses

Based on the preceding discussion of the relationship between experience, resources, and distance to the location of a FDI, three hypotheses are put forward:

H_1: There is a positive relationship between the economic distance between the home and the host country of a FDI and the level of general international experience, the operation specific experience and the resources of the investing company.

H_2: There is a positive relationship between the cultural distance between the home and the host country of a FDI and the level of general international experience, the operation specific experience and the resources of the investing company.

H_3: There is a positive relationship between the geographic distance between the home and the host country of a FDI and the level of general international experience, the operation specific experience and the resources of the investing company.

Methodology

Data

The unit of analysis in this study is a given FDI in manufacturing. Data on foreign direct investment are taken from a survey carried out by the Norwegian Industrial Federation on Norwegian companies' foreign manufacturing establishments. The survey covered operative manufacturing subsidiaries in 1984 in which the Norwegian parents' stake was at least 10 per cent. In addition, information on a number of variables relating to the parent companies and the host countries have been compiled from various sources and included in the data base. In total, the data base consists of 254 cases representing investments made by 104 Norwegian companies. Unfortunately, missing data on various variables reduced the usable sample to 203 cases. The final sample covers approximately 60 per cent of total Norwegian foreign direct investment in 1984 (Hansen, 1984).

Operationalization of variables

The dependent variable in this study is distance between the home country of an investor company and the location (i.e., host country) of a given foreign investment. Distance is a multifaceted concept, and this study focuses on three particular dimensions of distance, namely geographic, cultural and economic distance. Of these, cultural distance is probably the most complex and therefore problematic dimension to measure empirically. The approach taken in the present study is to follow several recent studies (e.g., Erramilli, 1991; Benito and Gripsrud, 1992) and use an index for cultural distance developed by Kogut and Singh (1988). The Kogut-Singh index, which is based on the study conducted by Hofstede (1980) on cultural dimensions of work organization, measures cultural distance as the sum of variance-corrected score differences along four cultural dimensions (i.e., uncertainty avoidance, individuality, power distance and masculinity-femininity) for each country pair (i.e., the home country of the parent company and the host country of a given subsidiary). The Kogut-Singh index for cultural distance is defined as,

$$\text{Cultural distance}_j = \sum_{i=1}^{4} \{(I_{ij} - I_{iN})^2/V_i\}/4,$$

where I_{ij} = index value for the cultural dimension i of country j, V_i = variance of the index for dimension i, and N = Norway (the home country in this study). Scores on the four dimensions for the various countries were obtained from Hofstede (1984).

Geographic distance was operationalized as the air distance in 1,000 kilometers between Oslo, the capital of Norway, and the capital of a focal host country. A similar measure has been used in several other studies (e.g., Terpstra and Yu, 1988;

Yu, 1990; Veugelers, 1991). The values for this variable were taken from *IATA's Air Distance Manual* (1986).

Economic distance refers to disparities between countries in terms of standards of living, development of an infrastructure etc. Following Teece (1977) this variable was operationalized as the absolute value of the difference in GNP per capita in a given year (in 1,000 US$) between Norway and a host country j,

$$\text{Economic distance}_j = | \text{GNPcap}_{\text{Norway, 1983}} - \text{GNPcap}_{\text{j, 1983}} |$$

Data for this variable (for the year 1983) were taken from *European Marketing Data and Statistics* and *International Marketing Data and Statistics*, both published by Euromonitor.

Turning to the explanatory variables, experience is according to the internationalization process framework an important determinant of firm behaviour (Johanson and Vahlne, 1990). Firms with scant international experience are expected to act cautiously, and to be unwilling to take any great risks in the development of their international operations. The internationalization process approach suggests that the first international operations undertaken by a company typically take place in a country that is close to the home market. Accumulation of experience gradually expands the set of opportunities taken into consideration by a company, and entry into more distant markets may therefore take place as more experience is acquired. Two types of experience are examined in this study. One type of experience relates to the extent to which a company has been exposed to international activities in general. General international experience was operationalized as the ratio of export sales to total sales for a given parent company in the year prior to undertaking a focal foreign direct investment. These data were taken from the annual publication *Norges Største Bedrifter* (Norway's Largest Companies).

The other type of experience investigated here is of a more specific kind in that it relates to experience acquired through management of manufacturing subsidiaries in foreign locations. Operation specific experience was measured by two indicators; i) the number of years since a company undertook its first foreign direct investment in manufacturing, and ii) the number of foreign direct investments undertaken by the company prior to a focal investment. The relatively high correlation ($r = 0.71$) between the two indicators suggests that they map the same underlying construct, but somewhat different aspects of it. In order to arrive at a single measure for operation specific experience, an index composed of both indicators was constructed. Standardized scores (mean = 0, std.dev. = 1) were used due to the different scales of the indicators[4]. The variable is thus given as,

$$\text{Operation specific experience} = (Z_1 + Z_2) / 2$$

where Z_1 denotes the first standardized indicator (number of years), and where Z_2 is the second indicator (number of investments). The reliability measure - coefficient alpha - for this two-item variable is 0.83.

Finally, foreign direct investment is a risky undertaking that involves a substantial commitment of financial and managerial resources. Thus, resources are hypothesized to influence the location choices made by internationalizing firms. The resource base of the parent company was measured by two size indicators; i) total sales, and ii) number of employees. These data were collected from *Norges Største Bedrifter* (Norway's Largest Companies) for the year prior to a focal investment[5]. The Pearson correlation coefficient between the indicators is 0.82. The standardization procedure used for the experience index was also applied for the resource index. Again, the reliability coefficient for this variable is very high (coefficient alpha = 0.91).

Method

The hypotheses can be expressed in three equations;

$$(1) \quad Y_1 = \alpha_1 + \beta_{11} X_1 + \beta_{12} X_2 + \beta_{13} X_3 + \epsilon$$
$$(2) \quad Y_2 = \alpha_2 + \beta_{21} X_1 + \beta_{22} X_2 + \beta_{23} X_3 + \epsilon$$
$$(3) \quad Y_3 = \alpha_3 + \beta_{31} X_1 + \beta_{32} X_2 + \beta_{33} X_3 + \epsilon$$

where,

Y_1 = Economic distance: difference in GNP per capita
Y_2 = Cultural distance: Kogut-Singh index
Y_3 = Geographic distance: kilometers between capital cities
X_1 = General international experience: export sales/total sales
X_2 = Operation specific experience (index)
X_3 = Resources (index)
α, β = Coefficients
ϵ = Error term

Equations (1)-(3) were estimated by ordinary least squares regression analysis. According to the hypotheses all βs are expected to be positive.

Results

Table 4.1 reports means, standard deviations, and the correlation matrix of the variables included in equations (1)-(3). Inspection of the correlations between the dependent variables reveals, expectedly, that the various dimensions of distance are quite interrelated; in other words, the countries most similar to Norway in terms of culture tend, overall, to be other affluent countries located nearby. However, the correlations suggest that the fit between different measures of distance is far from perfect. Culturally and/or economically similar countries may lie far from each other in geographical terms (a good example is Norway and New Zealand), and conversely, considerable cultural and economic differences may be found between countries that

Table 4.1
Means, standard deviations, and Pearson correlation coefficients (n = 203)

	Mean	SD	Y_1	Y_2	Y_3	X_1	X_2	X_3
Y_1	4.75	3.10	-					
Y_2	1.90	1.42	0.69	-				
Y_3	3.22	3.34	0.58	0.72	-			
X_1	44.02	29.65	-0.07	-0.03	-0.05	-		
X_2	0.00	1.39	0.08	0.09	0.07	0.22	-	
X_3	0.00	0.96	-0.12	-0.10	-0.17	0.42	0.59	-

Table 4.2
Multiple regression of equations (1)-(3), OLS-estimation (n = 203)

Independent variables	Coefficients (t-values) (1)	(2)	(3)
α	4.441[b] (9.724)	1.621[b] (7.191)	2.693[b] (5.262)
$Log(X_1)$	0.031 (0.428)	0.096 (1.328)	0.086 (1.198)
X_2	0.224[a] (2.614)	0.229[a] (2.686)	0.257[a] (3.058)
X_3	-0.265[b] (-3.038)	-0.267[b] (-3.069)	-0.351[b] (-4093)
F=	3.486 (p=0.017)	3.946 (p=0.009)	5.996 (p=0.000)
Adj R^2=	0.04	0.04	0.07
D-W=	1.60	1.45	1.65

Notes: a) p<0.05 (one-tailed); b) p<0.05 (two-tailed)

Table 4.3
Multiple regression of equations (1)-(3) for subsample consisting of FDIs with investment number five or less. OLS-estimation (n = 147).

Coefficients (t-values)

Independent variables	(1)	(2)	(3)
α	4.447[b] (8.796)	1.670[b] (6.447)	2.790[b] (4.747)
$Log(X_1)$	0.024 (0.275)	0.106 (1.249)	0.082 (0.979)
X_2	0.079 (0.926)	0.136 (1.610)	0.187[a] (2.236)
X_3	-0.067 (-0.764)	-0.038 (-0.444)	-0.144 (-1.685)
F=	0.409 (p=0.747)	1.407 (p=0.243)	2.370 (p=0.073)
Adj R^2=	0.00	0.00	0.03
D-W=	1.79	1.58	1.73

Notes: a) p<0.05 (one-tailed); b) p<0.05 (two-tailed)

are relatively close geographically (the case of Norway and Turkey illustrates this point).

Turning to the independent variables the correlation matrix shows that, apart from the relatively high correlation between resources and operation specific experience ($r = 0.59$), there is no apparent reason to suspect serious problems due to intercorrelation. Nevertheless, although it may not be surprising that large companies have more experience from managing foreign subsidiaries than smaller companies, the magnitude of the correlation between these variables indicates that a confounding problem might be present. Moreover, collinearity can affect the estimation of the parameters. Therefore, the values for the tolerance of a variable, an often used measure of collinearity, were inspected[6]. It turned out that the lowest tolerance found was 0.56, which does not suggest any serious collinearity problems.

The results of the regressions are shown in table 4.2[7]. Since the data material includes cases where individual parent companies may have made several FDIs, the question of serial correlation must be addressed. The estimated Durbin-Watson statistics are 1.60, 1.45, and 1.65 for equations (1), (2) and (3) respectively. The Durbin-Watson test is therefore - using a 0.01 level of significance - inconclusive with regard to the null hypothesis that serial correlation is not present in equation (3). On the other hand, positive serial correlation is indicated in equations (1) and (2). The estimated parameters in these equations must therefore be interpreted with caution, and the results should be regarded as tentative.

Since the F-statistics are significant, a closer examination of the regression coefficients is warranted. It should be noted, however, that the quite modest R^2 statistics imply that the proportion of variance in the dependent variables actually captured by the models is fairly low, thus suggesting that location decisions are influenced by - probably many - factors not taken into account by the internationalization process model.

Turning to the significance of the various variables, the results only give mixed support to the hypotheses[8]. First, general international experience does not seem to have any decisive impact on the various dimensions of distance. Although the coefficients for this variable are positive in all regressions, as was expected, they are not significant in equations (1) and (3) and only weakly significant ($\beta_{21} = 0.096$, $p < 0.10$) in equation (2). Second, all coefficients for the operation specific experience variable are positive and highly significant. This result is in accordance with the hypothesis that companies seek out more distant locations as they gain experience from conducting foreign production activities. In particular, strong support is found for a positive relationship between operation specific experience and geographic distance to FDI locations ($\beta_{32} = 0.257$, $p < 0.01$). Finally, the coefficients for the resource variable are negative in all regressions. This suggests that the effect of company resources on the distance to a foreign establishment may be in the opposite direction of what was expected.

As noted earlier, however, there might be confounding problems associated with the resource and the operation specific experience variables. An inspection of the correlations between the indicators used in constructing the indexes reveals that there is a high correlation between the number of investments undertaken by a company prior to a focal investment and the two size indicators ($r = 0.74$, and $r = 0.66$), while the number of years since the first investment was made is not particularly highly correlated with size ($r = 0.48$, and $r = 0.39$). A closely related problem is that the number of investments undertaken by a few large multinationals is far higher than the average. For example, four companies in our sample owned ten or more foreign manufacturing subsidiaries, while the average number of subsidiaries owned by a company in our sample was considerably lower (2.4 subsidiaries per company). It is therefore probable that location strategies specific to a limited number of large companies may influence the overall location patterns observed in the data material.

In order to control for such effects, additional regressions including only the first five investments undertaken by any company were conducted. Although this procedure must admittedly be considered as rather ad hoc, it turns out that it remedies any potential intercorrelation problem quite well[9]. In addition, the Durbin-Watson statistics improve considerably. The null hypothesis that serial correlation is not present is accepted for equations (1) and (3) using a 0.01 level of significance. The

Durbin-Watson test is, however, still inconclusive for equation (2). The regressions are presented in Table 4.3.

The estimations for the subsample provide some interesting results. First, it is clear that the performance of the models drops considerably. In fact, as seen from the estimated F-values only equation (3) calls for any further examination. Secondly, the signs of the coefficients are unchanged when compared to the regressions reported in Table 4.2. Again, the partial regression coefficient for general international experience - measured as a firm's export ratio - shows a positive sign in accordance with the hypotheses, but the coefficient is not significant. In a similar vein, the coefficient for the operation specific experience index remains positive, and is significant ($\beta_{32} = 0.187$, $p < 0.05$).

On the other hand, the sign of the parent company resource index coefficient is still negative, but the coefficient is only weakly significant ($\beta_{33} = -0.144$, $p < 0.10$, two-tailed test) when higher-order investments are excluded from the analysis. This suggests that the strong negative relationship between resources and distance reported in table 2 is indeed partly due to the particular location strategies followed by some large companies. When the influence of these companies on the overall pattern is controlled for, the results are no longer clearly contradictory to the hypotheses.

Summary and discussion

This study has taken an empirical look at the internationalization process approach to decisions regarding the location of FDIs. The internationalization process framework is a general model that explains various aspects of firms' internationalization - including location choices - as the outcome of a continuous process of learning and commitment of resources to international markets (Vahlne and Nordström, 1993).

Overall, this study gives limited support to the internationalization process approach. The findings support the notion of a positive relationship between the level of experience related to prior involvement in international production activities - termed operation specific experience in this study - and distance to the chosen locations for FDIs. Only weak support was found for a similar relationship between general international experience (measured by the export ratio of a company) and distance. Moreover, no support was found for the hypothesized positive relationship between company resources and distance to FDI sites. Various specifications of the dependent variable - economic, cultural, and geographic distance from the home country to the host country - provided basically the same results. However, the clear results were found for geographical distance as the dependent variable.

Since this study only provides limited support for the internationalization process model, and some other recent studies also finds only weak or no support at all for the model (Benito and Gripsrud, 1992; Engwall and Wallenstål, 1988), the validity of the internationalization process model as a general explanation of firms' internationalization behaviour must be questioned. In order to explain the lack of support reported in recent studies, Vahlne and Nordström (1993) argue that the process model is probably more valid in the early stages of the internationalization process of a company. Although this argument may have some intuitive appeal, it is not corroborated by our findings. A notable finding in this study is that the results for the subsample containing only the first five FDIs made by any given company, give even less support to the process model than the results obtained for the total sample.

Nevertheless, our results show that there is a positive relationship between operation specific experience and, in particular, geographical distance. This suggests that experience may act as a determinant of location decisions regarding FDIs. Thus, the internationalization process model provides a contribution towards understanding location choices. However, as indicated by the low explanatory power of the regressions, the internationalization process model is apparently - perhaps not surprisingly - a rather partial model.

While traditional economic and geographic approaches to FDI focus primarily on factors that are external to the individual companies, such as demand conditions and competitive structure in the various markets, and factor availability and production costs in different locations, the internationalization process model focuses almost entirely on factors that are internal to the company. In other words, the process model is mainly supply-side oriented. Basically, the model relies on the assumption that company growth is the driving force behind FDI, and predicts that growth takes place along an experiential path. Little attention is paid to the underlying motives for FDI. Thus, the reasons for undertaking a FDI in a given situation instead of, for example, exporting are not accounted for. The same applies to the question of why a given market or country was targeted in the first place.

Both demand-side and supply-side factors must be included in order to explain the location of FDIs. In particular, it has to be acknowledged that firms move into foreign countries for different reasons. Some FDIs are based on resource-seeking considerations, and investments are made in order to gain control over important - often immobile - inputs to upstream activities. Other FDIs are of an export substituting kind, where foreign production activities serve to supply a market with finished goods in the presence of trade barriers such as high tariffs and/or transportation costs. Still other FDIs are predominantly motivated by cost considerations; production activities are moved to another country mainly to take advantage of low labour costs in that country. Clearly, the set of countries considered as potential locations for a foreign direct investment is likely to vary depending on the motive for investment. For example, a Norwegian firm that is planning to make a foreign direct investment in order to achieve lower production costs will probably not consider countries close to Norway - regardless of how the concept of distance is measured - as viable alternatives. Experience effects may of course influence the actual choices made by companies, but mainly to the extent that a given site belongs to the set of feasible locations defined by the nature of the business and the rationale for foreign investment. Experience effects, as well as the effect of company resources, may therefore be difficult to detect in a cross-industry study like the one presented here. Our findings should accordingly be regarded as preliminary. This limitation in our study provides an opportunity for future research based on the internationalization process model that controls for different types of foreign direct investment.

Notes

1. It should be clear, however, that determinants of location do not alone explain why an FDI is undertaken since the question of who owns the productive assets is left unanswered. Thus, the theory of international production must explain both location choices and why companies would own and control operations abroad. The latter question has been analysed quite successfully by a number of scholars using an internalization (Buckley and Casson, 1976) or a transaction cost approach (Rugman, 1981; Williamson, 1981; Teece, 1986). A general economic framework encompassing both location and ownership aspects of international production is set out in Dunning's (1981, 1988, 1993) so-called eclectic theory.
2. Although we acknowledge that country-specific experience can be an important location determinant, the effect of such experience will not, due to limitations in our data, be examined empirically in the present study.
3. An additional reason why larger firms can be expected to be more adventurous is that if a distant location is to be considered at all, a firm must possess a certain market scanning capability.
4. Standardized scores (Z_i) are calculated as, $Z_i = (X_i - \bar{X}) / \sigma$ where σ is the standard deviation.
5. Data from different years were used. The total sales (TS) figures had to be adjusted in order to make them comparable over time. Using the consumer price index (CPI) for 1979 as the base year the following adjustment was made; $TS_{adjusted} = TS_{nominal} / CPI \cdot 100$
6. The tolerance of a variable I is defined as $1\text{-}R_i^2$, where R_i is the multiple correlation coefficient when the ith independent variable is predicted by the other independent variables. A low tolerance value means that a variable is a linear combination of the other independent variables (see, for example, Hair et al., 1992).
7. Inspection of normal probability plots revealed some deviation from normality for the general experience variable (X_1). This was solved by a logarithmic transformation.
8. In assessing the significance of the individual coefficients, we use one-tailed tests when the coefficient is in the predicted direction, and two-tailed tests if the direction of the coefficient is opposite to the one predicted.
9. The correlations between number of investments and the size indicators (sales and employees) drop to 0.31 and 0.28 respectively, when only the first five investments made by any company are included in the analysis. The correlation between the operation specific experience variable and the resource variable drops correspondingly to 0.21.

5 Silicon Glen – Fifty years of the electronics industry

Ewan Sutherland

Introduction

The Scottish economy has suffered badly through most of the twentieth century as a result of the collapse of the heavy engineering industries which had been built up through the nineteenth century by local entrepreneurs. There was little compensating growth from the rise of other sectors, except in electronics, oil and, most recently, in services. So great was the apparent success of the electronics and computer industries that in the early 1980s the most populous part of Scotland was designated Silicon Glen, both in conscious imitation of California's Silicon Valley and also in a desire to emulate its success. This chapter analyses the role of Foreign Direct Investment (FDI) in the development of those industries from the 1940s to the present day. An assessment is made of government intervention to sustain the Scottish economy in general and in particular the electronics and computer industries. This is followed by consideration of some of the multinational corporations (NCR, Wang Laboratories, Timex and DEC) and finally by a comparison with Scottish entrepreneurial activity including the Scottish Electronics Scheme and Rodime PLC.

Scotland and electronics

Scotland is an integral part of the United Kingdom with free movement of people, goods and capital, with the same tax rates, interest charges and so on. Yet Scotland is demonstrably a separate country, with fiercely expressed nationalism and a distinct culture, possessing its own religious, legal and educational systems, in effect, its own civil society. Therefore Scotland and the Scottish economy have to be seen on the one hand as part of the UK and of the UK economy while on the other hand they must be seen as entities in their own right. It is also essential to realize that Scotland is no more a homogenous nation than is the United Kingdom, there are considerable contrasts and can often be tensions between the highlands and lowlands and between Glasgow and Edinburgh.

As early as the 1940s efforts were made to build up the electrical and electronics industry. Although encouragement of indigenous firms was ultimately to achieve little of lasting value, Scotland was remarkably successful in attracting multinational corporations. However, the attraction of footloose multinational corporations was attempted elsewhere, making Scotland part of a fiercely competitive global market in locations in which, despite many years of work, no real differentiation has been achieved.

It was long argued that once the foreign corporations had developed their local presence, a critical mass would be attained after which the sector would be self-sustaining. Not only has this not happened, but a report by Monitor (management consultants) in 1993 raised fears that the whole basis of Silicon Glen could easily slip away, with a worst case scenario of the loss of forty percent of existing jobs in only five years. The underlying problems being:

- changes in the practices of multinational corporations;
- changes in the computer and electronic industries;
- a failure to develop competitiveness through integration of the industry in Scotland;
- too little research and development;
- too much reliance on imported components and sub-assemblies.

If nothing else, this raised the level of debate on the future of Silicon Glen; what can reasonably be expected from it and what the alternatives might be.

Industrial revolutions

Checkland (1981) has characterized in stark terms the economic development of the period of more than a century when Clydeside was dominated by vertically integrated heavy industry—iron to engineering and shipbuilding. The strategic over commitment to heavy engineering and shipbuilding meant that it took a remarkably long time to realize that something had gone wrong and to discover that the position was seemingly irrecoverable. Only a very small minority took the view that perseverance with the traditional industries could have been seen through to success (Harvie, 1977).

A Second Industrial Revolution had occurred at the end of the nineteenth century, based on three industries: cars, chemicals and electrical equipment (Chandler, 1990). The failure in Scotland to exploit the opportunities this created led to a seemingly inevitable economic decline, heavy engineering had killed off or discouraged the growth of more modern industries. Business was fixed in its historical pattern of iron and steel, marine and railway engines, shipbuilding and other forms of heavy engineering. The reputation of 'Clydebuilt', epitomized by the liners the Queen Mary and the Queen Elizabeth, was achieved by industries that operated at the level of one-off and small batches. The skilled workers were individuals unfamiliar with mass production and the dull routine of assembly lines, there was little understanding of the mass production, distribution or advertising which were revolutionizing industry in the USA and Germany. These small workplaces were dominated by strong-willed individualists—both owners and foremen—who could often be myopic and parochial. Management continued to be dominated by the founding families rather than by a managerial meritocracy; it had not been necessary to create teams of expert managers to run large corporations. There was no mass market in Scotland and it was far from any of the large consumer markets.

The contrast with the USA is most obvious in the person of Andrew Carnegie who emigrated from Scotland to the USA in 1848. His industrial success was based on economies of scale, permitting low-cost production, allowing him to push down prices and so drive up demand, allowing a further increase in scale, facilitating further cost savings (Livesay, 1976). By comparison, the Scottish steel industry operated on a much smaller scale and the degree of integration was very limited. Manufacturers participated in cartels allocating quotas, penalizing those who overproduced and compensating those who underproduced. Small firms survived, but at the cost of the economies of scale and the development of modern management practices. Effective diversification was discouraged and economic growth retarded. An integrated steel works was not in operation in Scotland until Ravenscraig opened in 1957, by which time it was many decades too late (Payne, 1992).

By the outbreak of the Second World War the flaws and failings of the Scottish economy could no longer be hidden. In terms of technology and management it had made little progress since the beginning of the century. The result was an absence of the economic growth necessary to sustain Scotland's place in the world and its growing population. One consequence of this was the continuing flow of migrants to England and overseas. The position of the Scottish economy was at least as bad as that of any other peripheral region of the UK and often worse. A sequence of crises hit the Scottish economy in the 1960s, of which the grandest was the drawn-out collapse of shipbuilding on the Clyde which absorbed so much emotional and political energy in the late 1960s and early 1970s. Attempts at reorganization had been too slow and had failed, because of a blind refusal to compromise, with the result that in 1967:

> When the Queen Elizabeth II steamed down the Firth it left a river which was only marginally more lively than the Styx (Harvie, 1977, p. 174).

The information revolution of computers and electronics came to Scotland almost exclusively as the result of the actions of foreigners, aided by the government and the Scottish establishment. Without the intervention of multinational corporations there is no reason to believe that there would be significant activity in this sector of the economy.

Government intervention

In the face of near terminal economic decline, an obvious lack of entrepreneurial efforts, continuing factory closures and latterly goaded by the intermittent but spectacular electoral successes of the Scottish National Party, it became increasingly important for the government to avoid economic collapse and to be seen to be trying to stimulate growth. A succession of ministers set important political and economic aims:

- to contain emigration;
- to increase employment;
- to modernize the technological base;
- to encourage Scottish-owned industry.

The principal form of intervention was the encouragement of foreigners to make good the deficit in the performance of Scottish companies in adopting new technology and in creating new jobs. This was intended both for its immediate effect and as an example to local industry:

> I also do not disguise that I have thought, as indeed I think you too have thought, that the introduction of I.B.M. methods to the Clydeside would be an exceedingly healthy thing. (Hector McNeil to Harold Wilson, 3.iv.1951, PRO/BT 177/905[1]).

Industrial locations were to become a competitive market, with different nations, regions and cities fighting for foreign direct investment (Encarnation and Wells, 1986). Rivalry has grown with the proliferation of technopoles, science parks, free trade zones and so on (Massey et al., 1992). In order to attract the multinational corporations, it has become commonplace to offer a range of incentives such as tax holidays, grants, skilled labour and free factories. It became essential for the agencies involved to increase their understanding of the individual corporations, their industries, their suppliers and their markets. Understanding their customers was vital in a market where the competition was so fierce that countries and regions fight over potential factories. A conspicuous example of this was when Motorola, already established in Scotland with a microprocessor plant at East Kilbride, announced plans for a plant somewhere in Europe to manufacture customer equipment for mobile telephony. Scotland won this but only after considerable competition from other countries and at the expenditure of great effort, including a rapid response team which flew to the USA.

The result of such competition is to drive down the costs for the multinational corporations, with the host countries paying the price, through direct subsidy and lost tax revenues. These pressures are also liable to encourage inexperienced firms to make overseas investments before they need to and without the necessary experience.

Locate in Scotland (LIS) operates in California to encourage companies to build factories in Scotland. In effect, it is part of the feeding frenzy, of hyper-active venture capitalism, concerned to get some new industry, by offering relatively low cost labour (in European terms) and incentives up to and including investment capital, before they are snapped up by another country. As a result, the future of a significant sector of the Scottish economy had become reliant on games of chance being played in California's 'silicon casino'.

While a fresh supply of foreign direct investment remains important, it has also been important to maintain contact with existing corporations. This 'aftercare' has played a significant role in maintaining employment, with significant new investments and increases in employment notably at Motorola and NEC.

Whether in support of lame ducks or sunrise industries, UK governments have spent considerable sums of money on various forms of regional assistance which in many ways has been of considerable value to Scotland. However, this expenditure cannot be seen in isolation, it is essential to compare it with related spending, specifically on defense procurement contracts. This changes the picture quite dramatically, if for no other reason than that defense procurement contracts have been ten times the size of regional assistance (see Table 11.1). In this light, regional assistance can be seen to be little more than a palliative. Similarly, government research establishments are almost all in the South-East of England. Clearly the 1990s have brought significant changes to this as the effects of the 'peace dividend' have begun to turn into plant closures, for example, the naval dockyard at Rosyth in Fife.

From agency to enterprise

The Scottish Development Agency, Scottish Enterprise and Locate in Scotland have been the institutions through which government has operated to supplement and encourage the market. The Scottish Development Agency (the Agency) was created in 1975 to coordinate economic development in Scotland. Specifically it was to:

- provide finance for business;
- assist in the development of industry;
- provide and manage sites and premises;
- renew land.

The Agency inherited the work of various government bodies and part of the work of the voluntary Scottish Council (Development and Industry). The circumstances at the time of its creation were that the Agency:

> ... found itself inhabiting a political environment influenced by three prominent groupings: a deeply skeptical business community, made wretched by its own lack of self-confidence; a deeply anxious political and civil service corps, made nervous

by its own failures with economic performance; a deeply cynical electorate, made impatient by the evident inability of either to haul Scotland out of this mire. (Cunningham, 1990, formerly Industry Director, SDA).

To which should be added a trades union movement which was often bloody-minded and which had become enamoured of central planning.

In the scramble for foreign direct investment in the late 1970s, the activities of the Scottish Office, the Scottish Council, SDA, new town development corporations, regional and district councils were often overlapping and the failure to coordinate these activities led to more than simply confusion. The government created Locate in Scotland (LIS) in 1981 as a joint venture between the SDA and the Industry Department for Scotland to oversee the search for FDI. This brought its activities more closely under Civil Service control and made it easier for ministers to claim credit. It was to be a fast response, one-stop shop for: grants, loans, advice and access to experience (Committee on Scottish Affairs, 1980).

Table 5.1
Per capita expenditure by UK region in 1983 and 1990

Region	1983			1990		
	Reg. assist.	Defence contracts	Total	Reg. assist.	Defence contracts	Total
North	29.66	44.64	74.30	27.64	276.39	304.03
South-West	2.72	174.55	177.27	1.93	203.58	205.51
South-East	-	220.39	220.39	-	166.11	166.11
North-West	21.19	118.33	139.52	9.00	140.88	149.88
Scotland	43.00	80.49	123.50	31.18	117.59	148.77
East Anglia	-	110.37	110.37	-	97.13	97.13
West Midlands	-	53.61	53.61	3.45	86.22	89.67
East Midlands	4.58	90.24	94.82	1.37	74.65	76.02
Wales	40.46	24.74	65.20	46.40	17.35	63.75
Yorkshire & Humberside	7.23	28.27	35.50	5.94	30.29	36.23
UK	13.11	123.34	136.45	8.66	130.64	139.30

Under the Thatcher Administration (1979-1990) the Agency was officially constrained to be involved only where the market would not produce the desired policy outcomes, to improve the workings of the market and to avoid creating any dependency on government intervention (IDS, 1987). The case for using the Agency was that it had to be more efficient than the central or local government alternatives. Yet Hood (1991) argues convincingly that the SDA was able to pursue what amounts to an industrial policy targeted on a handful of industrial sectors, of which the most important was in electronics and computers.

The perception in Westminster was that the Agency was not 'one of us', not truly imbued with the spirit of radical Thatcherism. It was too inclined to intervention, while the staff contained too many bureaucrats and academics, rather than captains of industry. In some ways it was too Scottish, too much part of a civil consensus from which the government itself was excluded.

The Agency was reformed as Scottish Enterprise in 1992, by merging it with the Training Agency. The development corporations for the new towns were also phased out. The new structure of Scottish Enterprise, Highlands and Islands Enterprise and a network of Local Enterprise Companies (LECs) was intended to improve the services provided with its explicit link to training and its greater focus on local requirements. Many of the functions of the SDA were transferred to a network of twenty-three Local Enterprise Companies. However, integrating such a complex set of organizations and policy objectives has proved far from simple. Leading industrialists, once installed in LECs and SE have faced two problems. Firstly, they must avoid seeing government money as a bottomless pit from which they can always draw more. Secondly, they must acquire new skills in the development of long term programmes which are both creative and customer orientated.

For electronics, it is not possible for the skills and competencies to be developed in each of the LECs, thus policy has remained in Scottish Enterprise. One area where subsidiarity has been evident is in the encouragement of the software business, with LECs developing their own incubator projects for software start-ups at East Kilbride, Glasgow, Livingston and Stirling.

A branch plant economy

By the late 1970s an economy had emerged and, in part, had been designed, which was largely without the control of Scotland and the Scots. It was dependent on the decisions—sometimes the whims—of non-Scottish managers and overseas investors. When faced with economic problems, multinational enterprises seemed invariably to close their factories in Scotland, rather than those at home, a well-known weakness of this type of economic development. Scotland lost jobs at Caterpillar Tractors, Goodyear Tyre, Massey-Ferguson Tractors, Monsanto Chemicals, Singer Sewing Machines and in the closure of the Linwood car plant (Hood and Young, 1982). The reasons for this were a mixture of low productivity, over staffing, restrictive practices or poor labour relations. In most multinational corporations comparative plant performance is closely monitored with poor performers vulnerable to closure. Few plants in Scotland had unique products or production capacity and they lacked the R&D necessary to make themselves self-sustaining.

The feeling of Scottish economic helplessness was reinforced by the continuing loss of control of leading Scottish firms through mergers and acquisitions, of which the most dramatic was the acquisition by Guinness of Distillers. In the electronics sector, Pilkington plc acquired the old-established opto-electronics firm of Barr and Stroud, Mitsubishi acquired the multimedia software house Office Workstations Limited, and Laporte Industries acquired Compugraphics, which makes masks for chip fabrication (Ashcroft and Love, 1993).

Figure 5.1 shows the number of people employed in overseas-owned manufacturing plants in Scotland since the 1950s. From the mid-1970s it is clear that the number of jobs was declining, though the percentage of the total manufacturing workforce was rising, indicating a rather better performance in the overseas-owned sector than in the UK-owned sector. Computers and electronics comprised almost one quarter of the overseas owned manufacturing plants and some 36 percent of the employment.

The incomers

There can be little doubt about the superficial success of the foreign direct investment policy (see Table 5.2).The first instances of foreign direct investment were in the light manufacturing sector, corporations which were to face the painful evolution into manufacturers of computers and electronic systems. In the intervening fifty years there have been enormous changes in the structure of the industry and the participants. Early investments in Scotland came from England and the USA, now both are the recipients of inward foreign direct investment and thus in competition with Scotland. The wheel of fortune has turned against many of the initial investors, who have been forced into contraction or liquidation. The nature of international business has also changed with much greater reliance on strategic partnerships between companies, as an alternative to integrating the activities within the business. In the mean time the US-based multinational corporations were much more confident in their attitude to other European countries and followed the logic of the single market of the European Union by consolidating their operations into single plants, often in continental Europe. Sometimes this has worked in favour of Scotland, as in the case of Hoover. Similarly Japanese companies now seem willing to locate in any of several European Union member states.

The reasons why foreigners came to Scotland to build factories appear to have been:

- English language;
- low labour costs;
- ancestral and cultural connections;
- scientific and engineering tradition;

- access to markets;
- governmental encouragement and support.

The Scottish scientific and engineering tradition may, in practice, have been largely or wholly irrelevant, but an image was still there from the era of 'Clydebuilt'. The idea of the Scot as engineer was revived in the television series and films of *Star Trek* where the chief engineer on the USS Enterprise was 'Scotty' complete, on occasion, with kilt and bagpipes.

A factory in Scotland opened the way for a multinational corporation to be included in preferential purchasing for UK defense contracts and more generally to markets in the UK, the British Empire, the Commonwealth, the European Free Trade Area and, after 1971, the European Community. However, access to the public non-defense sector in the UK markets was problematic, with organizations under strong pressure to buy British, primarily to support national champions in the 1960s and 1970s, to the disadvantage of Burroughs, Honeywell and IBM, all then established in Scotland.

The UK government encouraged almost anybody with a plausible proposal to come to Scotland as an expedient to revive the Scottish economy, offering tax relief, automatic grants, selective financial assistance and so on. By comparison, the French government was at best neutral and often anti-American, especially in the defense sector, though recently it has been much more welcoming. The Germans believed, perhaps correctly, that they could do without inward investment. By comparison, Scotland shared the same language, was cheap and was welcoming. As the companies and individual executives gained experience in European operations and marketing they were tempted to look at other non-English speaking locations, including the new

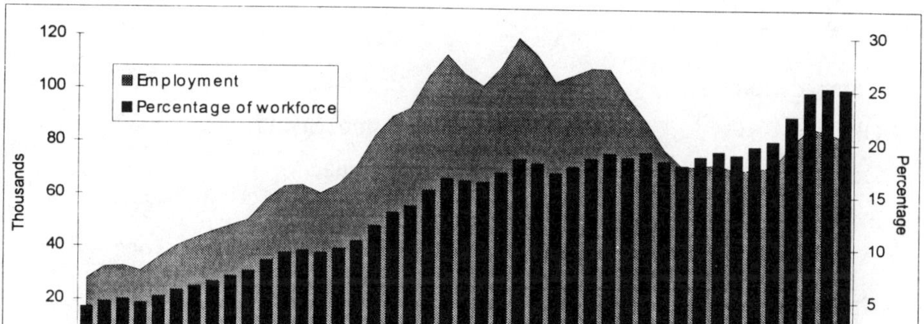

Figure 5.1: Employment in overseas-owned manufacturing plants

Table 5.2

Branch plants opened in Scotland

Company	Nationality	Location	Date
Remington-Rand	USA	Hillington	1937
Ferranti	England	Edinburgh	1943
NCR	USA	Dundee	1946
Timex	USA/Norway	Dundee	1946
Honeywell	USA	Blantyre	1948
IBM	USA	Greenock	1951
Hughes Microelectronics	USA	Glenrothes	1960
Hewlett-Packard	USA	S Queensferry	1964
General Instrument	USA	Glenrothes	1968
Motorola	USA	East Kilbride	1969
National Semiconductor	USA	Greenock	1969
Burroughs	USA	Livingston	1971
DEC	USA	Ayr	1976
NEC	Japan	Livingston	1980
Sun Microsystems	USA	Livingston	1984
Wang Laboratories	USA	Stirling	1984
DEC	USA	S Queensferry	1986
Compaq Computer	USA	Erskine	1987
Oki	Japan	Cumbernauld	1987
Delta	Japan	Inchinan	1990
Seiko	Japan	Livingston	1990
Fuji Electric	Japan	East Kilbride	1992
Canon	Japan	East Kilbride	1993
Escom	Germany	Prestwick	1993
Exabyte	USA	Falkirk	1994
Elonex	UK	Cumbernauld	1994
Teledyne	USA	Cumbernauld	1994

member states of the European Community. This was made more important as it moved to complete the single European market, which acted as a major stimulus for the Europeanization of corporations, emphasizing production for the pan-European market from a single location. Scotland had acted as a staging post, somewhere for US-based multinational corporations to learn about Europe before they move on to the continent.

Once it was decided to look overseas for solutions, the initial problem was how to attract multinational corporations to a remote part of the world and one shrouded in *clichés*, either as some kind of Brigadoon[2] never-never land, or a damp depressing expanse of grey tenements, with high unemployment and Marxist workers (Committee on Scottish Affairs, 1980, p. 15).

Figure 5.2 shows the breakdown of employment in the electronics and computer industries by product grouping, which has been relatively stable for the last decade, seemingly kept in equilibrium with closures balanced by new arrivals. The decline in the 1990s is significant and is more a reflection of a global downturn in the industry.

In the ten years to 1993, the number of overseas owned plants rose from 185 to 190, but this involved some 53 expansions of existing plants as against 43 contractions, some 93 plants being opened and 88 being closed. There was no net change in employment over the ten years (SOID, 1994, p. 3).

Table 5.3 shows the leading companies in Silicon Glen, how long they have been

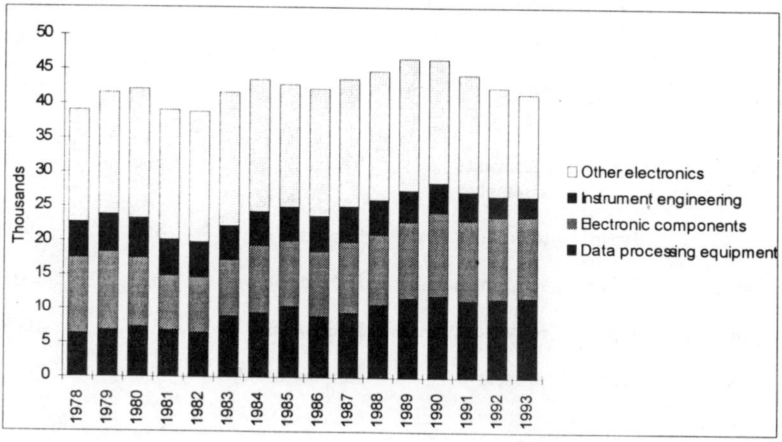

Figure 5.2: Employment by industry grouping in the electronics sector

Source: IDS, 1989, p. 2 and SOID, 1994, p. 2

Table 5.3
Leading companies in Silicon Glen

Company	Nation	Products	Location	Workforce	Opened
IBM	USA	PCs and monitors	Greenock	2,300	1951
Motorola	USA	semiconductors	East Kilbride	2,000	1969
Motorola	USA	mobile telephones	Easter Inch	1,600	1990
AT&T GIS[1]	USA	automatic teller machines	Dundee	1,600	1946
DEC	USA	workstations	Ayr	1,600	1976
National Semiconductor	USA	semiconductors	Greenock	1,300	1969
Hewlett-Packard	USA	communications systems	S Queensferry	1,000	1964
NEC	Japan	semiconductors	Livingston	850	1980
Polaroid	USA	cameras	Dumbarton	800	1950
Compaq Computer	Japan	PCs	Erskine	700	1987
SCI	USA	electronics assembly	Irvine	800	1990
JVC	Japan	televisions	East Kilbride	700	1985
Motorola[2]	Japan	semiconductors	S Queensferry	550	1986
Mitsubishi[3]	Japan	televisions	Haddington	515	1968
Oki	Japan	printers	Cumbermauld	500	1979

1. Formerly NCR.
2. Opened as DEC, subsequently acquired in 1995.
3. Opened as Tandberg, acquired in 1987.

established in Scotland and type of products currently manufactured. Motorola is now the largest employer, a position achieved as a result of recent and rapid expansion.

Figure 5.3 shows the changing composition of ownership of plants in Scotland It reflects the decline of the European Union (excluding the UK) and the growth of employment by firms from Japan. The USA overtook the UK as the largest employer in 1991, the result of the disproportionate decline in the instrument engineering and 'other electronics' groupings in which the UK had been strongest.

From before the Act of Union in 1707, Scots had been emigrating to and trading with North America. This included a massive tobacco trade in the eighteenth century and in the nineteenth century the financing of the trans-continental railways. The first companies to reverse the historic relationship between Scotland and North America, by making a direct investment in Scotland, were Uniroyal in 1856 and Singer Sewing Machines in 1867. At the end of the Second World War, the number of US-based firms in Scotland was still only six but rose rapidly with the arrival, for example, of National Cash Registers (NCR) in Dundee and Honeywell in Blantyre. The factories of the late 1940s and 1950s were light industrial manufacturing, usually relying on low cost unskilled or semi-skilled female workers. These were usually opened to overcome currency problems in a Europe still struggling to recover from the war and at locations chosen by a mixture of chance and government direction.

Despite many years of work in developing the computer industry, the inability of firms to find local suppliers is a serious problem, as figure 5.4 shows. The appearance of growth in output from the computer and electronics industries is comprised mainly of components and sub-assemblies bought in from overseas, notably from South East Asia. Some of the evidence of this problem could be seen in the earlier calculations of the input-output data for the Scottish economy, so that policy makers must have been aware of this issue in the mid-1980s.

The problem of the low level of local supplies is being addressed by Scottish

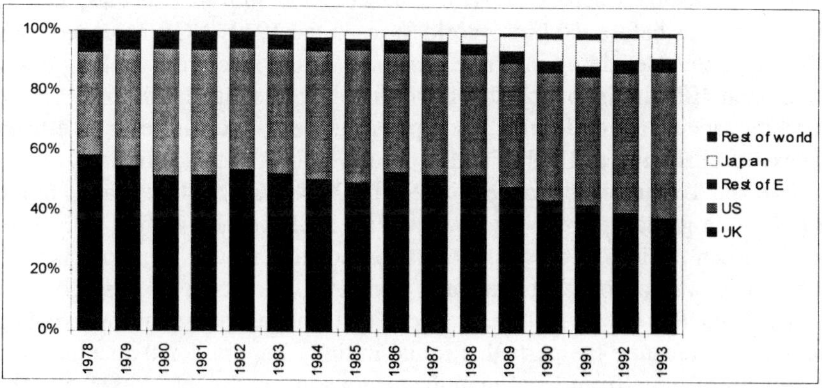

Figure 5.3: Employment in the electronics sectors by country of ownership
Source: IDS, 1991, p. 4, SOID, 1994, p.3

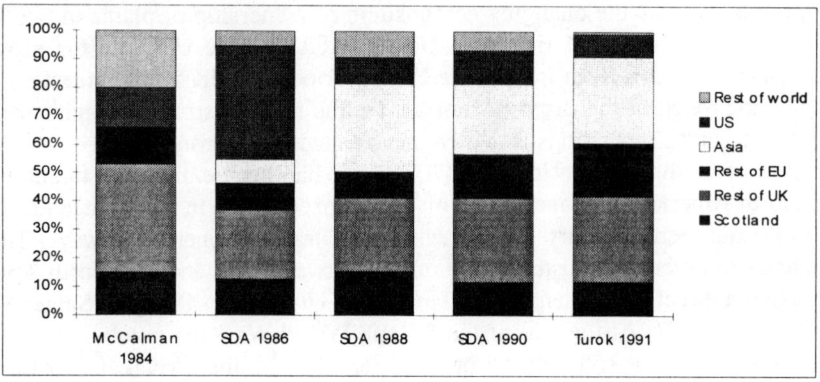

Figure 5.4: Source of materials imputs by value

Note: McCalman includes Asia in rest of the world
Source: McCalman, 1987 and Turok, 1993

Enterprise and by Scottish Electronics Forum, a consortium of leading companies. However, there are no easy or immediate solutions.

National Cash Register

National Cash Register (NCR) was created in 1884 by John Patterson when he bought the National Manufacturing Company. Based in Dayton, Ohio, NCR rapidly developed its business across the USA, and quickly moved overseas, having ten foreign operations before the First World War. In the 1920s NCR extended its range of products to include adding machines and accounting machines, making it a direct competitor of IBM in the punched card business. In the late 1950s and 1960s NCR made significant efforts to develop a computer business, but was never able to mount a successful challenge to IBM. Finally, in 1991 NCR was acquired by American Telephone and Telegraph and in 1994 it became AT&T Global Information Solutions.

In 1946 with guidance from the government, NCR opened its first UK factory in Dundee, chosen for its low operating costs, especially labour. The factory produced cash registers and accounting machines for the UK market by assembling parts imported from the USA. NCR expanded its Dundee operations by creating the capacity to manufacture the parts that it had initially imported and also increased its procurement of parts from local manufacturers and, by the late 1960s, the Dundee operation was largely self-sufficient.

At its peak in 1969-70, NCR employed 6,500 people and operated 120,000 m^2 of space in nine factories. This was just as the UK was decimalizing its currency, switching from £sd to £p, requiring vast numbers of new adding machines and cash registers and the conversion of existing equipment. Thereafter, NCR went into decline as the manufacturers of electro-mechanical machines came under considerable attack from Texas Instruments, Wang Laboratories and a number of Japanese manufacturers, cutting into NCR's traditional market with transistorized calculators. Whereas, in the manufacture of electro-mechanical systems it had been feasible to use vertical integration, with electronics this was impractical. The change meant that costs were turned upside down, from being largely labour costs to being the purchase of components and sub-assemblies. Product lifespan collapsed, requiring enormous efforts in the design of new products and much greater flexibility in manufacturing, while the relationship with customers had to switch from selling and maintenance to quite sophisticated marketing. As old products were phased out, so the worldwide workforce was cut, with the closure of four European factories to concentrate at slimmed-down plants at Augsburg and Dundee, though even these faced successive redundancies. NCR conscientiously sought to retrain staff for the new jobs in the plant, even if the changes were enormous.

As part of a global restructuring of manufacturing NCR concentrated on smaller plants with a group of related products for which the plant would hold a 'global charter.' In the late 1970s, Dundee was the supplier of mainframe computers to Europe, Middle East and Africa and a second source for the USA. Dundee also held the sole charter for banking terminals, initially producing to a US-design, but with funding for the R&D to develop it. Dundee became the centre of NCR's global business in Automatic Teller Machines (ATMs). Today, it is run by Jim Adamson, a Scot originally head hunted from ITT, and with a staff of some fifteen hundred of whom four hundred are engaged in R&D. NCR Dundee markets, designs and manufactures its own products—a business currently worth nearly one billion dollars per annum. In 1990 it was selected as Britain's Best Factory.

Timex Corporation

One of the early investors in Scotland was what became the Timex Corporation, a US-based part of a complex off-shore corporate structure owned by Fred Olsen, a Norwegian businessman. Timex developed from the Waterbury Watch Company into a mass-producer of clocks and watches. In 1946, Timex's first plant outside the USA was in Dundee. Later factories were opened in England, France, Germany, Portugal and beyond Europe in the Philippines.

In January 1944 what was then Waterbury (Britain) Ltd approached the Board of Trade looking for a factory of about 80,000 ft^2 in which to manufacture watches and clocks. The government was keen to encourage the clock and watch industry since it was an area in which the UK had little capacity and consequently relied on imports. Fred Olsen visited the Board of Trade in February 1944 where a typical range of development areas was discussed: Wigan, South Wales, the North-East and Scotland. It was only in late 1945 that sites were visited, as they were being released from wartime manufacturing. Representatives of Timex (by then called UK Time) visited Dundee on 21st November 1945. By January 1946, Timex had decided to open at Dundee and a factory of 35,000 ft^2 had been found at Camperdown. The factors in selecting Dundee appear to have included availability of labour, low labour costs and the ready availability of a factory with space for expansion. In November 1947, Timex sought an additional 50,000 ft^2 of factory space to manufacture parts previously imported from US Time. It was neither possible to obtain the dollars to continue importing the parts nor to subcontract the manufacturing in the UK, so that Timex was forced to make the parts itself. By 1947, Timex employed 238 workers, by 1957 the workforce had risen to 731 and in 1966 stood at almost 3,500.

The product line had been allowed to remain in traditional mechanical watches. In the late 1970s, when digital watches from the Far East rapidly dominated the mass market, Timex faced a marked decline in sales, requiring them to invest in product development, new plant and to look at diversification. Significant efforts were made by Timex to move to lower cost labour locations, notably in the Philippines and Portugal.

Timex Dundee had undertaken subcontracting assembly work from the Polaroid Corporation as early as 1952—building around fourteen million cameras in the period up to 1979. The Dundee factories contracted to manufacture the Nimslo camera which took three-dimensional pictures, though the work was eventually transferred to Simpac and Ricoh in Japan and subsequently abandoned. Timex Corporation won contracts from Sinclair Research and Amstrad to manufacture the Sinclair ZX81, ZX Spectrum and later the Sinclair QL computers, but these also failed. Both the Nimslo and Sinclair Research projects were recipients of considerable government support. In 1982-83 production of both watches and the Nimslo camera were closed, cutting the workforce by 1,900 to 4,200. The Milton plant was closed after a bitter work-in, being demolished to make way for a McDonald's hamburger outlet and a supermarket. Watch production was switched to France and Dundee made the painful transition to electronics assembly. There was a gradual decline in the workforce to just over 300 in 1993 (Young, 1984, pp. 119-120).

February 1993 saw a resurgence of problems in industrial relations at Timex with a clash between unions and management. Fears of redundancies in the autumn and suspicions about a more abrasive new managing director had seen the election of more militant shop stewards aggravating industrial relations. The management dismissed and locked out the workforce of 320 following a twenty-day dispute over provision for lay-offs and employed 200 new staff in their place. The decision was taken by senior management from the USA who had flown to Scotland in an abortive attempt to negotiate a deal with the trade union, the Amalgamated Electrical and Engineering Union (AEEU). The legal limit of six pickets was broken by supporters of the strikers—who came from as far away as Yorkshire—mounting demonstrations and mass pickets of the plant which sometimes became violent; thirty-eight people arrested on the worst day. A parliamentary committee interviewed both sides in the dispute and tried to set up talks (Employment Committee, 1993). In the middle of the dispute the managing director, P W Hall, resigned.

Timex finally closed the Camperdown factory in the autumn of 1993, bringing to a rather sad end a story of almost fifty years. Fred Olsen claimed the plant had lost £10 millions in the preceding ten years and cost around £3 millions in redundancy payments. The management of Timex had failed to make the difficult transition to a new product line and thus the factory closed and jobs disappeared, though Timex remained successful in watches.

Wang Laboratories

The most famous of the electronics closures was that of Wang Laboratories. It was announced in June 1989 that Wang Laboratories would close its plant beside the campus of the University of Stirling. While some of the ensuing controversy arose from the combative nature of British politics and from the usual posturing, there was genuine surprise at the closure and the government was caught making payments only a few weeks before the announcement. The plant manufactured personal computers, an area where Wang Laboratories was weak and the closure was the result of a poor strategy combined with an over-engineered product.

When Wang Laboratories first came to Europe it selected Limerick in the Republic of Ireland—only later did it opened at Stirling (both were university campuses). The apparent reason for the move to Scotland was growing demand in Europe for its products combined with the belief by the founder Dr An Wang, that plants should not exceed 200 persons if they were to be properly managed. The financial assistance from the government was an attraction to come to Stirling, though this could have been more had it chosen a special development area. There was a less clearly stated desire to improve the share of the public sector market in the UK held by Wang Laboratories, which required a manufacturing operation in the UK, after which it would be treated as 'British'. Once the factory was announced, Wang was awarded the last of the government's Office Automation Pilot Projects, a fully operational demonstrator system at the National Coal Board (subsequently British Coal), worth £250,000 plus considerable publicity value. Wang Laboratories claimed the link to the University of Stirling would be important, though it was limited to the funding of a research fellow. In order to encourage Wang Laboratories, Central Regional Council funded a professor in information technology.

The closure of the Stirling factory in 1989 was no very great surprise to observers in the industry. A factory in Scotland for the production of personal computers was not what Wang Laboratories required. The manufacture of personal computers is a relatively unsophisticated activity; at that time over one hundred and fifty firms worldwide were making and selling clones of the IBM Personal Computer and PS/2. Where skill was required was in the development and introduction of new models. The Stirling closure in 1989 was linked to a failure of business strategy (or lack of one) and the high price of products:

> Wang did not understand it was a software company. If Wang had moved at the right time to move its software across multiple vendors' boxes, if it had realized that the software was going to run the PC as opposed to the reverse then it could

be in an entirely different position today. ... They had the first PC but they marketed the hardware box. Instead of moving the [Office Automation] application across to the PC and selling the solution they tried marketing the PC hardware. Nobody was interested (Chambers, 1992, p. 44).

Wang Laboratories had allowed itself to become embroiled in the fiercely competitive personal computer market and had become, albeit inadvertently, 'Just Another PC' manufacturer.

Wang Laboratories was founded in 1954 by Dr An Wang who retained control of the business until his death. Wang jumped with considerable success from one area of business to another; from computer memory to electronic calculators and on to minicomputers and word processing systems (Wang, 1986).

Politicians leapt fearlessly onto the closure, denouncing the lack of constancy of foreign multinational corporations and decrying the government which had been given notice of the closure only one week before the event. To make matters worse for the government, the factory was located in the constituency of a particularly disliked government minister and the government had made a payment to Wang Laboratories shortly before the announcement of the closure. To some extent the bad news was offset by the decision to expand the Compaq plant at Erskine at about the same time. Compaq also took over the Wang factory, though not for manufacturing, but as its European repair and maintenance base. Nonetheless, the response of the politicians was over-reaction, given that such closures were a characteristic of the computer industry (*Hansard*, 27.vi.89 (C) 155 cols. 833-840).

Wang Laboratories was temporarily saved by a subsequent joint venture with IBM but this fell through and Wang Labs filed for Chapter 11 'protective bankruptcy' in 1992. It emerged in late 1993, a much smaller company, shorn of its manufacturing activities and with a very uncertain future.

Digital Equipment Corporation

From the late 1950s Digital Equipment Corporation (DEC) grew rapidly under the guidance of its founder, Ken Olsen to become the second largest computer company in the world. Its ranges of minicomputers allowed it first to create and then to dominate the global minicomputer market. As demand grew, so DEC followed the example of the older mainframe computer manufacturers into overseas operations. Digital Equipment Corporation (DEC) opened its first office in the UK in 1964 at Reading where it maintains it UK headquarters. In 1976, Digital opened a manufacturing plant near Ayr, in a rural setting overlooking the Firth of Clyde, where initially it undertook final assembly and testing of PDP-11 and later VAX minicomputers.

The plant moved from final assembly of customized systems to the volume production of small standardized systems, reflecting a shift in emphasis towards mass and semi-custom manufacturing. This had been made possible by much easier installation at customer sites. The European parts of DEC fought for greater autonomy:

The company literature spoke of supplying its European market from British and European plants, using components bought locally. But the Ayr management, and colleagues in France and Germany, had actively driven corporate strategy in this direction in the face of opposition and indifference. The operation at Kaufbeuren was comparatively expensive to run, but was justified on the 'local manufacturing presence' argument by European management. The product charter for small computer systems was given to Ayr, and not to an American or Far East plant, because Ayr managers were able to convince corporate decision makers that they could make the products profitably at a competitive European 'landed cost' (Buchanan and McCalman, 1989, p. 67).

In 1989, DEC launched the MicroVAX 3100, the first machine to have been designed in Scotland.

Business for DEC peaked in the late 1980s as its VAX range of minicomputers reached the end of its life cycle. Thereafter, DEC fell into decline (see figure 5.5), though it remained a large computer company. There was talk of Chapter 11 bankruptcy, of parallels with Wang Labs and finally the board forced the founder, Ken Olsen, to retire. There followed massive retrenchment with a substantial reduction in the workforce. The key to the survival of DEC was increasingly Alpha, a high-power RISC chip developed at DEC to power a post-VAX generation of computers (DEC annual reports).

An unpleasant public controversy broke out in early 1993 over whether DEC would close its factory in Ayr or its factory in Galway, Ireland, they were evidently too similar for both to survive. The battle was conducted very much in public, with Irish government ministers apparently seeking to blame the perfidious British for the

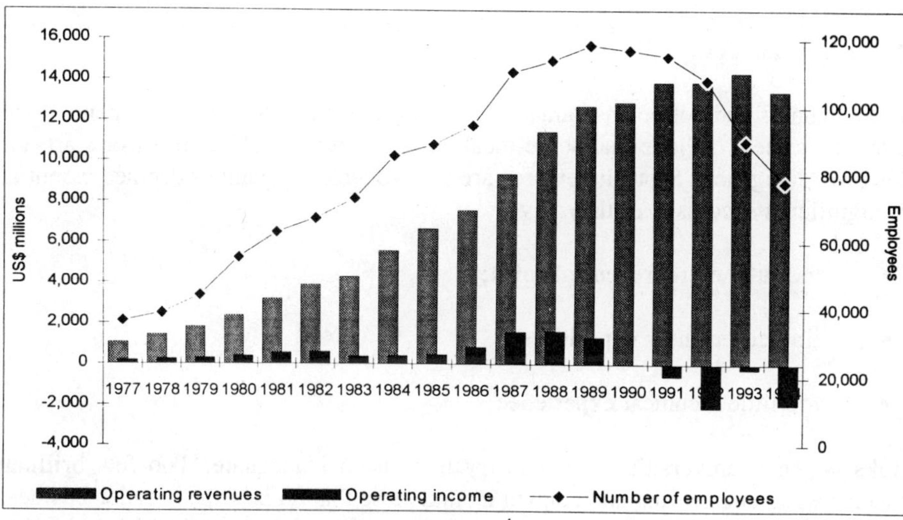

Figure 5.5: DEC financial results (1977-1994)

Source: DEC annual reports

eventual loss of their factory. Accusations were made that the UK Government had placed or would place very large contracts with DEC but this remains unproven and improbable, though Locate in Scotland did admit to talks with the Corporation. The UK represents around a quarter of DEC's turnover in Europe, worth US$ 1 billion. The cause of the closure lay in the shake-out in the market in general and in the restructuring within DEC. The closure of the Galway plant came after a review of manufacturing in the USA and the closure of several factories there in order to cut overheads. In its home base of Massachusetts, DEC cut some 6,500 jobs in the early 1990s. DEC has found it cheaper to buy in supplies, rather than manufacture them.

The DEC plant in Galway had been a mainstay of industry in the West of Ireland since it opened in 1971, at the close employing 780, down from 1,100 in 1990. In 1991 a DEC network products factory at Clonmel, County Tipperary, closed. The European Software Supply Business, opened in 1976, remained in Galway, employing 350.

In 1985 DEC announced its intention to expand its operations in Scotland with a plan for a semiconductor factory at South Queensferry near Edinburgh. The reasons given for the choice of the site were the availability of skilled labour and the chip research being carried out at nearby universities. The opening of the plant suffered a two year delay to allow for changes in the process technology, and production of their prestigious new Alpha RISC chip finally began in 1992. In January 1995, DEC announced the sale of its South Queensferry plant to Motorola, a company already well-established in Scotland and in need of chip-making capacity for its nearby plant manufacturing mobile telephones. DEC did not need the capacity of the South Queensferry plant where, latterly, it had been using some of its production capacity to manufacture 486 clone chips for AMD.

The entrepreneurs

While planners and politicians came to rely on the inward flow of investment, there remained a view or hope that some local entrepreneurs would spin-off or start-up. However, indigenous Scottish ventures are seen to lack the qualities deemed essential for significant success, i.e. they have:

- too little entrepreneurial spirit;
- limited business experience;
- too little technical experience.

Links between universities and industry have been inadequate. Too few brilliant students study engineering and computing and those that do lack the broader business skills and role models of their counterparts in the USA. Many of the better students in Scottish universities, especially doctoral students, are not Scottish and usually return overseas on completing their studies.

In California the governmental support mechanisms are much less than in Scotland, but the culture is far more positive towards entrepreneurship and more forgiving of failure—the rewards are also greater. Indeed one of the great successes of Silicon Valley has been its ability to generate and propagate new businesses.

The Scottish Electronics Scheme became famous through the work of Burns and Stalker (1961) and remains indicative of the problems faced in revivifying Scottish industry. Rodime PLC is discussed to show how a rare Scottish start-up which was able to go overseas failed.

The Scottish electronics scheme

In the late 1940s the Scottish Council (Development and Industry) recognized that Scotland had missed out on the motor car and aircraft industries and that something had to be done if this was not to be repeated for electrical and later electronic industries. The Ministry of Supply and the Admiralty played influential roles in the UK electronics industry through development contracts placed with commercial manufacturers. While the government was spending money through the Board of Trade successfully encouraging firms to locate in Scotland, the Ministry of Supply and the Admiralty were not helping by placing almost all their contracts in the South of England. In 1948 the Scottish Council proposed to the Secretary of State for Scotland that Ferranti Ltd, a large UK manufacturer in defence and later computer electronics, be used as a leader in contracts, allowing staff from other firms to be trained in design. The intention was not to build up a radio and television manufacturing industry, rather it was to help in the adoption of electronics technology in the engineering industry in the hope of creating new applications.

A joint venture was established with Ferranti Ltd, the Ministry of Supply and the Admiralty in May 1951 in order to build up the Scottish electronics industry. Initial contact for companies was through the Scottish Council who arranged visits to Ferranti's laboratories, followed by discussions with the management of Ferranti—thereafter the defence ministries were approached in search of a suitable joint contract, though Ferranti subcontracted some work on their own initiative. The design teams were to work initially with Ferranti, later moving to their own premises. Ferranti hoped to gain insights into the broader applications of electronics in the engineering industry.

The project ran into difficulties in the 1957 with the defence cuts after the Suez Crisis. At the same time the viability of the Scheme had changed since 1949, because the products being designed by Ferranti were much more complex and it was more important to have in-house control of the design. The project foundered in part because the government saw the growth in Scotland of multinational corporations in the electronics sector and partly because defence spending was now contracting. The Ministry of Supply did not see the need to take 'abnormal' measures to help companies in the Scheme. To do so it would have had to justify the increased cost of the relative inefficiency of the fledgling firms and also to counter criticism from established companies. (SRO/SEP 4/2082[3])

The six companies[4] involved in the Electronics Scheme, which can now be identified, had workforces ranging from 150 to 1,500 and although seen as sound businesses, some were already in difficulties with obsolete products or were operating in markets which were collapsing:

> With the advantage of hindsight it can be suggested that the attempt to impose a dynamic technology upon organizations adapted to a stable or declining market environment and firmly rooted in a *regional* engineering complex was insufficient. The types of organization necessary to translate technical advances into successful products in a more dynamic, diffuse and *international* market context were not created to support the technology transfers achieved by the Scottish Council-Ministry of Supply Scheme (McDermott, 1979, p. 293).

Before the war the companies were small and operated without research; where design teams existed they were often distinct units poorly integrated into overall production. Fundamental problems existed in their planing functions:

> More important than the explicitly stated reasons seems to be the fact that the middle-distance future was obscured by extreme preoccupation with the short-term future. Firms in the radio and television business are geared to annual cycles of new designs-production-sales, each successive activity rising to a peak in early spring, the summer and autumn (Burns and Stalker 1961, p. 66).

Ferranti remained in Scotland with a substantial presence mainly in the defense sector until the story finally and tragically ended in 1994. The company went into liquidation, not least because of its FDI activities in the USA.

Rodime Limited

Rodime was a rarity, a Scottish spin-off. It was founded in 1980 by two Scottish and two American engineers from Burroughs (subsequently merged into Unisys), led by Dr Leonard Brownlow. In October 1991, Rodime called in the receivers for their operations in Glenrothes and Singapore and filed for 'Chapter 11' bankruptcy protection for its plant in Boca Raton, Florida; despite a rescue in 1989 with the introduction of new management from the USA and a substantial injection of cash. Rodime was not being paid royalties for its hard disc patents, which were often disputed. Even though it no longer manufactures disc drives, Rodime remains in the legal business.

Rodime had initially produced 5.25 inch hard discs and was the first company to develop the smaller 3.5 inch hard disc drive, found in most personal computers in the early 1990s. Manufacturing at Glenrothes, Fife, was expanded first to Singapore and then to Boca Raton, Florida. The design and manufacture of disc drives is, like so much of the IT industry, a cut-throat business, where new products must be brought to market as soon as humanly possible. The cutting edge of the industry moved on from 3.5 inch drives to 2.5 inch and 1 inch drives for use in laptop and portable PCs.

Moreover, the well-known difficulties faced in the personal computer industry with the downturn in demand in 1991 led to a collapse in disc drive prices.

The key question is why Rodime failed. It seems to have been too far from its market, the headquarters of the PC manufacturers, despite their substantial manufacturing presences in Scotland. Moreover, there were too many rival start-ups, there was enormous competitive pressure for business and the technological pace was fast and accelerating. A successor company, Calluna, supported by Scottish Enterprise, seems to be carrying on the work of Rodime in the design and manufacture of hard disks. This raises questions about the failure of Rodime, suggesting that it is not an impossible activity to conduct in Scotland.

Conclusion

A strong case has been made against the introduction of multinational corporations into local economies, in that they cause distortions by (Dunning, 1970, pp. 270-290):

- drawing on local capital to the disadvantage of indigenous firms and straining local capital markets;
- siphoning off technical and managerial expertise;
- reducing the ability to plan and control the economy.

The extent to which these apply to Scotland is limited, primarily because so much control has already been transferred to London and beyond, with long-established and continuing outward flows of capital and human resources.

In any event the continuation of past policies and practices seems unlikely to yield any significant results. The Agency and Locate in Scotland seem to have operated on the 'panther principle'—sitting in a tree waiting for something nourishing to pass by on to which they could jump.

Factory closures in Scotland have less often been the result of Machiavellian scheming by foreign multinational corporations than a failure of their strategy or of corporate vision. Scottish factories remain on the periphery of the operations of the multinational corporations and consequently have been and are today vulnerable to the effects of recession. Moreover, as a result of the accelerating pace of technology-based competition many investing corporations have been liable to sudden, even catastrophic, collapse. To survive, companies have had to make massive and revolutionary advances in their products and their process technologies. The global electronics and computer industries are in turmoil—firms which were once bitter rivals are now in joint ventures. There has been a flurry of often fiercely contested mergers and acquisitions, while programmes of rationalization have led to large numbers of redundancies. Once-great corporations have been cast down or are struggling to survive. Foreign direct investment has been replaced by foreign joint ventures and strategic partnerships. IBM has been noticeable in spinning off its printer business as Lexmark and its UK hard disk business as Xyratex, as management buy-outs.

Many of the benefits of individual foreign direct investments have been short term and that time period is getting briefer as product life-cycles contract and corporations become less stable. Nonetheless the creation of direct jobs in the electronics and computer sector has been very beneficial to the Scottish economy—over 40,000 jobs and over 40% of Scottish manufactured exports. Without foreign direct investment there would be no electronics and computer industry in Scotland.

There is no compelling evidence of Scotland being outbid by other countries. The failure to win battles for specific opportunities for foreign direct investment has seldom been due to the limitations of control from London or the absence of a few more dollars, rather it has been a reflection of the complexities of this type of marketing exercise. The requirements of multinational corporations are often very specific and the focus is more likely to be on human resources and logistics than on grants and taxes.

The long desired, much touted, but ill-defined critical mass has not been achieved and seems ever less likely. The failure lay in not stating clearly what the critical mass was to be and then systematically developing it and, in particular, what was required of the indigenous sector. The atomistic Californian model of Silicon Valley was inappropriate—a great diversity of unrelated firms in Scotland was unlikely to permit the interactions necessary for the mass to go critical, this was made worse by the local perception that the plants were scattered across Scotland. Although dispersion was a plausible policy both for the government and the firms themselves, it was one which reduced the likelihood of interaction. The firms wanted a safe and secure labour supply, while the government wanted good news for each of the new towns, encouraging geographical fragmentation. The foreigners seem to have thought they were close together.

The success of Pacific Rim economies such as South Korea and Japan has been achieved by quite different means from those in Silicon Valley. Alliances have been forged between government and industry, sharing the costs of research and development, protecting domestic markets and targeting export markets. Inward investment played a modest role in the early stages, but once the pump was primed the indigenous conglomerates quickly took over. This was never contemplated and there is no way this could have been done in Scotland.

Much of what has been done in the name of policy has been *ad hoc* measures, dressed up in talk of critical mass. Bad news has been cast aside in favour of good news, creating an unduly rosy picture of a sector with growing imports, declining employment and a fragile future.

Labour and nationalist politicians demand the right to give bigger and better grants, while denouncing foreign governments and agencies for doing just that. The Conservative Party is different only insofar as it tries to achieve the same result by lowering the costs of employment. In reality it is not that important. Scotland has been accused of having a 'dependency culture', reliant on grants from Westminster. Combined with the almost miraculous achievement of parity in unemployment with

Table 5.4
Summary of Scottish electronics and IT industries

	Ownership				
	Scotland	Other UK	Other EC	USA	Japan
Semiconductors	none	niche	none	Strong	NEC and suppliers
Computers	none	defence only	Groupe Bull	PCs and workstations	Apricot
Consumer electronics	weak	weak	none	none	strong
Tele-communications	none	none	Philips BCS	Motorola	none
Components	limited	limited	limited	limited	limited
Software	many, but small	limited	limited	sales-operations	OWL

South-East England it does not suggest a long term willingness to sustain grants in Scotland. Of course, possibilities exist which would cause dramatic changes, such as the election of a Labour government committed to the creation of a Scottish parliament or the withdrawal from the European Union by a Conservative government. The overall status of the sector is shown in Table 5.4.

The failure to develop an integrated local supply industry is difficult to explain and severely undermines the future success of the sector; there is little point in the sector dominating Scottish exports, if this is largely constituted by components imported from Asia. One confusion was that a strong semiconductor industry developed, but seems not to have been supplying the other sectors, so that even though there was the appearance of a whole range of activities, but it was not self-evident that the industry was not linked together. As a long-term strategy, the branch economy has performed poorly and has been difficult to sustain. Like the painting of the Forth Bridge which has gone on since it was opened over one hundred years ago, the attraction of foreign direct investment, seems doomed to go on for ever. Given the fierce competitive struggles in the industry and the increasingly desperate struggle for foreign direct investment it seems unlikely that Scotland can continue to draw in investments to match its likely losses. Moreover, given the changes in the industry the opportunities will be significantly fewer, with greater reliance being placed on those companies already established in Scotland.

Notes

1. Papers held in the Public Record Office.
2. Brigadoon was a Broadway musical in which the image of Scotland was tweed and cloyingly sentimental. Two Americans find a ghost village in Scotland which awakens one day every one hundred years in which the actors were swathed in tartan and the actresses bedecked in heather. It was first produced in 1947, then turned into a film in 1954 by Alan Jay Lerner, the author, and director Vincente Minelli. While the stage version had been seen as whimsical and charming, the New York Times found that the film was as "pretty weak synthetic scotch", despite the talents of Cyd Charisse and Gene Kelly.
3. Papers held in the Public Record Office.
4. Atkins, Robertson and Whiteford Limited, Barr and Stroud Limited, Bruce Peebles and Company Limited, Dobbie McInnes Limited, Robert Maclaren and Company Limited, James Scott (Electrical Engineers) Limited and G & J Weir Limited.

Acknowledgments

The author gratefully acknowledges the comments on drafts of this work from John Beaumont (Energis and formerly University of Bath) and Professor Tom Carbery (OFFER and formerly of the University of Strathclyde). An earlier version of this material was presented at a seminar at the Wirtschaftsuniversität Wien, Austria, for which thanks are due to Dr Gunther Maier of the Interdisziplinäres Institut für Raumordnung Stadt- und Regionalentwicklung.

6 Japanese manufacturing companies in southern Ontario and NAFTA

David W. Edgington

Introduction

Increasing globalization of trade and investment, and the recent emergence of new free trade zones in North America, Europe and the Asia-Pacific region, represent significant discontinuities in the nature of multinational (MNC) location decision making. This chapter addresses specifically the impact of the North American Free Trade Agreement (NAFTA) on Japanese owned manufacturing subsidiaries in Canada's industrial heartland - southern Ontario. Within North America, Japanese manufacturing foreign direct investment (FDI) has overwhelmingly located in the USA, due mainly to the dominant size of this market (Kenney and Florida, 1993). Yet since the high yen period (*endaka*) a wide range of Japanese companies have also been drawn to southern Ontario (Edgington, 1994). Previous work on Japanese investment in NAFTA, based on aggregate FDI statistics, suggested that Japanese firms would increasingly gravitate to Mexico and the south of the USA (Edgington and Fruin, 1994). But there is a need to balance this judgment with micro-level studies which try to understand the strategic orientation of Japanese firms to the newly signed NAFTA. For instance, the existence of NAFTA will clearly increase the locational options of Japanese companies considering serving the Canadian market, as well as existing manufacturing subsidiaries located in Ontario. The question arises whether Japanese subsidiaries will take advantage of NAFTA, by exporting out of Ontario to markets in the United States and Mexico, or whether they will disinvest as tariffs decline, and import more products into Canada from their Mexican factories and other lower wage North American regions.

Within this above broad concern the research reported here is based on a survey of Japanese-controlled manufacturing companies in southern Ontario which was conducted during 1994, the first year of NAFTA's operation. Structured interviews (obtained through both site meetings and telephone conversations) were conducted with 39 Japanese manufacturing firms, selected at random, which had set up in Ontario and were listed in data bases assembled by the Ontario Government and the

Japan External Trade Organization (JETRO) (see Government of Ontario, 1992; Japan External Trade Organization, 1993). The majority of these subsidiaries had been established since the mid-1980s. The survey questionnaire was designed to elicit responses on issues such as investment motivations and mode of entry, levels of exports and research and development, linkages to local suppliers, relative autonomy from headquarters in Japan, and the perceived impact of NAFTA.

The overall aim of this chapter is to examine the profile of Japanese manufacturing companies in a Canadian industrial region, and try to position their operations within the broader context of the North American triad economy. The chapter proceeds as follows; the subsequent section examines briefly the conceptual issues involved in the emergence of regional trading blocks for the geography of multinational investment. This is then followed by examining the profile of Japanese manufacturing operations in southern Ontario. The link between these investments and the wider continental situation is also considered through a look at the production networks of four groups of Japanese MNCs across Canada, the United States and Mexico. The chapter concludes by reflecting on how NAFTA has impacted on existing Japanese manufacturing subsidiaries and their future investments in southern Ontario.

Multinational regionalism: Japanese FDI in NAFTA

Japanese companies have moved over time to a full top-to-bottom manufacturing system within each of the global triad economies (Edgington, 1993). As with Europe and the West Pacific, Japanese FDI in NAFTA is aimed increasingly at transferring R and D, design engineering, finance, regional management and other necessary functions to allow corporations to become fully-fledged insiders (Edgington and Fruin, 1994). In theory, economic integration offers a wider locational choice to incoming companies over how to arrange their activities. In addition, for firms who have operated in NAFTA for some time, the net effect of regional integration allows the restructuring and relocation of existing activities in order to coordinate production facilities among a number of countries and to serve the wider market. In other words, trade liberalization arrangements such as NAFTA and the European Union allow MNCs to move from a philosophy of one market, one factory (often known as the United Nations theory of foreign direct investment, see Ohmae, 1985) to one of multinational regionalism (see Mitchell-Weaver and Bremm, 1993).[1]

A number of geographic strategies suggest themselves under the new regional free trade regimes (Dunning, 1993b, chp.17). For example, regionalization might present opportunities for economies of scale and the full rationalization of investment networks into a hub and spoke arrangement (see Figure 6.1a). In this case, higher order design and production activities are largely centralized, leaving lower-order assembly or distribution operations to peripheral market locations. By contrast, a more traditional parallel paths model might be necessary for political reasons, or where distinctive markets and difficult distribution channels demand local and relatively autonomous production units within each country (Figure 6.1b). A further variation, one established on national complementarity, is for multinationals to

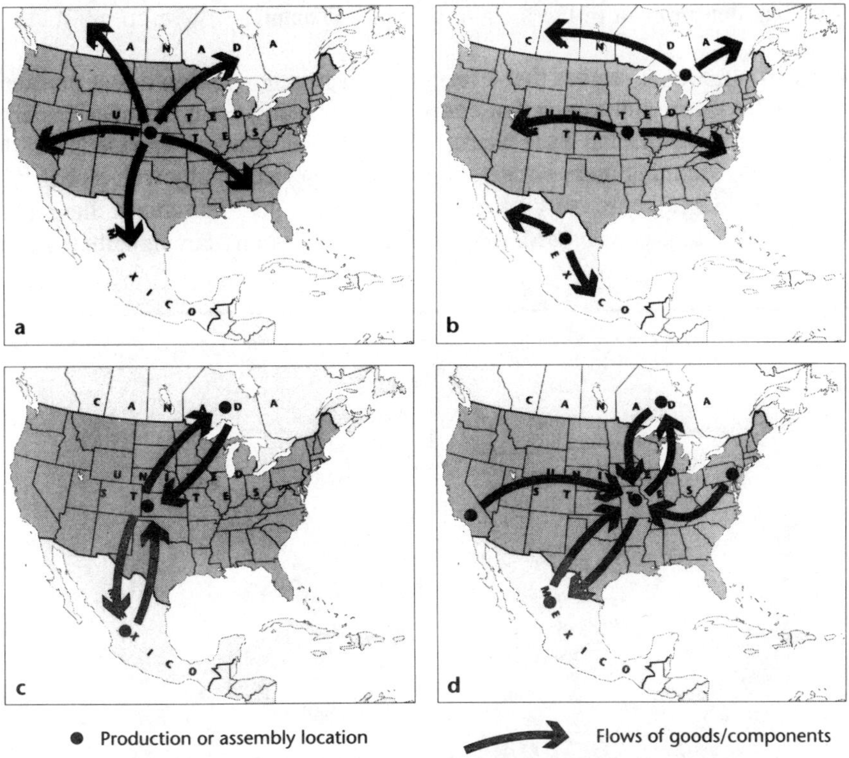

Figure 6.1 Four potential foreign direct investment configurations in NAFTA: (a) hub and spoke; (b) parallel paths; (c) national complementarity; and (d) national specialization

specialize their models (or parts of models) among countries, so that each country focuses on just one or a limited range of products for the entire region (Figure 6.1c). Yet another option is to engage in national specialization among a continental-wide value-added production chain, taking advantage of each country's (or subregion's) comparative advantage such as cheap wage labour, access to raw materials or technology and so on (Figure 6.1d). More generally:

> It might be expected that integration would promote a more hierarchical division of labour, with high value activities being concentrated in one or two central locations, and lower value-added activities being dispersed...Sometimes specialization is based on traditional factor endowments, sometimes on the need to take advantage of economies of scale and sometimes on the macro-organizational policies pursued by governments. Research, however, suggests that the need to reduce transaction costs

(including transport), rather than production costs, is becoming an increasingly important determinant of the locational choice (Dunning, 1993b, p. 488).

Rugman (1990) also argues that a major motivation for foreign direct investment is the need to overcome transaction costs. Paradoxically, as it becomes easier and cheaper to serve continental trade blocks from a central location, knowledge of local markets often becoming more important in competing successfully with global rivals, not less. Consequently, strategies and production configurations that address significant differences of cross-border consumer tastes and buying cultures remain

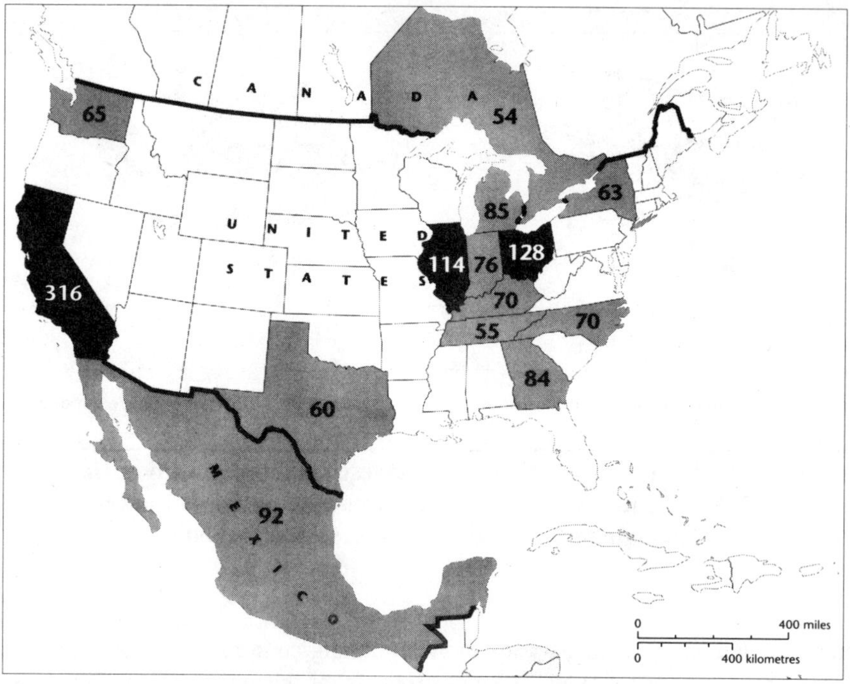

Figure 6.2 Number of Japanese factories by provinces, states and Mexico, 1992

Note: Only units recording more than 50 factories are shown.

Source: Government of Ontario, *Japanese Investment Profile*, Tokyo, Ontario House, 1992; Japan External Trade Organization, *1993-94 Directory: Japanese-Affiliated Companies in USA and Canada*, Tokyo, Jetro, 1993; Toyo Keizai Shimpo, *Japanese Overseas Investments*, 1992, Tokyo, Tokyo Keizai Shimpo (in Japanese)

important. In these cases, integration is often likely to make little difference to corporate strategies. As a result, at least some MNCs will continue to be nationally, rather than regionally, oriented.

This particular inference was confirmed in a previous study by the author which showed that reductions in tariffs under the Canada-Japan Free Trade Agreement - the predecessor to NAFTA - by itself had little effect on Japanese investment strategy (Edgington, 1990). To understand how the more extensive NAFTA impacts upon Japanese investments already made, and the likelihood of attracting new investments in the future, there is a need to investigate the production chains which Japanese firms have woven across the entire North American continent. The chapter now turns to the results of the empirical based survey of Japanese manufacturing firms in southern Ontario.

Japanese companies in southern Ontario

General studies of Japanese manufacturing investment in Canada have been carried out by Wright (1984), Blain and Norcliffe (1988), Morris (1989, 1991a,b), and Edgington (1992). The United States remains the dominant source country in terms of foreign direct investment in Canada, and at the time of this study still accounted for about 70 per cent of total FDI. By contrast, Japan accounted for only a fraction of cumulative FDI in Canada, but through the 1980s it had been the fastest growing of the major source countries investing in the country (Investment Canada, 1993).

Within the NAFTA triad, southern Ontario has captured substantial manufacturing investment from Japan, most within the last 10 years (see Edgington, 1992, 1995). The province is one of a dozen or more North American locations which had attracted considerable numbers of Japanese affiliated plants during the last decade (see Figure 6.2). As the industrial core of Canada, southern Ontario has a market area served by one day's trucking of around 103 million people (Richardson, 1990). An analysis of data bases compiled by the Ontario Government and the Japan External Trade Organization (JETRO) indicated that during the 1980s and early 1990s over 50 factories with majority Japanese equity (or minority equity where a Japanese executive was dispatched) had set up in Ontario (Government of Ontario, 1992; Japan External Trade Organization, 1993). The author has elsewhere identified these firms as part of a new wave of Japanese investment into Canada (Edgington, 1994). Within Canada, Ontario not surprisingly accounted for about 90 per cent of Japanese manufacturing investment other than timber mills or pulp mills. Apart from a handful of high technology plants in and around Ottawa, most of the Japanese investments have been located in southern Ontario, particularly in the corridor between metropolitan Toronto and the US border. The author's survey identified 54 Japanese manufacturing companies in southern Ontario existing during 1994 with a total direct employment level of over 18,000. They could be classified into four groups (see Table 6.1), each having different responses to locating in Ontario and, as will be shown later, each having a different response to the arrival of NAFTA.

Table 6.1
Profile of Japanese manufacturing companies in Ontario, 1994

	No. of Establishments	Employment Numbers
Group I: Auto Assemblers	3	5105
Group II: Auto Parts	19	5750
Group III: Industrial Products	31	6090
Group IV: Consumer Electronics	4	1080
TOTAL	57	18025

The first group, auto assembly, has been the second most significant Japanese investment in Canadian manufacturing behind timber products, pulp and paper (Edgington, 1995). The three Japanese autoplants operating in Canada are all located in Ontario. A Honda plant in Alliston, Ontario, opened in 1986, and produces both Coupe and 3-door models of the Honda Civic model. A Toyota facility in Cambridge, Ontario, began production in 1988, and manufactures 4-door Corollas. CAMI Automotive, a joint venture between Suzuki and General Motors Canada opened at Ingersoll, Ontario, in 1989, concentrating on small cars and four-wheel-drive utility vehicles. At the time of their inauguration these plants together accounted for about 25 per cent of Japanese total auto assembly investment in North America, and about 20 per cent of continental production in so-called transplant Japanese auto production factories. This was even though Canada constituted only 10 per cent of the joint US /Canada market (Edgington, 1992). However, more rapid investment by Japanese auto producers in the United States following the mid-1980s subsequently diluted this figure to about 11 per cent. Nonetheless, up to the end of 1993 these three ventures invested around $1.5 billion in Canadian production facilities, and in 1992 they produced an estimated 319,000 units, exporting around 78 per cent of their output to the United States and contributing significantly to Canada's trade balance (Japan Automobile Manufacturers Association of Canada, 1993). As a group, the Japanese car assemblers tended to engage in a complementarity strategy, specializing their model production between each NAFTA country.

Besides these three assembly plants a number of Japanese parts suppliers also set up in southern Ontario. Many of this second group of Japanese companies set up joint ventures established under the aegis of the Pacific Automotive Cooperation Inc, established in Toronto in 1984 by eleven Japanese automakers and a major auto parts manufacturer. The organization's aim was to encourage both investment and technology transfers by acting as an intermediary between suppliers to the Canadian and Japanese automotive industries (Japan Automobile Manufacturers Association of Canada, 1993; Pacific Automotive Co-operation Inc, 1993). In general, those Japanese parts makers which located in Ontario have not been tied solely to Japanese car assemblers in Canada; they also came to take advantage of possible contracts with the US Big Three car makers and other Japanese auto transplants in the United States. Hence they chose locations alongside Highway 401 between Toronto and Detroit as these were convenient to the Japanese assembly plants in Group 1 (Edgington, 1992). This group as a whole engaged in a mix of locational strategies; either the hub and spoke type in order to take advantage of continental economies of scale, or the more local parallel paths strategy in order to remain close to car assembly complexes and to engage in just-in-time (JIT) delivery operations. During interviews, Japanese firms in Group II reported that Japanese just-in-time (JIT) requirements necessitated relative close proximity between in-coming parts suppliers and existing assembly factories. Accordingly, Japanese assembly plants in the United States, being larger, had attracted the vast majority of Japanese parts plants which have set up in NAFTA. Nonetheless, Japanese parts manufacturers based in Ontario were attempting to secure further supply contracts from the Big Three and other producers, and NAFTA should help in this endeavor (interview with Hisanori Kobayashi, Senior Vice President, Kohan Kobayashi Canada, Breslau, Ontario, April, 1994)

The third group comprised the largest size in the survey, both by number of Japanese subsidiaries as well as direct employment numbers (Table 6.1). It was made up of a diverse group of industrial parts makers and full production companies - ranging from metallised films, color pigments, computer floppy discs and industrial gases. In the main, these subsidiaries engaged in both hub and spoke strategies, serving the North American market from a Canadian base, as well as parallel paths locational models, due to need to be close to Canadian markets. Most companies in this group were medium-sized Japanese firms, many of which set up Canadian manufacturing units in the full knowledge that their major market was in the USA - as a result, NAFTA has again been a positive outcome. Overall, their output strategy was inclined to be based on the orders of individual customers, rather than predicated on standardized production. Consequently their operations tended to compete on quality and accessibility to markets rather than on price alone. For some Japanese companies in this category, acquiring a Canadian company which was up for sale was seen as a quick way of establishing a beachhead into North America. For others, the Canadian plant was acquired as part of a takeover of a much larger United States headquartered enterprise, in which case the Japanese company's entry into Canada was indirect and their locational patterns largely predetermined. By way of illustration, the large Bridgestone industrial textiles plant in Woodstock, Ontario, was inherited from the Firestone corporation in 1990. In fact, about 66 per cent of all this group consisted of takeovers of existing Canadian plants or the Canadian branch plants of acquired US companies (computed from the author's survey). Where small-to-medium firms were able to make so-called green fields investments, then Canada often became the preferred location because the Ontario government had been rather aggressive in attracting Japanese companies, and could often offer land for development at cheaper rates than those which applied in the USA (interview with Fuminori Inagaki, Consul, Consulate General of Japan, Toronto, April, 1994.). Some companies in this group had gone as far as to establish world export mandates for their products (e.g. Kao Didak's floppy disks, and Lumonics laser equipment).

The final type of company comprised four consumer electronics firms (Matsushita Electronics, Sony, Mitsubishi Electronics and Hitachi).[2] Compared with the other groups these firms arrived in Canada somewhat earlier than the other three. They were attracted to Ontario from the 1970s onwards because of the relatively large market and high growth potential in Canada at that time (Wright, 1984). Yet under then Prime Minister Trudeau's Foreign Investment Review Agency (FIRA), set up in the 1970s, Japanese companies wishing to establish substantial new distribution networks were requested to create a factory to provide jobs in the market they were selling into. Moreover, they faced relatively high tariff levels for imported electronics products (historically set at high levels, between 10-15 per cent). Accordingly, this group set up small-scale plants in Ontario aimed at producing color TVs or audio products (Sony assembles speakers and headphones in Willowdale, Ontario) primarily for the local Canadian market under the parallel paths model. For Matsushita Electronics this matched its corporate philosophy of providing a local manufacturing capacity in each major market (Richardson, 1990). Previous research by the author (Edgington, 1990) found that the output of these Japanese consumer electronics operations were predisposed to be price-sensitive, and consequently their long-term viability was challenged by other cheaper cost locations in North America. For example, the price competitiveness of color televisions and other audio-visual products increased in the early 1990s due to the entry of large-scale discount stores into Canada such as Woolco. Accordingly, the tariff reduction provisions under NAFTA was likely to accelerate the adjustment of these subsidiaries to operate within a North American as opposed to purely Canadian marketplace. Canadian subsidiaries in this group were therefore expected to reduce the range of TV sets produced and integrate with other North American operations in the United States and Mexican macquiladoras under a national complementarity and/or national specialization pattern of production (interview with Tadashi Nishiuchi, Senior Manager Merchandising, Hitachi (HSC) Canada Inc, Mississauga, Ontario, May, 1994).

Case studies of production networks in North America

The chapter now examines the role played by these Canadian subsidiaries within the broader context of the wider North American triad economy. Edgington (1990) and Morris (1989, 1991a) already noted that many Canadian subsidiaries of Japanese manufacturing plants were already well integrated into an overall North American network of sales and production before the inauguration of NAFTA in 1994. The author's structured interviews with Japanese-controlled companies in southern Ontario allowed a more detailed picture of how their Canadian operations fitted into the broader NAFTA factory, as well as their perceptions of what changes were afoot due to their head office regionalization initiatives. Following work on commodity production chain analysis, carried out by Gereffi (1992), Dicken (1994) and Kenney and Florida (1994), this examination focussed on understanding the changing configuration of Japanese corporate production networks across Canada, the United States and Mexico. Four representative case studies are reported in this section, based on the author's survey.

Auto assembly: Honda Motor Corporation

Figure 6.3a shows the production network of Honda in NAFTA. Honda essentially views its US and Canadian operations as part of a tightly integrated unit in which the border is irrelevant. Nonetheless, it is generally acknowledged that politics, rather than the need to find an efficient North American location, played a major role in Honda's decision to build an assembly plant in Canada. In the early 1980s, almost a decade before NAFTA was introduced, a key reason for these investments was the need to preserve long-term access to the Canadian market while retaining relatively unhindered access to the United States. Consequently, Honda built a middle-range assembly plant (originally 80,000 units per annum, then expanded to 100,000) concentrating on a slightly lower-valued added three door Honda Civic, leaving the more popular four door Civic and Acura models to Honda's larger factories located in Ohio. The Canadian plant, with its workforce around 1,600 employees, depends upon access to the United States market for its existence, as the Canadian market alone is not large enough to support efficient production (usually taken at around 200,000 units per annum). Engines for the Canadian Honda Civic are supplied from plants in the United States which have a total capacity of 500,000 vehicles a year (Edgington, 1992). Honda of Canada's R and D is shared between Japan and the USA, and it has to pay five per cent to either headquarters or the USA company for its overhead. There is a very small local R and D team in the Toronto sales office to cover market research and new model development, as well as a small team in Halifax, concentrating on cold weather research (interview with Vaughn Hibbets, Vice President Administration, Honda of Canada Manufacturing, Alliston, April, 1994).

Events since 1993, especially the increased yen-based costs in Japan caused by an appreciating currency and ballooning unit labour costs, impelled Japanese auto companies to seek even higher levels of production within NAFTA markets. As a result, Honda released plans in 1994 to increase total Canadian assembly output by about 20 per cent to 120,000 units annually by 1997. A new model was proposed to be made at the Ontario plant for release in 1996 (a Canadian version of the Acura model), which comprised the first vehicle exclusively for the Canadian market from a Japanese manufacturer. An additional capacity investment of $20 million was expected to bring the total investment in the Ontario facility to around $490 million, involving an additional 80 new jobs, and plans were made to export Canadian made Civics to Taiwan and Brazil (*Honda Announcement*, 19 July, 1994).

At the same time, however, Honda announced a much larger US$245 million expansion to its Ohio operations in the United States, involving 600 people, mainly to develop a 50 per cent increase in engine manufacturing capacity and to set up a new production line to raise output by 18 per cent to around 720,000 vehicles. In addition, a further 250 workers were hired at Honda's US research and development facilities in Ohio and California, and US$50 million invested in a new Mexican assembly plant, which was expected to create 250 jobs and start making cars in November 1995. Honda publicly stated that its proposed Mexican output would not be directed towards sales in either the United States or Canada, and so would not be affected by the domestic content provisions of NAFTA. Honda explained its decision to located in Mexico by citing a local regulation requiring auto makers who wanted to sell imported vehicles to assemble them in Mexico as well. Under the terms of NAFTA, this regulation was to be phased out over a period of 10 years (Matsumoto, 1994).

The heavy US prejudice in this new round of investment by Honda, compared with its previous bias towards Canadian production in the mid-1980s, was seen as an attempt to appease US irritation over Japan's huge trade imbalance in auto vehicles and parts (*Financial Post*, 20 July, 1994). By comparison, exports from the three Canadian-based Japanese plants exceeded the number of vehicles imported into Canada from Japan during 1993 (Japan Automobile Manufacturers Association of Canada, 1993).

Autoparts companies: Honda's suppliers; Bellemar Parts Industries, F and P Manufacturing, and Yachio

Figure 6.3b shows the production network of three of Honda's directly affiliated first-tier parts suppliers located in Canada. Each is a subsidiary of primary suppliers to Honda in its home market. Thus F and P Manufacturing, located in Tottenham, Ontario, is a joint venture of Honda and two Japanese firms (with about 375 employees) and makes over 35 types of structural assemblies, such as brake pedals and struts, for all brand of cars and engines produced by Honda's North American plants. As the focus of the F and P's work is metal stamping, this subsidiary began at a Canadian location due to the cheaper cost of steel, which comprises about 65 per cent of its input cost. Yet although their factory is just 15 km from Honda's Alliston plant, it is located 10 to 12 hours truck delivery time across the border from Honda Marysville and East Liberty. As a key JIT supplier to Honda as well as other North American auto assemblers, F and P Manufacturing had little choice but to expand into the United States, and so it opened a branch factory in Ohio during 1993 (note that Honda released its suppliers from exclusive arrangements in 1991 in order to allow them to be more competitive). Following NAFTA and Honda's advance into Mexico during 1994, this Canadian-based subsidiary also considered opening a Mexican sales office (interview with Eric Broger, Executive Vice President, F and P Manufacturing Inc, Tottenham, Ontario, 5 May, 1994).

Bellemar Parts Industries, a manufacturer of car seats, is in many ways a mirror-image of F and P Manufacturing. It too has plants close to Honda in Ohio and Ontario because it must match its products to particular cars on the assembly line - primarily to ensure that colors are properly coordinated. Initially, Bellemar supplied both Canada and the US from Ohio, but the JIT organization required a site in Ontario, just 2 km from the Honda plant. In 1994, Bellemar Canada supplied around 420 units of seats, tyres and wheel assemblies daily, and employed around 100 employees (interview with Rudy Klaming, Vice President, Bellemar Parts Industries Canada Inc, Alliston, Ontario, April, 1994).

Yachiyo of Ontario Manufacturing Inc, the third affiliated supplier, produces fuel

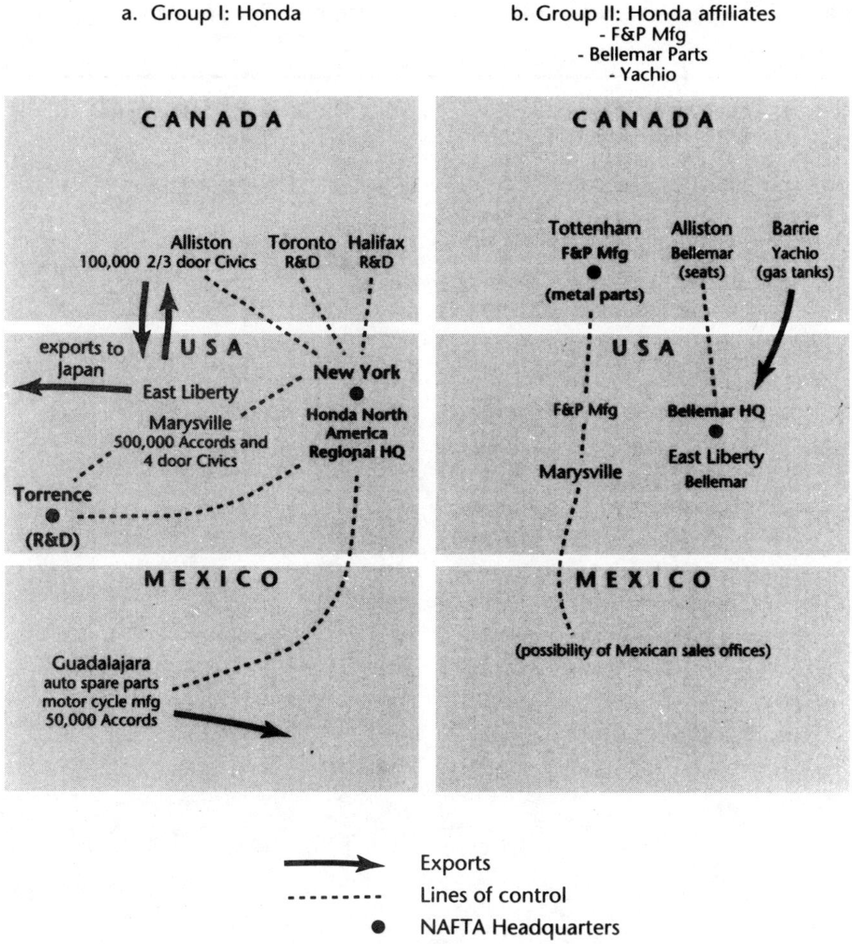

Figure 6.3 Japanese production networks in NAFTA I: (a) Honda Motor Corporations; (b) Honda's suppliers, Bellemar Parts Industries, F and P Mfg, and Yachio of Ontario Manufacturing Inc

Source: Author's survey and company reports

tanks and body parts. As with F and P, it commenced its Barrie, Ontario, production in the knowledge that the cost of steel and energy to press metal was cheaper than in the United States. No longer tied to Honda, Yachio has started to aggressively export to the USA, as well as supply Honda's competitors such as CAMI (interview with Rick Strouth, Manager Associate Services, Yachiyo of Ontario Manufacturing Inc, Barrie, Ontario, April, 1994).

Although Honda has about 33 suppliers in North America, only these three affiliated companies supply the Canadian assembly plant on a just-in-time basis. In contrast, Honda has to keep about 2-3 days worth of USA parts and engines in its

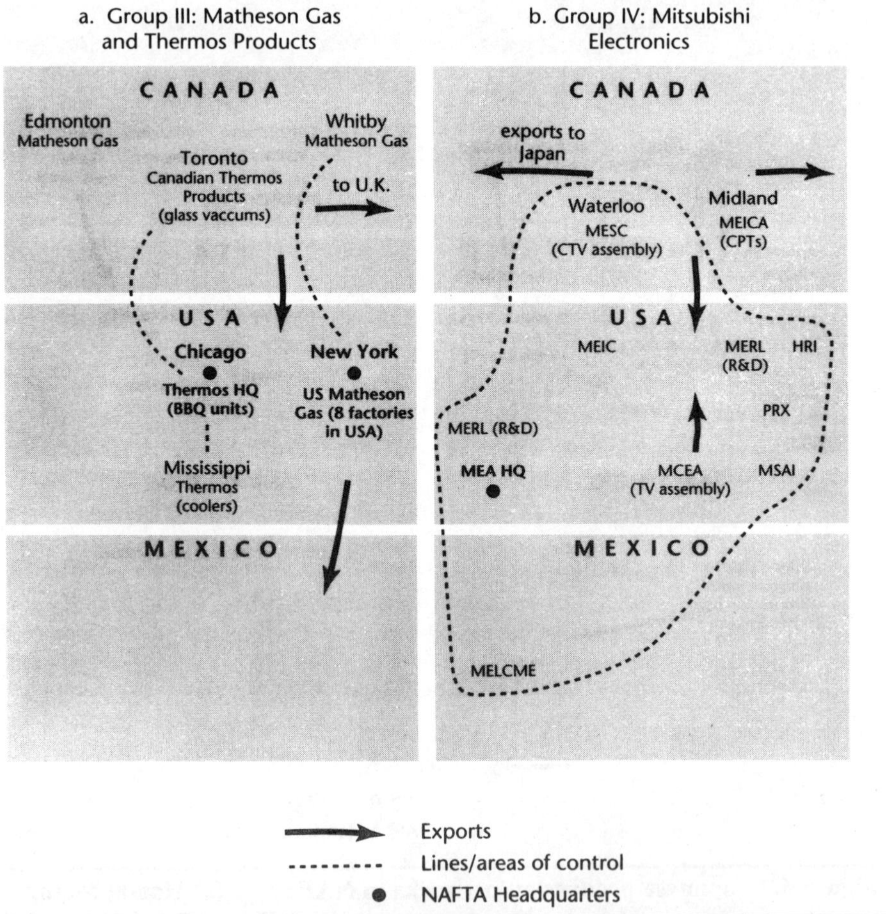

Figure 6.4 Japanese production networks in NAFTA II: (a) Matheson Gas and Thermos Products; (b) Mitsubishi Electronics

Source: Author's survey and company reports

Alliston factory (Stinson, 1991). Most of Honda's North American suppliers are located in the United States, not least because it is simply more economical for suppliers to set up closest to the heart of the North American network. Its two Ohio plants together assemble five times as many cars as Honda of Canada, and many times the annual production of the 15,000 Accords earmarked for Honda's Mexican plant.

Industrial products: Matheson Gas and Thermos Products.

As examples of this rather diverse group, the Canadian subsidiaries of Nippon Sanso - Matheson Gas and Thermos Products - are shown in Figure 6.4a. Nippon Sanso KK of Japan, is a major manufacturer of industrial gases, such as oxygen and nitrogen, and during the mid-1980s it began to expand into consumer goods, including frozen foods and stainless steel vacuum bottles. The same strategy saw Nippon Sanso move aggressively into the North American market through acquisitions, based upon extensive access to investment capital during the time of Japan's bubble economy (1987-91).

Matheson Gas was formerly a United States-owned company with eight factories for its gases in the US and two in Canada (at Whitby, Ontario, and Edmonton, Alberta). The demand for its specialty gases and gas equipment mainly comes local research laboratories, and as gas is very bulky it has to be produced close to the market. Consequently the cross-border trade provisions of NAFTA have had little effect. All bulk gases produced by Matheson Canada continue to be bought in their unprocessed form in Ontario, while the more uncommon gases and gas appliances come from Matheson's operations in the USA. Overall, Matheson has very little integrated North American structure as each factory tends to be relatively independent, and at the time of the survey there was no Mexican subsidiary (interview with Doug Bonnar, Branch Manager, Matheson Gas Products Canada, Whitby, Ontario, June, 1994).

Canadian Thermos Products was initially the Canadian subsidiary of Thermos Products Inc, a United States company owned by Household International, headquartered in Chicago. It had two US plants and one each in Canada and Britain - all making a wide range of products for local markets (Little, 1991). Nippon Sanso was a number of suitors for Thermos Products Inc. and acquired the entire North American operations in 1989, establishing its headquarters in Chicago. Originally the Canadian factory was built to service the Canadian market, but over the subsequent five years Nippon Sanso rationalized the North American production network, closed one factory in Connecticut, and distributed product mandates to each remaining facility. Following this shift to an integrated regional focus, and with new investment, employment in the Scarborough, Ontario, location doubled to about 200 and sales more than doubled to C$45 million. Canadian Thermos rationalized its product lines and by 1994 exported almost 65 per cent of its output, compared with almost none before the shift in corporate strategy. For the Canadian market, Thermos has substituted United States products for ones previously made in Canada. In the decision to close the Connecticut factory and move its production to Canada, wages in Ontario and Connecticut were evaluated to be about the same, but total compensation was higher in Connecticut, mainly because of the bill the company paid to private insurers for health care and workers compensation (these costs are paid for by the Onatario Province out of taxes). Beyond that, Connecticut's energy costs were about three times those in Ontario. As a result, the Canadian factory focused on the manufacture of glass vacuums and coolers (ibid.). Exports to the United States grew from virtually nothing to around 50 per cent of production. In this case the NAFTA agreement was seen as vital in boosting output and employment in the Canadian factory. Nippon Sanso has also extended the product mandate approach (originally initiated by Household International) to global markets. Thus exports of products to the United Kingdom and Pacific Rim markets now make up nearly 15 per cent of production. Conversely, NAFTA has allowed the rationalization of Thermos Canada's suppliers, and all the required plastic resin and propylene is now sourced from the United States, together with the BBQ units which used to be produced in Canada. Thermos currently ships to the Mexican market from either the USA or Canadian operation, and no Mexican factory is contemplated while the dollar remains so low (interview with Grant Ross, Director of Operations, Canadian Thermos Products Inc, Scarborough, Ontario, June, 1994).

Consumer electronics: Mitsubishi Electronics

Figure 6.4b shows the commodity chain of Mitsubishi Electronics in NAFTA. It indicates that Mitsubishi Electronics America (MEA), headquartered in San Diego, California, is the United States regional coordination headquarters for a group of 20 subsidiaries, spanning the entire continent and which includes Mitsubishi Electronics Sales Canada (MESCA), a medium-sized color television assembly factory located in Kitchener, Ontario. This facility commenced production in the early 1980s originally as a joint venture with Electrohume, and now produces big-screen color televisions with traditional wooden cabinet design (CTVs) as well as medium-size CTVs, primarily for the Canadian market. Prior to NAFTA, Canadian, Mexican and US models had different specifications, and this continues to give the Canadian operation a degree of insulation from any immediate rationalization with the production networks of other Mitsubishi Electronics subsidiaries on a North American-wide basis. In Mexico, for instance, the broadcast technology is Black and White and there is only a relatively small middle income group of consumers.

Notwithstanding, Mitsubishi Electronics executives consider that in the future NAFTA will facilitate the standardization of the North American market for consumer products as a whole and this is likely to have several effects on the Canadian assembly operation. Thus it is conceivable that the more popular bigger screen sizes will come into Canada from the large United States factories located in San Diego, California, and Atlanta, Georgia, which can achieve economies of scale. Nonetheless, as long as the Canadian dollar remains low against the US dollar (one Canadian dollar equalled just 75 US cents in mid-1994) Mitsubishi Electronics realizes this makes little economic sense. Moreover, the long-term viability of the Canadian operation is enhanced due to its capacity to produce several TV models in small quantities on batch production lines, hence it can continue to fill a niche in the Mitsubishi Electronics family for a flexible manufacturing capability making small sized screens and medium-scale output for the North American market. Yet another long-term affect of NAFTA is that more of Mitsubishi's local engineering design and market research will be concentrated in the United States rather than Japan, and more sourcing of chassis and plastic cabinets will be done either in Mexico or in the United States, replacing Canadian wood parts for TV cabinets and southeast Asia electronic subassemblies (interview with S. Goldstein, Vice Chairman, Mitsubishi Electronics Sales Canada, Inc, Markham, Ontario, June, 1994).

In contrast to MESCA's situation, Mitsubishi Electronics headquarters in Japan has chosen its plant at Midland, Ontario (known as Mitsubishi Electronic Industries Canada, or MEICA), to produce to a world product mandate for its high quality medium-sized color picture tubes (CPTs) (see Innami, 1986; *Financial Times of Canada*, 1993; Rankine, 1994). This subsidiary is rather unique as Mitsubishi Electronics is the only consumer electronics firm which to date has given one of its Canadian subsidiaries a world product mandate. The plant was acquired from RCA in 1983, who tended to treat it as merely a Canadian branch plant. Yet, following increased capacity, more automation and higher quality improvement, production and global sales subsequently increased to over 1 million units per year, and 75 per cent of sales are now exported (40 per cent to Japan). Exporting to Japan commenced in 1990 due to delays in reducing tariffs into the United States and anti-dumping duties, combined with Mitsubishi Electronics' need to source cheaper parts into Japan to retain competitiveness there. The Midland plant's first shipment of 10,000 tubes to its Japanese parent in 1990 saw 25 per cent rejects; in 1992, fewer than 1 per cent of the 100,000 shipped tubes failed the inspection. Southern Ontario now has the largest overseas Mitsubishi Electronics CPT factory (interview with H. Kitagawa, President, Mitsubishi Electronics Industries Canada Inc, Midland, Ontario, April, 1994).

Conclusions

This chapter has argued that new political and economic spaces shape the geography of multinational investment, and the restructuring of the world economy into regional economic blocks needs to be incorporated into established models of foreign investment behavior. Multinational regionalism and the link between trade liberalization and direct investment allow MNCs a degree of locational flexibility, yet as shown in this study Japanese firms in NAFTA often traded off the full exploitation of continental economies of scale against political considerations, as well as the benefits of flexibility and proximity to national or local markets as suggested by Dunning (1993b) and Rugman (1990). Gereffi (1992, 85) notes that these new regional configurations 'contain their own cores and peripheries with particular sets of unequal transactions, dependencies, and development possibilities.' This final section reflects therefore on the role played by the existing range of Japanese controlled factories in southern Ontario within the NAFTA block, and also the future opportunities and constraints on Japanese FDI in this location.

To begin with, the author's survey allowed a detailed examination of patterns of exports and local sourcing (see Table 6.2). With regard to exports, Table 6.2 shows that there was enormous variation in the percentage of total sales recorded as being sent to export markets. Nonetheless, most of the major companies in each group, such as Honda, Bridgestone and Mitsubishi Electronics Industries Canada, had substantial sales into the United States. Similarly, there was a wide range of North American local content (that is the percentage of parts and materials sourced from either Canada, United States or Mexico), yet levels were nearly always above the 50 per cent minimum necessary to conduct trans-border trade in the NAFTA region during for the first four years of the Agreement (Group I recorded a level above the 62.5 per cent long-term NAFTA local content minimum for automobiles). The levels of purely Canadian local content, however, were much less (see Table 6.2). Still, local content of the Canadian subsidiaries appears to have risen over time in line with the build up of production volumes and closer relationships with local suppliers. As noted by previous studies (Edgington, 1990; Morris, 1991a) these results suggest that the vast majority of Japanese factories in Ontario were already well integrated into continental networks of sales and production prior to the implementation of NAFTA. By and large, the Japanese manufacturers in southern Ontario were attracted by this region's comparative advantages, such as a low-cost yet skilled labour force and cheaper energy costs. Since 1991, the lower value of the Canadian dollar has also helped win export markets. In the future, this study suggests that the new free trade agreement should assist the further penetration of products made by the Ontario-based plants into the United States markets, and in some cases into Mexico. Although local content regulations have been increased from 50 per cent under the previous Canada-US Free Trade Agreement to 62.5 per cent over the next eight years, the ambiguity surrounding their definition appears to have been resolved to the advantage of Japanese firms located in Canada.

Another finding is that, by itself, NAFTA does not present an overall threat to the continued viability of existing Japanese subsidiaries in southern Ontario. As noted earlier, all companies except the color television and audio product plants of Group IV made high quality products which were not price sensitive or threatened by relocation to cheaper wage regions in North America, such as Mexico. Indeed, recent research by Kenney and Florida (1994) appears to suggest that, to date, Mexico has been only able to attract Japanese plants which had production processes that required cheap labour and which were in markets that suffered from intense competition. The results of their study throws doubt on whether more capital-intensive production processes that rely on high-skill levels can be relocated to Mexico in the short-term. This is confirmed by Table 6.3 which shows that Mexico, up to financial year 1992, had captured very little Japanese direct manufacturing investment in NAFTA. In the consumer electronics sector, rationalization of Group IV assembly firms could occur as the Canadian tariff drops, under NAFTA arrangements, and as technical standards harmonize to North American-wide levels. Both the US and Mexico have price advantage over southern Ontario due to the size of their markets, transport costs, and scale economies[3].

Table 6.2
Exports, local content and research and development

	Group I (N=3)	Group II (N=10)	Group III (N=22)	Group IV* (N=4)
Percentage of Exports	76-83	0-90	0-95	0-70
Percentage of Local Content**				
- range	55-85	35-100	4-100	50-80
- average***	67	83	70	66
Percentage Canadian Content				
- range	11-30	20-100	4-100	0-43
- average***	20	42	54	28
R and D as Percentage of Sales				
- range	0-1	0-2	0-15	0
- average	0	0	2	0

Note: Group I = Auto Assemblers; Group II = Auto Parts; Group III = Industrial Products; Group IV = Consumer Electronics. * excludes MEICA which is included in Group III; ** refers to total North American local content; **** unweighted averages for each group.

Source: author's survey, 1994.

Significantly, Honda and Nissan, which have both invested in car assembly plants in Mexico recently, appear to be affected by the politics of NAFTA and have decided not to export from a Mexican base into either the United States or Canada (Matsumoto, 1994). Toyota, for its part, has recently confirmed its confidence in its Ontario assembly subsidiary with new investments, rather than propose any expansion into Mexico. It is thought that NAFTA's more explicit rules defining allowable levels of local content for transborder trade, the cheaper Canadian dollar and the elimination of Canadian tariffs on auto parts imported from Japan and elsewhere, together accounted for this willingness to make further investments in Ontario (Mahood, 1994). Moreover, Toyota's plant at Cambridge has established itself as one of the highest quality automobile plants in North America and has been honored

Table 6.3
Annual Japanese manufacturing FDI in NAFTA: Canada, USA and Mexico, percentage shares
(Financial years, April-March)

	Canada	USA	Mexico	TOTAL	(value $USmill.)
1952-81	10.5	80.3	9.2	100.0	(3,784)
1982	4.4	82.2	13.4	100.0	(944)
1983	2.0	87.7	10.3	100.0	(1,104)
1984	7.5	88.7	3.8	100.0	(1,291)
1985	1.6	93.9	4.6	100.0	(1,281)
1986	2.5	88.9	8.5	100.0	(2,405)
1987	9.7	90.0	0.3	100.0	(4,864)
1988	3.8	95.5	0.6	100.0	(9,249)
1989	13.3	86.5	0.2	100.0	(10,256)
1990	14.0	84.0	2.0	100.0	(7,601)
1991	12.2	85.4	2.4	100.0	(6,510)
1992	16.6	82.3	1.2	100.0	(4,550)
Cumulative 1982-92	10.1	87.8	2.0	100.0	(50,086)

Note: This data excludes all raw materials and services investments. However, it includes investments in paper and pulp (thus inflating the Canadian percentage), which were excluded in the author's surveys of Japanese firms in southern Ontario.

Source: Bank of Japan, unpublished data.

Table 6.4
Decision making in Japanese subsidiaries, Southern Ontario, 1994

	Group I	Group II	Group III	Group IV
A. Financial Independence:				
i. ability to raise finance	1.0	2.9	3.7	2.8
ii. upper limit of spending	1.3	1.9	2.0	1.0
iii. signing of contracts	2.0	1.7	1.6	1.0
iv. banking	1.3	3.7	1.9	1.0
v. accounting services	1.0	1.2	2.0	1.8
B. Routine Managerial Responsibility				
i. legal advice	1.0	1.2	1.4	1.0
ii. technical advice	2.3	2.6	1.8	3.0
iii. personal hiring	1.0	1.2	1.3	1.0
iv. shipping	1.6	1.0	1.1	1.0
v. freight mgt./warehousing	1.0	1.0	1.1	1.0
C. Strategic Decisions				
i. Pricing policy	4.3	2.0	1.3	1.5
ii. Production Volumes	3.7	1.6	1.1	1.8
iii. New products	4.3	3.2	1.9	1.0
iv. New markets	3.3	2.2	1.4	1.0
v. New sources of Raw Materials/Parts	2.6	2.1	1.6	1.3

Note: Company interviewees were asked to rank each decision making factor on a scale of 1 to 5, so that 1 or 2 = decision normally is taken locally and totally independent of parent company; 3 = decision normally is arrived at by negotiation and varies case by case; 4 or 5 = parent company normally makes decision or has final say. Recorded scores are the unweighted average for each of the four major groups of Japanese companies.

Source: Author's survey, 1994.

on several occasions with J.D. Power and Associates Awards (*Canada-Japan Trade Council Newsletter*, Sept-Oct, 1993, 4). At the end of 1994, Toyota announced that the continuing increase in the value of the Japanese yen required a boost in North

American production by about 50 per cent by 1996. At the same time it announced a planned C$600 million expansion which would more than double its annual production capacity in Cambridge to 200,000 Corollas per year from its 1994 level of around 80,000. Toyota will no longer export Corolla sedans to the US and Canada from Japanese when this proposed expansion is completed. This addition, which includes an engine assembly facility, compares relatively favorably with the planned expansion of at its Georgetown, Kentucky, plant to around 400,000 Camry and Avalon units per year (Mahood, 1994).

Table 6.4 indicates that Canadian subsidiaries were relatively autonomous from their Japanese headquarters in most areas of decision making (as demonstrated by the large number of average survey scores falling below 2.5). Interestingly, Table 6.4 reveals that Group I (the auto assemblers) had the least degrees of freedom over strategic decisions such as new products and product volumes, no doubt reflecting their ties to an overall North American regional scheme. Conversely, Group III (industrial parts and goods producers), many of whom were oriented towards local Canadian markets, appeared to have the most decision making flexibility.

The major adverse finding from this survey was that the vast majority firms in Ontario continued to depend on Japan or the United States for their research and design facilities (Table 6.2), as well as for much of their technology and production engineering (see Table 6.4). For instance, where the Japanese owner took over the American headquarters, then the R and D continued to be carried out in the United States. By way of illustration, the research and regional headquarters operations of Matsushita Canada, Canadian Thermos Products and Bridgestone Canada takes place in Chicago. In a similar vein, it became apparent from survey results that in the case of the auto assembly group (Group I) United States parts suppliers were more important. Thus all three firms in Group I reported that it was very hard to find first tier car assembly suppliers in Canada. Beyond semi-processed metal, plastic and wooden parts, most component supplies came from the United States. In turn, this has contributed to the development of a clear continental spatial division of labour in which the Canadian component of the North American product chain focused on medium value production with a relative dearth of higher order regional management or technology activities. Exceptions exist, such as Lumonics (a Canadian-based laser technology company with global markets acquired by Sumitomo Heavy Industries), and some adaptive R and D, quality control and analytical capacity also takes place in Canada.

In the future, Japanese firms will continue to look at ways to increase overseas production and will establish additional assembly and major component plants in North America over the next few years (Tejima, 1993). It is also clear that this will involve further localization of both R and D and parts supplies. What is less clear is where the plants and new investments will be located. In theory, under the NAFTA, the plants could be located in Canada, the United States or Mexico. While Mexico has lower costs and a growing market in its favour, Canada has more developed infrastructure and a broader range of parts and suppliers. Consequently, while Ontario is extremely unlikely to attract NAFTA regional headquarters or research and design functions it can attempt to attract more Japanese parts suppliers and assembly plants oriented to North American or even global product mandates. Nevertheless, analysis of the JETRO data base suggests that Ontario has in fact lost pace recently as an attractive investment destination for Japanese investors. Thus while Japanese manufacturing investment levelled off in Ontario after 1990 (the onset of the recent Japanese recession), Japanese companies continued to add new factories in other North American locations such as California, Georgia, New York, Ohio, Illinois, Indiana, Kentucky and North Carolina (Japan External Trade Organization, 1990-1993). This study has shown that Canada's role to date within NAFTA has emphasized medium technology assembly and component operations. To continue to attract these and other Japanese investment Ontario must retain its competitive position. This will be best achieved by upgrading its overall technological infrastructure, and introducing new equipment and process innovations, as well as the production of engineering talent (see Gertler, 1991; Britton, 1993).

Notes

1. For a discussion of multinational investment in the European Union see Dunning and Robson (1987). For a summary of the evolution of Japanese strategies in the European Union see Dunning (1993a, chp6).
2. Hitachi Sales Canada is headquartered in Mississauga, Ontario, although its Canadian assembly plant at the time of the survey was located in Montreal, Quebec.
3. In fact, subsequent to the author's survey two Japanese electronics firms (Hitachi and Sanyo) announced they would move their television assembly operations out of Quebec, Canada during 1995, with one switching production to the United States and the other to Mexico (*Mainichi Daily News*, 9 March, 1995).

7 Japanese corporate groups and the locational strategy of Japanese auto and component parts makers in the United States

Neil Reid, Andrew Solocha and Breandán Ó hUallacháin

Introduction

The purpose of this chapter is to examine the locational strategy and resultant spatial patterns of Japanese automobile assembly and component parts manufacturing facilities in the United States. The level of Japanese direct manufacturing investment in the United States has increased dramatically since the early 1970s. At the beginning of 1970 there were only thirteen Japanese-owned manufacturing plants in the United States. By the end of 1990 there were 1,778. Japan, after the United Kingdom, is the second largest foreign direct investor in the United States (United States Department of Commerce, 1991). The United States is the most important destination for Japanese direct investment (JDI), accounting for forty-two per cent of the value of the total (Japan Economic Institute, 1992). The rapid increase in the level of JDI in the United States is primarily attributable to two factors - US-Japan trade friction and fluctuations in the yen-dollar ratio (Webley 1979; Cole and Yakushiji 1984; Dicken 1988).

The rapid increase in JDI in the United States has attracted the attention of academics from a variety disciplines. Much of this academic research has focussed, not surprisingly, on the automobile industry. Japanese direct investors have invested heavily in automobile and automobile-related industries in the United States. In 1982 Honda became the first Japanese automaker to assemble automobiles in the United States. Today there are nine Japanese-owned automobile assembly plants and over three hundred Japanese-owned automobile component parts makers in the United States. These nine assembly plants and three-hundred plus component parts makers are geographically concentrated in seven states - California, Illinois, Indiana, Kentucky, Michigan, Ohio, and Tennessee. Ohio has three assembly plants and each of the other six states have one each. Sixty-three per cent of the component part makers are located in the states with an assembly plant (Table 7.1). Six of the seven states with an assembly plant (California is the exception) are geographically contiguous and form what in the literature has become known as the auto-alley. The auto-alley runs from Michigan in the north to Tennessee in the south.

Table 7.1
Geographic distribution of Japanese auto-related direct investment in the United States

State	Number of Parts Suppliers	Auto-related Plants as a % of Total Japanese Plants	Greenfield Auto-related Plants as a % of Total Auto-related Plants
California	36	11	54
Illinois	20	20	43
Indiana	26	38	81
Kentucky	27	44	93
Michigan	28	33	59
Ohio	39	33	76
Tennessee	20	34	62
Auto Alley	160	32	71
Seven States	196	23	68
United States	313	18	63

Notes: Calculated from data in MacKnight 1992. The auto-alley comprises Illinois, Indiana, Kentucky, Michigan, Ohio, and Tennessee.

Japanese auto-related direct investment comprises a significant proportion of overall JDI in the United States. Eighteen per cent of all Japanese-owned manufacturing plants in the United States are auto-related, either an assembly plant or a component parts maker (Table 7.1). This proportion increases significantly in the auto-alley, where thirty-two per cent of the Japanese plants are auto-related. Japanese automobile assembly and component parts plants are predominantly greenfield investments (newly constructed manufacturing plants). Nationally, sixty-three per cent of Japanese auto-related plants are greenfield. In the auto-alley seventy-one per cent of Japanese auto-related plants are greenfield. The concentration of Japanese direct auto-related investment in greenfield plants in the auto-alley is no accident. It is the result of a carefully thought-out locational strategy, designed to both maintain long-standing inter-firm business relationships and industrial practices and to minimize uncertainties associated with doing business in an alien economic and cultural environment.

The remainder of this chapter is divided into three sections. The following section argues that firm-specific assets are a key contributor to the successful penetration of foreign markets by multinational corporations. A crucial firm-specific asset enjoyed by many Japanese multinationals is membership in one or more corporate groups. Three major types of corporate group exist in modern-day Japan - keiretsu, enterprise group, and vertical distribution group. We describe each of these. We follow with an assessment of the advantages of corporate group membership. Corporate groups enable Japanese manufacturers to simultaneously lower manufacturing costs, improve product quality, and quicken the pace of both product and process innovation.

Finally, we discuss the implications of corporate groups for the locational strategy and resultant spatial distribution of Japanese automobile assembly plants and component parts makers in the United States. This strategy is designed to replicate long-standing business and geographical relationships between customers and suppliers who, very often, are members of the same corporate group. Maintenance of the intensive inter-firm material and information linkages, which are a defining characteristic of corporate groups, results in geographic proximity between assemblers and component parts producers.

The organizational structure of Japanese industry: corporate groups and networks

Foreign direct investment theory argues that firm-specific assets are a key factor in the successful penetration of foreign markets by multinational corporations (Rugman 1980; Caves 1982; Helpman 1984). Such firm-specific assets include managerial skills, corporate organization, marketing and distribution channels, and product specific research and development. Multinational firms choose to exploit their firm-specific assets through FDI if transaction costs favor direct control over contractual agreements. Multinational enterprises with firm-specific assets also prefer direct ownership in the foreign market over licensing because of problems in monitoring business performance (Horstmann and Markusen, 1987; Rugman, 1980). Caves (1982) contends that transaction costs in servicing a foreign market may be considerable. These costs include gathering information about the foreign market and adapting the product to that market. By choosing direct investment as their mode of entry into foreign markets firms can reduce their transaction costs. The manufacture of products that embody high levels of firm-specific assets in the host country may facilitate efficient product design for the special requirements of foreign markets (Caves and Jones, 1985). A firm engaged in FDI is assisted in product modification by direct information on consumer acceptance in the host country market.

Corporate organization is a crucial contributor to the competitive advantage enjoyed by many Japanese manufacturers with production facilities in the United States. Japanese corporate groups facilitate penetration of foreign markets by reducing the uncertainty of doing business in an alien economic environment. By facilitating both the identification of customers and suppliers corporate groups provide a support infrastructure for manufacturers. Group membership gives manufacturers control (both perceived and real) of the transactional environment. Anderson and Gatignon (1986) argue that the level of control a firm has over its transactions is the single most important determinant of risk and return. As will be discussed in more detail below, membership in corporate groups also contribute to lower manufacturing costs and faster rates of both process and product innovation.

A variety of different types of corporate group exist in Japan, making the organizational structure of Japanese industry somewhat difficult to comprehend. Difficulties of comprehension are exacerbated by researchers using inconsistent nomenclature when discussing corporate groups. Thus, different authors use the same term to describe different types of corporate group, or different terms to describe the same type of corporate group (for example, see Okumura's (1982) and Ostrom's (1990) use of the terms keiretsu and enterprise group). Confusion also arises from firms being able to belong to more than one type of corporate group. To simplify our discussion of Japan's corporate groups we employ a single nomenclature, that of Ostrom (1990). Ostrom (1990) identified three types of corporate group in modern-day Japan - keiretsu, enterprise groups, and vertical distribution groups.

Keiretsu

Ostrom (1990) defined a keiretsu as a group of firms organized around a large bank. There are six keiretsu in modern-day Japan - Dai-Ichi Kangyo, Fuyo, Mitsui, Mitsubishi, Sanwa, and Sumitomo (Okumura, 1982; Anchordoguy, 1990; Ostrom, 1990).

Member firms of a keiretsu are linked primarily by finances rather than products (Ostrom 1990). Financial links are based on mutual stockholding. Stockholding is 'matrix-like' with firms in one keiretsu not only holding stock in member firms of the same keiretsu, but also holding stock in firms who are members of other keiretsu (Ostrom 1990, p. 3). Between twelve per cent and twenty-seven per cent of the stock of keiretsu members is held by other members of the same keiretsu. The remainder (between eighty-eight per cent and seventy-three percent) of the stock is held by members of another keiretsu or by independent companies (Ostrom, 1990). Interlocking stock ownership means that control relationships between group members are interdependent, with no one member having the capability of controlling the business activities of another member (Okumura, 1982). One-way control relationships are also restricted by a law that limits core banks to ownership of not more than five per cent of nonfinancial group members (Ostrom, 1990). Firms can be members of more than one keiretsu. For example, Hitachi Limited belongs not only to the Fuyo keiretsu, but also to the Sanwa and Dai-Ichi Kangyo keiretsu.

Keiretsu have wide ranging business interests. For example, the business activities of the Mitsui keiretsu include banking, life insurance, coal mining, construction, chemical manufacture, and retailing. Their wide ranging business interests means that the structure of keiretsu take on a conglomerate, rather than a vertical or horizontal, nature (Ostrom, 1990). The importance of keiretsu firms in the modern Japanese economy can be illustrated by a few simple statistics. In the late 1980s over half of the largest 100 firms in Japan belonged to a keiretsu. Keiretsus earned eighteen per cent of the total net profits accruing to Japanese business, had nearly seventeen per cent of total sales, held over fourteen per cent of paid-up capital, and employed almost five per cent of the Japanese labor force (Anchordoguy, 1990).

Enterprise groups

Ostrom (1990) defined an enterprise group as a group of firms organized around a single independent firm. In most cases the core firm of the enterprise group is a manufacturer, but can be another type of firm such as a retailer. Modern day Japan is home to dozens of enterprise groups. Core firms include the Sony Corporation, the Nissan Motor Company Limited, and the Toyota Motor Corporation. Enterprise groups tend to be most strongly developed in the automobile, electronics, and machinery industries (Anchordoguy, 1990). In contrast to keiretsu, stockholding in enterprise groups is pyramidal in nature. The core firm owns the largest share holdings in other group members, which has the effect of strengthening the level of control exercised by core firms. Unlike keiretsu where interlocking stock ownership ensures interdependent control relationships, relationships in an enterprise group tend to be characterized by control and subordination (Okumura, 1982).

Ostrom (1990) identified three types of enterprise group based upon variation in levels of vertical integration between members. First, there are enterprise groups whose members belong to the same industry and display high levels of vertical integration. In such groups, the production output of one member firm becomes the input to another member. The Toyota Motor Corporation and its hundreds of affiliated subcontractors are an example of this type of enterprise group. The main source of competitive advantage provided by this type of enterprise group lies in the network of suppliers and the material and information linkages established between network members. Second, there are enterprise groups whose members are involved in different industries and whose outputs may or may not be inputs to another group member. Thus, the level of vertical integration is less than in the first type of enterprise group. For example, members of the Hitachi enterprise group are involved in a wide range of economic activities including construction, consumer electronics, and financial services. Networks, based upon material and information exchanges, again provide the main source of competitive for this second type of enterprise group. Third, there are enterprise groups whose members display no vertical integration. In these enterprise groups, members produce the same good or service as the core firm. For example, members of the enterprise group headed by the Matsushita Electrical Industrial Company Limited are almost exclusively involved in the manufacture of audio and video equipment such as videocassette recorders (Ostrom, 1990). Technology sharing, resulting in the elimination of redundant research and development, is the major source of competitive advantage for this third type of enterprise group.

Complicating our understanding of the organizational structure of Japanese industry is the fact that some members of enterprise groups (both core and noncore) are also members of keiretsu. For example, the Toyota Motor Corporation is a member of the Mitsui keiretsu, while the Nissan Motor Company is a member of the Fuyo keiretsu. Nissan Fire and Marine Insurance Company, which belongs to the Nissan Motor Company enterprise group, also belongs to the Dai-Ichi Kangyo keiretsu. Thus, the Nissan Fire and Marine Insurance Company belongs to a different keiretsu than the Nissan Motor Company. Similarly, Mitsubishi Heavy Industries Limited is a member of the Mitsubishi keiretsu, but is also a core firm in an enterprise group (Ostrom, 1990).

Vertical distribution groups

Vertical distribution groups refer to distribution channels such as retail outlets which manufacturers establish for their products. Control of these distribution channels constitute a key firm-specific asset. In many ways, vertical distribution groups can be considered an extension of enterprise groups. The major difference between enterprise and vertical distribution groups is that in the latter case the upstream supplier firm is likely to exercise control through such means as exclusive sales arrangements in addition to, or in place of, stock ownership. Nevertheless, vertical distribution groups allow firms to maintain their competitive advantage when penetrating new markets.

Advantages of corporate group membership

Manufacturing a product requires the combination of a number of different inputs. These include firm-specific assets, materials, labor, and capital. A firm has two options for obtaining the inputs to its production process. Either it can purchase the input internally or it can purchase the input from another firm (Coase, 1937; Sheard, 1983; Williamson, 1979). Hood and Young (1979) noted that in perfectly competitive markets all inputs are externally produced. In imperfect markets costs arise in purchasing inputs from other firms. These include the costs of finding the appropriate price, the costs of negotiating a separate contract for each exchange transaction which takes place, and the cost of taxes which must be paid on market transactions (Coase, 1937; Hood and Young, 1979). Hood and Young (1979) suggested that if transactions can be carried out at a lower cost within the firm than through the market place, they will be internalized and conducted within the firm.

Between these two extremes of obtaining inputs externally or producing them internally there lies a third option. Suppliers who are vertically quasi-integrated into the purchasing firm's production system can provide the inputs (Blois, 1972; Richardson, 1972; Sheard, 1983). Unlike a vertically-integrated supplier, a vertically quasi-integrated supplier is not a wholly-owned subsidiary of the customer. The customer does, however, exert a considerable amount of control over the supplier because the latter depends upon the former for a large proportion of its sales (Blois, 1972). Control can include dictating which suppliers a firm may do business with, having access to the records of the supplier firm, and having influence over whom the supplier firm appoints to its executive staff. Thus, vertical quasi-integration allows the customer to maintain the advantages of vertical integration while at the same time avoiding the risks and rigidity associated with full ownership. Advantages of vertical integration include stability and certainty of input supplies and tighter quality and inventory control. Potential disadvantages of vertical integration include disparities between productive capacities at various stages of production, inflexibility of operations, and lack of direct competitive pressures on the costs of intermediate inputs (Blois, 1972). The benefits of entering into a vertically quasi-integrated relationship are not limited to the customer firm. There are advantages for the supplier firm. These include the opportunity to obtain technical expertise from the customer firm, the possibilities of attaining economies of scale due to the volume of the customer's input requirements, and the stability of longer term contracts. Aoki (1990) argued that vertical quasi-integration and the inherent autonomy of supplier firms is the key to industrial mastery.

An important Japanese firm-specific asset is knowledge in production. An overriding goal of Japanese manufacturers is the manufacture of high quality products at reasonable cost to the consumer. Contrary to traditional western thinking, Japanese manufacturers view the relationship between product quality and costs of production to be a negative one (Oliver and Wilkinson, 1988). In Japanese industry the apparent paradox in which production costs and product quality are seen to be inversely related is solved by viewing quality as 'freedom from waste' (Oliver and Wilkinson 1988, p. 30). Giunipero and O'Neal (1988, p. 36) defined waste as 'anything other than the minimum amount of equipment, material, parts, and workers which is essential to production', while Rao and Scheraga (1988, p. 44) defined waste as 'any incurred cost, such as inventory, set up, scrap, and rework that does not add value to the product'.

Japanese manufacturers have been very successful at eliminating substantial amounts of waste from their manufacturing processes. Inventory cost reduction is one area where the Japanese have been particularly successful. Costs associated with inventory (e.g. warehouse storage costs) can be a significant component of a company's overall production costs (Sayer, 1986; Ptak, 1988). Zero inventory at the point of production is the theoretical goal of JIT delivery (O'Neal, 1989). This is achieved by the delivery of small batches of material inputs on a frequent and regular basis (Hannah, 1987; Malley and Ray, 1988; Jordan, 1988). Zero inventory necessitates the delivery of zero-defective material inputs. The delivery of defective parts to an assembly line has the potential to slow down production. Thus, the delivery of high quality material inputs is integral to the success of any JIT inventory control system. In turn, attainment of satisfactory quality levels provides a source of competitive advantage by allowing further cost savings to be realized. If quality of incoming material inputs is guaranteed the receiving facility can considerably reduce inspection, rework, and warranty repair costs (Jordan, 1988). Having little or no inventory at the point of production leaves the customer susceptible to disruption in the incoming flow of material inputs. Strikes at suppliers can be particularly problematic for manufacturers having material inputs delivered JIT (Oliver and Wilkinson, 1988; Reid, 1990).

The necessity for trustworthy suppliers encourages Japanese manufacturers, by using suppliers who are members of the same corporate group, to internalize their markets for material inputs. Japanese manufacturers develop long-term, cooperative relationships with such suppliers (Ansari and Modarres, 1987; Burton, 1988; Giunipero and O'Neal, 1988; Lubben, 1988; Malley and Ray, 1988). If suppliers perform satisfactorily they are given long-term contracts and become part of a larger supplier network. Satisfactory performance includes meeting the stringent delivery requirements of JIT.

The long-term nature of supplier-customer relationships in Japanese industry was illustrated by Arnesen, Cole, and Krishna (1987). They showed that approximately one-third of Toyota suppliers have been supplying them since the 1930s, two-thirds since the 1940s, and all but seven per cent since the 1950s. One implication of the Japanese preference for using suppliers who belong to the same corporate group is that it is extremely difficult for a US company to become a supplier to a Japanese company (Holstein, Treece, Crock and Armstrong, 1990). A study by the United States General Accounting Office (USGAO) (1988) supports this contention. The USGAO (1988) found that US companies have experienced severe difficulties in obtaining business from Japanese-owned automobile assembly plans located in the United States. The most frequently cited difficulty was overcoming preexisting relationships between Japanese automakers and their suppliers. Japanese automakers prefer to purchase component parts from suppliers with whom they already have long-standing organizational and financial relationships back in Japan. Maintaining and strengthening these relationships is viewed as integral to successful penetration of the US economy via direct investment. For example, manufacturing plants in the United States who are members of the Mitsubishi keiretsu rely heavily on other members of the keiretsu to supply them with both material inputs and industrial machinery (*Business Week*, 1990; Holstein, Treece, Crock, and Armstrong, 1990). One estimate suggested that as much as 50% of the trade of a keiretsu or an enterprise group member is conducted with another group member (Anchordoguy, 1990).

The organizational structure and resulting long-term relationships which are characteristic of Japanese industry also have important implications for both product and process innovation. Product and process development occurs as a result of the generation of new knowledge. New knowledge, in turn, is generated by combining relevant pieces of information (Imai and Itami, 1984; Imai, 1987-88). This information, which is embodied in individual employees, is usually technical and proprietary in nature. It is often ambiguous and subject to refinement (Ó hUallacháin, 1991). Such proprietary technical knowledge is a key source of firm specific assets (Gruber, Mehta, and Vernon, 1967; Caves, 1974; Lipsey, Karvis, and O'Connor, 1983).

According to Imai and Itami (1984, p. 306) Japanese manufacturers excel at what they term 'incremental innovation'. This involves relatively minor process and product innovations, each of which contributes ever so slightly to a better product or a more efficient manufacturing process. In contrast, US manufacturers have tended to excel at 'radical innovation' (Imai and Itami, 1984, p. 306). These are innovations where there is a major breakthrough in either the product or the process. Incremental innovations take place on the factory floor, while radical innovations tend to be the product of research and development laboratories.

A philosophy of fostering incremental innovation in Japanese industry dates back to the 1940s when, due to low market demand, Toyota began rotating workers between a variety of different tasks (Cusumano, 1988). Rotating between different tasks allows workers to acquire a broad range of skills, to become generalists rather than specialists, and to develop a more comprehensive understanding of the entire manufacturing process. In short, workers become flexible and gain the necessary expertise to rotate between tasks (Pascale and Rohlen, 1983; Dohse, Jurgens and Malsch, 1985; Aoki, 1986; Sayer, 1986). For example, sixty per cent of assembly line workers are capable of undertaking routine line maintenance (Pascale and Rohlen, 1983). Suzuki (1985) cited the example of the Toyota worker who handled thirty-five different production processes in a cycle lasting eight and a half minutes. Aoki (1986) argued that this flexibility and exposure to a wide variety of tasks makes production workers key participants in the innovation process.

Economically useful knowledge is not only found in blueprints, books, or the minds of management. It is also found in the minds of those on the assembly line. Such knowledge remains untapped until the coming together of its possessors. The clearinghouse for information exchange in Japanese factories are quality circles; regular and frequent factory floor meetings of small groups of workers who come together to discuss a whole range of production-related issues including ways in which particular products or processes may be improved upon (Pascale and Rohlen, 1983). This sharing of undefined tacit knowledge plays a key role in the incremental innovation process.

Information sharing occurs, not only between workers in the same factory, but also between firms within the same corporate group (Imai and Itami, 1987-88; Taylor, 1990). Interfirm information sharing has the same implications for innovation as the sharing of information between workers within the same firm. Unlike the United States where frequent switching of suppliers discourages interfirm information sharing, the long-term customer-supplier relationships which are characteristic of Japanese industry encourages the sharing of proprietary technical information and collaboration on coordinated research and development (Imai, 1987-88). Collaboration exploits the unique talents of both customers and suppliers and also eliminates duplication of efforts (Asanuma, 1985; Florida and Kenney, 1990b). Long term business relationships allow the establishment of mutual trust, provide time for customers and suppliers to glean knowledge about each others products and production processes, and eliminate the possibility of proprietary information being lost to competitor firms. Lubben (1988) and Ó hUallacháin (1991) have argued that such information, which is often ambiguous and subject to refinement, is most efficiently and effectively exchanged via face-to-face contact rather than via either telephone conversations or written communication.

The implications of corporate groups for the spatial distribution of Japanese direct investment in the US auto industry

Penetration of a foreign economy via foreign direct investment (FDI) is fraught with risk and uncertainty. Two key contributors to risk and uncertainty are the need to find suppliers of material inputs with whom satisfactory business relationships can be established and the need to find a labor force endowed with the requisite skills and work ethic. Minimization of risk and uncertainty is one of the keys to successful FDI. Japanese automakers have minimized the risk and uncertainty of assembling automobiles in the United States by:

1 maintaining long-term business and geographical relationships with Japanese suppliers who have served them well in the past, and

2 replicating, using American workers, the type of employee and labor-management relationships which have contributed to their firm's success back in Japan.

A key contributor to the successful attainment of these objectives has been the locational strategy employed by both Japanese automakers and their component parts suppliers.

The decision by Japanese automakers to locate in Midwestern and upper southern states is consistent with broader locational trends in the US auto industry. Rubenstein (1986) showed that since the mid-1960s US automakers closed down assembly plants in geographically peripheral regions of the country (East and West Coasts) and opened new assembly plants in the geographic interior (Midwest and Upper South). He argued that market fragmentation, increased foreign competition, and improvements in transportation infrastructure favored concentration of automobile production in the Midwest and Upper South. A Midwestern location allows automobile assembly plants serving a national market to minimize distribution costs of assembled automobiles. Perrucci (1994) suggested that the existence of a well developed infrastructure of US parts makers in the Midwest was also a factor in the decision of Japanese automakers to locate their assembly plants in these states. He argued that, until Japanese automakers had their own supplier base established in each state, access to domestic suppliers was an important consideration in their location decision.

Perruci (1994) found a key variable distinguishing states which were successful in attracting a Japanese automobile assembly plant from those which were unsuccessful in attracting one was the existence of an infrastructure of component part makers. Woodward's (1992) finding that Japanese greenfield manufacturing plants (auto and nonauto) constructed in the auto alley during the 1980s were attracted to counties with a large manufacturing base provides additional evidence that agglomeration economies are clearly important determinants of the location of Japanese direct investment. Although Midwestern states such as Ohio and Michigan were particularly well positioned to take advantage of this early need of Japanese automakers for domestic suppliers, the growth of component parts suppliers in Southern states since the early 1970s clearly made states such as Kentucky and Tennessee also viable candidates for Japanese assembly plants (Glasmeier and McCluskey, 1987).

In deciding where to locate in the United States Japanese automobile component parts makers are strongly influenced by corporate group ties. Automakers often ask key suppliers to follow them to the United States to provide them with material inputs (Rubenstein, 1992). Ó hUallacháin (1993), for example, argued that corporate group ties between auto assemblers and steel producers strongly influenced the decision by

Japanese steel firms to invest in production capacity in the midwest. Kenney and Florida (1992) found that the primary reason why Japanese automobile component part makers invest in US production capacity was a request from a Japanese customer that they do so in order to maintain an already existing relationship. In some cases suppliers are directed to locate in the same state as their major customer. The state of Ohio is perceived both by Japanese bankers and automakers as 'Honda's state' (Rubenstein, 1992, p. 212). Suppliers of other Japanese automakers, such as Toyota, are discouraged from locating production facilities in Ohio (Rubenstein, 1991). Assembly plants act like magnets, attracting parts suppliers to locate in close geographic proximity. Geographic proximity allows assemblers and component parts makers to take advantage of the firm-specific assets associated with corporate group membership.

Research dealing with the issue of the geographic relationship between Japanese automobile assembly plants and their suppliers of component parts has focussed overwhelmingly upon the spatial implications of just-in-time (JIT) inventory control. Although the spatial implications of JIT have been the subject of some debate (for a summary of this debate, see Reid, 1995), there does appear to be an emerging consensus that the use of JIT encourages the spatial clustering of the members of a JIT network (see for example, Schoenberger, 1982; Scott, 1983; Sheard, 1983; Piore and Sabel, 1984; Estall, 1985; Sayer, 1986; Ansari and Modarress, 1987; Dicken, 1987; Mair, Florida and Kenney, 1988; Florida and Kenney, 1991; Kenney and Florida, 1992). Spatial clustering is encouraged by the necessity to have material inputs delivered on a frequent and regular basis and by the need to achieve line haul economies in the delivery of small batches. Estall (1985) argued that JIT inventory control requires suppliers to be no further than 100 kilometers from their customers. Mair, Florida, and Kenney (1988) suggested that JIT suppliers need to be within two hours driving time of customers. Use of JIT is widespread among Japanese automobile component parts makers in the United States. Eighty per cent of first-tier and forty-three per cent of second-tier suppliers deliver material inputs according to a just-in-time schedule (Kenney and Florida, 1992). Forty per cent of first-tier suppliers are within a two hour driving radius of their major customer (Kenney and Florida, 1992). Spatial proximity to assembly plants was the most important site selection criteria for ninety per cent of Japanese automobile component parts makers in the United States (Kenney and Florida, 1992). Spatial proximity between customers and suppliers, resulting from use of JIT inventory control, ensures the development of strong backward material linkages with the local economy. Reid (1995) found that Japanese manufacturing plants receiving material inputs according to a JIT schedule purchased a greater proportion of their material inputs from their county economy than plants not using JIT inventory control. The second most important site selection criteria for Japanese automobile component part makers was proximity to major transportation routes (Kenney and Florida, 1992). The Japanese automotive complex which emerged in the Midwestern United States is well served with transportation infrastructure. Interstate-75 and Interstate-65 link Michigan, Ohio, Indiana, Kentucky, and Tennessee, while in an east-west direction Ohio, Indiana, and Illinois are serviced by Interstates 70 and 80. Woodward (1992) found that the presence of an interstate highway in a county was a key locational determinant of Japanese greenfield plants in the auto alley.

The spatial clustering of the members of a JIT network is also encouraged by the need to exchange design and engineering information on a regular and frequent basis (Schoenberger, 1982; Lubben, 1988; Jones and North, 1991). Forsgren (1989) argued that successful implementation of new technology is related to the strength and distance of linkages between a firm and its suppliers and customers. Lubben (1988) has argued that information sharing may be a stronger agglomerative force that the need to have material inputs delivered on a just-in-time basis. Spatial clustering of network members allows engineering and design personnel from both the customer and supplier to visit each others' facilities on a regular and frequent basis to discuss design and engineering issues as well as problems pertaining to material inputs provided by the supplier. Kenney and Florida (1992) found that eighty-six per cent of Japanese-owned automobile component part makers received regular visits from their customer's engineers to assist them with quality control or production problems. The same authors also suggested that Japanese-owned machine tool plants are in close geographic proximity to the automobile assembly plants (their major customer) to make close interaction in the development, installation, and maintenance of their machinery easier.

Labor issues are also important components of the locational strategy of Japanese automobile assemblers and component parts producers. Japanese manufacturers with production facilities in the United States invest considerable amounts of time and money in their employee selection process (Child Hill, Indergaard and Fujita, 1989; Doeringer and Terkla, 1992; Rubenstein, 1992; Woodward, 1992). They prefer to hire workers who are well-educated, have a good history of attendance in both high school and previous jobs, have little or no previous association with trade unions, and are flexible, adaptable, loyal, and motivated (Cole and Deskins, 1988; Mair, Florida and Kenney, 1988; Florida and Kenney, 1991; Kenney and Florida, 1991, 1992; Doeringer and Terkla, 1992). Possession of such characteristics is viewed by many Japanese manufacturers as essential to the successful implementation of both innovative labor-management relationships and flexible production practices (Woodward, 1992).

To access their desired labor force many Japanese manufacturers have located in small towns. Woodward (1992) found that the population density of a county was a statistically significant variable in explaining the intercounty distribution of Japanese greenfield investment outside, but not inside, the auto alley. He concluded that Japanese greenfield investment is more rural-oriented inside the auto alley than it is elsewhere in the United States. Five of the Japanese automobile assembly plants and over half of the component part makers are located in towns whose populations are under 20,000 (Reid, 1990; Florida and Kenney, 1991).

Small towns provide Japanese automakers and component parts makers with the type of employee they prefer. To begin with unions and union sympathies tend to be weaker. Previous association with the automobile industry is also less likely. Five of the nine Japanese-owned automobile assembly plants in the United States and over ninety per cent of automobile parts suppliers are nonunionized. Only nineteen per cent of workers in Japanese-owned automobile component part makers have previously belonged to a trade union (Kenney and Florida, 1992). Likewise, many employees have never held jobs in the auto industry. For example, at the Mazda automobile assembly plant in Flat Rock, Michigan only twenty-five per cent of employees have previously worked in the automobile assembly or component parts industry (Child Hill, Indergaard, and Fujita, 1989), while a survey of two hundred employees at the Chrysler-Mitsubishi assembly plant in Bloomington, Illinois revealed that only eighteen per cent had previously held jobs in the industry (Elhance and Chapman, 1992). Hostile labor-management relationships has been problematic for manufacturers wishing to establish JIT inventory control in the United States. The potential for worker militancy at a JIT supplier to disrupt production at the customer's manufacturing facility is a very real threat. For example, a strike involving 7,700 workers at the Delco radio plant in Kokomo, Indiana in 1986 resulted in thousands of temporary layoffs at General Motors' assembly plants throughout the United States because the latter had only a small inventory of radios (Reid, 1990).

Charges of racial discrimination have haunted Japanese manufacturers in the United States ever since a 1986 comment by the Japanese Prime Minister that 'Japan's racial homogeneity made it a more intelligent society than the US where there are more blacks, Mexicans, and Puerto Ricans' (*US News and World Report*, 1988). Japanese perceive small towns as advantageous from a racial perspective. With regard to hiring practices The Equal Employment Opportunity Commission (EEOC) requires that the racial composition of a manufacturing facility's workforce be representative of the local area or the surrounding laborshed. Locating in small towns, with their predominantly White populations, allows Japanese manufacturers to hire small numbers of Blacks without violating EEOC guidelines (Kenney and Florida, 1992; Rubenstein, 1992). Despite locating in small towns Cole and Deskins (1989) found that Japanese automobile assembly and component part plants still hired a lower percentage of Blacks than laid down by EEOC guidelines. Woodward (1992) shed further light on the racial issue. He found that Japanese greenfield investors in the auto alley avoided counties with high Black population densities. For counties outside of the auto alley Woodward found no significant relationship between the number of Japanese greenfield plants and Black population density.

Locating in small towns also has implications for mode of entry. As noted in the introduction to this chapter, the majority of JDI in automobile assembly and component parts plants in the United States are greenfield investments. There are a number of reasons for this. First, small towns have a smaller number of acquisition candidates than larger towns and cities. Second, many Japanese automobile assemblers and component parts makers prefer greenfield investments because it allows them to start afresh with regards to the labor force, labor-management relationships, capital equipment, and manufacturing techniques and practices. In other words, by investing in greenfield production capacity they avoid problems associated with an acquisition. These include inheriting unproductive employees, outdated labor-management relationships, and inappropriate production practices.

Conclusion

Understanding Japanese direct investment requires a knowledge of Japanese inter-firm relationships within corporate groups. This chapter has focussed upon Japanese direct investment in automobile assembly and component parts production in the United States. This investment is dominated by greenfield plants, located in small towns, and geographically concentrated in a handful of states in the Midwestern and upper southern United States. This geographic pattern is no accident. It is an outcome of Japanese automakers' desire to replicate, in an alien economic and cultural environment, long-standing business and geographical relationships with their suppliers of component parts. Assemblers and suppliers are often members of the same corporate group. Corporate groups provide the institutional structure for the development of material and information networks, while spatial concentration provides the geographic framework for efficient and effective exchange of material inputs and distance-sensitive design and engineering information. Constructing greenfield plants in small towns allows Japanese automakers and suppliers to avoid inheriting outdated capital equipment and undesirable labor. They are thus able to hire *virgin* employees, train them to their own specifications, and instill in them appropriate attitudes and values.

8 Causes of foreign takeovers in the United States: A real sector imperfections model

M. Wayne Marr, Sanjeev Mohta and Michael J. Spivey

Introduction

In the late 1970s, the United States entered a new era of industrial deregulation that grew to much larger proportions in the 1980s. The deregulation prompted the decade of the 1980s to witness one of the largest waves of mergers in the history of United States. The continuing merger boom caused a renewed interest among academicians and nonacademicians alike to investigate the causes and effects of a merger.[1] A further consequence of the deregulation has been a massive increase in the foreign direct investment activity in the United States.[2]

Mergers and acquisitions, especially those that are hostile, have always been controversial and there is always immense pressure from the anti-takeover lobby on regulators to restrict this activity (Jensen, 1988). The boom in foreign direct investment activity has also been also very controversial. The anti-foreign direct investment lobby argues that foreign direct investment has focused on acquiring an access to high technology industries in the United States. For example, Goldstein (1988) says it is feared that 'US industry may be liquidating its technological edge at bargain-basement prices.' On the other hand, proponents of foreign direct investment activity argue that foreign ownership of United States' assets reflects confidence in the long term economic outlook of the United States. Also, as Peter Truell reports in *The Wall Street Journal*, foreign direct investors are 'less likely to cut and run in bad times - and more likely to invest extra capital, introduce new capital and create jobs'. The controversy surrounding foreign companies taking over US firms is especially sensitive since a flavor of nationalism is added.[3]

Takeover of US companies by foreign bidders is not a new phenomenon. According to Bradley and Korn (1982) this phenomenon started gaining importance as far back as in 1973-74. *Mergers and Acquisitions* reports that in the 1980s, other than a period of three years between 1982 and 1984, foreign buyers accounted for at least 12 per cent of the total takeover activity in the United States if the dollar amount is considered. In 1987 and 1988 foreigners accounted for more than one-fourth of the total takeover activity.

Given the large volume of foreign takeover activity in the United States and the controversy surrounding it, an interesting question is what are the causes and consequences of foreign takeovers in the United States? The decision of a foreign takeover is different from a domestic takeover in that it involves foreign direct investment. The theories that explain foreign direct investment have developed independently from the ones that explain mergers/acquisition. However, in a broad sense, both foreign direct investment and mergers/acquisitions can be explained by the existence of market imperfections. These imperfections can be in the real sector or in the financial sector. Theories based on real sector imperfections imply that a foreign takeover is one of the many modes of entry or expansion into a foreign market. These theories predict that the motives of foreign takeovers in the United States are 1) to enter or expand the United States' market, and 2) to obtain synergistic gains by acquiring an appropriate target. The theories based on financial imperfections imply that a foreign takeover is portfolio investment.

The business press has argued that strategic goals drive foreign takeovers or, put differently, that exploitation of real sector imperfections motivates foreign takeovers.[4] Also, the theories and the empirical evidence since the mid 60s have supported the view that real sector imperfections motivate foreign direct investment. In this paper, we investigate whether real sector imperfections motivate foreign takeovers by examining causes and consequences of domestic takeovers by foreign firms.

To accomplish our study, we have compiled a database of US firms that were targets of foreign takeovers between 1975 and 1987. We empirically examine the foreign takeovers in the pre-takeover stage. By examining the pre-takeover stage we can assess whether the imperfections in the product and factor markets prior to the takeover contribute to foreign takeovers in this country. We develop a set of hypotheses about the expected characteristics of the foreign takeover targets and then test them by comparing characteristics of foreign takeover targets with a control sample of nontargets and domestic takeover targets.

To summarize, this paper provides 1) a theoretical framework for foreign takeovers based on real sector imperfection theories, and 2) an empirical analysis of causes of foreign takeovers. The analysis also jointly tests the validity of foreign direct investment and mergers and acquisition theories based on real sector imperfections. In addition, the paper also provides insight into whether foreign firms buy US corporations because of their intangible assets or whether they simply want to buy such assets.

Our results show that the foreign bidders acquire firms in markets characterized by high degree of marketing skills, as measured by advertisement expenditures. Also, more takeover activity is targeted in industries which themselves have high levels of foreign direct investment implying that the bidders use takeovers as a vehicle of quick entry to counteract rival firms' moves. The surprising result is that takeovers do not take place in high technology (as measured by R and D expenditures) industries. Another result pertaining to the target firms' industries shows that these takeovers take place in more mature, low growth industries. The foreign targets, on average, are smaller than the nontargets. The foreign bidders takeover firms with very low levels of intangible assets, as measured by the market-to-book value.

The results are consistent with the contention that foreign bidders are motivated by real sector imperfections. The foreign bidders are interested not only in the target but the market in which the target operates. The results also imply that exploiting financial sector imperfections is not the only motive for foreign takeovers. Inasmuch as the financial sector imperfection theory is a competing theory, the results are inconsistent with the financial sector imperfections theory. The results also show that the motive of the foreign bidders is not to buy intangible assets, rather it is to use their own intangible assets.

A theory of foreign takeovers

Foreign takeovers : a theoretical background

A foreign takeover occurs when a firm merges with or acquires a firm incorporated in another country. Foreign takeovers fall into the realm of foreign direct investment and allow theories of foreign direct investment and theories of mergers/acquisitions to explain them. Theories of foreign direct investment say that foreign direct investment occurs to exploit market imperfections. These imperfections could be in the financial sector or in the real sector.[5] The theories based on financial sector imperfections implies that foreign takeovers are a means of adding to the investment portfolio of a firm. The focus of this paper is on the theories based on real sector imperfections.

The theory of foreign direct investment, based on real sector imperfections, says that a firm will choose foreign direct investment over the alternatives if it has special advantages to exploit product and factor market imperfections in the host market.[6] The alternatives include exports, licensing, and cooperative ventures. Although foreign takeovers also fall under the broad theory of foreign direct investment, it makes only a casual reference to direct entry and takeovers as distinct alternatives to entry or expansion in foreign countries.[7]

The mergers/acquisition theories that have tried to explain the phenomenon of takeovers have been primarily domestic in nature (Mandelker and Nachtmann, 1990). To summarize, in Calvet's (1982, p. 45) words:

> Foreign direct investment theories have dealt at length with the determinants of international production but have somehow neglected the study of specific means by which firms engage in international investment, in particular through takeover of an existing local firm. On the other hand . . . merger theories have approached acquisition activity in a domestic context but have failed to provide an explanation for a widespread international phenomenon, i.e. the takeover of host country firms.

Only a handful of researchers, like Dubin (1976), Wilson (1980), Lindgren (1982), Calvet (1982), and Caves and Mehra (1986) have recognized this inadequacy of the foreign direct investment literature. They have tried to develop a theory of foreign takeovers by extending the foreign direct investment theories using the literature on strategic management.[8] This literature recognizes direct entry, and takeovers as competing modes of entry or expansion. The purpose of this literature on foreign takeovers is to find factors which make foreign acquisition a better choice than direct entry.[9]

The literature on foreign takeover is still incomplete. It only defines the conditions under which takeover is the better alternative. It does not elaborate on how to select an appropriate takeover target when takeover is the better alternative. One needs to integrate the literature on takeovers, which tells us how to choose an appropriate takeover candidate, with the existing theory to form a complete theory of foreign takeovers.

Foreign direct investment Foreign direct investment occurs when a firm owns and controls the operations of physical assets, such as plant and equipment, in a foreign country (Shapiro, 1982, p. 594). A firm involved in foreign direct investment is called a multinational firm. Lately, foreign direct investment has become very important in the United States' economy. Since the mid-1970s it has increased by more than 10 per cent each year. In 1988, the foreign holdings in the United States exceeded the United States' overseas holding for the first time. At the end of 1989, the foreigners held $US390 billion in plants and property in United States. The corresponding figure for United States' holding abroad was $US368.1 billion (*Wall Street Journal*, 1990, p. A1).

Till the early 1960s the theories of foreign direct investment relied 'exclusively upon a neoclassical financial theory of portfolio flows' (Dunning and Rugman, 1985). These theories explained foreign direct investment as international capital movement. They argued that capital will flow from one country to another to reap benefits from imperfect financial markets. These gains could come from, for example, favorable exchange rates, differential rates of normal profits, or reduction of risk. This capital arbitrage view implies that foreign takeovers are made for the purpose of adding to an investment portfolio. Kindleberger (1969, p. 2) points out several peculiar phenomena which were not consistent with these theories. He says:

> investors often failed to take money with them when they went abroad to acquire control of a company; instead they borrowed in the local market. Capital movements would take place gross - the acquisition of an asset (an outflow) and the incurring of a liability (an inflow) - but not net. Or the investment would take place in kind, through the exchange of property - patents, technology, or machinery - against equity claims, without the normal transfer of funds through the foreign exchange associated with capital movements. And direct investment would proceed by the reinvestment of profits, with the capital outflow matched by earnings on past investment, but again no movement of funds through the foreign exchange market.

This shows that the theory of capital movement cannot fully explain the phenomenon of foreign direct investment. Also this theory, as Teece (1985) points out, cannot explain the evidence of large cross flows of foreign direct investment and its concentration in particular industries.[10] Teece (1985) says that a portfolio investment is a much superior substitute to foreign direct investment if the motive is to exploit financial sector imperfections.[11] This is because a portfolio investment does not involve the fixed costs of foreign direct investment. Financial sector imperfections, by making foreign assets more attractive, can affect the volume of foreign direct investment. However, they do not affect the nature of foreign direct investment. Therefore, one must look somewhere else to find plausible motives for foreign direct investment.

In the late 1960s, the modern theory of foreign direct investment started looking at real sector imperfections for possible explanations. The basis of this theory was Stephen Hymer's seminal dissertation in 1960, published in Hymer (1976). Later works by Kindleberger (1969) and Caves (1971) add to this literature. The essence of this theory, which Rugman (1982, p. 11) calls the internalization theory, is that under conditions of real sector imperfections a firm is better off using its internal market for production and distribution than by using the regular market. These real sector imperfections could be in the form of

> market failure associated with the pricing of knowledge, or similar firm specific intangible advantages. These occur in the areas of technology, managerial skills corporate organizational structures and other aspects of the internal market of the firm.

Other forms of these imperfections are existence of transactions costs and government created distortions, like specific wage policies, tariffs and quotas.

The firm, according to this theory, is a substitute to the market. The firm 'develops its own managerial hierarchy to solve the allocational and distributional decisions that a regular market makes automatically' to earn higher rents (Rugman, 1982, p. 11). The higher rents come from the special advantages the firm has in the areas of technology, knowhow, patents, brand names or managerial skills. Empirical evidence supports the internalization theory. Reichhold Chemical Inc.'s takeover by Dainippon Ink and Chemicals Inc. of Japan in 1987 is a case in point. Dainippon's president, Mr. Kawamura, said that by infusing technological input Dainippon could save the sick product lines of Reichhold, such as chemical coatings and reactive polymers (Nathans, 1987). A lot of researchers have also found empirical support for this theory. For example, Grubaugh (1987), who uses a sample of 300 American multinational and purely domestic firms, confirms that firms become multinational to exploit their firm specific advantages. Morck and Young's (1989) findings also support this theory.

The modern literature on foreign direct investment is simply an extension of the internalization theory. One such extension is Dunning's (1981) eclectic theory of international production. The internalization theory focuses on the ownership specific advantages of the firm. Dunning introduces location specific advantages of the host country as additional factors which explain foreign direct investment. Some examples of the location specific advantages are the relative cost of resources, the relative quality of resources, and the size of the market in the host country. The findings of Ajami and Ricks (1981) supports the eclectic theory. According to them, the search for new markets and the need for growth motivate foreign direct investors when they invest in the United States. The size of the US market makes it a very attractive locale.

Knickerbocker (1974) and Graham (1974) used the oligopolistic reactions of the firms to extend the internalization theory. They base their theories on one of the predictions of the internalization theory that multinational firms are oligopolists. According to them a firm becomes multinational either to follow the industry leader or to exchange a threat from its competitor. This argument explains the evidence of large cross flows of foreign direct investment and its concentration in particular industries, which the capital movement theory could not. Dunning and Rugman (1985) say that the internalization theory can be linked to the literature on strategic management. The internalization theory, according to them, predicts that a firm investing abroad will 'identify entry and exit barriers, and then operate generic strategies based upon price competition, product differentiation, or the seeking of market niches'. To evaluate foreign direct investment as a viable strategy one has to compare it with alternative strategies. The major contribution of the internalization theory is that it recognizes foreign direct investment as an alternative to exports, licensing and cooperative venture. Foreign direct investment involves certain fixed costs which are almost nonexistent in the alternatives. These costs include search costs, startup costs and also some nonobservable costs like cultural and political costs. A firm has to weigh its costs and benefits to decide on the better alternative.

Exporting involves only arms length transaction between two firms. It is a very low risk venture. Kindleberger (1969) says that in a world of free trade, perfect competition and no transactions costs, exporting is a much superior alternative to foreign direct investment. In this perfect world the 'local firms are at no relative disadvantage and international firms have no special incentive to direct their investments abroad.' However, with market imperfections, foreign direct investment becomes a superior alternative. Errunza and Senbet (1985) say that a firm would choose foreign direct investment over exports if it can exploit the ownership specific and location specific advantages to earn higher rents than those achieved by local competitors.

Contractual agreements, such as licensing and cooperative venture, are alternatives to foreign direct investment.[12] The principal advantage of the contractual agreements over foreign direct investment is that it requires minimal investment. However, foreign direct investment becomes a better option if there is a chance of losing firm specific advantages by the use of contractual agreements. This could arise due to the market failure associated with pricing of proprietary information like knowledge, technology, entrepreneurial or marketing skills (Rugman, 1982, p. 10). Also, if the motive of the firm is to acquire intangible assets, foreign direct investment and contractual agreements are alternative strategies. Again, the failure in the market for intangible assets may make foreign direct investment a better strategy.

To summarize, the internalization theory implies that a firm will choose foreign direct investment if it is a superior strategy to both exports and contractual agreement. The firm will choose foreign direct investment if it has special advantages which overcome barriers to entry in the host country market to earn economic rent. The firm may also choose foreign direct investment to counter the strategies of its competitors. Finally, the firm may choose foreign direct investment as a means to buy intangible assets in a foreign country. As discussed earlier, a firm choosing foreign direct investment, can do so in two ways. It can establish a new subsidiary in the foreign country or it can take over an existing firm.

Strategies of entry and expansion: takeover versus new establishment The internalization theory recognizes foreign direct investment as a method of entry or expansion in a foreign market. Takeovers and new establishments are two strategies of foreign direct investment. The strategic management literature recognizes takeovers and new establishment as competing modes of entry or expansion.[13] However, as mentioned earlier, there is a relatively sparse literature on this topic in an international context. Foreign firms have relied heavily on takeovers as the strategy for foreign direct investment in the United States. By dollar amounts spent, acquisitions made by foreign companies in the United States far outweighs the amount spent on new establishments. For example, in 1986 the outlays on acquisitions by foreign firms was around $US31.4 billion while the outlays on new establishments was only $US7.7 billion (*Survey of Current Business*, 1987).

The choice between new establishment and acquisition will depend upon the consideration of risks and costs, according to Caves (1982). The acquisition route is very quick and has an immediate impact on the revenue and market share of the foreign firm. The foreign firm that buys the local firm also buys access to a stock of valuable information and an existing distribution network. It gets an operating local management who are aware of the national market environment. These factors reduce the uncertainty about how well the subsidiary will do. A foreign firm starting a new establishment avoids paying the going concern value for an existing enterprise, which it may not value highly if it wants to install its own management practices from the start (a strong preference of Japanese multinational firms according to Tsurumi (1976). It also does not face the problems of replacing a management team or phasing out irrelevant areas, which firms using takeover as the entry route face. However, direct entry typically requires a long time to achieve the desired size and profitability.[14] This, coupled with the uncertainty of its success, makes new establishment a much riskier proposition than acquisition entry. For example, a major reason why Blue Arrow PLC of Britain acquired Manpower Inc. was to gain a quick entry in the temporary service market and avoid the risk of a new establishment. Blue Arrow sources said that it would take years and cost far more to build from scratch (*Wall Street Journal*, 1987, p. 14).

This implies that the choice of appropriate strategy of the foreign firm might depend upon how soon it wants to establish its presence in the local market.[15] Time could especially be important if the motive was to counteract a rivals move. In such a case acquisition would be a better strategy. This is one explanation of Matsushita Electric Industrial Co.'s takeover of MCA Inc. in 1990. Matsushita, a Japanese firm, was counteracting Columbia Pictures' takeover by Sony Corp. of Japan in 1989 (*Wall Street Journal*, 1990, p. A1). In certain cases, however, the unavailability of suitable candidates targets, in a particular market, may limit takeovers. For takeover to be a viable alternative a well developed market for corporate control is required. Yip (1982) says 'more acquisition candidates should be available in more mature, low growth markets'. This is because as the market matures, with growth rates falling, the firms tend to reorganize and consolidate.[16] This increases the availability of acquisition candidates.

To summarize, the choice of appropriate strategy depends on the time factor, which in turn is related to the risk and cost issue. Unavailability of appropriate target may, however, constrain the choice. The analyses in the last two subsections have not said anything about the firm which is chosen as the takeover target. Although references were made to appropriate target but these theories do not address problem of how to find one. The next subsection tries to solve this problem.

Mergers/acquisitions A takeover, which involves the absorption of one company (the target) into another (the bidder), can be accomplished by a merger or by an acquisition. A merger requires transfer of the assets and liabilities of the target or the selling company to the bidder or the buying company. An acquisition, on the other hand, can take place in two ways. The buying company can either acquire the stocks of the target or some of its specific assets.[17] The acquisition of stock of the target, the more common form of transaction, can be done in exchange for cash, shares, or other securities issued by the buyer. In this latter case, a possible scenario, which has become somewhat popular of late, is when the target's management objects to a merger. In such a situation the buying firm can appeal directly to the selling firm's shareholders. Proxy fights and unsolicited tender offers are two ways of doing this.

In a proxy fight the bidding firm can challenge the existing management and bid for a transfer of control at the target's next annual meeting. Proxy fights are expensive and difficult to win.[18] The alternative strategy is to make a tender offer directly to the target's shareholders. The shareholders will normally tender their shares to the bidder if the tender offer is generous enough. If the bidder can get 50 per cent of the voting stock of the target then it has control over the target and the ability to force a merger.[19]

From the financial standpoint the decision of a merger is like any other investment decision. Assumption of profit maximization requires that not only should it make a net contribution to the shareholders' wealth, but, the contribution should be more than that by any alternative strategy.[20] However, the evaluation of a merger is quite complex when compared to that of, say, equipment. A merger involves addressing legal and accounting issues in addition to the issue of benefit and cost. Ravenscraft (1987) points out that a lot of research has been done on finding the potential motives for a takeover. Morck, Shleifer and Vishny (1988) divide the motives of takeovers into two broad categories: 1) synergistic and 2) disciplinary.

In category 1, the hope of achieving synergy motivates a takeover. Synergy occurs when the value of the firms, after the merger, becomes greater than the individual values of the two firms before merger. Jensen and Ruback (1983) say economies of scale, vertical integration or employing better techniques are sources of synergies. For example, synergy was the motive when West Germany's AEG Aktiengesellschaft acquired Modular Computer Systems Inc. in 1986. AEG sources said that AEG would provide Modular with the necessary technology to pursue the industrial automation strategy to end a three year era of losses and layoffs at Modular (*Electronic News*, 1986, p. 1).

Acquisition of complementary assets is another source of synergy. For example, Contractor (1987) in a study of ten largest Japanese takeovers in the United States concludes that the Japanese firms, with superior technology, invested largely in nontechnical fields mostly buying companies with established market share and an extensive distribution network. Bradley, Desai and Kim (1983, 1988) argue that mergers result in synergies. They provide evidence to this effect. Based on the empirical findings of Ravenscraft (1987), bidders look for firms which fit their strategies and strength. This finding is also consistent with the existence of synergies.

In category 2, eliminating the inefficiencies created by the existing management motivate takeovers. Two major reasons for these inefficiencies are: a) divergence of the goals of the managers and the shareholders and, b) lack of managerial skill. Jensen and Ruback (1983) view the market for takeovers as a market for corporate control, which disciplines inefficiency in management in the same way as the 'internal and the external managerial labor markets'. Manne (1965) argues that the market of corporate control mitigates to a large extent the agency problems arising due to separation of ownership and control. Palepu (1986), who uses a sample of 163 targets and 256 nontargets, provides empirical evidence which supports the disciplinary model in the domestic setting. He finds that the negative returns are a measure of inefficiency, and increase a firm's chance of becoming a target.

It is hard to rationalize a foreign takeover whose only motive is to discipline an inefficient management team. This is because the foreign firm is at a disadvantage when compared with any domestic firm. The foreign firm has to incur additional costs of operating in a foreign country compared to the domestic firms.[21] Other things equal, the foreign bidders will not be able to make the same offer as the domestic bidder. A foreign management team is able to compete with other domestic buyers only if these costs are compensated. Also, this motive is not different from the synergistic motive if the foreign bidder possesses superior management skills and acquires an inefficient target to utilize its management skills. Thus, under the real sector imperfection framework, expectations of synergy should motivate a foreign bidder, in its choice of an appropriate target.

The decision to takeover a firm is similar to the decision to buy any other capital asset. The choice of an appropriate takeover target depends on the motive for the takeover and the net present value of expected post takeover cash flows of the potential target. Dietrich and Sorensen (1984) say that the 'factors tending to increase the net present value of the cash outflows associated with a merger tend to increase the attractiveness of a particular merger candidate.'

The synergistic motives will cause firms to acquire other firms producing related products. Dutz (1989) says that this is because synergy can be realized by reorganizing the assets of the participants into 'more efficient configuration'. The appropriate target will also depend on the motive of the bidder. The appropriate target will differ depending on whether the bidder wants to exploit its own intangible assets or it wants to buy intangible assets. A few other factors like transactions costs, and government regulations will also affect the choice of an appropriate target. Transactions costs for a bidder in a takeover include cost of integration of the target and the possible cost of fending against an uncooperative target. Palepu (1986) says that these transactions costs are likely to increase with the size of the target. Therefore, bigger the target more inappropriate it is for takeover.

The acquisition in the United States are restricted by the antitrust and security laws. These laws include the Sherman Antitrust Act, the Clayton Act, the Hart-Scott-Rodino Act, the National Cooperative Research Act and the Webb-Pomerene Act. The foreign firms who acquire firms in the US are subjected to the same laws.[22] Additionally, the federal law prohibits or restricts foreign direct investment in certain areas. Foreign direct investment is prohibited in the nuclear industry and restricted in the radio, television, telegraph and telephone, coastal and inland shipping, domestic air transportation, and hydroelectric industries. Foreign involvement is restricted on classified government contracts or mining on federal lands.

To summarize the bidder should choose firms which provide synergy. However, factors like transactions cost and government regulations put a constraint on the appropriate choice. We now develop a complete model of foreign takeovers based on the analysis of the last three subsections.

A model of foreign takeovers

Let $X = (x_1, x_2, \ldots\ldots, x_n)$ be a vector of all possible tangible and intangible resources that a firm uses where $x_j \geq 0$ for all $j = (1,2,\ldots\ldots n)$.

Assumption 1: The net present value of a firm is a function of X, i.e., $V = V(\mathbf{X})$.[23]

V is the net present value (NPV) of a firm. Let F be a foreign firm which wants to enter United States. The NPV of this firm is $V^F = V^F(\mathbf{X}^F)$. Since the firm wants to enter United States it faces many choices. Earlier, we discussed that a firm can enter United States by i) exports (E), ii) licensing (L), iii) a cooperative venture (C), or iv) foreign direct investment (D). Let V^{FE}, V^{FL}, V^{FC}, or V^{FD} be the respective NPV's of the firm F if it chooses E, L, C or D as the method of entry. If the firm decides not to enter then its NPV remains as V^F.

Assumption 2: The firm F's goal is to maximize its NPV.

Under this assumption, the analysis implies that F will choose foreign direct investment as the method of entry only if the following inequality:

$$V^D \geq \max \{ V^{FE}, V^{FL}, V^{FC}, V^F) \qquad (1)$$

is satisfied.

If the firm, F, chooses foreign direct investment as the method of entry, it faces two options. New establishment or takeover of a local firm. Let V^{FN} be the NPV of the firm if it chooses new establishment as entry route and V^{FT} if it chooses takeover as the mode of entry. Under the assumption of value maximization , the firm will choose takeover over new establishment if

$$V^{FT} \geq V^{FN} \qquad (2)$$

Since takeover is a form of foreign direct investment, and it is chosen as the best strategy, we rewrite (1) as

$$V^{FT} \geq \max \{ V^{FE}, V^{FL}, V^{FC}, V^{F}) \qquad (1a)$$

Combining (2) and (1a), we get :

$$V^{FT} \geq \max \{ V^{FE}, V^{FL}, V^{FC}, V^{FN}, V^{F}) \qquad (3)$$

This is where the existing theory of foreign takeovers stops. We extend this by using the theory of mergers/acquisitions.

Once takeover has been chosen as the best strategy, under the assumption of NPV maximization, F will choose that target which maximizes V^{FT}, subject to the inequality (3). Let there be m domestic firms, which are possible candidates for takeover. Let $\mathbf{X}^i$ be the vector of resources for the ith firm for i = 1, 2, …., m, and let $V^i = V^i(\mathbf{X}^i)$ be the NPV for the ith firm. The gains from a takeover of the ith firm to F can be defined as

$$G^{Fi} = V^{Fi}(\mathbf{X}^F,\mathbf{X}^i) - V^F(\mathbf{X}^F) - V^i(\mathbf{X}^i) \qquad (4)^{24}$$

where G^{Fi} is the gains to F from the takeover of the ith firm. $V^{Fi}(\mathbf{X}^F,\mathbf{X}^i)$ is the NPV of the combined firm and it depends on the pretakeover assets of both the firms. $V^F(\mathbf{X}^F)$ is the NPV of F before takeover. $V^i(\mathbf{X}^i)$ is the NPV of i before takeover.

Assumption 3: The firm F pays a fraction k ($0 \leq k \leq 1$) of the gains as a premium for takeover to the stockholders of the ith firm.[25]

This assumption implies that

$$V^{FT} = (1-k)G^{Fi} \qquad (5).$$

Therefore, under this assumption maximizing V^{FT} is the same as maximizing G^{Fi}. The firm F faces a choice of m firms. The firm F obviously knows its $\mathbf{X}^F$'s. In this scenario, choosing the firms is like choosing the right $\mathbf{X}^i$ which maximizes

$$G^{Fi} = V^{Fi}(\mathbf{X}^F,\mathbf{X}^i) - V^F(\mathbf{X}^F) - V^i(\mathbf{X}^i) \qquad (6)$$

subject to

$$(1\text{-}k)G^{Fi} \geq \max \{ V^{FE}, V^{FL}, V^{FD}, V^{FC}, V^{F}) \qquad (7).$$

The constraint (7) formally summarizes the existing theory of foreign takeovers. This theory says that firm F will choose the takeover route if it is more profitable than the alternatives. As discussed above, this theory specifies some exogenous attributes (like market characteristics) which makes takeover the best strategy. Let $\mathbf{I}^*$ be a vector of attributes that makes takeover the best strategy, in a particular market. Therefore, if $\mathbf{I}^*$ exists for a certain market the constraint (7) will not be binding. In such a scenario, choosing an appropriate target is like choosing the $\mathbf{X}^i$ that maximizes (6) unconstrained. The solution implies the following function form:

$$G^{Fi*} = Gfi(XF,Xi*,I*) \qquad (8),$$

that is, the optimal gains from takeover G^{Fi*} depends on the attributes of the target, the attributes of the bidder and the attributes which make takeover the best alternative.

Empirical implications

Equation (8) can be empirically tested to find the if the real sector imperfections causes foreign takeovers. The test of this equation is also a joint test for theory of foreign direct investment and that of mergers/acquisitions. Also, this model implies Yip's (1982) contention that when takeovers are used as a mode for entry or expansion, the bidder is interested not only in obtaining synergy but also in the market in which the target operates. This also has a testable implication. The empirical testing of this equation may also throw light on the question whether the motive of the foreign bidders is to buy intangible assets or to utilize their own. The empirical testing requires knowledge of firm- and industry-specific characteristics of both bidders and targets. Unfortunately, the information on foreign bidders is not readily available. However, one can still obtain substantial insight into the causes of foreign takeovers by analyzing the information available on the takeover targets.

The pretakeover stage

The real sector imperfections model developed earlier says that a takeover is a mode of entry or expansion. As mentioned, when a bidder uses takeover as a mode of strategic entry or expansion, rather than as portfolio investment, it is interested in exploiting synergy. Also, along with the target, the bidder is interested in the industry of the target. Therefore, observation of systematic differences in the characteristic of the foreign takeover targets, compared to other firms, would be inconsistent with the view that takeovers are used as portfolio investments. Another interesting question that is answered by this empirical analysis is that if the real sector imperfections model is true, whether the foreign firms takeover domestic firms to use their intangible assets or to buy intangible assets.

The theoretical background

The purpose of this section is to develop a theoretical framework to empirically investigate the pre-takeover stage. As previously discussed, the foreign firm F, which enters United States by the takeover route solves the following problem. The firm F faces a choice of m firms. The firm F chooses the appropriate target by choosing the appropriate $\mathbf{X}^i$ which maximizes:

$$G^{Fi} = V^{Fi}(\mathbf{X}^F,\mathbf{X}^i) - V^F(\mathbf{X}^F) - V^i(\mathbf{X}^i) \qquad (9)$$

subject to,

$$(1\text{-}k)G^{Fi} \geq \max \{ V^{FE}, V^{FL}, V^{FC}, V^{FN}, V^F) \qquad (10)$$

where $k.G^{Fi}$ is the premium for takeover to the stockholders of the ith firm and $0 \leq k \leq 1$. G^{Fi} is the gains to F from the takeover of the ith firm. $\mathbf{X}^F$ is the vector of all possible tangible and intangible resources that a firm F uses. X^i is the vector of all possible tangible and intangible resources for the ith firm for i = 1, 2, …., m. V^{Fi} is the NPV of the combined firm and it depends on the level of pre-takeover assets of both the firms. V^F is the NPV of F before takeover. V^i is the NPV of the ith firm before takeover. V^{FE}, V^{FL}, V^{FC}, and V^{FN} are the respective NPV's of the firm F if it chooses exports, licensing, cooperative venture or new establishment as the method of entry.

The first order conditions for this maximization problem can be re-written in the implicit form as follows:[26]

$$\begin{aligned} F^1(\mathbf{X}^{i*},\mathbf{X}^F) &= 0 \\ F^2(\mathbf{X}^{i*},\mathbf{X}^F) &= 0 \\ \ldots\ldots & \\ F^n(\mathbf{X}^{i*},\mathbf{X}^F) &= 0 \end{aligned} \qquad (11)$$

where, $\mathbf{X}^{i*}$ is the optimal $\mathbf{X}^i$ chosen by the foreign firm, and F^j's are the implicit form of the first order conditions. Since we observe the foreign takeover targets, we know the $\mathbf{X}^{i*}$. However, we do not know the $\mathbf{X}^F$, since we do not observe the characteristics of the foreign bidders. This problem can be solved since both $\mathbf{X}^{i*}$ and $\mathbf{X}^F$ are, by construction, vectors of the same dimension (n), and as such, we can solve the $\mathbf{X}^F$'s, in terms of the $\mathbf{X}^{i*}$'s. We can write this in the following functional form:

$$\mathbf{X}^F = \phi(\mathbf{X}^{i*}) \qquad (12).$$

We already know from earlier discussion that the optimized gains from the takeover can be written in the following functional form:

$$G^{Fi*} = Gfi(Xi*,XF,I) \qquad (13)$$

where, G^{Fi*} is the optimal gains from takeover and **I** is a vector of attributes that makes the constraint nonbinding. By substituting (12) into (13) we get:

$$G^{Fi*} \;=\; G^{Fi}(\mathbf{X}^{i*},\ \phi(\mathbf{X}^{i*}),\mathbf{I}) \;=\; f(\mathbf{X}^{i*},\mathbf{I}) \qquad (14)$$

The optimal gains from takeover depends on the characteristics of the chosen takeover target and the attributes that make takeovers preferable to other modes of entry. The empirical analysis in this chapter tests the validity of equation (14).

Development of hypotheses

To test the validity of equation (14) we need to develop some hypotheses about $\mathbf{X}^{i*}$ and **I**. From the earlier discussion we suggest certain relevant hypotheses.

Attributes that make takeover the best strategy Hypothesis 1: the intangible assets hypothesis - the internalization theory implies that foreign takeover, which is a form of foreign direct investment, is a mode of strategic entry into a foreign market. A foreign takeover, under this theory, can play two opposite roles. On the one hand a firm chooses foreign takeovers over exporting or cooperative ventures if it has special advantages in the form of intangible assets (like technological and marketing skills) to overcome barriers to entry in the host country market to earn economic rent (Errunza and Senbet, 1981). On the other hand, foreign takeovers can be used to buy firms which have high level of intangible assets. Therefore, under the internalization theory, industries which require high levels of intangible assets are very attractive for foreign takeovers for three major reasons. Firstly, a foreign bidder may use a takeover in industries with high levels of intangible assets as a way to exploit its intangible assets in local markets through the local firm.[27] Secondly, if the bidder lacks the appropriate intangible assets it can acquire such assets by acquiring a firm in an industry characterized by high levels of such assets.[28] Thirdly, high level of intangible assets act as a barrier to entry in an industry, which is a source of economic rent.[29] Foreign direct investment, hence a foreign takeover, is incompatible with perfect competition. In fact, high barriers to entry would attract foreign takeovers.[30] Formally, the intangible assets hypothesis says that industries which are characterized by high levels of intangible assets (for example high-technology industries or industries with high level of product differentiation) are more attractive for foreign takeovers.

Hypothesis 2: the defensive hypothesis - the work of Knickerbocker (1974) and Graham (1974) says that part of foreign direct investment can be explained as a reaction to the strategies of the other firms in the industry. In other words, a firm chooses foreign direct investment to counter the strategies of its competitors. Therefore industries which themselves indulge in high level of foreign direct investment will also be a recipient of high level of reverse foreign direct investment. Therefore, the defensive hypothesis says that foreign takeovers will be higher in industries which themselves indulge in foreign direct investment.

Hypothesis 3: the time hypothesis - the choice of appropriate strategy of the foreign might depend upon how soon it wants to establish its presence in the local market. A takeover is the fastest way to establish a presence in a foreign market. Lindgren (1982) says that time is the most important factor in choosing takeover as the best strategy. Time could especially be important if the motive was to counteract a rivals move. In such a case acquisition would be a better strategy. The time hypothesis says that takeover is the best strategy if time is a very important strategic factor. This hypothesis augments the defensive hypothesis. The defensive hypothesis only says that foreign direct investment is a good counter strategy. This hypothesis goes a step further and says that foreign takeover is the preferred route for countering moves.

Hypothesis 4: the availability hypothesis - in certain cases the unavailability of suitable candidates targets, in a particular market, may limit takeovers. More acquisition candidates should be available in more mature, low growth markets. Yip (1982) and Dutz (1989) say that this is because as the market matures, with growth rates falling, the firms tend to reorganize and consolidate. This increases the availability of acquisition candidates causing more takeover activity in low growth industries. Therefore, the availability hypothesis says that foreign takeovers will take place in declining, or low growth, industries.

Choice of an appropriate target The hypotheses discussed in the previous sub-section deals with foreign takeover process at the industry-level. These hypotheses are based on the existing theory of foreign takeovers. We extend this theory to include the choice of an appropriate target as an equally important decision in the foreign takeover process. The decision to takeover a firm is similar to the decision to buy any other capital asset. The choice of an appropriate takeover target depends on the motive for the takeover and the net present value of expected post takeover cash flows of the potential target. Dietrich and Sorensen (1984) say that the 'factors tending to increase the net present value of the cash outflows associated with a merger tend to increase the attractiveness of a particular merger candidate.' In other words, a firm which results in maximum operating synergy is the best candidate for takeover.

Hypothesis 5: the synergy hypothesis - The synergy argument is an extension of the internalization theory from the industry-specific level to the firm specific level. The internalization theory of foreign direct investment says that under conditions of real sector imperfections a firm becomes multinational either to use its intangible assets or to acquire them.[31] The model in the theory section suggests the following proposition. A bidder with higher level of intangible assets will acquire a firm with low level of intangible assets and bidders with low level of intangible assets will acquire firms with high level of intangible assets to maximize profits.[32]

We integrate the internalization theory and this proposition to form the synergy hypothesis. This hypothesis says that the foreign takeover targets will be characterized by low level of intangible assets if the bidders possess high levels of intangible assets.[33] The targets will be characterized by high level of intangible assets if the motive of the bidder is to acquire such assets.

Hypothesis 6: the size hypothesis - Transactions costs for a bidder in a takeover include cost of integration of the target and the possible cost of fending against an uncooperative target. Palepu (1986) says that these transactions costs are likely to increase with the size of the target. Therefore, the bigger the target the more inappropriate it is for takeover.

Hypothesis 7: the relatedness hypothesis - The synergistic motive of takeovers implies that the target should be in a business related to the bidder.[34] This is because realization of synergy generally requires the integration of the participating firms' business.[35] Integration is possible only if the firms involved are in related business. Also one can expect that the more related the operations of the target with that of the bidder, the easier it would be to either adapt its intangible assets to the local firm or the local firm's intangible assets to itself.

To sum up, if the real sector imperfections model of foreign takeovers holds the bidder will be interested not only in the firm but also in the market itself. As such foreign takeovers will take place in industries characterized by high levels of intangible assets and industries which themselves heavily participate in foreign direct investment. If the motive of the bidder is to use its intangible assets it will acquire a target which has low levels of such assets. If, however, the motive is to acquire intangible assets the appropriate targets will be the firms with high level of intangible assets. The availability of appropriate targets and the transactions cost will act as constraints in the choice of the appropriate targets and as such firms which are in low growth industries and are small will be more easy to takeover. The alternative theory of foreign takeovers, based on financial market imperfections, says that takeover is a mode of enhancing a firm's portfolio. In this case the above hypotheses would not hold.

The data

The sample includes 73 foreign takeover targets taken over the period 1975-1987 where data used in our empirical analysis were available from the COMPUSTAT tapes. We also compile a control sample of non targets and a control sample of domestic takeover targets. The control samples do not include firms in the industries classified by SIC numbers between 4000 and 4999 since they are not allowed to be taken over completely by foreigners. The nontargets are those firms which have not been taken over as of 1987. After deleting the firms in the industries classified by SIC numbers between 4000 and 4999 in the COMPUSTAT tapes and deleting firms for which values of all the variables are not available, we obtain a sample of 363 nontargets.

The domestic takeover targets include only tender offers, during the period 1979-1987. Only tender offers are used because almost all the foreign takeovers are tender offers. After deleting the firms in the industries classified by SIC numbers between 4000 and 4999 in the COMPUSTAT tapes and deleting firms for which values of all the variables are not available, we obtain a sample of 148 domestic takeover targets.

The methodology

As the first step, we observe the major lines of businesses of the target and the bidder to find if they operate in related areas or not. The relatedness hypothesis says that they should be operating in related areas. Although, only a casual observation, it will be a major step in establishing the theory of foreign takeovers put forward in this paper. To test the other hypotheses, we use a logit model. The logit analysis is well suited to the problem of finding whether the characteristics of foreign takeover targets differ from other firms. The empirical specification of the logit model is as follows:

Let W_i be the expected wealth of the foreign firm F resulting from the takeover of the ith firm (i= 1,2,....., m). The wealth will be a function of the deterministic component G^{Fi}, discussed above, and a random one, ϵ. The random component ϵ includes the characteristics of the target and the bidder, which cannot be measured and firm specific idiosyncracies. We write this as:

$$W^i = G^{Fi} + \epsilon \qquad (15).$$

We assume a linear specification for equation (14). Therefore,

$$G^{Fi} = \beta_1'\mathbf{X}_i + \beta_2'\mathbf{I} \qquad (16).$$

Under certain assumptions, like a large number of profit maximizing bidders, ϵ will follow a Type I extreme value distribution.[36] The foreign firm will choose the ith firm if:

$$W^i > W^k \quad \text{for all } k \neq i. \qquad (17).$$

In this case the ith firm's probability of being a foreign takeover target follows a logit distribution.[37] In other words, the probability(firm i is a foreign takeover target) = $\exp(\mathbf{Z}\beta)/(1 + \exp(\mathbf{Z}\beta))$ where $\mathbf{Z} = (\mathbf{X}^i, \mathbf{I})$. The parameters β's are estimated using maximum likelihood estimation.

The proxy variables The industry specific variables are calculated using four-digit industry code. For each firm in the sample, the firm specific variables are matched with their corresponding industry specific variables using the industry codes and according to the year. Following Palepu (1986) all the proxy variables are calculated as at most five year averages using COMPUSTAT tapes.[38] For the firms that are takeover targets (foreign or domestic) the variables are averaged for five years prior to the takeover. For the non targets the variables are averaged over the period 1982-1986. The description of proxy variables used to test the hypotheses is as follows.

The intangible assets hypothesis - as measures of level of intangible assets of an industry, we take the average industry level of research and development expenditure as a proxy for technological skills and the average industry level of advertisement expenditure as a proxy for marketing or product differentiating skills. This is consistent with the standard literature.[39] RNDIND, this variable is a proxy of average level of technological skill in an industry. We calculate this variable by taking the industry average of research and development expenditure as a percentage of total sales. ADVIND, this variable is a proxy of average level of marketing or product differentiating skills in an industry. We calculate this variable by taking the industry average of advertisement expenditures as a percentage of total sales.

The intangible assets hypothesis predicts that these variables will be higher than average for the industries targeted by foreign bidders.

The time hypothesis/the defensive hypothesis. We combine the time hypothesis and the defensive hypothesis to say that if foreign direct investment is used as a defensive reaction, due to its speed a foreign takeover is the best method for such a reaction. We do not use a separate proxy to test the time hypothesis. We use the following measure to jointly test these two hypotheses: FOREIGN, this variable measures the average level of foreign direct investment by a particular industry. The COMPUSTAT does not provide the level of foreign investment for the firms, however it does provide the level of foreign taxes paid. For an individual firm the level of taxes might not be a good measure of foreign involvement because of firm specific idiosyncracies. However, for the industry as a whole it would be a better measure since the individual firm idiosyncracies will average out. Therefore, as a proxy for foreign involvement of a particular industry, we take the average level of foreign taxes paid (as a per cent of total assets) by an industry.

The defensive hypothesis and the time hypothesis predict that this will be higher than average for target industries.

The availability hypothesis. We use the following variable to test this hypothesis, INDGROW. This variable measures the average industry growth per year. We use the average nominal growth in industry sales as the measure for this. The availability hypothesis says that growth will be lower than average in target industries.

The synergy hypothesis. The synergy hypothesis says that firms with low levels of intangible assets are good targets for bidders which possess high level of such assets. If the bidders want to buy such assets then firms with high level of intangible assets are more appropriate targets. These intangible assets include technical skill, marketing skill and managerial skill. One possibility is to take three different measures for all of these. The research and development expenditure and the advertising expenditure could be used as proxies for the technical skill and the marketing skill. However, because COMPUSTAT data for these expenditures are available for only a few firms we lose a lot of observations.[40] Also, it would be very convenient if there is one combined measure for the level of intangible assets. Morck, Shleifer and Vishny (1988) say that Tobin's q is a good measure of the level of intangible assets of a firm. Intangible assets yield rents to a firm (Caves, 1982, p. 4). We use the market-to-book value as a proxy for this measure, MTB. This variable is a measure of the level of intangible assets possessed by a firm. Our justification for using this as a good measure for the firm's intangible assets is further

Table 8.1
Summary statistics of foreign takeover targets and control samples[1]

	MEAN (MEDIAN)		
VARIABLE[2]	FOREIGN-TARGETS	CONTROL SAMPLE 1	CONTROL SAMPLE 2
ADVIND	1.91% (1.24)	1.74% (0.94)	1.63% (0.90)
RNDIND	1.46% (0.52)	1.77% (0.70)	1.64% (0.61)
INDGROW	10.97% (10.88)	15.05% (13.91)	14.52% (13.71)
FOREIGN	0.40% (0.28)	0.36% (0.20)	0.36% (0.19)
MTB	1.27 (0.96)	1.80 (1.40)	1.68 (1.26)
FIRMSIZE	$US0.27 BIL. (0.08)	$US1.18 BIL. (0.18)	$US0.95 BIL. (0.14)

[1]Complete data available from Compustat tapes on 73 foreign takeover targets, which were taken over during the period 1975-1987. Control Sample 1 includes 363 firms that were not taken over as of 1987. Control Sample2 includes 148 domestic takeover targets, which were taken over during the period 1979-1987, in addition to the nontargets in Control Sample1. The number of firms in Control Sample 2 is 511.

[2]The variables are defined as follows:
ADVIND : The industry average of yearly advertising expenditure as a percentage of total sales.
RNDIND : The industry average of yearly R & D expenditure as a percentage of total sales.
INDGROW : The industry average of yearly growth rate of sales.
FOREIGN : The industry average of level of foreign taxes paid as a percentage of total assets.
MTB : The average market - to - book ratio for the firm.
FIRMSIZE: The value of total assets of the firm (in $US billions)

(The variables have been averaged over a period of at most five years: 5 years prior to takeover for the targets and 5 years prior to 1987 for the nontargets. All the data items were not reported for all the firms every year. The industry variables are calculated using the 4-digit SIC codes for the firms.)

bolstered by the evidence that the market-to-book value is highly correlated to the advertisement and the research and development expenditure of the firms in the sample.[41] The synergistic hypothesis says that targets will have either low levels of intangible assets or high levels of intangible assets. Hence, the targets will have either lower than average market-to-book values or higher than average market-to-book values.

The size hypothesis. To test this hypothesis, we use the following variable, FIRMSIZE. This variable measures the size of a firm. We take the book value of the assets as a proxy for the size of the firm. The size hypothesis predicts that the size of the takeover targets will be lower than average.

The results

Relatedness Out of 94 firms transactions, in which the industries of the target and the bidder were identified, 78 were in related industries. The concept of relatedness is also consistent with the barrier to entry hypothesis. A foreign bidder which has operations similar to that of the target is better suited to overcome the barrier to entry than another potential entrant who operates in unrelated areas. Related takeovers could be used to enhance market power. For example this seemed to be one of the motives in the takeover of New Hampshire Ball Bearing Inc. by Minebea Co. of Japan in 1985. Both the firms made ball bearings. This acquisition gave Minebea a 50 per cent share in the world market for miniature ball bearings.

Relatedness is used, in some cases, to obtain synergy by cutting operating costs. For example, International Thomson Organization Ltd. of Canada, which publishes books and newspapers has a strategy of taking over publishing firms and then using their expertise to cut the costs to the bone.[42] This was one of the reasons why International Thomson took over Cordura Corp., which publishes auto repair manuals, in 1986.

Relatedness can also be used to acquire complementary resources, a source of synergy. A case in point is West German firm AEG Aktiengesellschaft's acquisition of Modular Computer Systems Inc. in 1986. Both firms produce electronic components. Modular Computer's CEO, Mr. Gabriel Rosica, said that AEG will bring in 'the missing elements and resources necessary to enable Modular to pursue (its) industrial automation strategy' (*Electronic News*, 1986). Also AEG, in turn, will use Modular Computer's sales and service organization to market its products.

The results are consistent with the relatedness hypothesis, which is the first step towards establishing the validity of the theory of foreign takeovers presented earlier. In other words the evidence on relatedness supports the claim that the foreign takeovers are motivated by real sector imperfections and are not a means of portfolio enhancement.

Other characteristics: summary statistics Table 8.1 presents the means and medians of the variables of interest by the type of firms. The observed values of ADVIND, the average industry expenditure on advertisement as a percentage of total sales, are consistent with the hypothesis that foreigners target firms in industries which use above average level of intangible assets, especially marketing skills which enhance product differentiation. The mean ADVIND for foreign targets is 1.91 per cent. The corresponding values for control sample 1, which includes only nontargets, is 1.74 per cent. The inclusion of domestic takeover targets lowers this mean further. For control sample 2, which includes nontargets and domestic targets, the mean is 1.63 per cent. The medians are much smaller compared to the means. For foreign targets, for example, the median of ADVIND is 1.24 per cent. However, the medians relate the exact same story as the means.

The observed values for RNDIND, the industry average R and D expenditure as a percentage of total sales, are not consistent with the intangible assets hypothesis. In fact, the mean of this variable is lower(1.46 per cent) than for control sample 1 (1.77 per cent) and control sample 2 (1.64 per cent). The medians, although much smaller, follow the same pattern as the means. This suggests high technology industries are not necessarily good targets for foreign takeovers.

The means and medians of industry growth are consistent with the hypothesis that foreign targets are more easily available in more mature industries. The foreign takeover targets lie in industries with average nominal growth rate in sales of 10.97 per cent. The corresponding figure for control sample 1 is 15.05 per cent. Control sample 2 shows an industry growth rate of 14.52 per cent. The medians, although lower are not very different from thee means. Again, the medians follow the same pattern as the means.

The evidence on the final industry specific variable, the foreign involvement of a particular industry, is consistent with the oligopolistic reaction models and the argument that a takeover, which has an almost immediate impact, is a desirable mode to react to a threat of foreign competitors. The industry average of foreign taxes as a percentage of total assets paid is 0.40 per cent for foreign targets. The corresponding figures for both control sample 1 and control sample 2 is 0.36 per cent. Again, the medians, although lower, convey the same information.

The averages of market-to-book value, which is taken as a proxy for Tobin's q shows that foreign takeover targets are characterized by low level of intangible assets. This is consistent with the hypothesis that foreign bidders takeover firms to utilize their own intangible assets and that they are not here to buy intangible assets. The mean market-to-book value for foreign targets is 1.27 which is exactly 53 percentage points lower than the mean market-to-book value for control sample 1 (consisting of nontargets only) which has a mean of 1.80. The corresponding value for control sample 2 is 1.68. This shows that the inclusion of domestic targets decreases the mean for the control sample. Therefore, the domestic targets of tender offers are also characterized by lower than average market to book values. Interestingly enough, the median market to book value for foreign targets is 0.98, which is less than one, indicating that the market value for an average target firm is less than its book value. Glen Gery Corp. had the lowest market-to-book value of 0.41 in the sample of foreign targets. Budd Co. (0.43), Koehring Corp. (0.44), Norin Corp. (0.45), Lehigh Portland Cement (0.47), and General Portland Inc. (0.47) were other firms with market-book-value below 0.50. The medians are consistent with the information conveyed by the means.

Table 8.2
Logit model estimation of foreign takeover targets versus control samples[1]

	MODEL 1			MODEL 2		
VARIABLE[3]	COEFF.	STD-ERROR	P	COEFF.	STD-ERROR	P
CONSTANT	-0.468	.3313	.158	-1.212	.3079	.000
ADVIND	0.112	.0745	.132	0.141	.0732	.053
RNDIND	-0.028	.0925	.759	-0.024	.0883	.784
ADVRND	-0.047	.3380	.165	-0.045	.0336	.177
INDGROW	-0.016	.0101	.111	-0.017	.0103	.108
FOREIGN	0.689	.3467	.047	0.534	.3002	.975
MTB	-0.586	.1687	.000	-0.442	.1572	.004
FIRMSIZE	-0.072	.0280	.010	-0.058	.0251	.021
Log Likelihood		-175.67			-204.46	
N =		436			584	

[1]Complete data available from Compustat on 73 foreign takeover targets, which were taken over during the period 1975-1987. Model 1 uses control sample 1 that consists of 363 firms which were not taken over as of 1987. The foreign takeover targets are at value 1 and the firms in Control Sample 1 are at value 0. Model 2 uses control sample 2 that consists of 363 firms that were not taken over as of 1987 and 148 firms that were taken over by domestic bidders during 1979-1987. The foreign takeover targets are at value 1 and the firms in Control Sample 2 are at value 0.
[2]The variables are defined as follows:
ADVIND : The industry average of yearly advertising expenditure as a percentage of total sales.
RNDIND : The industry average of yearly R and D expenditure as a percentage of total sales.
ADVRND : ADVIND * RNDIND.
INDGROW : The industry average of yearly growth rate of sales.
FOREIGN : The industry average of level of foreign taxes paid as a percentage of total assets.
MTB : The average market - to - book ratio for the firm.
FIRMSIZE: The value of total assets of the firm (in $US100 millions)
(The variables have been averaged over a period of at most five years: 5 years prior to takeover for the targets and 5 years prior to 1987 for the nontargets. The industry variables are calculated using the 4-digit SIC codes for the firms.)

The average size of the firms clearly show that larger a firm gets more difficult it is to acquire it. The mean size of control sample 1 ($US1.18 billion), consisting only of nontargets, is more than 4 times the mean size of the foreign targets ($US0.27

billion). The inclusion of domestic targets substantially reduces the mean size of the firms. The means size of firms in control sample 2 is 0.95 billion. The medians, which are much smaller, convey the same information. The biggest foreign target was Celanese Corp. with assets worth $US2.9 billion. Carnation Corp.($US1.64 billion), Texasgulf Inc. ($US1.61 billion), Cheseborough Pond's Inc. ($US1.55 billion) and Santa Fe International ($US1.14 billion) were the other firms in the billion dollar category. The smallest foreign target was Stanley Aviation Corp. with assets worth $US4.8 million.

Other than for RNDIND, the summary data supports all the hypotheses, which are being tested.

Results of logit estimates Table 8.2 shows the results for the logit model with foreign takeover targets taking the value 1 and control sample 1 taking the value 0 in model 1 and control sample 2 taking the value 0 in model 2. A positive (negative) sign for an estimate signifies that an increase(decrease) in that variable increases a firm's probability of becoming a foreign takeover target. The signs of the coefficient estimates are consistent with the casual observation of summary statistics in all the cases. Since we have hypothesized the sign for all the variables, it is possible to do a one-tailed test. However, since these are proxy variables, we report the two-tailed P-Values. We have included a variable ADVRND (which is the product of ADVIND and RNDIND) to control for the cross effects.

Model 1 shows that for the industry-specific variables the signs of FOREIGN, INDGROW, and ADVIND are consistent with the hypothesized sign. However, for a two-tailed test, only FOREIGN, with a P-Value of 0.047, is significant at a standard level of significance (in this case 5 per cent level). The P-Values for ADVIND and INDGROW are 0.132 and 0.111, which are not significant at 10 per cent level respectively. The sign for RNDIND is opposite of the hypothesized sign. However, it is highly insignificant with a P-Value of 0.759. For the firm specific variables, both market-to book value and firm size not only have the right sign but are highly significant (both at 1 per cent level).

Model 2 tests with a much larger control sample. The control sample includes nontargets and domestic takeover targets. The coefficients have the exact same sign as the ones in model 1. However ADVIND, with a P-Value of 0.053 becomes statistically significant. The INDGROW variable, with a P-Value of 0.108 is almost significant. The firm specific variables are again highly significant with the right sign, but as expected, they become slightly less significant due to the inclusion of domestic takeover targets in the control sample.[43]

Interpreting the results

The results show that 80 per cent of the foreign bidders acquired targets operating in businesses related to their own. This is the first step in establishing that foreign bidders are interested in the market of the target. Also, since some intangible are particular to some business the evidence shows that foreign buyers want to use or buy intangible assets. The results of the logit models are consistent with the real sector imperfections of foreign takeover.

Foreign takeovers and the industry of the targets The results regarding the industry specific variables are consistent, albeit weakly, with the contention that foreign takeovers are used as a mode of entry into a new market or expansion. The significance of FOREIGN suggests that foreign acquisitions are a good vehicle of entry or expansions in markets especially when the motive is to react the strategies of the rival firms. This is consistent with Knickerbocker's (1974) findings. This is also consistent with the hypothesis that acquisition is preferred over direct investment if time is an important component of the business strategy. The results here echo Dubin's findings.

The ability of acquisition to provide a firm with quick access to new markets reduced the level of risk of investing abroad during these periods when investments in similar markets were undertaken by competing multinationals (Dubin, 1976). However, for various reasons, one has to be careful in making a strong statement. For one, level of foreign taxes may not be a good measure of foreign involvement. A firm can be involved abroad without making any profits and hence not paying any taxes. Also, tax laws are different for different countries which makes the measure less reliable. Finally, taxes generally depend on accounting measures of profits, making it a less attractive measure. Keeping, these limitations in mind, we conclude that for the sample considered here, the probability of foreign takeovers in an industry increases with the foreign involvement of that industry.

The significance of ADVIND can be interpreted in the following ways. Firstly, it shows that more the levels of product differentiation in an industry, higher the probability of that industry being a target of foreign takeovers. This result is consistent with the evidence in the foreign direct investment literature. Secondly, it is consistent with the contention that acquisition in industries with high average level of advertisement expenditure may bring the advantage of an established distribution system. Thirdly, inasmuch as product differentiation is a barrier to entry, the result shows that foreign acquisition is a way to circumvent barriers to entry in a market. This is consistent with the argument that foreign firms either possess intangible assets, which they want to utilize to earn rents or they want to buy such assets.

The highly insignificant RNDIND is not consistent with the hypothesis that industries which require high level of technological skills are good targets for foreign direct investment. This is contrary to the findings of many researchers. One explanation for this result may be that foreign bidders possess technological skills that cannot be adapted to the US industries and hence they do not seek such industries. Also, it shows that the motive of the bidders is not to buy highly developed technological skills. One of the reason for the different results could be the sample design. We do not limit the sample to manufacturing industries, which has been done by most researchers.

The significance of INDGROW shows that availability of targets acts as a constraint to takeovers. This follows from the argument that more mature, low growth industries have more takeover targets because of reorganizations and restructurings.

To summarize, the results regarding industry specific variables confirm the hypotheses and empirical evidence of the existing literature. We would like to make a note of caution about the structure of the data. The source of data is the COMPUSTAT tapes, which consists of only firms listed on the stock exchanges. The industry does not consist of only these firms. If the firms in this data set are good representatives of the industry then there is nothing to worry about. However, if this is not so, these results are less interesting.

Foreign takeovers and the target The results are highly supportive of the synergistic theory of takeover. The results show that the foreign targets, when compared to the control samples, are characterized by very low levels of intangible assets, as measured by the market-to book values. This result is highly robust. It remains highly significant in all the cases even when compensation for choice based sampling is made.

This result shows that a) the motive of the foreign buyers is to use their own intangible assets and not buy intangible assets, b) foreign buyers are interested in synergistic gains.

This result is consistent with empirical evidence on domestic acquisitions. Hasbrouck (1985) using a sample of 86 takeover targets and a control sample of 172 firms finds that takeover targets have significantly lower q than that of the control sample. Servaes (1988) also finds exactly the same result. If q (and hence market-to-book value) is taken as a measure of managerial inefficiency, which is generally assumed in the corporate control literature, one can say that the market for corporate control is not confined to domestic barriers, in fact we have a global market for corporate control, in which management teams vie for control of resources.[44]

However, as mentioned earlier, market-to-book value is not only a measure of managerial skills, but also a measure of technological and marketing skills of a firm. If the market-to-book value is low because of a lack of these skills, the result can be interpreted as showing that foreign firms want to adapt their highly developed skills to increase the operating efficiency of the target.[45]

Despite the strong results, a word of caution is warranted. Many researchers have argued that market-to-book value is not a good measure of q. Some researches (for example Palepu (1986)) say that the book value does not reflect the replacement value of the assets. Others have pointed to the noninclusion of debt, a much more serious problem, making it a suspect measure. However, one can hope, that these shortcomings cause a systematic bias for all the firms alike in the sample, mitigating this problem.

Finally, the firms are limited in their ability to acquire by the size of the firms. On an average, larger a firm gets more difficult it is to acquire it.

Summary

To summarize, the results do show that foreign takeovers targets are systematically different from the control sample. Also, the systematic differences are close to what is hypothesized by the real sector imperfections model. These results further validate the importance of the internalization theory of foreign takeovers. Also, it shows that the mergers and acquisition theories that are pertinent in the domestic setting also apply to the foreign bidders. Although, we do not directly test the financial sector imperfections hypothesis, the results disprove the contention that foreign takeovers are done purely for enhancement of a portfolio. Finally, foreign bidders wish to use their own intangible assets to achieve synergy, rather than buy targets which possess such assets.

Notes

1. For example, Federal Reserve Bank of Boston organized a conference to discuss the various reasons and implications of the current merger wave in October 1987. The conference was attended by financial economists, industrial organization specialists, government officials and representatives from the business community. Proceedings of the conference are recorded in Browne and Rosengren (1987).
2. *The Wall Street Journal* (April 9, 1990) reports that the foreign direct investment activity has increased by more than 10 per cent each year since mid-1970s. In the late eighties, the foreign holdings in the United States exceeded the United States' overseas holdings for the first time since World War 1. At the end of 1989, the foreigners held $US390 billion in plants and property in the United States. The corresponding figure for United States' holdings abroad was $US368.1 billion.
3. *Electronic News*, March 23, 1987 reported that 'the House Energy subcommittee voted 11 to 2 to direct Commerce Secretary Malcolm Baldrige to investigate whether any proposed foreign takeover 'would impair the national security and essential commerce.' The drive was, in essence, to set up a national policy to curb foreign takeovers of high-technology companies in the United States. This recommendation was adopted, in part, with the passage of Exon-Florio Amendment in 1988, which allows the President to restrict foreign takeovers on the grounds of national security.
4. For example see the 'Roundtable: Perspectives of Strategic Transactions in 1990', *Mergers and Acquisitions*, May/June 1990. The participants in this roundtable are eight business personalities, all of who agree that foreign buyers believe in strategic transactions.

5. See, for example, Errunza and Senbet (1981). Errunza and Senbet argue that foreign direct investment occurs due to financial sector imperfections, real sector imperfections or government created distortions. Since the government creates distortions in either of the two markets, we do not list government created distortions as a separate imperfection.
6. See, for example, Morck and Young (1990). The theory of foreign direct investment, based on real sector imperfections, is popularly known as theory of internalization.
7. See, for example, Caves (1982, p. 81). Caves brings in elements of strategic management in his book, but deals with the issue of acquisition versus direct entry at a very superficial level.
8. This was the logical extension because, as Dunning and Rugman (1985) point out, the internalization theory was closely related to the literature on strategic management.
9. For example, Lindgren (1982) says that time is the most important factor that makes companies to choose acquisitions over new establishments.
10. An example of Teece's argument can be seen from the following observation reported in the *Survey of Current Business* (1987). The share of the affiliates of foreign firms in terms of total assets in 1986 was 12.1 per cent of the total assets in the manufacturing sector in the United States. However, the corresponding share in the Chemical industry was 32 per cent.
11. Little (1988) defines portfolio investment as a short term investment in financial instruments such as corporate stocks, bonds, government issued securities and bank deposits. From a strategic point of view Portfolio investment differs from foreign direct investment in that it has no entrepreneurial purpose or connotation.
12. Under licensing the parent company rents a license or permit in return for royalties and other form of payments. Licensing gives a foreign firm the right to use processes, techniques, or brand names for manufacturing or selling a product. Cooperative venture is a contractual agreement between two or more firms. It may or may not involve formation of a separate entity. The participating firms often provide knowhow, initial capital investment, management personnel, production facilities and patents, etc. Typically these ventures are created for a very limited mission for example production of a particular product in a specific geographic area.
13. For example, Yip (1982) devotes a full chapter discussing takeovers and new establishments as competing modes of entry.
14. For example Biggadike (1979) estimated that a new establishment takes an average of eight years to become profitable.
15. Lindgren (1982) says that time is the most important factor that makes companies to choose acquisitions over setting up new subsidiaries.
16. For example, Dutz (1989, p. 14) says that 'in an oligopolistic industry where each firm has a mix of outmoded state-of-the art technology, two firms may have an incentive to merge to combine the better part of each firm's plant when industry demand declines'.

17. In the case of acquisition of assets the buyer acquires individual specific assets and the payment, which is made to the selling firm and not shareholders, can be in the form of cash, the buyer's shares or other securities issued by the buyer. The selling company can then dissolve itself. If it does so the receipts from the sales are paid to the shareholders.
18. For a detailed analysis of difficulties faced by the bidder in a proxy contest see, for example, Pound (1988). Pound claims, backed by empirical support, that a proxy contest might be overly biased towards the incumbent management making it very difficult, if not impossible, for the bidder to actually win the contest. These biases may be in the form of cost disadvantages, inefficiencies in the system of vote solicitation or even lack of support from institutional investors, which a bidder might face.
19. In some cases acquisition of 50 per cent of stock might not be enough for a merger. If the target expects an unsolicited tender offer, or a hostile takeover, it may decide to make certain amendments in its charter. Supermajority amendments, which set the minimum approval required for a merger to two-thirds or even nine-tenths of the total votes, is one example of such an amendment. This would require acquisition of 66 per cent to 90 per cent of the target's shares. There are a host of other defensive strategies, like super-majority amendments, which make it difficult for bidders to takeover a firm. Poison pills, greenmail, fair price amendments are some other examples of these strategies. For a good empirical survey of these strategies see, for example: Jarrell, Brickley, and Netter (1988).
20. A lot of researchers have questioned the assumption of profit maximization. For example, Jensen and Meckling (1976) show that managers may diverge from profit maximization goal due to agency problems. In the context of takeovers, in particular, Roll (1986) hypothesizes that managers are overly optimistic in evaluating mergers due to animal spirits or hubris. However, Jarrell, Brickley and Netter (1988), in a survey of empirical evidence of takeover studies, say that the evidence supports the assumption of profit maximization.
21. For example, Caves (1982) says that 'investment and search costs are quite high for foreign investment as compared with other investment decisions, what with overseas site visits, the cost of acquiring the necessary approvals from the foreign governments, and the like'.
22. One exception is the Exon-Florio Amendment which is part of Conference Committee's version of omnibus trade bill (HR 4848) passed in late 1988. The amendment allows the President to restrict foreign mergers/acquisitions on the grounds of national security.
23. This assumption is another way of saying that financial markets are efficient. For a similar treatment of firm value, see Morck and Young (1989).
24. When financial markets are efficient $V^i(\mathbf{X}^i)$ is the market value of the ith firm. Therefore, equation (4) suggests that if the bidder pays exactly the market value for the firm G^{Fi} is the gains from takeover of the ith firm to F.

25. The fraction k depends on the nature of the takeover. Empirical evidence shows that premium depends on the method of payment and on whether the takeover is friendly or hostile. The transaction stage section of the paper deals with the determinants of the premium.
26. The first order conditions are based on the assumption that the constraint is not binding. As mentioned earlier, the existing theory of foreign takeovers suggests some attributes, **I**, which make foreign takeover the best strategy, and hence the constraint nonbinding.
27. For example, Caves and Mehra (1988) say that a takeover would be 'an attractive takeover route in a high research industry, if the going firm's research capacity helps to adapt the parent's technological assets to the local market'.
28. For example, Cebenoyan, Papaionnou and Travlos (1989) say that the 'knowledge seeking theories attribute foreign direct investment in the(..) US economy to the need of multinational corporation to acquire information and knowledge in technology, marketing, and managerial skills.'
29. Several studies have shown high level of intangible assets act as barriers to entry. See, for example Bain (1956) and Mueller and Rogers (1980).
30. Foreign takeovers, rather than new establishment, will particularly be attractive in industries with high barriers because, as Yip (1982) says, an acquisition is the best way to overcome a barrier to entry.
31. These real sector imperfections are in the form of market failures associated with pricing of intangible assets.
32. This is based on the assumption that intangible assets are substitutable.
33. For example, Vernon (1970), in his study of Fortune 500 corporations for multinationality, observed that firms that became multinational had better technological skills than the firms which did not become multinational.
34. By related we mean that the merger should either be horizontal or vertical. In other words the participating firms should be operating either in the same kind of business activity or in different stages of production. For a taxonomy of merger types and their definitions see, for example, Weston, Chung and Hoag (1990).
35. See Morck, Shleifer and Vishny (1988). The authors say integration of the bidder's and target's business is essential to realize synergistic gains which come from more market power, combined technology or marketing networks or elimination of common functions.
36. See for example Palepu (1986, p.15). The extreme valued distribution has the following cumulative density function: 1 - EXP(- EXP(-x)).
37. This follows from the standard result that the difference of two variables with type I extreme value distribution has a logit distribution. See, for example, Maddala (1987).
38. We use the words 'at most', because all the data items (at both industry-specific levels and firm-specific levels) are not available for all the years.
39. For example, Caves (1982) points out that as indicators of intangible assets 'economists have seized on the outlays for advertising and research and development undertaken by firms classified to an industry.'

40. The sample size is reduced to 393 from 683 if these expenditures are included.
41. We run a regression with the market-to-book (MTB) value as the dependent variable and the advertisement expenditure (ADV) and research and development expenditure (RND) of a firm as dependent variables. Both ADV and RND are measured as percentage of total firm sales. Also, all three variables, MTB, ADV and RND are averaged over a period of five years. The results of the OLS regression are:

$$\underset{}{MTB} = \underset{(0.075)}{1.29} + \underset{(0.019)}{0.04\ ADV} + \underset{(0.018)}{0.13\ RND} \qquad F = 28.62 \quad N = 357$$

The figures in the parenthesis are the standard errors. The coefficients on ADV and RND are significant at 5 per cent level of significance.
42. See Terry, Edith, 'A Media Giant Thinks to Get Bigger', *Business Week*, June 9, 1986.p. 48.
43. We also estimate a multinomial logit model with nontargets at 0, foreign takeover targets at 1, domestic takeover targets at 2. The results are consistent with these results. However, since the analysis here is based on foreign bidder trying to choose a target, we cannot theoretically justify the use of the multinomial logit model.
44. This seems highly plausible since the median of market-to-book value was less than one for the foreign targets and as Hasbrouck (1985) argues a q less than one is a sign of managerial inefficiency.
45. This is consistent with Servaes'(1988) finding that bidders generally have significantly higher q than the targets.

9 Trade regimes, foreign investment and the new liberalization environment in Indonesia

Thomas R. Leinbach

Introduction

Indonesia has enjoyed tremendous economic growth over the past decade, in part as a result of new government policies under the Soeharto New Order government and fortuitous market conditions. Indeed the country has come to be viewed by some as one of the 'new or second tier' Asian NICs. Despite this apparent success, there are those who argue that the development which has occurred is largely spurious and/or ephemeral (Clad, 1987; Kunio, 1988). Nonetheless it remains fact that Indonesia's GDP growth during the 1990-1993 period averaged nearly seven per cent and compares favorably to Singapore, Malaysia and Thailand within the region. While the per capita income of $US670 pales in comparison with that of Singapore ($US15,730) and Malaysia ($US2,790), it is a dramatic improvement for a nation which 30 years ago was considered impoverished and dominantly agrarian.

Oil and gas, the major revenue sources throughout the nation's history, still contribute significantly to the growth. However, the change is also the product of a strong structural adjustment effort in which liberalization measures have had an important role. These reforms, in part because of their newness, have not received critical attention and analysis. Within this changing development environment, the enlargement of manufacturing output has become a major goal. Such an objective is, of course, closely tied to the structuring and dynamics of trade regimes, foreign investment incentives, as well as, financial and other deregulation policies. Yet neither trade nor foreign direct investment and their interrelationship have been adequately studied in the Indonesian context. Thus given the progress of the industrial restructuring effort, the examination of the evolution of liberalization policies in regards to the trade regimes, especially, and their impact on trade flows, as well as, investment patterns holds great promise for understanding other LDCs and the complex interactions of the global economy.

Objectives

An initial objective of the paper is to carry out a brief but thorough review of liberalization efforts with respect to issues surrounding trade reform. This review begins with the situation in the early 1980s and includes the most recent, and in many ways, the most critical adjustments to date.

Following this as a second objective we examine the patterns of trade obtaining between 1980 and the current period. The intent is to interpret these patterns and relate them to the trade reform measures and more broadly structural adjustment and liberalization efforts. Of special interest is the performance of non-oil exports, their structure and an explanation of their behavior.

In addition we examine relations with Indonesia's dominant trading partners (both intra and extraregional) during the same period in an attempt to depict patterns in her involvement in the dynamic global economy. In this regard, the changing influence and behavior of Japan, the US and the East Asian NICs are of interest. But the intraregional components of the trade performance are also important and will be examined in light of the development dynamics within ASEAN and especially the emergence of the Growth Triangle concept (Toh and Low, 1993) and the ongoing discussion of an ASEAN Free Trade Agreement (AFTA) (Vatikiotis, 1993). In this regard the trade flows and relations with Singapore and Malaysia, Indonesia's nearest and most successful neighbors are especially important. Finally, critical too, are the trade positions of Thailand and the Philippines.

Given the importance to trade, a fourth objective is to analyze the pattern of foreign direct investment (FDI) over the same period. The temporal fluctuations in FDI as well as the investing nations and the location of the investment are of special interest. Linkages between trade growth, liberalization efforts and the behavior of investment patterns will be drawn.

Finally despite the strong progress to date with respect to trade liberalization, efforts have only just begun to position Indonesia with an 'efficiency enhancing' regime that will make her truly competitive in the global economy. Several criticisms have been launched at the reform efforts and deficiencies identified. One major question is the degree to which the system of deregulation has retarded the growth of an efficient export sector by encouraging the misallocation of resources for which Indonesia has no real comparative advantage. The additional reforms which are required as well as their intended impact will be discussed.

Background

Trade policy is an important instrument by which the pace and pattern of industrial development can be guided. But the exact form and sequencing of a trade strategy to carry out such development remains in debate. Some countries seek to promote growth through domestic industrialization and import substitution, that is where trade and industrial incentives are biased toward production for the domestic market. Such a strategy relies upon discretionary interventions which usually are characterized by controls, as well as, high and variable tariff protection and restrictions. Other countries aim to promote economic development through the expansion of foreign trade and by maintaining an 'open door' policy towards private foreign investment and foreign aid. This approach emphasizes linkages to the global economy through exports and enhanced import capacity. Further, it is critical that this strategy does not bias incentives toward the domestic market. Thus neutrality of incentives is desirable with respect to production for home and export markets. Yet this should not be construed to mean that government does not intervene. Indeed, many governments, especially among the East Asian NICs, rely heavily on government intervention to achieve market orientation.

The terms 'inward' and 'outward' looking trade strategies provide a convenient way to contrast these two different attitudes and policies (Myint, 1984; Bhattacharya and Linn, 1988). Thus pure outward-looking, in contrast to inward-looking, policies pursue free trade and export expansion goals instead of protectionist and import substitution policies. 'Open' type domestic and private foreign investment policies characterize the former while the latter's policies are more insulating and restrictive in this regard. An outward oriented strategy implies an undistorted import trade regime. Consequently reform of the import protecting regime provides a more direct route to achieving the objectives of an outward oriented trade strategy. Thus, for example, reducing and rationalizing import protection can produce:

1 a lessening of the antiexport bias resulting from protection and overvaluation of the exchange rate

2 a more efficient allocation of resources by aligning domestic prices with international opportunity costs

3 reducing 'rent-seeking' and unproductive activities associated with controls; and perhaps most critical

4 exposure of domestic firms to the positive effects of world competition (Bhattacharya and Linn, 1988).

Emerging Indonesian trade policies: 1970-1987

It is well known that in the late 1960s Indonesia under Soeharto's New Order government began to move away from older inward looking attitudes by implementing a long term recovery program. At the top of this recovery program was the objective of sound macroeconomic management with the intent of also improving the overall investment environment. But in addition a series of trade liberalization measures were carried out from 1966 to 1971. Legal under invoicing, which essentially subsidizes exports, and exchange rate unification, which eliminated discrimination in exchange rates among commodities, were among the measures applied. A devaluation of the rupiah in 1971, the first of a series of devaluations, marked the end of a period of liberalization that transformed Indonesia's trade regime from one of the most restrictive among LDCs to one in which there was full exchange convertibility and a complete absence of foreign exchange licensing (Pitt, 1991, p. 199). But despite the introduction of several important measures, macroeconomic stability was threatened by the period of the first oil boom (1973-1978) when abundant revenues permitted expansion of development expenditures. In order to stem inflation rather stringent credit controls were adopted. In this period inward-looking trade policies were in effect and these together with the proliferation of non-tariff barriers (NTBs) had a stifling effect upon non-oil and gas exports and the growth of efficient industry. Over the decade of the 1970s research has shown that Indonesia's trade regime became more restrictive and moreover there was a critical employment trade-off implicit in this choice of trade strategy. The employment cost of following an import substitution strategy was severe: one million dollars of increased value added from manufacturing exports generated 57 per cent more employment than an equivalent reduction in competing imports. Thus if manufactured exports were to increase by 15 per cent per year, the employment necessary to produce these exports would have risen from 370,000 in 1971 to 1.7 million in 1981 (Pitt, 1981, p. 225). This employment impact of the trade regime ultimately aided a stronger liberalization effort.

During the period 1973-1985 the World Bank, while sensing some improvement, still classified Indonesia as 'moderately inward-oriented' as a result of the emphasis on import substitution and technology based industries (World Bank, 1987). This was reflected by the adoption of import quotas, bans, licensing, surcharges, and duties (up to 200 per cent in some cases). But especially critical was the fact that non-tariff import restrictions had become very important: by 1982, 35 per cent of total imports were included within these restrictions. For example, as part of the trade regime milieu, the government issued licenses to approved importers for some goods and select importers for others. In addition, the local content of manufacturing was emphasized through special 'deletion' programs that forced producers of finished goods to source specific components locally (Barichello and Flatters, 1992). Moreover, export controls were imposed to protect downstream processing industries. This applied especially to the plywood and rattan industries where in the former fully restricted log exports were in effect by 1985. Unfortunately the overall effect of these trade restrictions and regulations on industry was to produce a high cost economy which reduced competitiveness and made the country ever more dependent upon petroleum and gas. And quite the opposite of the import substitution protagonists' argument, it was shown that investments encouraged by protection measures generated only one-quarter of the jobs as would the same investments in export production. These findings were actually unearthed in the early 1980s as a result of the government's determination to revamp Indonesia's tax system. Thus the beginnings of trade reform came from an unexpected, but logical, source.

Just as worrisome as the direct economic effects of these measures, were the ways in which they were interpreted and applied. So, for example, in the mid-1980s it came to be understood that firms which were willing to invest in priority sectors could expect guarantees that, given some minimal competition, investment in the industry would be closed thus protecting the investor from additional competition.

It would be misleading to suggest that no reforms in trade policies were attempted in the early 1980s. For example in 1981 the Ministry of Finance developed a new set of tariffs which would have produced a moderate reduction in the average levels but, these were never implemented. Four years later some reduction was finally achieved but it did not affect deeply the inadequacies of the overall tariff structure. However, several critical incidents took place within this time frame which triggered the beginnings of more meaningful change in trade reform.

Although not viewed at the time as part of trade reform, an important set of decrees issued under Presidential Instruction No. 4 (Inpres 4) in May, 1985 was to have monumental impacts. Like many other developing nations, Indonesia's port system, and especially the cargo clearance aspects, had become especially notorious resulting in long delays and high costs. The business community's frustration with escalating costs and corruption produced a significant response. The Inpres 4 legislation targeted port inefficiencies specifically and aimed at reducing the cost of goods clearance. The prime measure within this package was the replacement of Indonesian customs as the agent for customs processing. Under this order the responsibility of monitoring all Indonesian exports and imports was assigned to a Swiss surveying company which, on a contract basis, inspected, classified and valued shipments to and from Indonesia in the foreign port of export or import. In addition the Inpres 4 legislation also simplified port procedures by abolishing several onerous and costly port and shipping regulations. Finally shipping and freight forwarding activities were deregulated. The reforms had an immediate and positive impact on port costs and on trade in general. It is estimated that these measures have reduced port handling and shipping costs by as much as 30-40 per cent. The wider implications of such savings in a regional frame of reference have been noted in a recent study of ASEAN port facilities. This study shows that savings of over $US1.2 billion per year in shipping costs would be possible if container berth productivities in ASEAN ports were raised to levels equivalent to those currently employed in Singapore (Peters, 1986, p. 16).

Second, the US raised a complaint which accused the Indonesian government of twisting an export certificate program in the textile industry into a specific subsidy program for certain exporters. This incident forced the signing of the GATT accord and served as a powerful influence in support of the need for further policy reforms in trade.

Third, and most important, was the collapse of oil prices which began in 1981 but continued through 1985. With a dramatic 60 per cent reduction in barrel price over a few months time, the matter of trade reform was urgently brought to the surface for action. There was now an urgent need to stimulate nonoil export growth by removing barriers and introducing deregulation. A major discussion of trade reform thus began in earnest. These initial discussions produced, in principle, an agreement to discontinue non-tariff import restrictions, as well as, a decision to adjust a newly devised duty drawback program to extend import privileges for exporters to include the right to import required inputs free of any import licensing or quota restrictions.

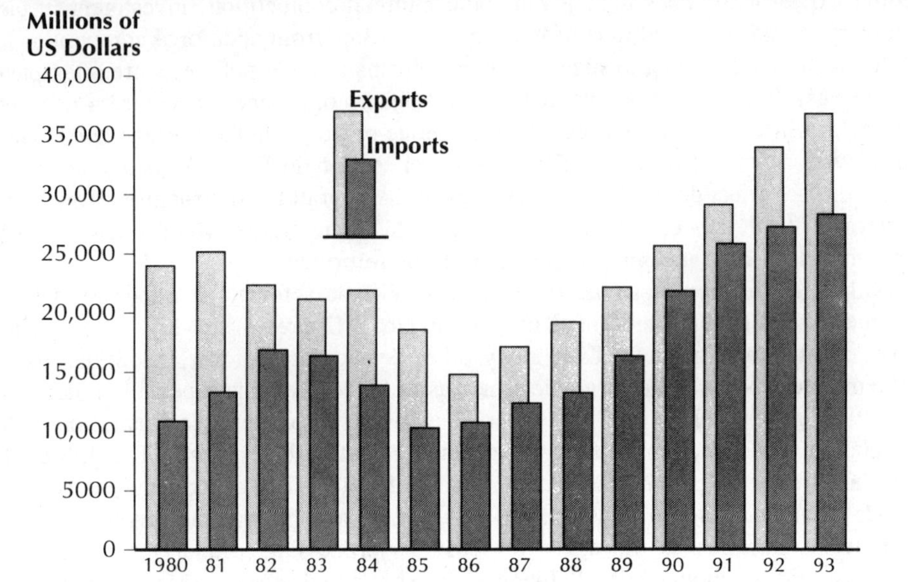

Figure 9.1 Indonesian trade: oil and gas included exports and imports, 1980-1993

Source: Central Bureau of Statisitics, Foreign Trade Statistics

New decrees on May 6th, 1986 included provisions for duty drawbacks and exemptions for exporters as well as a relaxation of import licensing regulations on inputs required for export production (Barichello and Flatters, 1992). Further, import licenses were removed on 539 items or 32 per cent of the items previously restricted.

Recent trade liberalization efforts

As can be seen from the above reforms, Indonesia's development strategy in the mid-1980s, shifted from inward-looking to outward-looking and indeed trade regime adjustments were critical to this transition. Since the mid-1980s the major changes in trade policies have been implemented through a series of annual packages. The dominant feature of these packages has been a continued attack on inefficiencies in the import environment. Especially important has been the reduction of coverage of non-tariff barriers (NTBs). These packages have reduced the share of production protected by NTBs from 41 per cent in 1986 to 22 per cent in 1992. The most dramatic changes have occurred with respect to manufacturing while the adjustments in agriculture, although important, have been smaller. The July, 1992 package (PAKJUL) reduced the number of NTBs further from 703 to 464. One of the important impacts of these reforms was to eliminate Krakatau Steel's monopoly rights in Indonesia. Almost directly as a result, the company's steel prices dropped 16 per cent in the year following the package. However, a significant share of output, especially in agriculture, agro-industry, paper products, steel and automobiles, was still protected by NTBs. This inefficiency has remained a high priority in reform efforts.

As the NTBs have been removed the challenge of further reform geared toward greater competitiveness and lower costs lies with the adjustment of tariffs. As a result of the annual measures between 1985 and 1991 the average tariff level was reduced from 37 per cent to 20 per cent. In the following year the elimination of 40 per cent of the tariff surcharges added further to the reform effort. But just as tariffs and NTBs alter domestic prices so too do export restrictions. In this regard controls on forestry products have been the most important restrictions. In the late 1980s very high export taxes were applied to sawn timber in an effort to drive raw materials into the secondary processing sector where value added would be higher. This expected expansion has now peaked while the number of sawmills have shrunk. The plywood industry has been the main beneficiary as a result of the increase in the supply of cheap logs. In 1992 the ban on log exports was replaced with export taxes. But, in fact, given the depth of the taxes, the effect has been negligible. Thus only processed products can be exported. As a result of the taxes, domestic log prices are well below international levels. For example prices for meranti logs from Indonesia are $US90 per cubic meter while those from Malaysia are over $US 300 per cubic meter. A clear impact of these artificially low log prices has been environmental degradation and inefficiency in both logging and wood processing industries (World Bank, 1993). Thus raising log prices would encourage lower consumption and could be accomplished by lowering export taxes to open foreign markets while increasing government rent collection. The RI government has begun the latter process by increasing both logging fees and royalties. The above illustration is significant for it demonstrates how trade policies can impact resource allocation by changing the returns in various sectors-- here export restrictions in the forest sector. We return to this theme below as we discuss further reforms which are required.

Continuing the deregulation process, the government announced two further economic reform packages in 1994. The first of these, PP 20/1994, was announced on June 2 and provided for the wide-ranging liberalization of regulations governing foreign direct investment. The second package issued on June 27 involved the further liberalization of the trade regime.

The liberalization of FDI package is significant because Repelita VI (the Sixth Five Year Development Plan) depends greatly on foreign private capital. Moreover such capital is also now being actively sought within the region by Vietnam, India, China, Malaysia, the Philippines and Thailand. The measures included a lifting of the existing ban on foreign investment in so-called strategic industries such as ports, telecommunications, power, water supply, education, railways, civil aviation and the mass media. Thus foreign investors may now operate in these areas in joint ventures with domestic enterprises. Coupled with this there was an easing of equity limits imposed on foreign partners in joint ventures.

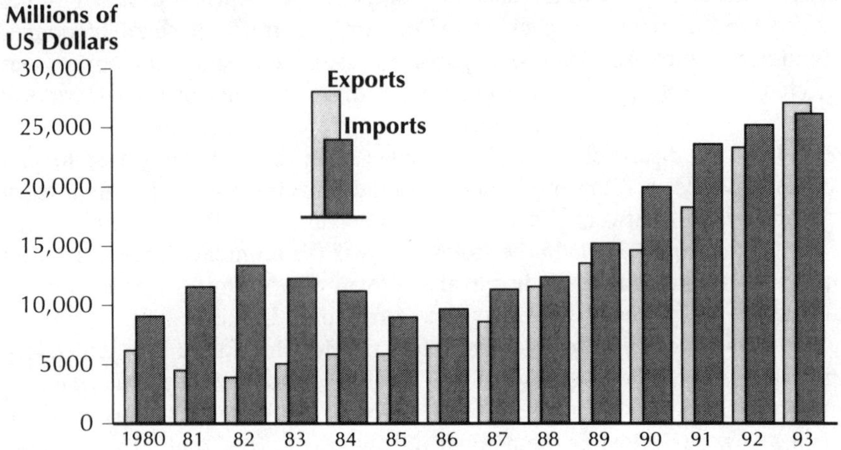

Figure 9.2 Indonesian trade: nonoil and gas exports and imports, 1980-1993

Source: Central Bureau of Statisitics, Foreign Trade Statistics

Such firms may now hold up to a 95 per cent equity share in such ventures as opposed to the previous restriction of 80 per cent. An important spatial impact of the foreign investment requirements relaxation is that 100 per cent foreign owned companies may now locate anywhere in Indonesia, not just in remote areas. This regulation also abolished the minimum paid-up capital requirement which previous to the package was $US50 million. In addition the length of business licenses has been extended from 20 to 30 years, the minimum capital requirement of $US250,000 has been dropped, divestment requirements are now merely token--as little as 1 per cent after 15 years, and operating conditions have been eased so that foreign companies may establish subsidiaries and acquire other foreign and domestic firms (EIU, 1994).

The reaction to this package, however, has been mixed. Some strongly nationalist interests claim it has gone too far and has exposed the country to excessive foreign influence. On the other hand, the proponents of liberalization say that it has provided 'too little, too late'. Moreover it has highlighted the strength of the conservative opposition to the technocratic reformers and some believe that the implementation 'tightness' which has been forced will severely weaken the intent of the legislation (Aziz, 1994). Thus it is still uncertain whether the measures will create the intended surge of investment.

The second reform package of 1994 also aimed to increase the competitiveness of manufacturing by reducing both the high cost of their imported inputs and the high level of protection. Tariffs on 739 items were reduced, surcharges were lifted on a further 108 products, import licensing procedures were simplified for several key products and restrictions on subcontracting firms in bonded areas and export processing zones were lifted. Unlike the first package these measures have received a very favorable response with the only caveat being that the reforms must be gradually deepened. The RI government has in fact restated its intention to continue the liberalization process with regards to the import regime and eventually to harmonize Indonesia's tariff structure with GATT and the proposed and potentially beneficial AFTA (ASEAN Free Trade Agreement) (Vatikiotis, 1993). This commitment must involve more than rhetoric and simply reducing tariffs. It must also include adjustments in the issues of intellectual property rights, trade-related investment measures (TRIMs) and trade in services. Indonesia, like many other developing countries has, however, expressed opposition to the attempt by some developed countries to link trade with environmental and social issues such as human rights.

Trade growth

The Southeast Asian region overall increased its share of world trade from the late 1970s to the early 1990s reflecting the area's growing importance in the international economy. More important for the purposes of this paper, however, is the changing pattern of Indonesia's trade. That foreign trade performance from 1980 through 1993 has been impressive but not without fluctuations (Figure 9.1). The exports component rises to a peak in 1981 and then begins a gradual decline to a low in 1986 reflecting the depressed oil market. Imports peak a year later but also join the decline as lower revenues force a stalling of imported goods. Beginning in 1987 both series reflect an upward trend that has not reversed since that date. Over the period from 1983 to 1993 the growth rate of exports was 57.4 per cent, while the growth of imports was slightly higher, 57.7 per cent (Indonesian Foreign Trade Statistics, 1993). The strong trade growth in the late 1980s clearly reflects the 'outward' orientation of the development strategy and the liberalization environment.

There is, of course, considerable value difference between the oil and gas included trade data and that without this critical revenue source. Unlike the previous series, the pattern of oil and gas excluded trade allows us to focus more directly upon the effect of government policies intended to diversify the economy. These data from 1988 onward reflect a changing emphasis to export goods. It is worth noting that the value of nonoil and gas exports in 1983 was nearly 24 per cent of total exports while in 1993 this proportion had reached 75 per cent (Figure 9.2).

Over the period from 1980 to 1986 Indonesia's average annual export and import growth were 2 and -1 per cent respectively. This performance is quite unimpressive when compared to the East Asian NICs and within ASEAN only the Philippines performed worse (World Bank, 1987). For example, Singapore and Malaysia, Indonesia's nearest trading partners, exhibited much stronger growth over this same period: 6 and 3.6 per cent for the former and 10.2 and 5.2 for the latter. The performances from competitors, along with the danger of relying on oil led revenues prompted further reforms in the trade regime. The impact of these adjustments in the liberalization effort can be seen if we examine the average annual export and import growth percentages over the extended period between 1980 and 1992. Reflecting the

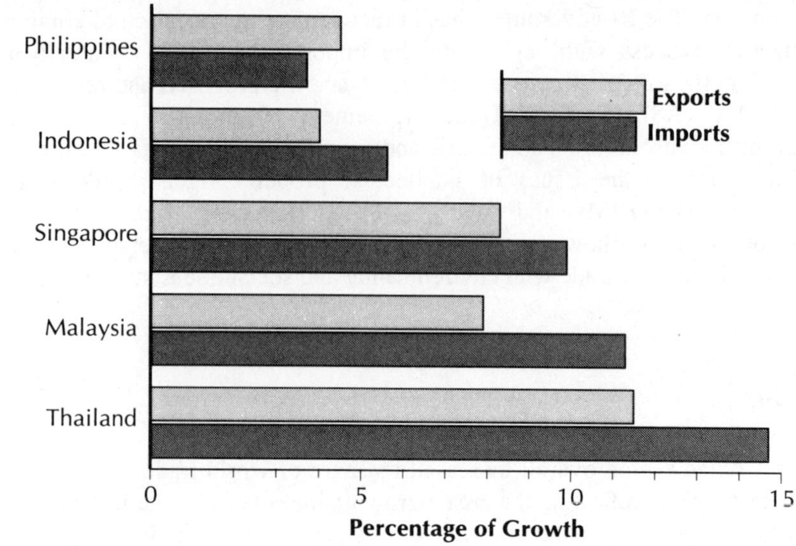

Figure 9.3 ASEAN average annual growth in trade, 1980-1992 (excluding Brunei)

Source: World Bank World Development Reports

new policy thrust Indonesia's performance in export and import growth was 5.6 and 4.0 per cent respectively (World Bank, 1994) (Figure 9.3). In only six years between 1983 and 1990 non-oil exports nearly tripled from $US5 billion to $US14.4 billion. It is important to note, however, that at least for the period 1987-88, the strong growth of non-oil exports is believed to have been impacted more by two major currency devaluations in 1983 and 1986, than the trade deregulation promulgated in May, 1986 (Aziz, 1994; Juoro, 1993). This specific illustration points up the complexity of determining and assigning impact in trade response where multiple tools are being utilized in a restructuring effort (see also Harris,et.al., 1994).

Yet, with the exception of the Philippines, in this 12 year period Indonesia lagged significantly behind the other members of ASEAN (Figure 9.3). Thailand led the group with average annual export growth of 14.7 per cent and import growth of 11.5 per cent (World Bank, 1994). More encouraging is Indonesia's share of exports from the ASEAN economies. For the 1987-1992 period, which reflects the strong growth in non-oil exports, the share of export trade was 18 per cent, only slightly less than Malaysia (21.9 per cent) and greater than that of Thailand (15.8 per cent).

Simultaneously the structural shift in exports can be seen in temporal perspective (Figure 9.4). Although there has been a concerted effort to diversify the economy, the contribution of mineral fuels remains quite important in the export pattern. Yet the growth of manufactured goods and the proportion of exports accounted for by this sector are dramatic especially from 1989 to 1993. This growth overshadows the

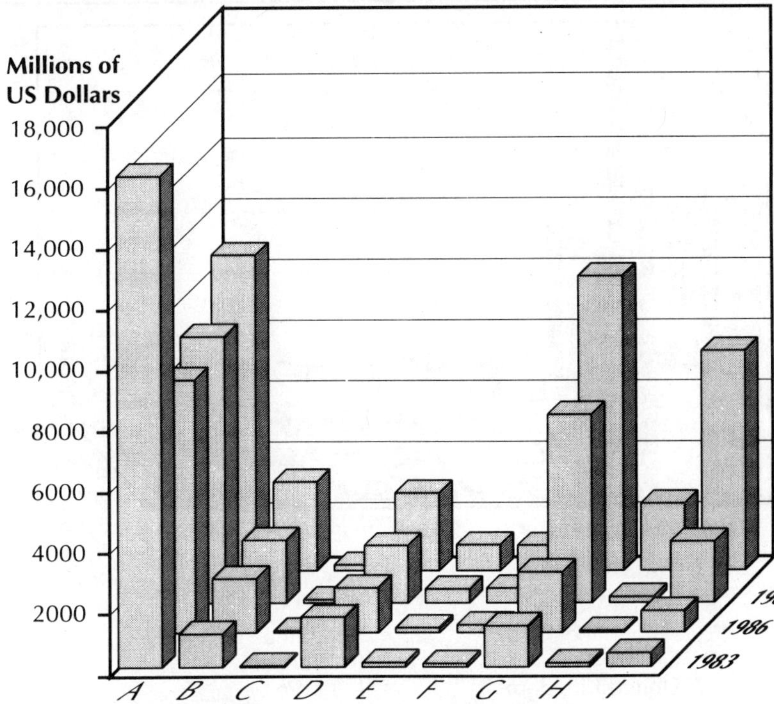

A. Mineral Fuels
B. Food
C. Beverage and Tobacco
D. Crude Materials
E. Vegetable Oils
F. Chemicals
G. Manufactured Goods
H. Machinery and Transportation Equipment
I. Others

Figure 9.4 Indonesian exports by SITC class, 1983-1993

Source: Central Bureau of Statistics, Foreign Trade Statistics

substantial changes in raw materials, vegetable oils, chemicals and machinery-transport equipment which have also benefited from the liberalized trade environment.

While nonoil export growth has been strong through 1992, the 1993 figures, the latest available, show a relative decline. Total exports of $US36.8 billion in 1993 represent an 8.4 per cent increase over 1992. But this was much lower than the 15.7 per cent and 14.3 per cent increases recorded in 1992 and 1991. The decline in the growth of nonoil exports to only 16.2 per cent from 25 per cent was the worst performance since the turnaround in 1987 (McBeth, 1994a). Imports grew only 3.2 per cent in 1992 leaving a trade surplus of $US8.66 billion.

Although a full analysis of this behavior is not yet completed, it appears that a combination of factors are responsible. First it appears that the weakening export

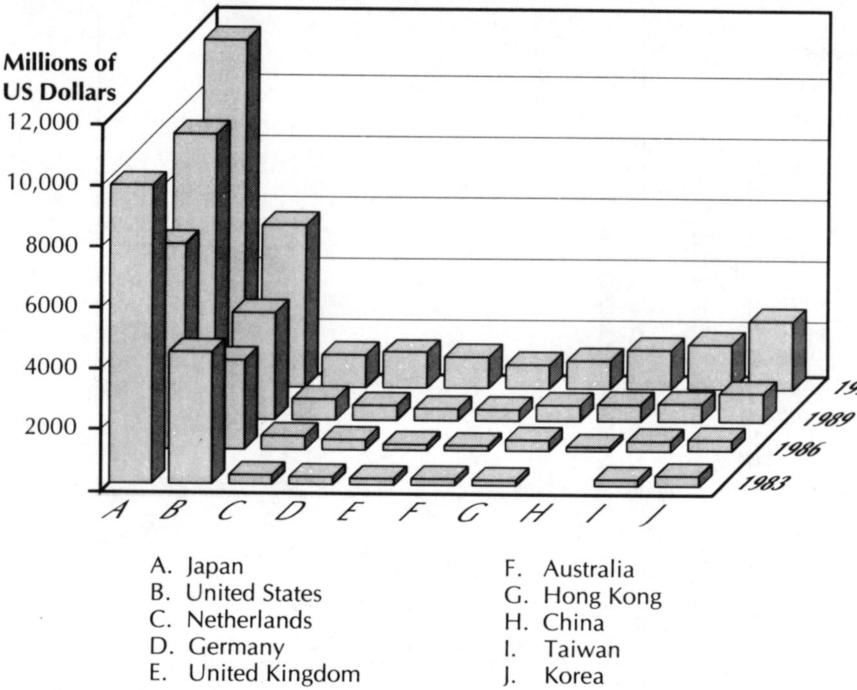

Figure 9.5 Indonesian exports to major partners, 1983-1993

Source: Central Bureau of Statistics, Foreign Trade Statistics

performance is certainly a function of terms of trade effects, with the prices of Indonesia's primary commodities having been particularly weak during the recent period. But another influence lies within the performance of the textile and apparel sectors which the Government hopes will be one of the major strengths in the immediate future in weaning the export base away from oil and gas. Investment in the industry, particularly in capital equipment, has been heavy but the response has also been significant: exports totaled $US6.3 billion in 1993, a figure 43 times that of 1980! While some firms are weathering the competition through use of high quality inputs and product improvements, others are not. Recession in major markets, increased competition from India and China, and alleged dumping by Taiwan and South Korea are responsible (EIU, 1994; Pangestu and Aziz, 1994).

Moreover it appears that internal factors are to blame as well. These include over expansion, inefficient production methods and failure to keep up with changing export market needs. The result is that while textile and garment exports are up by over 20 per cent from 1992, the value growth has been under 2 per cent (McBeth, 1994b).

In addition another possible cause of the weakening of non-oil exports is the decline in export-oriented investments (Pangestu and Aziz, 1994). This aspect will be discussed as we draw together the arguments and data surrounding foreign direct investment and how these link into the trade regime.

Given this weakening export performance the government has given new emphasis to export promotion efforts. One attempt is the decision to emphasize new markets in Southern Africa, Central Asia, and Eastern Europe. Nonetheless the fact remains that the weakening of textile imports undercuts the recent improvement in agricultural commodities, strengthening oil prices, as well as the recovery in overseas markets. Of some consequence also, since it is a major market, is the action taken by US negotiators in rejecting an Indonesian request for higher quotas in the American market. The explanation provided was that Indonesian exporters had circumvented the bilateral textile agreement between the two countries and further that any increase in quotas must be linked to easier access for US exports to the Indonesian market (EIU, 1994).

Trade flows

The data on trade flows over time with extraregional as well as regional partners is also an important source of information which contributes to our discussion of liberalized trade regimes and especially an increasingly outward oriented development posture. If trade destinations are viewed within a temporal perspective some interesting trends may be isolated which reflect the changing international division of labor. Over the past decade Japan and the US have been the most significant trading partners. As the graph depicts, Indonesia's exports to Japan are clearly dominant in comparison with the US (Figure 9.5). But of some significance is the fact that much of the export trade with Japan is in raw materials. For example, in 1993 54 per cent of the export traffic was attributable to oil and another 16 per cent to plywood. The continuing substantial trade surplus in Indonesia's favor ($US4.9 billion in 1993) has been of little consequence to date. This is especially so given Japan's need for raw materials from Indonesia and also her interest in maintaining a presence and strengthening markets in the ASEAN region. There is evidence, however, that Japan continues to explore new markets for both oil and wood products in an effort to seek diversity in suppliers. Over the period from 1986-1993 the average annual increase in imports was 14 per cent while that of exports only 9.7 per cent revealing some movement to counter the trade imbalance (Figure 9.6). While much lower in value, the US trade with Indonesia has been growing at a faster rate when compared with Japan: 11.4 per cent for exports and 17 per cent for imports over the same period as above. Of note too is the fact that in 1993 only 11 per cent of the exports to the US by value are oil related. The remaining 88 per cent of value is dominated by footwear, natural rubber, plywood and clothing. This trade is clearly related to the 'export platform' investment from the US which is discussed below.

Trade with individual countries in the European Community is, as expected, much lower in value but annual growth rates are higher when compared with the two major industrial partners (Figure 9.6). Both Germany and the United Kingdom have shown strong export growth over the period in part because change is measured from a lower base. The recent export trade for both countries, notably in the 1991-93 period, occurs in part as a result of a high demand for footwear. Textiles to Australia accounted for a major part of growth for that nation. Trade with the East Asian NICs has also grown dramatically over the seven year period as is evidenced by the figures for Hong Kong but, especially Taiwan and South Korea. The latter partner is especially conspicuous over the period where, at least recently, the bulk of the traffic is accounted for by both oil and plywood. Critical too is the dramatic expansion of trade with China as a result of the establishment of diplomatic ties.

Within the ASEAN region, Singapore's annual growth in exports, 25 per cent annually, is overshadowed by exports to Malaysia (88 per cent annually) and Thailand (66 per cent annually). The lower growth in part is reflected in the decrease in Indonesian exports of textiles to Singapore by over 13 per cent ($US285 million) in 1993 compared with the 1992 figure.

The interpretation of export trade between Indonesia and the ASEAN nations changes, however, if aggregate value is the measure (Figure 9.7). Clearly the most conspicuous partner is Singapore yet it must be borne in mind that much of the export traffic to the city-state is in fact reshipped onwards to other destinations and reflects her enduring role as an entrepot. The recent growth in the trade with Malaysia and Singapore indicates, in part, emerging cooperative development in the Growth Triangle or SIJORI, an area comprising Riau province of Indonesia, Johor state in Malaysia and Singapore (Lee, 1991; Toh and Low, 1993). Especially noteworthy in this respect is the development of Batam Island, part of Riau province and a free trade zone just off Singapore. Finally Indonesia's strengthening trade with Thailand and the Philippines is quite encouraging and provide some signs of progress toward Indonesia's participation in the creation of an integrated ASEAN market. In the past year the export value to ASEAN increased by about 9 per cent or $US385 million (Indonesian Foreign Trade, 1993).

These growth patterns reflect in one sense a regional effect of transactions in the global economy where Indonesia maintains a critical comparative advantage in certain raw materials. But in addition the data depicts external perception of the country as a base for global sourcing with a critical factor of production, labor. The dramatic expansion of trade over the past seven years at the same time mirrors a strongly reoriented development posture in which liberalization efforts have had considerable impact. We turn now to the foreign investment component of the development strategy and how it links into trade.

Foreign investment in Indonesia

Trade policy is an important instrument within the broader industrial strategy. But so too are policies with respect to foreign direct investment (FDI). While the trade regime is obviously one factor which influences foreign investment behavior, investment incentives, the degree and form of industrial regulation as well as licensing procedures and restrictions are important as well. Between 1986 and 1990 the government carried out a number of important reform efforts which had the intent of stimulating the inward flow of FDI. These included replacing a complex investment licensing list with one which was much shorter and simpler, simplifying investment approval procedures, providing incentives in the form of duty free imports and tax concessions for all new investments, and encouraging FDI by providing the same incentives as those given to domestic investors (World Bank, 1993).

The Investment Coordinating Board (BKPM) approves all private sector investment proposals which seek investment incentives (usually duty free imports of machinery and equipment for the first two years of production). These investments constitute about 75 per cent of all private sector investment. The actual imports of machinery and equipment provide reasonable estimates of the trend in realized investments. While there is some variation from year to year it is not unreasonable to assume 40 to 50 per cent as an estimate of the proportion of realized to total approved foreign investment.

It is fair to say that FDI has played an important role in the revival of private sector investment in general since 1986. The accompanying data in graphic form presents several perspectives on the approved foreign investment over the period from 1983 to 1993. First, the aggregate pattern of approved investments generally reflects the impact of a gradually liberalized environment and increasing incentives to investors (Figure 9.8). As a result of an active foreign exchange policy (the devaluation in

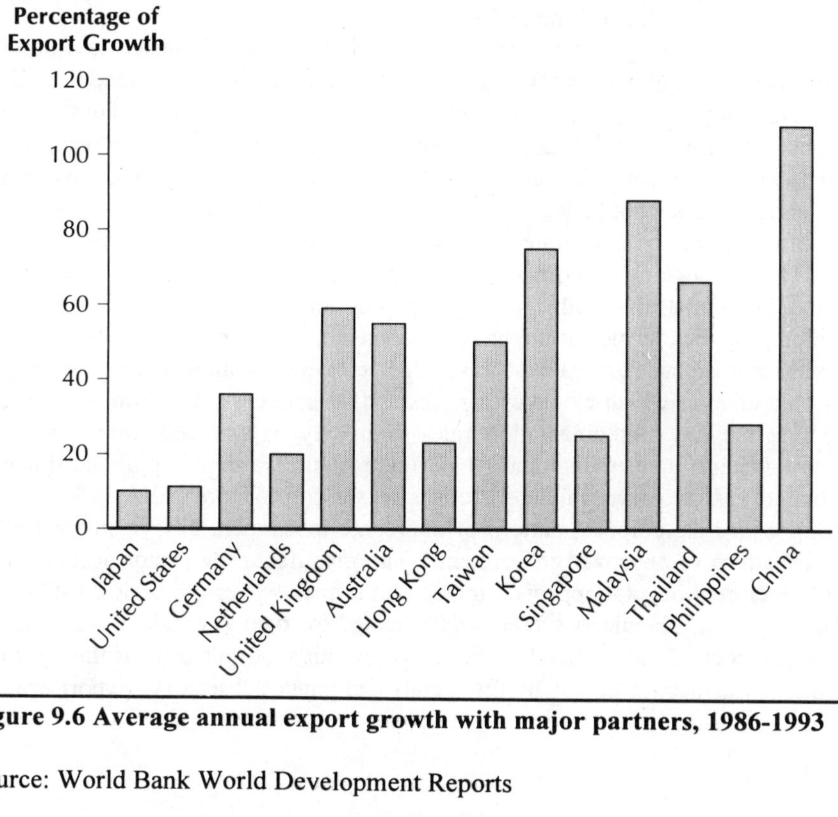

Figure 9.6 Average annual export growth with major partners, 1986-1993

Source: World Bank World Development Reports

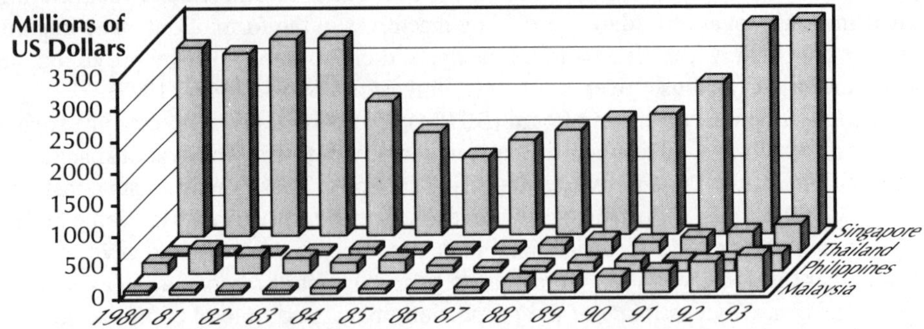

Figure 9.7 Indonesian exports to ASEAN nations, 1980-1993

Source: Central Bureau of Statistics, Foreign Trade Statistics

1986 and the increased flexibility of the exchange rate) (Juoro, 1993) and investment deregulation measures there occurred a boom in private sector investment approvals between 1987 and 1992 which totaled $US45 billion, including over $US16.5 billion in joint ventures with foreign investors. Of this about 45 per cent or $US20 billion had actually been realized through 1992.

After a disappointing year in 1993 in which the Japanese invested less heavily, foreign investment approvals through the first 10 months of 1994 exceeded $US23 billion. This surge of investment appears to be the result of an accumulating interest in Indonesia as liberalization has progressed but perhaps most directly a result of the PP/20 1994 package, which was discussed earlier. This latest surge of investment almost certainly does not reflect a more recent reform package of September, 1994 which lowered the top corporate tax rate to 30 per cent and allows firms to deduct research and technology spending from their taxable income. The corporate tax rate is now quite competitive with rates in Singapore and Thailand. However, the pro-regulation group and critics of the government's actions raise the point that much of the investment is concentrated in several large petroleum, mining and power projects rather than in areas which would create jobs and stimulate exports. Moreover critics argue that the low implementation rates with only 51 per cent of the value of approved foreign investments and 37 per cent of the value of approved domestic investments realized since the late 1960s is reason for concern (EIU, 1994).

Along with this temporal pattern of aggregate investment also of interest is the sectoral pattern of approved investment. The manufacturing sector accounted for about 70 per cent of total approved foreign investments over the period 1987-1993.

The textiles and chemicals subsectors accounted for over one-half of the approved and 48 per cent of the realized investments. Another 30 per cent of the approved investment was accounted for by the metals and paper subsectors. Export oriented

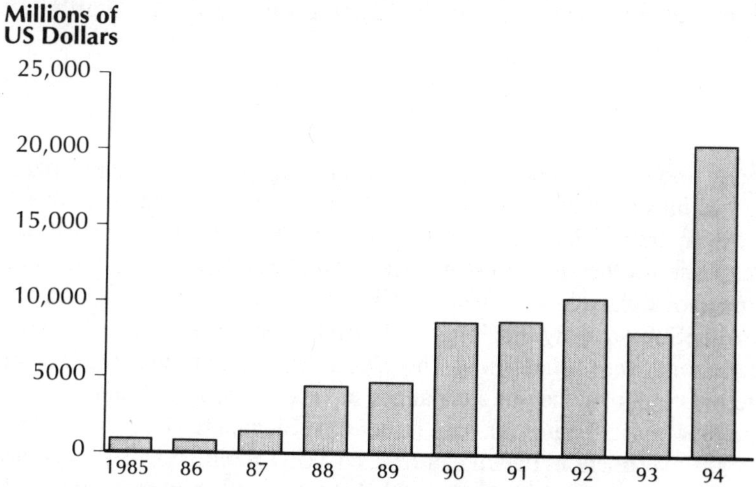

Figure 9.8 Indonesian approved foreign investment, 1985-1994

Source: Indonesian Investment Coordinating Board

industries attracted an increasing share of realized investments until 1990 when their share reached 62 per cent of total realized investment. But with the slowdown in investment since 1990, the share of these industries has declined to 38 per cent in 1992. In this decline, the textiles sector suffered most with its share declining from 40 per cent to 20 per cent (World Bank, 1993).

Finally, and especially given Indonesia's 'balanced development' goals, the spatial distribution of the approved foreign investment must be examined (Figure 9.9). The graphic pattern clearly shows that the bulk of the investment approvals are, not surprisingly, located in Java and especially West Java and the Jabotabek (Greater Jakarta) metro area since this is where the manufacturing sector remains heavily concentrated. Java's share in non-oil manufacturing value added approached 80 per cent in the early 1990s. While Sumatra and Kalimantan have several large resource based industries (fertilizer in South Sumatra, aluminum and rubber processing in North Sumatra, and fertilizer and plywood in East and West Kalimantan), the other provinces of the Outer Islands could be labeled non-industrial. The only trend that seems contrary to this continuing emphasis is the relocation of pulp and paper mills closer to the source of raw materials which are in Kalimantan. Thus the spatial pattern of industrialization reflects relative regional factor endowments. The discussion of factors involved in and strategies required to encourage relocation are beyond the topic of the current paper. But clearly efficient and low cost transport services are critical as are the enforcement of environmental laws (World Bank, 1993).

One further point needs to be made in regards to the location of investment and which at the same time points up a conspicuous exception to the lack of industrialization in the Outer Islands. Within the past six years Batam Island has received considerable attention as an investment destination and thus is worthy of a brief digression.

Batam

The island, about 30 minutes by ferry from Singapore, is actually part of Riau Province and thus is an integral part of the Growth Triangle encompassing Malaysia (Johor), Singapore and Indonesia (Riau). As early as 1970 Batam was designated as a logistical base for the oil and gas industry. Over the course of the following decade development took place in increments. This occurred first by focussing on the island's entrepot role. Subsequently the Batam Industrial Development Authority (BIDA) and a duty free zone were established. The area's development was actually stimulated on its present course by the policy changes in accounting and shipping which forced oil contractors to use Batam as a base rather than Singapore (Pangestu, 1991). By the end of 1990, investment in Batam had reached $US2.8 billion with private investment accounting for nearly 80 per cent of the total and the government the remainder. Only 31 per cent of the private investment is in the approved foreign category. The other investment is both approved domestic and domestic investment which does not require approval. The growth of investment has been more rapid here because of the lower

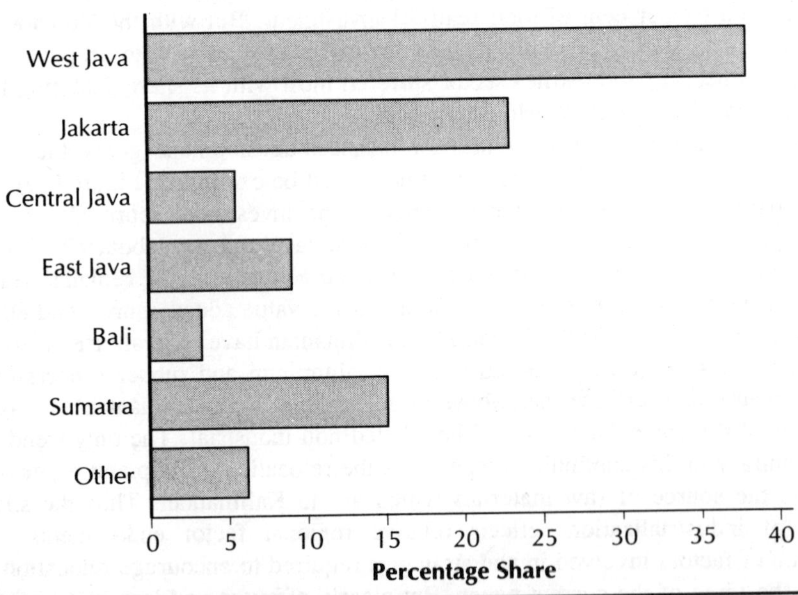

Figure 9.9 Average percentage share of approved foreign investment by location, 1985-1993

Source: Indonesian Investment Coordinating Board

base as well as policy changes which have made the investment extremely attractive, the most important of which was the allowance of 100 per cent foreign ownership. Five per cent of the investment must be divested within five years but if 100 per cent of the products are exported, no further divestment is required. Favored industries are those oriented to export using skilled labor, low water consumption, medium and high technology and are non-polluting. The decision to allow private companies to set up industrial estates produced a very strong response since this overcame the potential problem of the lack of or delays in government provided infrastructure.

While most of the investment in Batam prior to 1988 was oil-related, the present pattern reveals a shift to real estate, tourism, electronics and food. Many of these investments were undertaken with the Singapore market in mind. The city-state is clearly the major investor in the island as part of its 'second-wing' policy of involvement in trans-border projects to gain 'economic space' in order to overcome their lack of land resources. It is not clear however whether these investments are made by Singapore firms or multi-national corporations based in Singapore. The US is the second most important investor.

Investing nations

Over the period 1967-1990 approved Japanese investment totaled $US9.6 billion and represented one quarter of all investment. The next largest source was Hong Kong ($US3.7 billion) followed by Taiwan ($US2.3 billion) and the US ($US2.2 billion). It must be noted, however, that these figures from the Indonesian Investment Coordinating Board (BKPM) do not include investments in oil, gas banking, and insurance. If these sectors were included it is likely that the US investment would match that of the Japanese (Schwarz and Vatikiotis, 1991). Nonetheless, the distinction between the investment patterns between the two countries is evident from the graph depicting the trend over the last eight years (Figure 9.10).

If we broaden the view of the investment trend over this period, however, it is clear that a diversity of investors have sought out Indonesia including those within the European Community and the East Asian NICs (Figure 9.11). This appears in the trade flow data above and in large part reflects the role of these countries in Indonesia's export drive into labor intensive activities. Thus the export performance is clearly linked to foreign direct investment.

The case of US investment and potential alternative destinations is useful for illustrative purposes. Two major reasons prompt the flow from NAFTA and especially the US into Indonesia. First some FDI is combined with local resources to supply goods and services that are produced in, and exported from, Indonesia. This 'export platform' investment is obviously critical for Indonesia (as well as other ASEAN nations) in order to stimulate export led growth especially where it generates significant employment. But if trade diversion as a result of NAFTA diverts the source of imports to Mexico from ASEAN and Indonesia in particular, FDI would also likely be diverted. Thus FDI diversion would accompany trade diversion posing a threat to export led growth.

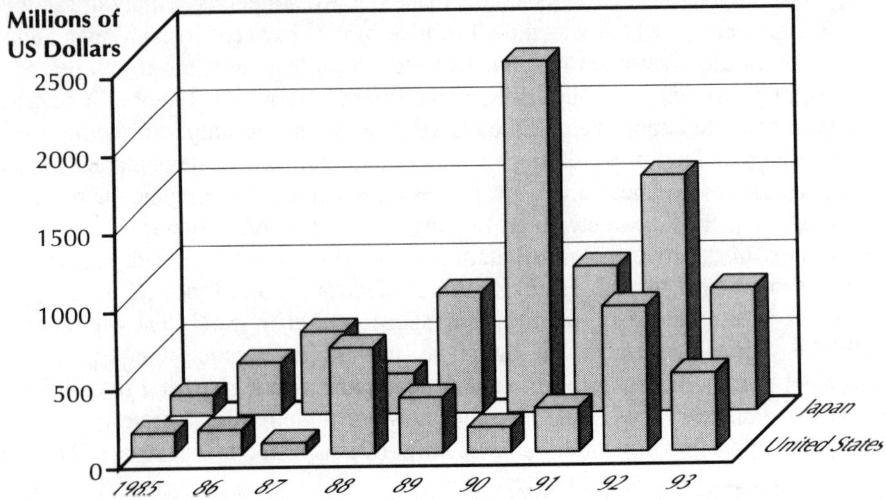

Figure 9.10 Approved foreign investment: United States and Japan, 1985-1993

Source: Indonesian Investment Coordinating Board

In addition US investment into Indonesia is prompted by an interest in combining investments with local resources in order to produce products and services destined for ASEAN and other East Asian markets. One implication of AFTA is that if trade is created through this mechanism, FDI flows would likely follow in search of opportunities.

Overall, the positive responses from foreign investors can be attributed to both push and pull forces. The deregulation of investment activities, duty drawback efforts, customs reforms, and low wage labor account for several of the more important pull forces. On the other hand, high wages in the NICs (including Singapore) and the lack of alternative destinations in the 1980s period were push forces.

Although the investment climate in Indonesia has been gradually improving, approved foreign investments declined from $US10.3 billion in 1992 to $US8.1 billion in 1993 (see Figure 9.8). This decline in approvals (and realized investment) may be another possible cause of the decline in non-oil exports. It must be noted, however, that the figure for 1992 is misleading since it includes two very large projects: the expansion of Freeport Indonesia's mining operations in Irian Jaya and the Candra Asri olefins plant (Pangestu and Aziz, 1994). The slowdown in investment interest, which is reflected also in the decline in imports of capital goods, is caused by several factors. First, Japanese investment approvals declined from $US1,511 million in 1992 to $US836 million in 1993. This decreased investment represents a decline of 45 per cent from the major investor (Indonesian Financial Statistics, 1994). Moreover the decline also calls attention to the ongoing process of competition for a limited pool of funds not only within the region but outside as well.

The globalization of economic relations and the competition among nations and firms have obviously made international trade and investment more competitive. This pattern will certainly intensify through the 1990s. The most significant evidence of the competition lies in the emergence and choice of China as a base point for global sourcing by an increasing number of nations. Foreign direct investment into China increased from $US3.5 billion in 1990 to $US11 billion in 1992. China has now overtaken Indonesia as the major destination of both South Korean and Japanese overseas manufacturing investment (World Bank, 1993). In order to maintain its share of FDI Indonesia will need to diversify its narrow export base into other labor intensive exports and move into higher value added products within the current production set by dedicating technology and other support infrastructure at both labor and resource intensive industries. Despite this pessimistic tone, Indonesia has apparently succeeded in attracting a record of foreign investment commitments in the current year thus reversing the trend. Through October, 1994 the government had approved 336 foreign investment projects with a total value of over $US23 billion. Even at the rate of 50 per cent realization, the resulting investment seems to indicate that the recent deregulation package is having some immediate impact.

Criticisms of trade reform

One final task remains in our broad discussion of trade issues and policies and that is the matter of current criticisms and future requirements. We know that trade policies may alter resource allocation by changing the returns in various sectors of the economy. This was illustrated above in respect to export restrictions in the forestry sector. Distortions brought about by trade policies may also be measured by effective rates of protection. Despite the real progress in liberalizing the trade regime, policies continue to be biased against exports. Essentially the prices of imports are raised relative to exports and thus act to shield high cost domestic industries from competition. If free trade were in effect there would not be a misallocation of resources to less efficient import competing activities. The food and beverage sector is one area where rates of protection are quite high. For example NTBs currently allow three state-owned trading companies sole import rights for over 450 food and beverage products (World Bank, 1993). These effective rates of protection must be reduced in order to create greater efficiencies and stronger exports.

It is critical that international trade restrictions be lowered in concert with domestic trade restrictions (World Bank, 1993, p. 71). One way in which this has occurred in Indonesia is in the deregulation of interisland shipping. But in fact this deregulation in the domestic environment has not been powerful enough to restrain domestic trade restrictions. Local level restrictions continue to hinder intraregional trade and efficient market growth. These restrictions are particularly critical in Indonesia where national policy is dedicated ostensibly to the improvement of spatial equity. The restrictions on domestic trade may have in some instances the effect of penalizing more distant producers, especially in eastern Indonesia which the government has declared a priority region in the development effort. Examples of these domestic trade restrictions include the clove trade which is monopolized by a sole marketing agency, a provincial tax in Kalimantan on processed rubber and inter-island shipping levies and institutional restrictions on vanilla producers in Bali (World Bank, 1993). While these restrictions seem to apply to only select commodities they have the effect of disrupting a basic principle: to develop a more integrated national economy.

Still another illustration of further need for reform lies in the Indonesian footwear industry. In this case there has developed significant export capacity in several specific footwear products, e.g. men's leather sports shoes. But despite the collapse of imports since the 1986 devaluation, tariff protection remains high. Hide export bans and export tariffs have effectively reduced the price of leather inputs to domestic producers by as much as 50 per cent in the late 1980s (Chapman, 1992). The result is that numerous large Indonesian firms are exporting successfully but enjoy substantial tariff protection in the home market. Most problematic is the fact that the export activities have not filtered back to smaller firms who subcontract to them in supplying thc local market. The lack of quality competitiveness constrains small producers from competing in the export market. In addition, it appears that the protection on hides is serving both Korean and Taiwanese firms that are selling into the domestic market. Further data shows that despite a doubling of domestic leather production between 1985 and 1988 there has been a declining contribution of Indonesian leather to footwear exports (Chapman, 1992). Still the bottom line effect

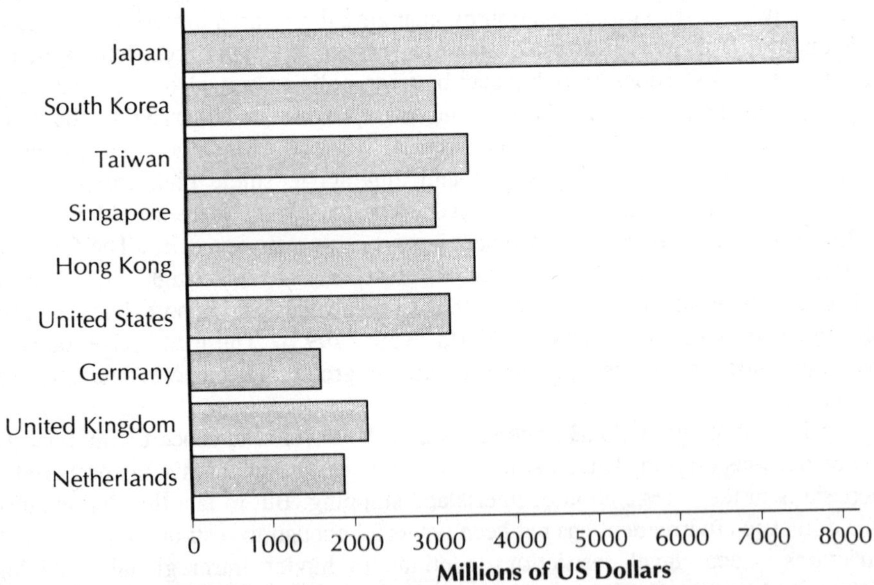

Figure 9.11 Approved foreign investment by major investor, 1985-1993

Source: Indonesian Investment Coordinating Board

of the continuing high footwear tariffs, bans and taxes on hide exports is to aid the development of a dichotomous industry in which the traditional domestic sector is in danger of stagnation. This is clearly another example of evidence which points to the need for continuing removal of protection.

Summary and conclusions

By the late 1980s Indonesia had begun to effectively address deficiencies in trade policy as a way of stimulating nonoil export development. In addition to the reduction in tariff levels and removal of import licenses, several other related measures proved effective. Especially important were the assignment of certifying customs procedures to the private sector and the deregulation of inter-island shipping. Since that time a series of nearly annual packages have served to further stimulate export development through modification of the trade regime. It is important, however especially in the Indonesian case, to view trade reform, not in isolation but, as part of a broader industrial policy and restructuring effort. Whether in the Indonesian case we are dealing with positive or defensive restructuring is not particularly germane here. There are numerous objectives that industrial policy may pursue. In Indonesia clearly a major goal has been to stimulate non-oil exports in order to further wean the economy from a dependence on oil and gas. But embedded within this industrial policy are also the objectives of employment creation, the development of 'strategic' industries irrespective of economic efficiency considerations as well as a more equitable regional development with emphasis currently on eastern Indonesia.

In addition, it is important to recognize the role not only of trade policies in the restructuring effort but also the way in which such policies mesh (or the converse) with financial sector policies, the tax structure, foreign direct investment and related policies as well as infrastructure upgrading. Our discussion above has summarized the progress in trade from the perspectives of aggregate growth, changing structure and continuing and emerging partners. Closely related to trade, of course, is foreign investment, which has grown dramatically under the liberalization effort. A continuing worry, in light of the balanced spatial objective in the industrial policy, is the strong concentration of such investment in the Jakarta metro area but more broadly the provinces of Java. The latest data on foreign investment approvals indicates that the country in 1994 will have experienced a banner year. However the euphoria associated with this outcome must be dampened by the recognition that Indonesia is facing an intense struggle in the competition for limited investment being allocated the region by the East Asian NICs, Japan and the US. Both China especially, and Vietnam as well as several economies in eastern Europe are attractive alternative destinations. The response to this competitive pressure must be a further deepening of trade reforms but especially additional tariff reductions and removal of protection in select sectors. The removal of bureaucratic obstacles, improved infrastructure and additional tax incentives will lead foreign investors to consider Indonesian destinations. But even substantial FDI flows are neither sufficient nor a necessary condition for rapid and successful industrialization. FDI is more likely to foster domestic development, including employment creation, where it is used in an outward oriented incentive system, such as that of Singapore, rather than where it aims to benefit from high input services such as in Indonesia (Bhattacharya and Linn, 1988). While the further manipulation of the trade regime will serve additional export expansion in the near future, Indonesia must increasingly look to and plan for a move into more diversified and higher value added production with an emphasis on technology in its long term development.

10 The location of foreign banks in Australia

April Wright and Peter Liesch

Banks from many countries have chosen to locate across national borders in the past several decades. This phenomenon is known as multinational banking. A multinational bank is an international financial intermediary which owns and controls branches and affiliates in more than one country (Jones, 1990). Developing an understanding of the location choice decision of multinational banks has gained increasing importance as banks continue to expand internationally and as they access new markets. Indeed, regulators, bank managers and academicians are interested in this line of enquiry because the activities of multinational banks affect domestic monetary policy and economic activity generally in both the home and host countries.

The increasing globalization of the world's money and capital markets has prompted some host countries, that previously imposed restrictions on foreign bank entry, to deregulate. This was the case for the Australian market. Sixteen new foreign banks began operating in the Australian financial market in 1985-86 following the removal of a long-standing government prohibition on foreign bank entry. Two foreign banks were already established in Australia at this time, having entered in the late nineteenth century. In this chapter, an analysis of the factors that motivated the decision by these foreign banks to locate in Australia is undertaken.

History of foreign banks in Australia

The history of multinational banks in Australia has been chequered. Colonial ties with Britain facilitated the entry of the first foreign banks into Australia in the 1830s (Butlin, 1953). By 1851, three British banks held two-thirds of the total bank assets in Australia, prompting the Australian banks to expand in response (Merrett, 1990). Foreign bank market share fell to approximately 30 per cent of total bank assets from a total of 43 banks operating in Australia in 1888 (*A Pocketful of Change*, 1991). However, bank failures in the 1890s, the Great Depression and wartime mergers caused a contraction in both British and domestic bank numbers in Australia.

A second group of foreign banks entered Australia during this period. The Bank of New Zealand arrived in 1872, France's Comptoir d'Escompte de Paris in 1880, Japan's Yokohama Specie Bank in 1915 and the Bank of China in 1942 (Merrett, 1990). Unlike the British banks, these government-owned banks did not have retail deposit bases. They provided financing exclusively for international trade between their home countries and Australia.

A significant barrier to foreign bank entry arose in 1945 when the Australian government began its subsequent long standing policy of refusing to grant banking licences to foreign banks (Campbell Report, 1981). Specific legislation for bank licensing was introduced in the original Banking Act, 1945. This was later revised in 1959 when the Reserve Bank of Australia, Australia's central bank, was established. The Banking Act restricts the use of the title 'bank' as a registered business name to institutions authorised under the Act. The exceptions are state banks, as state powers under S51(xiii) of the Commonwealth Constitution allow these banks to operate in all banking areas without being subject to the Banking Act. Authorisation as a bank allows the organisation to conduct general banking business. This conduct includes the borrowing and lending of money, accessing the domestic and international payments system and the provision of depositor protection with the Reserve Bank.

Both domestic and foreign groups are eligible for banking authorities as the Act does not distinguish between the two groups. Under Part II, Division 1 of the Banking Act 1959, written applications for a banking authority are made by body corporates to the Treasurer and granted by the Governor General. However, since 1945, the Commonwealth government has refused to grant licences to foreign banks (Martin Report, 1984). This policy was evidenced in 1963 when the government rejected a proposal by the London-based Chartered Bank to take over a local bank (Merrett, 1990). Nonresidents were further restricted, under the Banks (Shareholdings) Act, to holding less than 10 per cent of a bank's voting shares.

As a result, the only licensed foreign banks operating in Australia from 1972 were the Bank of New Zealand and Banque Nationale de Paris (previously named the Comptoir National D'Escompte de Paris). These banks were licensed as branches prior to the 1945 Banking Act. All other foreign banks had ceased operations. The retail activities of the remaining two foreign banks were restricted and government approval was required to open new branches.

During this period, the early 1970s, multinational corporations from America, Japan and Europe began investing directly in the Australian manufacturing, mining and energy industries (Merrett, 1990). Foreign banks were motivated to retain their relationships with these corporate clients by locating in Australia. To circumvent the embargo on foreign bank licensing, foreign banks entered Australia via correspondent relationships with Australian banks, representative offices and equity investments in Australian nonbank financial intermediaries (Campbell Report, 1981). These investments were made primarily in merchant banks, finance companies and general insurance companies. No restrictions existed on foreign ownership of Australian nonbank financial institutions until 1973, when proposals for new or increased nonresident investment were required to demonstrate economic benefit or involve Australian partnerships (Campbell Report, 1981).

Foreign bank entry attracted consideration on the political agenda in Australia in the 1980s. The Liberal government initiated the process in January 1979 with the establishment of the Campbell Committee to enquire into the Australian financial system (Pauly, 1987). The Committee's 1981 report recommended the removal of the embargo on foreign bank entry. In addition, compulsory resident equity participation requirements were not recommended.

The Campbell Report heightened market expectations of foreign bank entry and foreign groups subsequently expressed interest in obtaining bank licences (Martin Report, 1984). As a defence against the possibility of increased foreign competition in Australian banking, several Australian banks merged in the early 1980s. This led to four major trading banks dominating the Australian market. These banks were the Australian and New Zealand Banking Group Limited (ANZ), Westpac Banking Corporation, National Australia Bank (NAB) and the Commonwealth Banking Corporation.

The Australian Liberal government accepted the Campbell Committee's recommendations and, on January 13, 1983, announced a decision to allow the entry of ten foreign banks into Australia (Martin Report, 1984). However, prior to the extended June submission date for foreign bank applications, the Australian Labor Party was elected and replaced the Liberal government (Pauly, 1987). The Labor government refused to implement the previous government's policy on foreign bank entry and, in May 1983, commissioned a second review of the Australian financial system. The Martin Review Report was presented to Parliament on December 21, 1983 and, as did the Campbell Report, favoured foreign bank entry. The Martin Report recommended the granting of four, five or six foreign bank licences with foreign interests holding a maximum equity share of 50 per cent.

Following the release of the Martin Report, the Australian Labor government moved swiftly to facilitate foreign bank entry. A broad policy to accept foreign bank entry was determined by Caucus and was supported by the Australian Labor Party National Conference in the first half of 1984 (Hywood, 1984). A new era in Australian banking emerged on September 10, 1984, when the Treasurer announced the government's decision to accept licence applications from foreign banks.

Appropriate selection criteria were established. The foreign banks were to be locally incorporated subsidiaries, they were to maximise Australian equity participation or provide significant benefit to the Australian community, and to have minimum paid up capital of AUD 25 million. Foreign banks would be expected to operate within Australian prudential regulations and to provide a wide range of banking services. Additional considerations related to the nature and geographic spread of the bank's operations, and the extent of the commercial and economic relationship between the bank's home country and Australia. Finally, reciprocity for Australian banks abroad, and the foreign entrants' potential to contribute to Australian employment and industry development were also important.

The government, in 1984, announced amendments to the Banks (Shareholdings) Act which increased the threshold limit on individual or associated group shareholdings from 10 per cent to 15 per cent. However, exemptions to the 15 per cent threshold were permitted. This allowed the Federal Treasurer to approve exemptions needed to facilitate the entry of new foreign banks which could meet high prudential standards. The government also offered a branch licence to the Bank of China, because of trade considerations and the lapsing of its licence in 1972 (Hywood, 1984). Finally, the government also announced its decision to grant a 12 month moratorium on the application of foreign investment rules governing merchant banks to enable existing merchant banks to restructure their shareholdings and to permit new foreign entrants. The expectation of the banking sector at the time was that six to ten banking licences would be granted (Korporaal, 1984). Initial expressions of interest came from over 80 foreign banks. However, at the close of applications at the end of November, 1984, 42 licence applications were received from banks domiciled in 19 countries (Tingle, 1984). As the majority of applications met the government's requirements, the Treasurer campaigned to substantially increase the number of licences that were to be granted. The government finally decided on February 27, 1985, to allow the entry of sixteen foreign banks, with only eight of these incorporating Australian equity (Hywood, 1985).

The foreign banks that received licences to operate as legally incorporated subsidiaries of their parent group are presented in Table 10.1.

Fifteen of the approved foreign banks began operations in Australia during 1985 and 1986. Only J.P. Morgan and Co. had failed to take up its banking licence. Hence, after the removal of restrictions on foreign bank entry, as at the end of 1986, there were fifteen foreign banks operating as subsidiaries in Australia and three foreign banks operating as branches. These three were the Bank of New Zealand, the Banque Nationale de Paris, and the Bank of China.

Explanations of multinational bank location choice

The literature on domestic banking is well-developed (Santomero, 1984), with the multinational banking literature growing in the last decade as the overseas expansion of banks intensifies. Aliber (1984) identified two fundamental themes in the multinational banking literature. The industrial organisation theme explores the growth of foreign banks in terms of their advantage over local competitors, while in the international finance literature the impact of banking on cross-border and cross-currency flows is examined (Aliber, 1984). Goodman (1984, p. 681) further distills the industrial organisation theme into questions of '...locational and national cost advantages'. The literature reviewed in this section will address Goodman's locational question of, 'Why do banks of a given nationality locate themselves in a particular country?' (Goodman, 1984, p. 681).

As banks are firms, an appropriate point of entry to this question is the theories that have been developed to explain the multinationalisation of other firms. Multinational manufacturing firms have been well-researched and some authors have argued that the motives for foreign direct investment by manufacturing firms also explain banks' motives for investment abroad (Rugman, 1981; Casson, 1990). To this end, these authors apply the economic theories that have evolved to explain multinational enterprises generally to banks. Several authors have found that Dunning's eclectic

Table 10.1
Foreign banks in Australia

Name	Home country	Opening date	Structure	Assets 1986 $000	Capital Dec.1986 $000
Citibank	US	11/12/85	Sub.	4296449	321095
Bank of America	US	April 86	Sub.	665071	61410
Chase AMP	US	26/09/85	Sub.	2178362	191565
J.P. Morgan	US	No Entry	Sub.	-	-
Bankers Trust	US	25/02/86	Sub.	1546876	107029
Royal Bank	CANADA	26/02/86	Sub.	1932855	138448
Barclays	UK	19/11/85	Sub.	1833248	123147
Nat West	UK	06/02/86	Sub.	2418813	151368
Standard Chartered	UK	11/04/86	Sub.	1504596	136322
Bank of Tokyo	JAPAN	28/11/85	Sub.	515407	52155
Industrial Bank of Japan	JAPAN	18/12/85	Sub.	407488	158168
Mitsubishi	JAPAN	17/01/86	Sub.	345431	30233
Deutsche Bank	GERMANY	03/02/86	Sub.	324253	50003
Hong Kong Bank	HONG KONG	06/02/86	Sub.	1642190	154378
Lloyds	NEW ZEALAND	10/10/85	Sub.	1197381	83212
Bank of Singapore	SINGAPORE	April 86	Sub.	134392	48412
Bank of China	CHINA	16/12/85	Branch	84952	79278
Bank of New Zealand	NEW ZEALAND	1872	Branch	1413293	424924
Banque Nationale de Paris	FRANCE	1880	Branch	1173748	96657

Source: Batten, 1993 and KPMG Survey 1987.

paradigm (1980, 1988) is useful in explaining why banks choose to locate in foreign countries (Gray and Gray, 1981; Yannopoulos, 1983; Cho, 1986). The eclectic paradigm of international production postulates that a firm entering foreign markets must have a unique competitive advantage over host country rivals (ownership advantage); that this advantage is most efficiently exploited in foreign markets within the firm rather than via arm's length market exchange (internalisation advantage); and that the chosen foreign market allows the returns from the advantage to be maximised (location advantage). Clearly, location advantages are important factors in the country choice of multinational banks. Location advantages, relative to the location disadvantages of a host country, will help determine how well the multinational bank can exploit its ownership and internalisation advantages. This ultimately affects the bank's performance after entry.

The location advantages that a potential host country might offer to a multinational bank have received some research attention. This line of enquiry encompasses several academic disciplines because of the complex motivations for the multinationalisation of any firm. Consequently, the literature can be divided into four major strands as academicians, regulators and bank practitioners have employed a mixture of strategic, economic and more recently, historical and empirical analyses to determine the rationale for the location choice of a multinational bank.

Strategic literature

The strategic literature encompasses descriptive papers which rely on the identification of trends from official survey data to draw conclusions about the countries chosen for foreign banking. Explanations are of a general strategic nature and these stress environmental variables such as the market, the customer, and the economic and regulatory climate (Lees, 1974; Channon, 1988). It is argued in this literature that location choice arises from a complex interplay of individual bank management objectives, and expectations regarding not merely profit and risk but also political, economic, social and technological environments. The primary strategic objective of location choice is to maximise wealth (Coulbeck, 1984). Countries with expanding international capital markets present profitable opportunities for exploitation by an appropriately skilled bank and allow risk spreading through geographical diversification (Coulbeck, 1984). Attractive locations are those where incremental profits are anticipated (Phalen, 1977), where market demand for financial services is growing (Channon, 1988), and where taxes and regulations are favourable (Lewis and Davis, 1987). Countries may be ignored if there is insufficient market potential, excessive risk for expected return, and an over-presence of banks (Lees, 1974).

Several other strategic factors impact on multinational bank location choice. Banks follow corporate clients overseas to service their financial needs and to prevent losing them to international and local rivals (Eiteman and Stonehill, 1989; Channon, 1988). Hence, locations with a presence of multinational corporate customers from the bank's home country are chosen. Locations may be chosen to complete an international network, to create a foothold before or when foreign entry is limited, and to initiate a strategic position in preparation for future developments (Phalen, 1977).

Attractive locations for multinational banking are international financial centres (Park, 1989) for reasons of promoting maximisation of operating efficiency (Reed, 1980). These centres are characterised by social, political and economic stability; favourable banking and taxation laws; close proximity to international money and capital markets, other international financial centres, and multinational corporations; and sophisticated telecommunications (Park, 1989; Sing, 1989). Finally, location choice may be stimulated by nonrational reasons, including national prestige, corporate image and management's personal interests, and historical factors such as colonial ties (Coulbeck, 1984).

Economic theories

The economic literature can be classified as theoretical discussions, sometimes supported by analysis of descriptive statistics, which apply economic concepts of industrial organisations, foreign direct investment and international trade to multinational banking (Grubel, 1977; Gray and Gray, 1981; Yannopoulos, 1983). The focus of much of the economic literature is the importance of the maintenance of established customer relationships as a factor in a multinational bank's location choice. Gray and Gray (1981) proposed that all banks have a firm-specific advantage in information capital and if an existing customer is lost to another bank, then the ensuing information transfer reduces the former bank's advantage. To minimise this effect, a multinational bank chooses to locate in countries where its established customers operate. Casson (1990) similarly argued that personal contact with corporate customers created information network and goodwill advantages. The multinational bank could internalise these advantages and derive additional rents by opening branches in countries where these advantages can be capitalised upon. This would include countries where the bank's multinational manufacturing customers are located (Casson, 1990). Ultimately, the bank's close relationship with these customers differentiates the bank's product from its competitors (Caves, 1977). Furthermore, because of the 'orientation contact' nature of the information services provided to these customers, it is critical that the multinational bank is located in countries close to the information source (Yannopoulos, 1983). Similar explanations have been postulated for the less common multinational retail bank (Grubel, 1977; Yannopoulos, 1983; Tschoegl, 1987).

Aliber (1983), however, refuted the follow the leader motivation, noting that multinational corporations and banks historically have expanded sequentially. He proposed that this effect resulted from a common competitive advantage in that the cost of capital is lower in their home country than in the new host market. Corporations and banks from countries with a relatively low cost of capital, he argued, have tended to locate in countries with higher costs of capital, to exploit their advantage (Aliber, 1983).

Multinational banks are attracted to largely unregulated supranational markets, where unrestricted bank asset, liability, and foreign exchange management permit higher rates of return on equity than domestic regulation allows (Gray and Gray, 1981). In the absence of such regulatory barriers and other market imperfections,

Giddy (1983) argued that only arm's length international banking, through representative offices, would take place. Finally, as physical investment costs are relatively low for banks, multinational banks attempt to maximise network advantages by choosing principal locations around their headquarters (Casson, 1990).

Historical theories

Renewed interest in the ability of a firm's history to explain subsequent multinationalisation has spawned an historical literature strand (Dunning, 1988). Case studies of individual banks and/or countries are examined to identify whether the patterns of development are consistent with the multinational banking theories espoused in the economic and strategic literature (Jones, 1990).

Profit motives have impacted historically on multinational bank location choice. Wilkins (1989, 1990) concluded that, prior to 1914, European banks were located in the US to gain profits and information. Simultaneously, US banks established operations in those countries that facilitated capital movement to the home market. The dramatic growth since 1960 of foreign banks in the US and of US banks overseas was driven by economic growth, political stability, relaxation of exchange controls and trade barriers (Huertas, 1990). However, the results of historical studies on the issue of banks following their customers abroad are conflicting. While many authors support the view that banks historically followed their customers overseas (Merrett, 1990; Brown, 1990), some authors refute this argument (Wilkins, 1990; Jones, 1990).

Location choice has been driven historically by regulation and trade relationships. Multinational banks, particularly US banks, have chosen historically to enter countries where nonstringent regulations allowed them to exploit their competitive advantages (Huertas, 1990). Colonial ties influenced the location choices of British, and other, banks (Tschoegl, 1987). German banks chose locations that would foster German trade finance and overseas investment (Hertner, 1990), as did French and other European banks (Jacobs, 1975). Chinese banks became the conduit for South East Asian capital, networking through this region utilising cultural and language ties (Brown,1990).

Empirical research

Several authors have conducted empirical studies of multinational banks to determine how well the evolving strategic and economic theories withstand more rigorous testing. Early authors, investigating the factors motivating multinational bank location choice, analysed descriptive statistics collected by official organisations (Brimmer and Dahl, 1975; Terrell and Key, 1977; Rugman, 1979). Researchers then began formulating econometric models of multinational bank activities and utilising regression analysis of data aggregated across foreign banks to test the validity of their models (Nigh, Cho and Krishnan, 1986; Poulsen, 1986; Sabi, 1988; Hultman and McGee, 1989). Researchers are now testing multinational banking models utilising individual bank data (Ursacki and Vertinsky, 1992; Heinkel and Levi, 1992). The two major areas of study are foreign banks in the US, and US multinational banks overseas. Because of the difficulty of modelling expectations prior to choosing a location, empirical studies have investigated the determinants of a multinational bank's level of involvement after entering a host country location.

Many authors have tested empirically the profit motivation for multinational bank location choice. Data from the annual reports of banks were tested by Fieleke (1977) and Rugman (1981) with conflicting results as to the impact of profits on bank multinationality. Constraints on data availability forced other authors to utilise various proxy variables for profitability. Proxies reported to have a significant effect on the level of involvement in a location have included loan/deposit ratios (Terrell, 1979; Sabi, 1988); interest rate differentials (Khoury, 1979; Poulsen, 1986); operating costs (Khoury, 1979; Ursacki and Vertinsky, 1992); balance of payments (Goldberg and Saunders, 1980; Sabi, 1988); exchange rates (Goldberg and Saunders, 1981a); host country market size (Terrell, 1979; Tschoegl, 1982; Sabi, 1988); and market concentration (Tschoegl, 1982).

The follow-the-customer motive, where banks follow their home country corporate clients overseas, has been widely researched. A range of proxy variables to measure this motive has been tested successfully by different authors, supporting the conclusion that this is an important factor in location choice (Brimmer and Dahl, 1975; Fieleke, 1977; Goldberg and Saunders, 1980; Nigh, Cho and Krishnan, 1986; Jain, 1986; Sabi, 1988; Goldberg and Johnson, 1990; Ursacki and Vertinsky, 1992). The volumes of trade between the host and home country were also reported to have a positive influence on multinational bank level of involvement abroad by several authors (Terrell, 1979; Goldberg and Saunders, 1980 and 1981a; Jain, 1986; Poulsen, 1986; Heinkel and Levi, 1992; Ursacki and Vertinsky, 1992).

Host country regulation was reported by several authors to influence multinational bank level of involvement (Khoury ,1979; Poulsen, 1986; Nigh, Cho and Krishnan, 1986; Ursacki and Vertinsky, 1992). In addition, the size and geographical scope of the parent bank has been found to influence multinational bank entry (Tschoegl, 1982; Ball and Tschoegl, 1982; Ursacki and Vertinsky, 1992). Finally, the development of the host country's financial centre has influenced multinational bank involvement (Goldberg, Helsley and Levi, 1988; Heinkel and Levi, 1992; Ursacki and Vertinsky, 1992).

Synthesis of the arguments presented in the strategic, economic and historical literature strands with evidence of authors from the empirical literature suggests that the following factors shape the location advantages of a host country:

1 The expectation of profitable opportunity in the host country;

2 The degree of risk expected to be associated with profitability in the host country;

3 The activities of other corporations from the multinational bank's home country;

4 The extent of regulation of banking activities in the host country relative to the multinational bank's home country;

5 The ability of the host country to contribute to the global network that the multinational bank has established; and

6 The presence or otherwise of an international financial centre in the host country.

Consistent with Dunning's (1988) eclectic paradigm of international production, the decision by a multinational bank to locate in a particular host country is a function of the nature and strength of the bank's ownership and internalisation advantages in conjunction with the expected location advantages of operating in that country. The six major country-specific factors from which these location advantages ensue are profitability, risk, home country clients, regulation, network advantages and the presence of a financial centre. The eclectic paradigm is now applied to the special case of foreign banks' investment in Australia.

Location choice and foreign banks in Australia

As outlined previously, in 1984 the Australian government invited foreign banks to apply for bank licences to operate in Australia. The government accepted sixteen applications and these banks entered the Australian market in 1985-86. This chain of events suggests that foreign banks made two critical decisions during this period. First, the banks decided to apply for a licence. Second, the banks decided to accept the licence and enter the Australian market. The primary ownership, internalisation and location advantages underpinning these decisions will be explored now.

Ownership advantages

Several ownership advantages would have impelled the foreign banks, that eventually entered Australia, to apply for banking licences. The banks possessed the following ownership advantages over Australian domestic banks:

1 cost of capital (Aliber, 1983). As all applicants were in the world's largest 500 banks based on capital, the applicants had access to substantial foreign capital at low cost from their parent banks.

2 marketing (Hennart, 1982). The applicants were global banks with established international reputations in wholesale markets.

3 banker-customer relationships with multinational companies (Rugman, 1981). The applicants had broad customer bases in their home countries and widespread international networks.

Table 10.2
Location advantages of Australia

Profit Opportunity	* Net profits of Australian companies increased 38% in 1983/84 and 23% in 1984/85. * Net profits ofAustralian financial enterprises increased 22% in 1983/84 and 26% in 1984/85. * Australian interest rates were above bank lending rates in US, UK and Japan. * GDP increased 11% in 1983/84 and 1984/85. * Retail sales increased 8% in 1983/84 and 7% in 1984/85. * ABS production index was 101 in 1983/84 and 103 in 1984/85 (Base = 100 in 1976/77).
Risk	* Australia was economically and politically stable in 1983/84 and 1984/85.
Home Country Clients	* Total FDI in Australia increased by 55% in 1984/85, reaching $A 15 890 million. * FDI from the US increased by 135% and from Japan increased by 179% in 1984/85. * Major investing countries were US, Japan, UK and other Asia.
Regulation	* Regulation via Australia's central bank, theReserve Bank of Australia. Statutory Reserve Deposit Requirement (SRD) of 7% and Prime Assets Ratio of 12% (replaced LGS in 1985) were in place. However, the Australian financial system was being progressively deregulated, and prudential supervision was replacing direct quantitative supervision.
Network Advantages	* Australia's exports increased by 15% in 1983/84 and by 24% in 1984/85 (Total exports $A 29 440 million). * Australia's imports increased by 8% in 1983/84 and by 28% in 1984/85 (Total imports $A 30 104 million). * Major trading partners were US, Japan, UK and other Asia.

Table 10.2 (continued)
Location advantages of Australia

Financial Centre Advantages	* Sydney was classified as an international financial centre (Reed, 1980). * In 1983/84, the Australian financial system was comprised of 4 major banks, 4 state banks, 4 smaller banks (trading bank assets $65 billion, savings bank assets $ 38 billion), approx. 60 merchant banks (assets $ 18 billion), approx. 130 finance companies (assets $24 billion), approx. 75 building societies (assets $18 billion), and 170 credit unions (assets $ 4 billion). * The total number of Australian banks had fallen and deregulation was expected to enhance the role of banks. * Total lending by banks increased by 12.5% in 1983/84 and by 24% in 1984/85.

Source: various Reserve Bank of Australia Statistical Bulletins

4 economies of scale (Benston et al, 1982). The applicants had '...lower costs through economies obtained from using standard issuing, documenting and payment procedures within a single international banking organisation' (Campbell Report, 1981, p. 719).

5 product differentiation advantages (Grubel, 1977). This arises from the '...provision of international financial and sophisticated treasury products to large and small business, (which) involves substantial research and development' that domestic banks cannot afford (*Australian Bankers Submission*, 1990, p. x).

6 network advantages (McKay, 1990). The applicants had extensive international branch networks located in Australia's existing export markets.

7 experience and familiarity with the Australian market as a result of the applicants' prior presence in Australia through representative offices and shares in nonbank financial intermediaries. Consequently, the knowledge disadvantage of unfamiliarity with local practices normally incurred by multinational banks upon entry was significantly lessened (Grubel, 1977; Niehans, 1983).

Internalisation advantages

Following Dunning's eclectic paradigm, firms will internalise their ownership advantages in foreign markets when it is more efficient to engage in foreign direct investment than arm's length marketplace exchange. The knowledge advantage of banks can only be transferred to foreign markets by internalisation (Casson, 1990; Gray and Gray, 1981; Yannopoulous, 1983). The special bank-customer relationships are not patentable and therefore cannot be transferred into foreign markets through arm's length transactions because of problems of appropriability and protection of proprietary interests.

The possession of an Australian bank licence posed other internalisation advantages. Licensed banks could offer a full range of banking services, could structure operations in the most efficient manner, and could access some markets which at the time were exclusive to banks, in particular foreign exchange and cheque account transactions (Campbell Report, 1981). A licence therefore allowed foreign banks to compete more effectively with the Australian banks. A licence enhanced an institution's credit status because of a Reserve Bank guarantee to protect bank depositors, as outlined in Division 2 of the Banking Act 1959. This created the assumption that the government would not allow any of the newly licensed foreign banks to fail (Tingle, 1984a). Finally, ' ...the licence is extremely important to a bank's credit rating as it ensures larger limits within the money markets and for foreign exchange trading' (Brown, 1987, p. 98).

Location advantages

Consistent with Dunning's eclectic paradigm, firms will internalise and exploit their ownership advantages in locations which allow the derivation of maximum rents. The location advantages to multinational banks of positioning in Australia are summarised in Table 10.2.

The Australian Financial Review, November 12, 1984, conducted a survey of all foreign banks with representative offices in Australia which highlighted their perceptions of the advantages of locating in Australia. The survey revealed that foreign institutions regarded Australia as one of the most promising and stable environments in the world. Australia's business environment and dynamic economic growth were deemed opportunistic for both national banks and foreign banks with operations in the country. A further locational advantage of the Australian market was the ability to transfer business to the new foreign bank from the parent or from related nonbank financial institutions.

At the time of applying for a licence, the expectation of the applicants was that only six licences would be granted (Shepherd, 1988). This increased the advantage attached to possession of a licence, for it implied greater potential market shares and profitability for the banks that won licences. The combination of these factors led to the applicants projecting high return on equity figures for an Australian subsidiary. The applicants expected to acquire '...about 20% of the Australian banking market within five years of entry' (*A Pocket Full of Change*, 1991, p. 150).

The government announced in February 1985 that 16 foreign banks were successful in their applications for foreign bank licences. The banks chosen were the world's most prestigious banks. The ownership, internalisation and location advantages that motivated the submission of a licence application also underpinned the decision to enter. However, the number of invitations was higher than anticipated. The almost complete deregulation of entry and other rules affecting merchant banks, including the removal of foreign investment controls for one year, also occurred (Shepherd, 1988). Australia was now overbanked, with 33 banks servicing a population of 16 million (Brown, 1987). Despite the changed scenario, only one bank declined to take up its licence. The remaining 15 foreign banks were ' ...reluctant to decrease their expectations' and entered Australia in 1985 and 1986 (Brown, 1987, p. 135).

The invitation by government to enter Australia was the immediate stimulus behind the location choice decision, given each foreign bank's favourable predisposition and experience in Australia through representative offices and investments in nonbank financial institutions. The preceding discussion suggests that the decisions to apply for, and subsequently accept, a foreign bank licence to operate in Australia are consistent with Dunning's (1988) eclectic paradigm and other multinational banking theories.

Conclusions

Theory developed to explain multinational banking contends that a multinational bank will choose to locate in a host country where the bank's ownership and internalisation advantages can be exploited through the location advantages of the host country. The location advantages of a host country relate to expected profitability, a relatively low level of risk, the presence of home country clients, a favourable regulatory environment, network advantages and financial centre advantages. In this chapter, it was demonstrated that this theory can be applied to the case of foreign banks in Australia. Entry of sixteen new foreign banks into Australia occurred in 1985 and 1986, following an embargo on foreign bank entry which had existed for decades. Having made the decision to locate, an extension of the eclectic paradigm would suggest that the success of each multinational bank in Australia would be determined by the bank's ownership and internalisation advantages combined with their perceptions of Australia's locational advantages. Unfortunately, '...most new bank ...entrants over-estimated their ability to compete with the existing banks' (Shepherd, 1988, p. 135). Market share and profitability performance of the new foreign banks has been well below expectations. In June 1987, '...foreign banks represented some 9 per cent of the assets of all trading and savings banks in Australia, both old and new' (*Reserve Bank Bulletin*, November, 1987, p. 31). The total share in 1991 remained around ten per cent (*A Pocket Full of Change*, 1991, p. 150). Furthermore, although some new foreign banks are profitable in particular market segments, the overall profitability of the new foreign banks has been below that of the established banks (*Australian Bankers Submission*, 1990). Recent changes in foreign bank regulations, announced in the federal government's One Nation Statement in February, 1992, were designed to improve the competitiveness of foreign banks.

The poor performance of the foreign banks in Australia appears to have been a function of Australia's changed locational advantages following foreign bank entry. These factors include '...severe competition with low margins; high interest rates and an unstable dollar; lower economic demand; and Reserve Bank liquidity requirements' (Brown, 1987, p. 100). An important locational factor in the Australian market is the dominance of the four major Australian trading banks which has created an oligopolistic trading environment for the new foreign banks. The problem has been compounded by the requirement that '...new foreign banks operate as subsidiaries rather than branches ... (which) increased the cost of raising funds for the new banks' (*A Pocket Full of Change*, 1991, p. 150).

Locational factors have constrained the ability of the foreign bank entrants to exploit effectively their ownership and internalisation advantages. Australian locational advantages and disadvantages have been the critical influence on the performance of foreign banks following entry. At the time of applying for a licence, foreign banks perceived Australia to offer the locational advantages outlined in Table 10.2. Following entry, it became evident that the actual locational factors differed from the banks' perceptions, and this affected their performance. While ownership and internalisation advantages were important in the initial decision to locate in Australia, these advantages have a lesser impact post-entry when the strength of these advantages are tempered by the actual locational factors of the host country.

11 Transnational branch banking 1976–1986: An empiricist's approach

David M. Dahm and Milford B. Green

Introduction

Historically, large transnational banks (TNBs) tended to follow nonbanking firms in the search for underserved markets. This behaviour reflects the generally risk-averse nature of the transnational banking enterprise, and its basic interest in safeguarding the capital it manages on behalf of shareholders and depositors. More detailed reviews of the motivations underlying transnational banking are provided by Yannapoulos (1983), Coulbeck (1984) and Grubel (1989).

In the 1970s, TNBs began rapidly expanding their overseas activity in response to similar behaviour by nonbank transnationals. Additionally, declining rates of return in the domestic marketplace and the perception of better lending opportunities abroad accelerated the process of overseas expansion. During this protracted expansionary phase, which peaked before the 1990 recession, transnational banking was characterized by a basic shift away from informal banking ties (affiliate and subsidiary linkages), toward formalized branch bank services. While an abundance of theory and modelling attests to academic interest in understanding the expansion of global banking business, geographers have only started to measure and describe the spatial consequences of global capital flows.

Within the subdiscipline of corporate geography, research has tended to focus on one salient theme; the perceived inability of orthodox economic theory to anticipate the spatial complexity of global transactions (Hepworth, 1990). While this criticism is valid, geographers have not offered theoretical alternatives explaining the locational motivations of transnational enterprise, or a coherent framework for examining the complex transactional flows that characterize the global space-economy. Fundamentally, corporate geography must be concerned with developing a practical understanding - a realistic theory - of the complex factors that interact and give rise to the manifestation of economic activity in global space. For the subdiscipline, a necessary first step to developing a geographic theory of transnational enterprise is the empirical investigation of transnational firm behaviour on a very large scale.

This chapter contributes to the study of transnational banking, presenting empirical research documenting the spatial consequences of its evolution as a process. The research confines itself to a comprehensive examination of spatial change among 250 very large banks, and focuses on the changing structure of their operations using two base years: 1976 and 1986. Earlier works by Dahm and Green (1993) and Dahm (1994) examined spatial characterizations for affiliate, branch and subsidiary linkages. For brevity, this research confines itself to a presentation of branch banking activity. Where context is required, branch banking is compared and contrasted with both affiliate and subsidiary operations.

As the most powerful form of connection between two economic actors, branch banking provides a 'snapshot' of the nature of spatial evolution in the banking industry during the period studied. Thus, by examining the deduced economic space in both 1976 and 1986, an attempt is also made to link empirical results to contemporary theories of transnational banking. Additionally, general conclusions

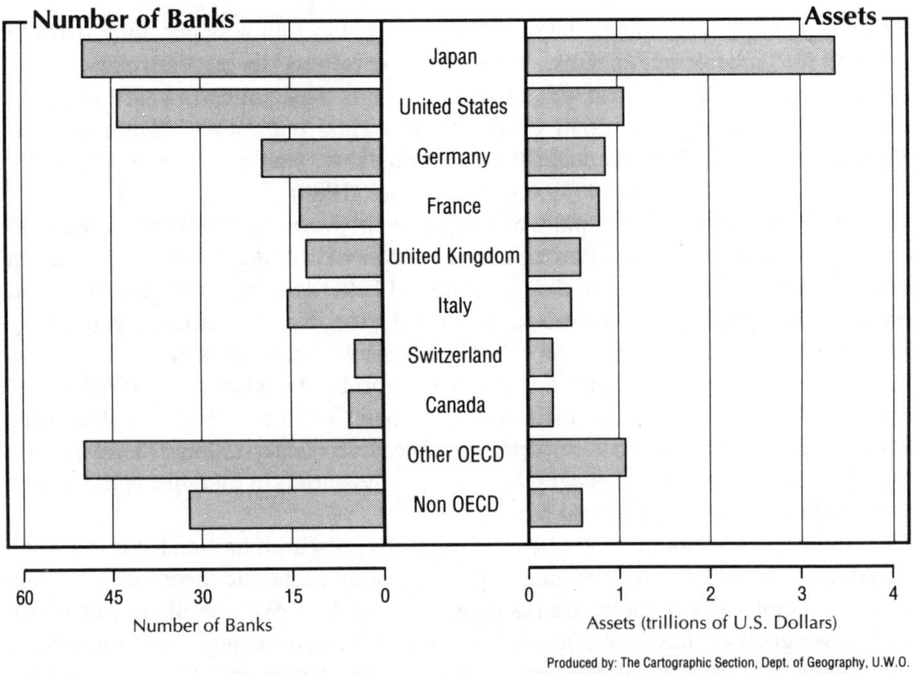

Figure 11.1 Number of banks and assets, principal banking nations, 1986 sample

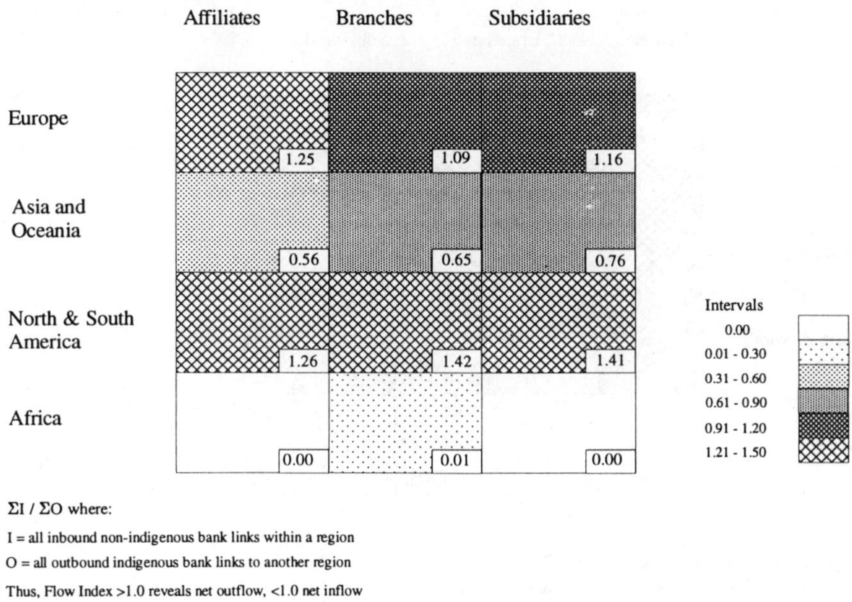

Figure 11.2 Regional banking flow index, 1976

are made as to the nature and direction of change occurring in the transnational banking system.

Origins of transnational banking

Many of the assumptions underlying contemporary transnational banking are closely related to the operational behaviour of firms which possessed elaborate colonial banking networks dating from the nineteenth century (Grubel, 1989). At that time, British, German, French, and Dutch banking institutions could easily penetrate foreign markets, reinforcing urban European control over colonial outposts. Critically, in most of these distant locations, no host banking systems had been established prior to the advent of colonialism.

Generally, colonial banking networks reinforced the patterns of trade that developed between the imperial heartland empires and their vast colonial hinterlands. Thus, the expansion of transnational banking during the mercantilist period mirrored growth in the level of global trade. At this time, the establishment of a viable enterprise in an overseas colony generated diffuse pecuniary needs, with the relative profitability of colonial business conditioned by the ability of an export staple to withstand the transportation costs imposed by physical separation from the market

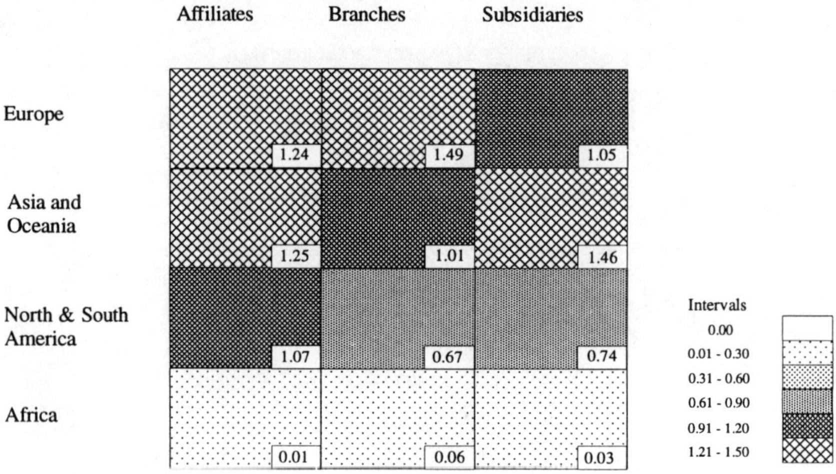

ΣI / ΣO where:

I = all inbound non-indigenous bank links within a region

O = all outbound indigenous bank links to another region

Thus, Flow Index >1.0 reveals net outflow, <1.0 net inflow

Figure 11.3 Regional banking flow index, 1986

(Crough, 1979). Thus, the expansion of transnational banking in the neocolonial period perpetuates many of the patterns that prevailed during the colonial era.

As transnational corporations expanded their global operations, large banks were carried on the wave of capitalist expansion. By 1913, four major American transnational banks had six foreign offices in Europe. From 1920 to 1950, this number grew to about 100 affiliates abroad (Dicken, 1986). By 1988, some 772 foreign affiliates had been established by American banks (Grubel, 1989). Clearly, this kind of expansion has fostered the popular image of the nebulous transnational bank prevalent in the twentieth century. Among the early American transnationals, none achieved the level of notoriety or broad-based power ascribed to the Morgan banking group. In *The House of Morgan,* Chernow describes that corporation as a far-reaching business empire with connections to foreign governments and to expanding transnational corporations:

> As the most mandarin of banks, it catered to many prominent families, including the Astors, Gugenheims, du Ponts, and Vanderbilts. It shunned dealings with lesser mortals, thus breeding popular suspicion. Since it financed many industrial giants, including US Steel, General Electric, General Motors, Du Pont, and American Telephone and Telegraph, it entered into their councils and aroused fear of undue banker power ... What gave the House of Morgan its tantalizing mystery was its government links. Much like the old Rothschilds and Barings, it seemed

insinuated into the power structure of many countries, especially the United States, England, and France and, to a lesser degree, Italy, Belgium, and Japan (Chernow, 1990, p. xii).

Large TNBs have always come from a prosperous group of nations. Seven countries that comprise the core of the OECD -- Japan, the United States, Germany, France, the United Kingdom, Italy, Switzerland and Canada -- are the principal banking nations involved in global finance today (Coulbeck, 1981; Semple and Rice, 1994). In 1986, these same nations accounted for US$9.5 trillion in deposits on hand, representing more than 80 per cent of the world's total banking activity. The sample examined in this study confirms a pattern of extensive global economic activity (Figure 11.1). Among headquartered transnational banks, the overwhelming representation of the OECD countries dwarfs the involvement of non-OECD countries, suggesting a strong and direct relationship between prolonged national prosperity and the presence of a mature transnational banking system.

Locational orthodoxy

From the perspective of large transnational banks, the most desirable locations for managing major foreign operations are those which offer political stability, historical involvement in the banking sector, and an existing communications infrastructure that supports pecuniary activity - features generally associated with the first world. Thus, while the development of a vast operational network requires exposure to the volatile economies of the developing world, most of the transnational banks limit their involvement to affiliate, subsidiary, or consortium arrangements. In turn, all of these forms can be easily directed from a first world branch which serves to co-ordinate regional operations.

Core banking activity, identified directly by those locations which support branch operations, signifies a transnational bank's willingness to assume greater legal responsibility for the business it conducts in a foreign locale. In general, the deep conservatism of large transnational banks makes it unlikely that any network would be skewed toward branch participation in the developing world. Thus, the presence of a foreign bank branch in the developing world is an exceptional occurrence denoting a considerable allocation of resources. Effective control of the transnational banking system is overwhelmingly restricted to the developed world.

In both 1976 and 1986, the strongest interregional banking connections remained those that occurred between banks and nations located in the developed world (Figures 11.2 and 11.3). In choosing to spread their risk over a range of relatively prosperous nations, large transnational banks can be simultaneously plugged into strong equity markets in expanding economies, while earning favourable rates of interest on government and corporate bonds issued in an alternative set of nations. By exploiting regional differences in the timing and duration of the business cycle, transnational banks are able to open and close global capital circuits in a manner that provides the greatest degree of security for the individual firm.

Wherever banking nations may fit on a continuum of banking power, the elite transnational banks have historically preferred concentrating their banking activities in particular regions. Transnational banks from the United States and Canada have focused their international activities upon Latin America and the Caribbean. Alternatively, European banks have been more inclined to have representation in ex-colonial possessions. This latter propensity is shown most clearly by the United Kingdom, which had fully 1,432 operational ties to Africa in the late 1980s (Grubel, 1989). Such figures support the arguments of authors who hold that colonial financing never truly disappeared; it simply remained as a neocolonial feature.

Another truism characterizing TNBs is that their knowledge of foreign markets, and their eventual establishment of international representatives, is characterized by a distance decay effect. As a bank's knowledge of a market becomes less exact, there are changes in both their physical ties to those places and the forms that those linkages take. Japan focuses most of its foreign banking upon the nations of the Pacific Basin, with fully 75 per cent of its 1986 foreign bank operations found in the United States, Canada, Latin America, China, Hong Kong, Singapore, Asian Pacific Islands, and other Southeast Asian nations. Some nations are clear exceptions to the 'distance decay' rule. Thus, Switzerland demonstrates a willingness to engage in transnational banking with a much more diverse portfolio of overseas holdings than other banking nations.

Despite the longevity of international banking, overseas business was a minor aspect of corporate activity until the 1950s. Even the largest TNBs limited their nondomestic business to one or two sites. Typically, these offices were located in traditional capital markets. Thus, Chase Manhattan Bank established offices in London in 1897, and in Paris by 1910 (Muro, 1984). Similarly, Citicorp showed an early willingness to consider global operations as a vehicle for growth, with 69 branches established abroad by 1915. Today, both of these banks remain dominant actors within the transnational banking sector.

Among American banking firms, part of the impetus for foreign expansion is rooted in legislation that limits interstate/intrastate expansion. As such, some 15,000 US banks remain highly restricted in their potential for domestic geographic coverage. Conversely, European and Japanese transnational banks have not been as restricted in their opportunities for domestic growth. Given such markedly dissimilar domestic environments, American membership among the largest transnational banks has steadily declined since 1956 (*The American Banker Yearbook, 1987*). While US TNBs rely upon overseas operations for a disproportionately high share of their business volume, Japanese and European banks have been able to exploit opportunities at home and use them as springboards to international activity.

Literature review

Most frequently, literature concerning transnational banking focuses on offering a plausible explanation for the expansion of transnational banking. The unidirectional nature of this research paradigm is not difficult to understand; prior to the 1990s, prolonged contraction in the transnational banking sector was unknown. Most overviews of global banking cite four principal macroeconomic realities as driving the expansion of TNBs:

- Increased financial requirements of expanding transnational corporations and the potential for intrafirm trade (Dicken, 1986; Morris, 1987);
- Proliferation of new currency markets in both Europe and Asia and the advent of continuous trading activity (Dicken, 1986; Grubel, 1989);
- Deregulation of the international banking environment and the accompanying mechanisms of tax evasion (Grubel, 1989); and
- Advantages afforded the bank that arise from embracing a broad diversification strategy, thereby permitting the exploration of new opportunities or the protection of existing international banking activities in a time of rapid economic change (Coulbeck, 1984).

Each of these factors represents a unique part of an overall strategy that serves to reduce a firm's exposure to one or two markets by spreading business risk over a spatially diverse range of markets. Formally, the portfolio theory of risk minimization does serve as an integrating framework for researchers examining the spatial behaviour of TNBs. According to Maxwell and Gitman, 'risk evaluation is fundamental to just about everything a banker, as well as a financial manager, does' (1989, p. 219). All of these features derive from Cohen's rationale (1981) for the explanation of international growth in transnational corporations. In that view, the expansion of corporations around the world is tied to the new international division of labour, which probably does affect the global strategies and locational decisions of TNBs. In turn, transnational corporations are seen as the reason for the international expansion of banking (Langdale, 1985).

Geographic views of international banking

Within geography, literature examining banking phenomena is relatively scarce. Moreover, many of the authors responsible for the geographic description of transnational banking imply that banking networks are somehow equivalent to computer networks. Thus, the geography of the information net has been construed as a surrogate for the geography of the bank.

Although descriptive studies of dedicated electronic banking networks are helpful, the recitation of empirical evidence is not matched by a corresponding level of theory. Among geographers, Langdale (1985) provides a representative example of this type of research by chronicling consortium and privately held global banking networks. Unfortunately, this work does not convey a sense of interdependency among the institutional actors. Explanations of cause and control are absent, with no cumulative sense conveyed by the author as to which companies 'command' the process of global expansion.

Other economic geographers with research interests similar to Langdale include Warf (1989), whose work is distinct in its focus on the collapse of time and space. In adopting this approach, Warf's work is strongly linked to the theoretical approach of Hägerstrand and the time-geography school. One contention advanced by Warf suggests a clear relationship exists between falling transactional costs and expanding electronic banking networks. While this relationship is not disputed, Warf does not discuss the important role that human contact plays in enabling contemporary telecommunications systems. Finally, Warf overlooks the potentially positive effect that global banking can have upon peripheral economic regions.

Several works that are concerned with geographic components of global banking are evident in the literature. Their focus is on examining the impact of banking on regional economies. Thus, Morris' (1987) case study of the effects of transnational banking on the labour force in South Wales is a representative work. Similarly, Hirst and others (1982) approach the geography of Australian trading banks from a regional perspective. Other examples are Ó hUallacháin's (1994) study of the effect of foreign banking on the American urban system and Semple and Rice's (1994) work on international bank headquarters cities.

Besides these geographic analyses, banking activity is given cursory treatment under the theme of 'capitalist systems in crises' by Marxist geographers (Corbridge, 1986). Alternatively, post-modern economic geographers usually present the global expansion of finance as yet another symptom related to the expansion of the information economy (Hepworth, 1990). Seemingly, instead of describing anything based on empiricism, theory is adjusted to fit the individual's world-view.

Indeed, some Marxist geographers describe the electronic connectivity of banks as symptomatic of underlying problems. They are portrayed as the latest capitalist approach to the maintenance of global efficiency and order. Other geographers generate hybridized views, mixing Marxist sensibilities with post-industrial landscapes, as typified by Ross' view of the nature of global capital (Ross, 1983). By employing the metaphor of the biblical Leviathan, Ross decries the transnational banks' ability to deskill and to exploit the new international division of labour. Unfortunately, the works of Ross and others (Hepworth, 1990; Roobeek, 1987) are based on weak empirical evidence and no sense of macro-techniques as organizing tools amenable to the study of transnational corporations.

Other disciplinary views of international banking

Several informative examinations of transnational banking are available from the perspectives of business, history, and economics. Each discipline views transnational banking from an aspatial perspective.

One work which is germane to this study is Coulbeck's (1984) rigorous account of the peculiarities of global banks emanating from within the G-7. Coulbeck provides an excellent synopsis of the domestic environments conditioning the growth of transnational banks prior to their globalization. As such, the reader receives a brief introduction to some of the formal aspects of transnational banking. However, as pivotal as the G-7 nations banks may be to lubricating the world economy, an incomplete sense of the extent and complexity of global banking is presented.

An older, but qualitatively different text is provided by Crough (1979). This examination chronicles the informal arrangements that banks have with one another, as suggested by the author's inclusion of research into the interlocking directorates of transnational banks. Crough also offers more than a summary description of the transnational banking process, but does not convey the web of social relationships that characterize interfirm contacts in succinct graphic representations. Similar criticism may be directed to Nagy (1983), who describes the international operations of Canada's 'Big Six' and their differing risk aversion strategies. Channon (1988) also examines the dynamic nature of global banking strategy and its variation among banks, but in a case study approach that does not convey a general picture of how transnational banks interact with one another.

One of the only studies which employs a formal statistical approach to testing a theory of banking behaviour is offered by Reed (1981). Using 41 key variables, Reed employs discriminant analysis to identify the emergence of 'prominent centres' in global banking. Ultimately, the theoretical context within which results are presented is based on theories of eminence and formation. Theories similar to Reed's advance the view that primate cities rise to their position of economic hegemony because of their ability to minimise time differences, leading to reductions in the costs of capital, communication, and transportation (Kindleberger, 1978; Nadler, 1955). Subjective evaluations, such as uncertainty and cultural differences, become less important determinants than the ability of a nation to command political power. These are exhibited as control over trade, transportation, communication, and pecuniary functions. In general, the work of these economic historians, and the explicit recognition of cities as nodes of differing influence and power, may be interpreted as equivalent to the urban historiography of Careless (1954), or the sociological paradigm typified by Rogers and Kincaid (1981).

Among economists and business analysts, many speculative discussions on banking have been produced; two of the most cogent transnational banking theorists have been Grubel and Yannapoulos. Historically, Grubel pioneered the study of transnational banking as a phenomenon worth an academic appraisal, while Yannapoulos has both criticized and extended Grubel's earlier assertions with his own observations about the nature of international capital movements and the growth of transnational banks.

Originally, Grubel (1977; 1989) held that a viable transnational banking theory would have to be able to consistently explain the emergence of different operational forms -- bank types -- in the international banking industry. While both Grubel and Yannapoulos use many of the same assumptions and ideas in framing their theories, Grubel places special emphasis on the doctrine of comparative advantage (after Ricardo) as part of an improved theory of multinational banking (Grubel, 1989; Crough, 1979). Three core functions are identified by Grubel; multinational commercial, retail and wholesale banking. Each function is said to absorb different kinds of surplus corporate energy; namely management technology, marketing knowledge and commercial intelligence.

Grubel suggests that the most basic reason underlying bank operations in a foreign nation derive from the expanding firm's need for high rates of return on capital deposited with the banking firm. In addition, the expanding transnational bank identifies those places in the global economy where its entrepreneurial resources are most effectively channelled (a corollary of comparative advantage, namely local receptiveness, underpins this assertion). Thus, by diffusing a banking firm's native talent, known market imperfections at points around the world are exploited, relaxing internal barriers to firm growth.

Grubel's general banking theory predicts that wholesale banking, and its focus on imperfections in currency markets and the subsequent potential for the firm to generate rapid rates of return on investment, is the initial foray that a transnational bank will make into a new market. Wholesale banking, which seeks to take advantage of the fluctuating values of a basket of currencies, is distinct from retail and service banking. Therefore, once a bank makes the decision to enter into a foreign retail market, it can be taken as a sign of two conditions:

- First, that the invading bank has arrived from a domestic banking environment that is saturated or constrained by intolerable levels of risk. Excess pools of capital must therefore flow to consuming regions in new parts of an evolving corporate network distributed around the world.

- Second, that the firm has probably established a wholesale banking presence, and still has surplus talent and capital that it can only consume internally.

According to Yannapoulos, Grubel overstates the case for comparative advantage as an 'intractable' causal explanation for the expansion of transnational banking. While conceding that location-specific advantages do play an important role in explaining TNB expansion, Yannapoulos contends that Grubel's theory is characterised by an inability to provide universal explanation for TNB behaviour. Thus, the use of theoretical subsets -- one each for multinational retail, service, and wholesale banking -- makes Grubel's multinational banking theory weak alongside a unified approach to the development of an eclectic banking theory (Gray and Gray, 1981). Yannapoulos criticizes Grubel's failure to acknowledge the importance of developing a unified theory as an explanatory framework for multinational banking, suggesting that a three-pronged theory limits the ability of analysts to simultaneously:

- Predict an Increasing interpenetration of the developed countries' credit markets by each others transnational banks.

- Account for an expanding number of different countries generating their own transnational banking services.

- Explain the rise of third world transnational banks and the preponderant role of very large firms among transnational banks.

- Reconcile the observation that some transnational banks start their business at the wholesale end of the banking market, while others start at the retail end, yet regardless of initial orientation, all find it necessary to universalise their services.

- Explain why some transnational banks can exploit offshore banking rules effectively while others cannot.

In a unified banking theory, Yannapoulos argues for the inclusion of *geography* as a master variable in explaining the redistribution of transnational banking markets in the period after 1945. Thus, a combination of location-specific, ownership-specific and international factor advantages collectively influence the time and place in which global expansion occurs (Morris, 1987; Yannapoulos, 1983). These include:

- Differences in regulatory frameworks for banking and in the fiscal treatment of income from deposits and borrowing, which in turn influence the cost of services;

- the desire by certain banks to separate currency risk from political risk by investing overseas;

- the internationalisation of manufacturing activities;

- labour migration;

- the need for close global contact and proximity to information;

- the necessity to obtain and retain skilled personnel;

- tax evasion and the globalization of traditional pools of American capital, i.e., Eurodollars and Asiadollars.

Responding to Yannapoulos, Grubel contends that unified transnational banking theory does not incorporate market imperfections and intrafirm trade as other factors influencing the growth of global banks. Thus, Grubel's latest general banking theory is appended with the portions of the model advanced by Yannapoulos, along with some new theoretical insights (Grubel, 1989). While the debate can be pedantic, both theorists have improved the state of knowledge concerning the growth of transnational banking. However, it seems unlikely that any theoretical construct could ever predict the range of possible banking networks that will appear at any place, in any business milieu at any point in time.

Unidirectional change and theoretical fallacy

One intriguing feature of the theories advanced by both Grubel and Yannapoulos is their preoccupation with the continuous expansion of transnational banking. Recently, this *a priori* assumption has proven to be a glaring error in the rush to establish a sound theory of transnational banking. Both Grubel and Yannapoulos have embedded logical assumptions in their theories that are based entirely on the prospect of unidirectional change. Yet, evidence is amassing that contraction has characterised the global banking system during the recessionary period associated with the early 1990s (*Globe and Mail Report on Banking,* 1992). As neither theorist considered the prospect of contraction in the 1990s, their efforts to explain an effect (transnational banking) as entirely dependent upon indicators of growth (independent variables) is a demonstration of *post hoc ergo propter hoc* - 'after this, therefore, because of this'.

Monolithic theories that overemphasize comparative advantage, surplus business acumen, or local market receptiveness cannot adequately explain why banks have found it necessary to establish operations in foreign locations. In time, transnational banking theory will identify a reliable mix of variables that can explain both the expansion and contraction of the transnational banking system. Predictive models will incorporate indicators shown to be sensitive to an economic downturn in the world's major banking economies.

In attempting to isolate indicators that are sensitive to a period of contraction in global banking, one good proxy measure would involve assessing the operations of transnationals at the most peripheral points in their networks. In general, these points are especially vulnerable to the vagaries of macro-economic cycles, reflecting a strong and direct relationship between local market knowledge and distance from home operations. In recessionary periods, the traditional advantages domestic banks enjoy in their home markets -- cultural and business knowledge of the internal market -- make domestic retrenchment a notable feature of global enterprise.

Finally, the identification of other components that have explanatory value in interpreting globalized banking includes works by Kim and Miller (1983) and McDougal (1985). As suggested in the *keiretsu* model, some authors hold that transnational banking in all cultural contexts represents a response to the capital needs of transnational corporations. To be sure, monolithic theories do explain much of the overseas activity of some American transnational banks. They do not, however, begin to account for the appearance of companies emanating from markedly different domestic regulatory environments.

In summary, the broad literature that deals with the evolution of globalized banking is remarkable for its limited interdisciplinary contact. Among economic geographers in particular, the practical adequacy of transnational banking theory as an organized approach to the interpretation of empirical research has not been exploited. Very little effort appears to have been expended in testing the assumptions of those theories that do exist. Some economists (Bannock, 1988), strenuously object to empiricism as a research approach. Alternatively, empiricists counter that models work better when they incorporate known behaviours observed in the real world. In choosing to engage in an empirical examination of transnational banking, some of the features deduced from observed banking relationships confront the assumptions of contemporary transnational banking theory.

Defining banking forms

The physical manifestation of transnational banking consists of three linkage types, namely affiliates, subsidiaries and branches. Other linkages encountered in assessing the literature include representative and correspondent banking offices. Both forms are services offered by local banks to other banks. As such, they should not be confused with bank activity that involves some degree of physical presence in an overseas market by a nondomestic bank. While no universal definition exists for any of the three basic linkage types, transnational banking is such a pervasive economic activity that each operational form can be generally described according to their operating characteristics.

Affiliates

As specialised corporations, affiliates typically receive less than 50 percent of their operating equity from the parent transnational bank. Usually, affiliate operations lend and transfer funds to firms engaged in business in the host nation, meeting the demand for commercial paper and accepting deposits to raise capital within the host country.

In Canada, for example, some 'Schedule B' transnationals use this organizational form to conduct specialised business. Typically, this would include such activities as financing foreign trade or engaging in interest rate arbitrage. As the simplest operational form available to an expanding transnational, the extent to which affiliates dominate a firm's network shows two conditions: the size of the bank and the bank's familiarity with the foreign banking market. Thus, when a bank is reluctant to establish an enduring presence in a foreign market, it may choose to operate an affiliate office. Similarly, a transnational bank network that is heavily weighted toward affiliate linkages may signify a bank's desire to improve corporate acumen in a new market.

Subsidiaries

Subsidiary relationships offer an alternate form of expansion to transnational banks. Ownership is distributed among several actors, which include firms or individuals that reside in the foreign nation and hold a substantial portion of the equity behind the business venture. Given its 'home content', the subsidiary sometimes gains the right to engage in banking activity that is not accessible to branch operations.

Table 11.1 Transnational linkages: operational and geographic characteristics

Affiliates	Subsidiaries	Branches
o Favoured by small to medium-sized TNBs; deployed by large TNBs in entirely new markets and converted to subsidiary or branch status when warranted	o Linkage type favoured by medium-sized TNBs; deployed by a few small but very well established TNBs engaged in specialised banking activities	o Favoured by large TNBs, with a substantial history of transnational business; mid-sized firms exploit this form in key global banking centres
o Connects peripheral points to larger centres	o Connects peripheral or intermediate points in the space-economy	o Forms an elite tier of connection between the largest centres in the space economy
o Early stage of TNB evolution	o Middle *or* late stage of TNB evolution	o Usually final stage in TNB evolution
o Signals lack of familiarity with new market; serves as a test market connection used to minimize potential for failure	o Signals growing or unique condition of familiarity with an established market	o Signals long-standing familiarity with local market
o Allows risk minimization while ensuring participation in potentially lucrative markets	o Firm accepts greater risk for the retention of local operations	o Firm accepts risk that accompanies business with both local and home-based TNCs
o Not a legal encumbrance for the transnational bank, as *de facto* control remains local	o TNB assumes greater legal responsibility relative to affiliate link; less legally encumbering relative to branches	o Branch entity fully incorporated into the TNB network, including legal responsibility for entity
o Allows TNB to engage in deposit taking and lending	o Allows TNB to engage in deposit taking and lending	o Allows TNB to engage in deposit taking and lending
o Signals limited presence of TNCs from home market	o Signals local concentration of TNCs from home market	o Signals extensive presence of other foreign TNCs
o Ephemeral form of connection: often a test linkage for extension of TNB services to overseas market	o Enduring form of connection: signals greater level of firm knowledge about local conditions	o Most complex and durable form of bank connection possible; linkage form indicative of surplus capital within the firm
o Power is ceded to partner; influence resides in *de jure* control by TNB	o *De facto* control resides with the TNB, not a local partner	o TNB retains complete control over all overseas office operations

NOTE: TNB = Transnational Bank,TNC =Transnational Corporation

Besides presenting the parent firm with a very basic strategic advantage over affiliate operations, subsidiaries also limit the transnational's local operating liabilities in a manner akin to affiliate bank operations. As an intermediate banking form, a subsidiary-based network shows TNBs that are larger and more familiar with foreign banking markets than firms whose overseas operations favour affiliate connections.

Branches

Branch operations signal the final extension of a TNB's overseas network. These suggest that a critical threshold of corporate knowledge has been achieved about sustaining business volume in the foreign market. When a bank's international network primarily consists of foreign branches, it is equally likely that the firm extends a consistently wide range of standard services in each of the host nations.

Generally, transnational banks own branch operations outright. Therefore, the parent bank treats the business of the foreign branch is treated as an integral part of its operations. This includes assuming complete liability for the business activities of the foreign branch operation. Unlike TNBs whose networks are weighted toward affiliate and subsidiary linkages, a transnational network favouring branch linkages is usually generating surplus internal capital that must be circulated to several overseas economies. Collectively, this wide circulation of funds ensures sustained demand for outbound capital.

Banking networks skewed toward branch operations typify very large transnational banks. Their headquarters are overwhelmingly located in the post-industrial economies of Europe, North America, and Japan. Compared to smaller TNBs, these exceptionally large banks sustain more than their expected share of branch offices abroad.

Other factors influencing banking networks

The choice of organizational form that a TNB establishes abroad reflects the exertion of market influences in both domestic and nondomestic economies. Some nations will not allow foreign transnationals to establish *de jure* banking, as exemplified by branch operations. Conversely, other nations limit the extent to which nationalised banks can engage in overseas lending operations.

A range of risks and opportunities derives from an individual bank's decision to operate as a universal or specialised TNB. A bank's international network can be extended into new markets by using each of the linkage types surveyed in this chapter. All three provide the bank with the ability to engage in deposit taking activities in the host country. Nevertheless, specialised banking activities favour the development of branch linkages abroad. Such activities include retail and wholesale lending, interbank lending, trade finance, fee earning services (trusts or direct equity participation), merchant banking and insurance underwriting.

Therefore, at any particular point in time, a strategic mix of linkage types, indicative of a range of geopolitical, economic, and firm-specific realities, will influence the shape of a TNB's foreign network. Table 11.1 provides a series of indicators that summarize the operational and geographic characteristics of affiliate, subsidiary and branch operations.

Network analysis and multidimensional scaling

The premise of this chapter is that the spatial characteristics of transnational banks can be described using the insights associated with a network-based approach. In this case, the technique of choice is multidimensional scaling (MDS). MDS reveals patterns of relations within a network structure based on the similarity of actors. By defining an objective function, and relating observations to one another in a fashion that minimizes aggregate distance (and, hence, maximizes similarities) among all scaled points, MDS conveys relationships between actors in succinct spatial maps of varying dimensionality and stress.

Dimensionality is a key concept in the language associated with MDS, and refers to the number of coordinate axes used to locate an actor or event on a spatial map.

Table 11.2 ALSCAL multidimensional solutions

	Actors	Dimensions	Iterations	Stress	R2
Bank to Bank					
Branches, 1976	37	3	6	0.240	0.590
Branches, 1986	53	3	24	0.250	0.620
City to City					
Branches, 1976	49	2	5	0.310	0.540
Branches, 1986	51	2	12	0.310	0.630

The determination of an appropriate number of dimensions is not an exact science; rather, two basic laws governing dimensionality help to explain its importance to an MDS solution. First, the greater the number of dimensions, the higher the R-squared; second, the higher the *stress* associated with the model outcome, the worse the fit of the data to the MDS configuration. All of the outcomes presented in this paper are two- or three-dimensional solutions. The specific stress histories of each solution are found in Table 11.2.

While the coefficient of determination, or R-squared, is a well-known multivariate statistical measure that refers to how successfully variation within a data set is explained by an equation or model, stress is less familiar concept. Put simply, stress can be thought of as a measure of the *goodness-of-fit* (sometimes called the *badness-*

of-fit) for data being modelled in the MDS exercise. For a more detailed explanation the reader is directed to Kruskal and Wish (1989).

Data and methodology

Data sources and data compilation The 1989 *American Banker Yearbook* contains a listing of the largest transnational banks, ranked by assets under firm control, for the fiscal year ended 1988. A sample of 250 large banks was developed from the top 500 asset-ranked banks in this listing. The first 200 banks found on this list were included in rank-order. Thereafter, the final 50 banks needed to complete the sample were randomly picked from positions falling between the 201st and 500th rank. This strategy provided banks from the developing world with a better chance for inclusion in the final sample. Figure 11.3 shows the national origins of the 250 bank sample used in this study, and the assets under their collective control in 1986.

The sample is comprehensive, with the 250 banks examined accounting for more than 70 per cent of the assets held by international banks in 1988. The accuracy of the information in the 1989 *American Banker Yearbook* was confirmed using the following sources:

- *Who Owns Whom* (Dun and Bradstreet, 1976, 1986)
- *Who Owns What* (Dun and Bradstreet, 1976, 1986)
- *Moody's Bank and Finance Manual* (Dun and Bradstreet, 1976, 1986)
- *Rand McNally International Banker's Directory* (Rand McNally, 1976, 1986).

For each of the banks included in this study, information was gathered on the location of all nondomestic bank affiliates, branches, and subsidiaries in 1976 and 1986. The headquarters location for each of the banks in 1986 was also noted. All of the data gathered on each of the banks included in this study was recorded as binary information.

At this stage of data collection, matrices were in their most elemental form. For all of the actors included in the base matrices, only two possible states could prevail; presence (indicated by 1), or absence (indicated by 0). Thus, a bank's presence or absence at a location was recorded in one of three base matrices, yielding eventual matrix dimensions of 250 banks (or actors) by 366 cities (or entities) over the two data years.

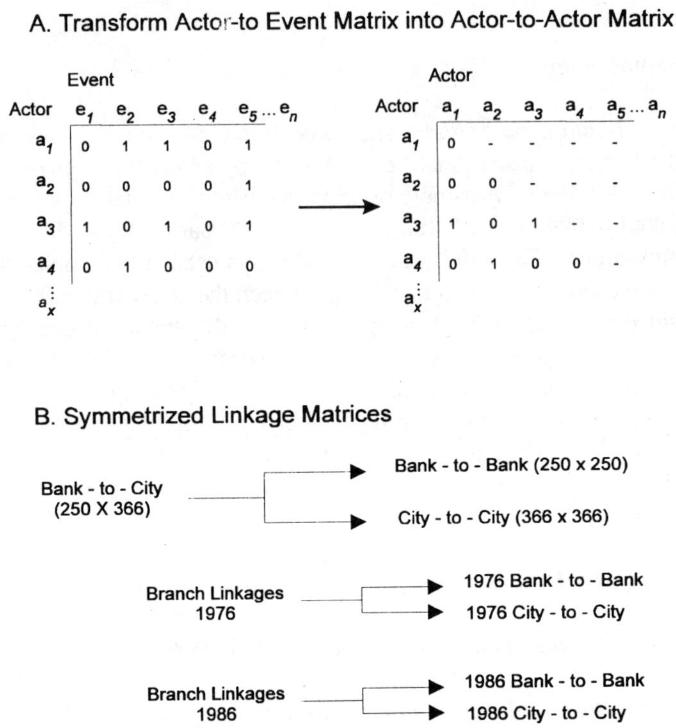

Figure 11.4 Matrix symmetrization

MDS data: preparation and output

In preparing the base matrices for submission to an MDS procedure, two additional steps were required. First, to simplify computing requirements and to keep the representation of the final configuration reasonably concise, all six of the base matrices were symmetrized. Symmetrizing involved turning the original actor to entity matrix into an actor to actor matrix (250 by 250) and an entity to entity matrix (366 by 366). Six base matrices of dimensions 250 by 366 became two sets of six symmetrized matrices. A schematic of this process is given in Figure 11.4.

In order to simplify the visual representation of the information contained in the 12 transformed matrices, a final matrix reduction was required. This process was determined by one principle: that the reduced matrices would have to contain a maximum amount of information and use a minimum number of cells. Thus, by determining how much activity an individual actor or entity accounted for in the non-

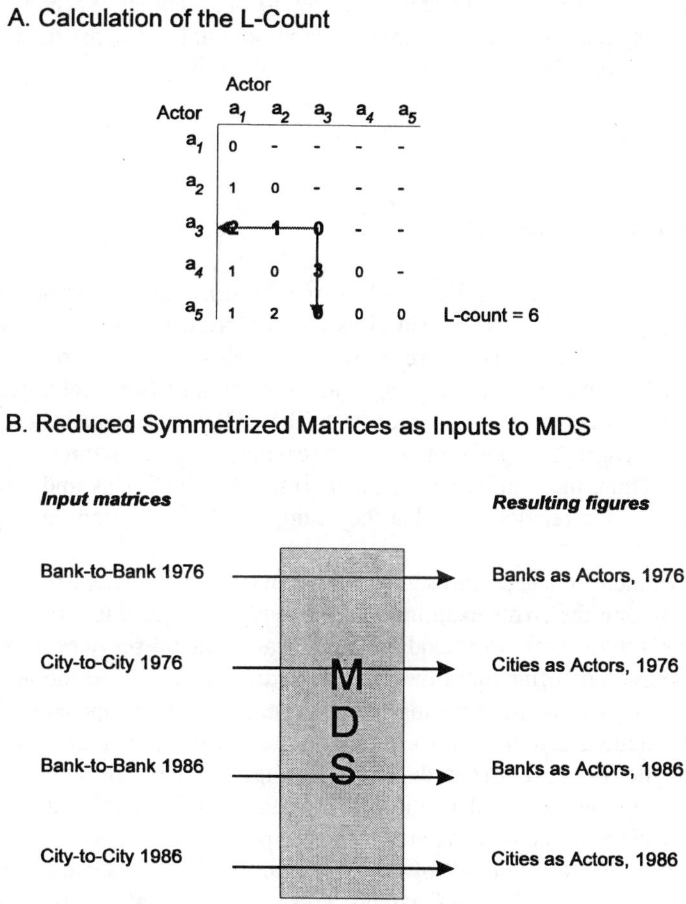

Figure 11.5 MDS input data transformations

reduced matrix (called a 'l-count'), it was possible to isolate the most heavily connected banks and cities. After some experimentation, cutoffs were established which captured 50% of the activity contained in all of the nonreduced matrix, but required the inclusion of 50 or fewer actors in each of the nonreduced matrices (Figure 11.5).

The final product is a series of spatial maps which serve to reveal the most active portions of two aspects of transnational banking networks. These were produced with the MDS program ALSCAL (Alternating Least Squares Scaling Algorithm), using the reduced matrices as the basic input.

All of the configurations presented in Figures 11.6 through 11.9 share one characteristic. Recalling that attributes are compared on an actor to actor basis, it follows that banks (or cities) appearing closer to one another are more alike than banks (or cities) that are further apart. This simple axiom forms the basis for all subsequent interpretations of the derived MDS solutions.

Results

Banks as Actors, 1976 and 1986

Occasionally, it is possible to intuitively name the dimensions that underlie a two-dimensional representation. However, it is much more difficult to ascribe names to solutions involving three or more dimensions; this normally requires lengthy exploration of the configuration, using other formal statistical techniques. In this instance the main concern is to demonstrate the utility of statistical techniques for portraying a geographic phenomenon, rather than with deducing the names of dimensions. Thus, the multidimensional representations of bank and city networks are examined for the relationships that they suggest within the transnational banking system.

In 1976, branch linkages represented the second most prevalent form of banking connection among the firms examined in this study. In general, branch operations reveal a bank's willingness to extend universal transnational services to markets that are well-understood, offer lucrative rates of return, and require the acceptance of higher levels of risk for the arriving bank. Therefore, the propensity of a bank to engage in branching activity is also related to the age of the banking firm.

Many of the banking firms depicted in Figure 11.6 are among the oldest transnational operators found in the world today. Collectively, their names are closely identified with the political and economic power structures of the nations from which they derive. Virtually all of the American banks represented in Figure 11.6 are highly recognizable; Morgan Guaranty Trust, the First National Bank of Chicago, the First National Bank of Boston, Chase Manhattan Bank, Bankers Trust Co., Bank of America and Chemical Bank all occur in the core of the 1976 MDS solution for bank branches.

Relative to their asset-based rankings, American transnational banks are clearly over represented in Figure 11.6. There is no incongruity attached to this finding; rather, the configuration underscores the important role that US transnationals have played in the post-World War II economy. Collectively, America's banks are seasoned global corporations that are broadly integrated into the world economy. As the nation that spawned the original wave of globalized banking expansion throughout the 1950s and 1960s, most of the transnationals that derive from the United States are mature firms with elaborate branch networks. While much of the impetus for American banks to engage in offshore banking is derived from legislated limits to domestic growth opportunities, the global diffusion of other US-based transnational firms, coupled with their demand for capital in support of opportunity abroad, served to accelerate the growth of US branch banking around the world.

In stark contrast to the United States, Japanese transnational banks were not well-represented in the 1976 branch banking core. Figure 11.6 contains just three transnational entries from Japan, consisting of the Bank of Tokyo, Mitsubishi Bank Ltd. (not shown) and Sumitomo Bank Ltd. Still, the assertion that branch linkage is a form best-suited to mature firms remains as true for Japan as for all of the post-industrial

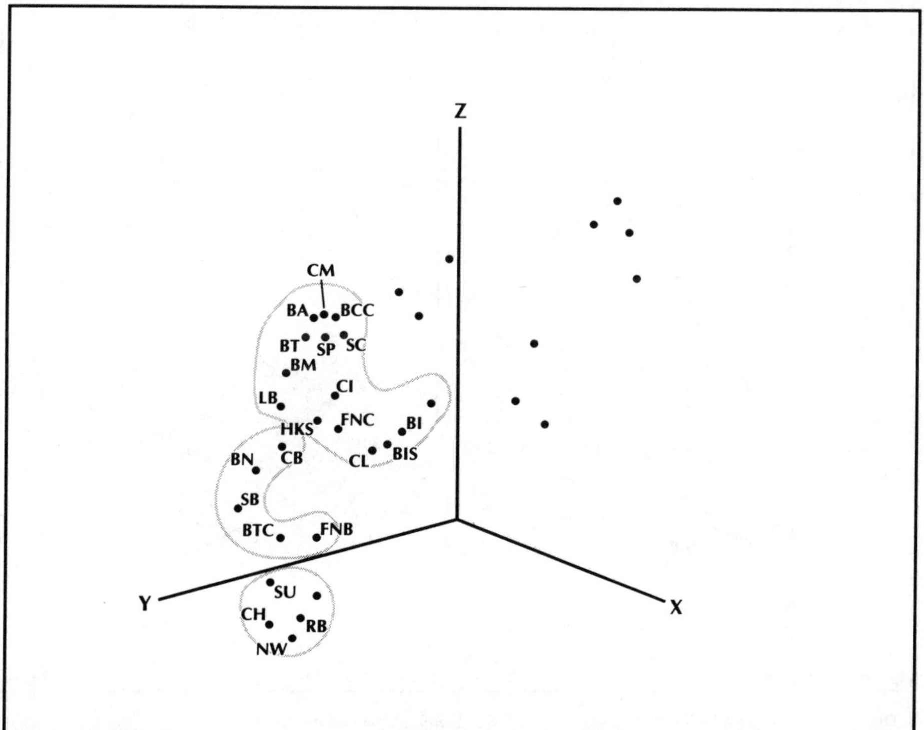

CODE	BANK NAME	RANK
CB	Citibank	9
BN	Banque Nationale de Paris	10
CL	Crédit Lyonnais	12
SU	Sumitomo Bank Ltd.	16
NW	National Westminster Bank PLC	17
BT	Bank of Tokyo	23
HKS	Hong Kong and Shanghai Banking Corp.	28
BA	Bank of America	29
SB	Swiss Bank Corporation	30
CM	Chase Manhattan Bank NA	37
LB	Lloyds Bank PLC	41
RB	Royal Bank of Canada	43

CODE	BANK NAME	RANK
BM	Bank of Montreal	53
CH	Chemical Bank	55
BTC	Bankers Trust Co.	63
SC	Standard Chartered Bank	69
SP	Security Pacifico National Bank	71
BIS	Banque Indosuez	77
FNC	First National Bank (Chicago)	87
CI	Continental Illinois National Bank & Trust	93
FNB	First National Bank (Boston)	111
BI	Bank of India	337
BCC	Bank of Credit and Commerce International	380

Produced by: The Cartographic Section, Dept. of Geography, U.W.O.

Figure 11.6 Banks as actors, 1976

nations. Thus, the average firm age of Japanese banks engaged in branch operations stood at 64 years in 1976, compared with an average firm age of 53 years for Japanese banks participating in the 1976 affiliate banking system, and 52 years for the subsidiary form.

All of the core banking systems identified in Figures 11.6 through 11.9 suggest that the propensity of a bank to be represented in each configuration is related to the size and longevity of the individual firm. Just as London's neo-colonial legacy and superb location reinforce the city's centrality in each of Figures 11.8 and 11.9, so too are

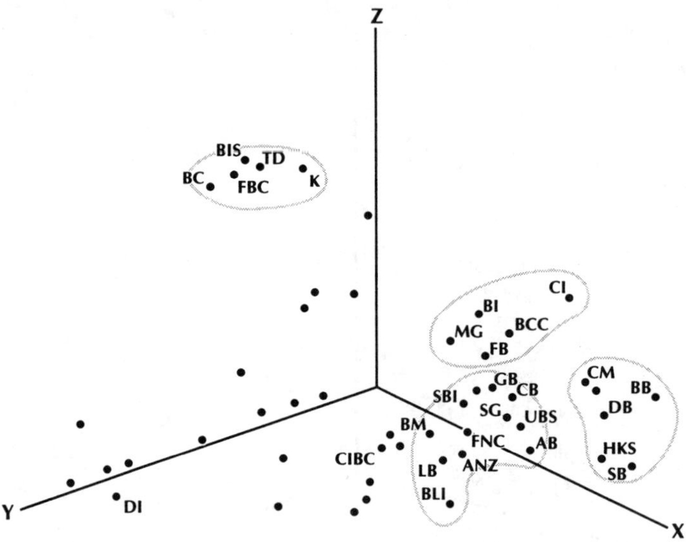

CODE	BANK NAME	RANK	CODE	BANK NAME	RANK
DI	Dai Ichi Kangyo Bank Ltd.	1	BIS	Banque Indosuez	77
FB	Fuji Bank Ltd.	3	WB	Westpac Banking Corp.	85
CB	Citibank	9	TD	Toronto Dominion Bank	86
DB	Deutsche Bank	13	FNC	First National Bank (Chicago)	87
SG	Société Generale	18	SBI	State Bank of India	90
BB	Barclays Bank PLC	19	CI	Continental Illinois National Bank & Trust	93
UBS	Union Bank of Switzerland	27	ANZ	Australia and New Zealand Banking Group	95
HKS	Hong Kong and Shanghai Banking Corp.	28	BC	Banco Central	99
SB	Swiss Bank Corp.	30	BLI	Bank Leumi Israel	113
CM	Chase Manhattan Bank NA	37	FBC	First Interstate Bank of California	124
LB	Lloyds Bank PLC	41	K	Korea Exchange Bank	153
MG	Morgan Guaranty Trust Co.	44	BI	Bank of India	337
AB	Algemene Bank Nederland	45	GB	Grindlays Bank PLC	364
BM	Bank of Montreal	53	BCC	Bank of Credit and Commerce International	380
CIBC	Canadian Imperial Bank of Commerce	60			

Produced by: The Cartographic Section, Dept. of Geography, U.W.O.

Figure 11.7 Banks as actors, 1986

banks with long transnational experience and large capital resources likely to appear in each of Figures 11.6 and 11.7.

In 1976, among banks emanating from Japan, the United States, Germany, France, the United Kingdom, Switzerland, Canada and the Netherlands, average firm age for affiliate linkages were substantially lower than average firm age for branch linkages. For the same group of nations, the average age of firms engaged in subsidiary operations was generally higher than for affiliate participation: Japan was a notable exception to this characterization of firms headquartered in the OECD nations.

Between 1976 and 1986, the transnational banking system redeployed its resources in response to the changing organization of the global space-economy. This period of rapid change culminated in the conversion of many nonbranch overseas operations to branch operations. The cause of network redeployment by the transnational banks is rooted in contemporary macroeconomic change (Dahm, 1994).

According to a United Nations study of transnational banks, the late 1970s and early 1980s were characterized by slack demand for loans in most of the post-industrial world, the proliferation of world trade by transnational corporations, and the expansion of Eurocurrency markets from US$59 billion in 1970, to US$1.8 trillion by 1982 (Bannock, 1988). Besides these evolutionary changes in the conduct of transnational banking, overseas branch managers of large transnational banks were vested with the authority to lend capital via interbank markets located in southeast Asia, North America, and Europe. Together, these four macroeconomic forces largely reshaped transnational banking during the study period (UNCTC, 1983).

Many specific features found in Figure 11.7 support the contention that the expansion of transnational corporations served to hasten the conversion of affiliate and subsidiary offices to branch operations. The clearest of these is the sheer number of firms participating in the core branch system, which rose from 37 in 1976, to 53 by 1986, an increase of 43.2 per cent.

The appearance of Asian-controlled subsidiaries in other Asian nations, the Americas, and Europe increased demand for capital from Asian transnational banks in new markets. Virtually all of the branch proliferation that occurred between 1976 and 1986 is attributed to Asian and European operators; only one North American firm, the Toronto Dominion Bank, appeared as an entirely new entrant in the 1986 branch banking system.

In examining specific bank groupings that occur in Figure 11.7, some interesting features can be deduced. Compared to their 1976 participation levels, several nations experienced enhanced representation in the 1986 branch banking system. Japanese firms increased their numbers in the core system, rising from just three entries in 1976, to six by 1986. Still, among the Japanese firms appearing as branch participants for the first time, the largest asset-ranked bank in the world, the Dai Ichi Kangyo Bank, occurs as an isolate at the edge of Figure 11.7.

Despite the general expansion of Asian headquartered banks between 1976 and 1986, transnationals from this region still only accounted for one-fifth of the firms represented in Figure 11.7. Between them, North American and European firms dominate Figure 11.7, accounting for 38 of the 53 firms comprising the core branch system.

Compared to 1976, the twelve American firms found in Figure 11.7 represent an increase of just one firm (First Interstate Bank of California) by 1986. More impressively, all eleven American entries that occurred in the 1976 configuration maintained their status as core actors in the 1986 branch configuration, suggesting that, even as early as 1976, the US banks had been mature players in the international banking area.

Five Canadian banks occur in the 1986 core branch structure, rounding out North American representation in Figure 11.7. The showing of the Canadian banks, especially given the size of Canada's economy relative to other OECD nations, hints at Canada's key role as a participant in international loan syndication (UNTNC, 1983). The Bank of Montreal and the Canadian Imperial Bank of Commerce appear close together. Along with the Banque Nationale de Paris, they occupy a space close to the busiest part of Figure 11.7. Canada's largest bank, the Royal Bank of Canada, occurs as an isolated firm, while the Toronto Dominion Bank forms a tight cluster with the First Interstate Bank of California, Banco Central (of Spain), Westpac Banking Corporation (of Australia) and the French-based Banque Indosuez. The Bank of Nova Scotia is tightly paired with the Chemical Bank of New York.

Historically, French transnational banks have not been prominent participants in branch banking activity but, by 1986, six appeared in the core of the branch system (Figure 11.7). Like France, German banks placed very little emphasis on branch linkages prior to the 1980s. Reflecting this reality, in 1976, there were no German banks participating in the core of the branch system. By 1986, three German transnational firms appeared in the core branch system.

One persistent grouping evident between 1976 and 1986 involves the appearance of the now infamous Bank of Credit and Commerce International, a transnational whose Luxembourg headquarters were established only in 1972, alongside the Bank of India and the Continental Illinois Trust and Banking Co. By 1986, these three banks formed a cluster that included the Morgan Guaranty Trust Co. and Tokyo-based Fuji Bank Ltd.

Only five transnational banks found in Figure 11.7 are headquartered in the developing world; two of these are from India. Both the State Bank of India and the Bank of India appear in the most densely populated area of the configuration, fortifying Indian participation in the world banking system. Finally, the disappearance of the Bank Melli-Iran by 1986, following its showing in the 1976 branch configuration, is consistent with political events that led to the isolation of the Iranian state from the world economy in the 1980s.

Cities as actors, 1976 and 1986

There was a rapid increase in the sheer number of cities involved in the branch banking system between 1976 and 1986. This points to a loosening urban hierarchy, with a more dispersed arrangement of cities serving as economic control points in the global economy. Even the concentrated activity-space shown in Figures 11.8 and 11.9 is indicative of the high degree of regional participation in the global economy in the 1970s and 1980s. In 1976, 49 cities accounted for 50 per cent of the branch linkages in the study sample. By 1986, 51 cities accounted for 50 per cent of the branch activity occurring in the 366 cities examined in this study. However, within the core and semicore regions defined in Figures 11.8 and 11.9, the number of cities participating rose from just 15 in 1976, to 23 by 1986.

In 1976, all of the cities enjoined in the branch banking network were notable for their size and prominent roles within the domestic economies from which they emanated. Unlike subsidiary and affiliate linkages, branch linkages tend to replicate the rank-order rules of the world urban system, with megacities and extreme conurbations from every economic region represented in Figures 11.8 and 11.9.

In the broadest sense, the spatial arrangement of cities occurring in both the 1976 and 1986 branch systems serves to reinforce the expectations of urbanologists;

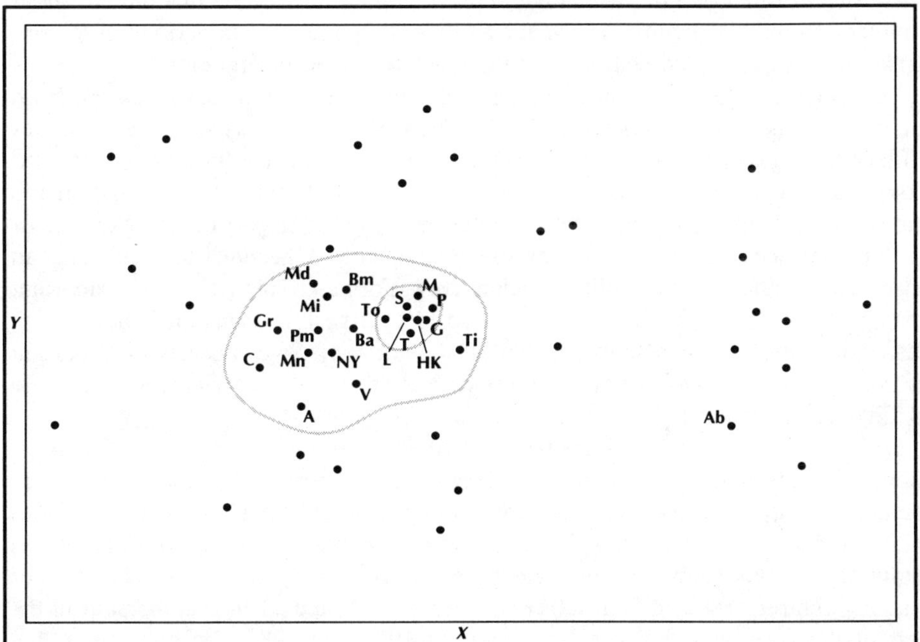

CODE	CITY	CODE	CITY	CODE	CITY
Ab	Abu Dhabi	HK	Hong Kong	Pm	Panama
A	Amsterdam	L	London	P	Paris
Bm	Bahamas	Md	Madrid	S	Seoul
Ba	Bahrain	M	Manilla	Ti	Taipei
C	Chicago	Mi	Milan	T	Tokyo
G	Geneva	Mn	Montreal	To	Toronto
Gr	Grand Cayman	NY	New York	V	Vancouver

Produced by: The Cartographic Section, Dept. of Geography, U.W.O.

Figure 11.8 Cities as actors, 1976

dominance in the world urban system, as measured by branch banking activity, tends to follow a rank-order rule. This generalization is tempered by recognizing the relative state of the domestic economy from which a large urban centre emanates; sprawling conurbations from the developing world may contain larger populations than large urban places in the developed world. Nevertheless, the tremendous per capita wealth differential that occurs between, say, Cairo and Toronto, renders the latter a more prominent branch banking city in both Figures 11.8 and 11.9.

Figure 11.8 is notable for its lack of tight structure, particularly in the regions lying beyond the core cities located around London. Besides the cohesion of the core and the dispersed periphery associated with Figure 11.8, one other remarkable feature is the barrier of empty space that separates the core from the edges of the configuration. In examining Figure 11.8, the absence of urban penetration in the space separating the core and periphery suggests that an important threshold differentiates the cities that reside in either part of the configuration. Figure 11.8 suggests that the threshold number of linkages required to change a city's designation from peripheral to core banking centre remained well beyond the reach of the peripheral city.

Two cities thought synonymous with global banking are conspicuously absent from the core branch banking system in 1976 -- New York and Tokyo. If one examines affiliate and subsidiary banking networks as well, it is clear that both New York and Tokyo perform roles that are distinct from London, Frankfurt and Paris in the transnational banking system (Dahm and Green, 1993). As part of its repertoire of banking services, London performs the role of both a headquarters city and an unrivalled destination city. Unlike London, New York and Tokyo are very important headquarters cities for many of the world's largest transnational banks. As destinations for banking activity, neither New York nor Tokyo is nearly as important as London, Paris, or any one of several other attractive urban places found at the core of Figures 11.8 and 11.9.

Both Figures 11.8 and 11.9 are best described as configurations with an arrangement of cities that follow a marked core-semicore-periphery pattern of branch banking activity. Still, the seemingly static structure of both solutions belies enormous changes that occurred within the core system of branch cities over the period examined by this study. While London remained the city around which all other banking centres arranged themselves in Figures 11.8 and 11.9, membership in the rest of the core and semicore was fluid. In 1976 and 1986, the only cities that persisted within the regions described as falling within the core and semicore were Geneva, Paris, Frankfurt, and Tokyo.

One direct conclusion can be drawn from this observation; cities that appear at or near the core of the transnational branch banking system in 1976 are not assured of inclusion in the core system at a subsequent point in time. In the MDS solutions presented here, only Manila manages to undergo the conversion from noncore to core player between 1976 and 1986. All of the other centres which were semi-core players alongside Manila -- Dusseldorf, Beirut and Amsterdam -- failed to find their way into the core system by 1986.

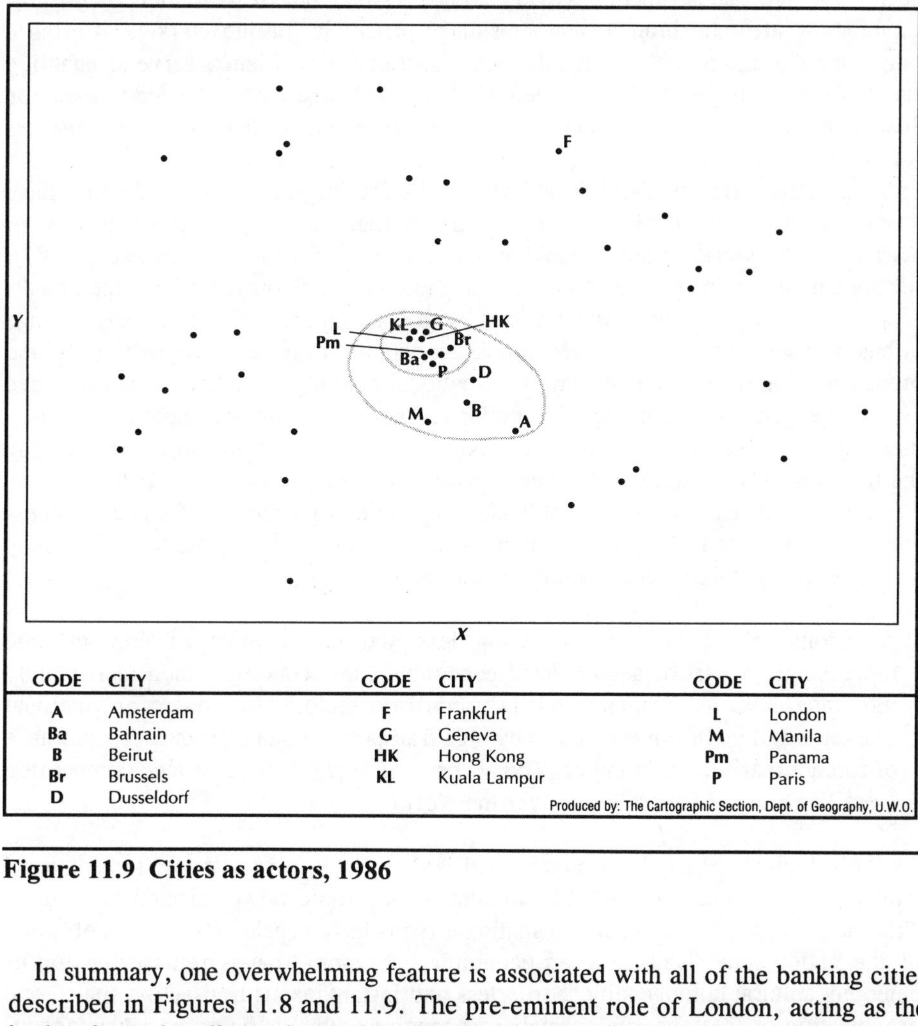

Figure 11.9 Cities as actors, 1986

In summary, one overwhelming feature is associated with all of the banking cities described in Figures 11.8 and 11.9. The pre-eminent role of London, acting as the broker for an inordinate share of the world's transnational banking, renders the city a peerless global banking centre. Reflecting its past and suggesting its future, the MDS solutions for the most important transnational banking linkage, branch operations, confirms the matchless power of London as the foci of human and non-human contact systems in the global banking system.

Summary and conclusions

Between the end of the Second World War and the late 1980s, some 10,000 corporations invested directly in the economies of foreign nations (Bannock et al., 1988). In turn, three-quarters of the benefits derived from these ventures have accrued to the five hundred largest transnational bank and non-bank enterprises. As core participants in the process of global economic integration, transnational banks serve a dual-purpose. First, banks function as very large transnational firms in their own right, establishing affiliate, branch, and subsidiary offices in foreign markets offering a range of risks and potential rewards. Second, transnational banks serve as enabling agents for other firms, possessing the knowledge and experience required to meet the diverse pecuniary needs of other transnational firms engaged in off-shore business activities.

As specialised transnational firms, the world's 250 largest transnational banks have dominated the global banking system, allowing them to gain control of roughly 70 percent of the world's global banking activity in 1986 (*American Banker*, 1987). Responding to the increasing complexity of the global economy, transnational banks are extremely sophisticated organizations, with contemporary firms offering a range of business services that far exceed simple conceptions of banks as deposit-taking and money-lending institutions. Today, transnational banking activity is inexorably tied to the emergence of Asian and Eurodollar markets, growing participation in equity markets, interbank lending, Edge Act banking, and, more than anything else, assuring the fortunes of other transnational enterprises engaged in business abroad.

While the impact of transnational banking upon the organization of global business is clear, characterizations of transnational banks as pernicious agents of social decay are not entirely unjustified. According to Lipsey:

> ...national economies are becoming less and less distinct as they become increasingly a part of a *globalized* economy -- an economy which increasingly integrates both its financial and its production sectors. No longer are national markets separated from each other by high transport costs and producers' ignorance of foreign market opportunities. Today, firms in many industries face competition from firms located literally all over the world.

As the principal vehicle by which capital is distributed across space, transnational banks quietly wield a remarkable amount of economic power around the world. Transnational banks and other transnational firms have accelerated the re-definition of the nation-state, leading to an economic geography that is remarkable for its emergent cultural homogeneity, borderless and instantaneous transaction space, and organization of regions into specialised economic subunits based on advantageous supplies of land, labour, or capital.

As transnational enterprise exploits the benefits of a globalizing economy, a basic requirement for the firm is the need to establish a presence in countries where the production process is located. Therefore, one basic feature of the emerging homogenous economic landscape is the proliferation of overseas offices -- affiliates, branches, and subsidiaries. Reflecting the similar nature of transnational banks to other forms of transnational enterprise, it is not surprising that a proliferation of global banking networks, and concomitant growth in foreign direct investment, occurred during the period examined in this chapter, which coincides with the early emergence of the post-Fordist paradigm.

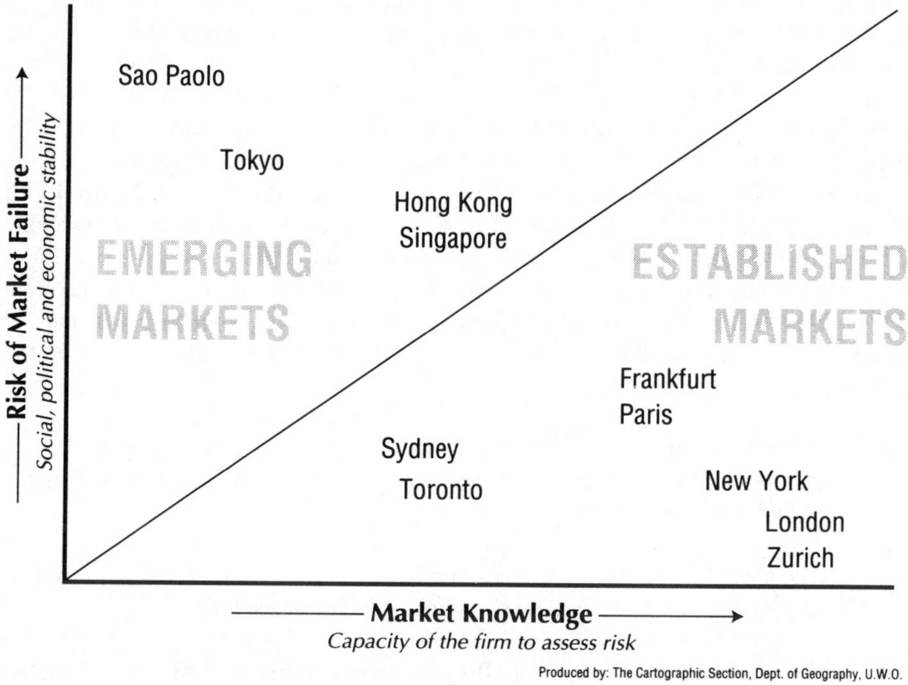

Figure 11.10 Relative positions of banking nodes, based on risk and market knowledge as perceived by firms

As both the hosts and recipients of transnational banking activity, cities act as control points in the global economy, marshalling the global flow of capital between macrogeographic regions. In general, the locational preferences of transnational banks, and the extent to which some cities serve as inordinately important foci for banking activity, reinforces the assertion that economic power emanates from a select group of urban power centres. In the tradition of Kuhn's structure of scientific revolutions, new paradigms emerge within the productive process and the organization of global trade that exerts profound influence upon the organization of the global economy. Occasionally, urban contenders emerge on the economic landscape with comparative advantages that render them sudden contemporaries of established heartland nodes. More frequently, emergent urban nodes exhibit little permanence, disappearing from the core of pecuniary power with the passing of a particular economic cycle or political calamity.

Collectively, the prominent urban nodes associated with transnational banking -- London, Paris, Sydney, New York, Tokyo, Zurich, Frankfurt -- are all points where trade, commerce, transportation, communications, and political power experience a remarkable degree of convergence. Yet within each of these cities, a complex milieu of political, economic, and technological factors leads to the endowment of each place with a unique risk profile.

While each of these urban agglomerations may seem more or less similar, the variable performances of their stock markets, coupled with occasional outbreaks of nationalist fervour or real estate collapse leads to a simple proposition. For those transnational banks interested in self-perpetuation, all of these heartland cities must be regarded as unique entities with particular risks, and therefore they must be approached with caution. This basic axiom becomes even more important when the transnational bank considers establishing operations in hinterland nodes. Figure 11.10 provides a graphical representation of how transnational banks likely viewed the world's pre-eminent banking centres between 1976 and 1986.

Besides advancing some basic ideas about the locational behaviour of transnational banks, this chapter offers several approaches to corporate geography that can be replicated in future studies of the multinational enterprise. These include the following:

- It is shown that the linkages established by banks serve as a reasonable proxy for deducing the most powerful economic nodes extant within the global urban hierarchy.

- The specific emergence of cities and banks from Southeast Asia, and Japan in particular, is readily conveyed by the MDS procedure.

- The research heeds the call for macrogeographic assessments of global circuits of capital, and provides a method for the empirical examination of emerging theoretical paradigms, including Lipsey's technical-economic paradigm.

This research underscores the importance attached to the extension of branch operations into all of the world's economic regions. It is reasonable to suggest that, as a final extension of transnational banking into the overseas marketplace, the emergence of the branch linkage as *de rigueur* within the banking community is indicative of the final stages of corporate evolution within the technical-economic paradigm. In general, the growth of branch operations between 1976 and 1986 is shown to be closely tied to the need for the more efficient export of excess capital to nonsaturated markets abroad. Clearly, the expansion of the transnational banking system mirrors rapid macroeconomic change in the world economy and offers researchers many avenues for further study.

In conclusion, this study reinforces the value of geography as an approach to understanding the manifestation of banking activity in the global economy. By providing a succinct snapshot of transnational banking activity, several macroeconomic changes associated with the 1970s and 1980s are clearly revealed. These included the rise and fall of OPEC, the geographic consequences of political conflict, increased involvement by developing countries in the economic activity of their more industrialised neighbours, the persistence of neocolonial relationships in shaping the pattern of banking linkages, and, overall, the rapid expansion of transnational banking between 1976 and 1986 as a consequence of fundamental change in the organization of the global economic system.

12 Concentration and dispersion of global control links and changes in the multinational quaternary place system

Kee-Bom Nahm and R. Keith Semple

Introduction

The global economy faces a period of rapid change. The forces driving this change are advances in information technology, telecommunications, and transportation. In response, large business organizations find it necessary to reorganize and decentralize towards a flatter network-like structure (Powell 1990; Amin and Dietrich, 1991; Dicken 1992). Globalization of the world economy entails international economic interdependence and financial deregulation. Corporations surviving change widen their activity base and expand operations globally to function as true multinational corporations (MNCs) and to prosper in a borderless society (Ohmae, 1990). Two important but contrasting trends characterize the global economy of the 1990s. First, a small number of larger and more powerful MNCs control international economic resources (Taylor and Thrift, 1986). Second, MNCs find internal corporate functions more decentralized (Miles and Snow, 1986).

Recent mergers, acquisitions, and strategic alliances contribute to the reorganization of capital into larger units. Oligopolistic business organizations, rather than nation states or competitive market mechanism, manipulate and control both national and international economic domains. The world increasingly becomes a single market place and global interdependence intensifies as MNCs rapidly expand their sphere and volume of trade and foreign direct investment (FDI). At the same time, these MNCs reorganize in order to cope efficiently with the changing economic environment as well as to respond quickly to functionally more complex and larger organizations. Corporate headquarters functions, such as command, control, co-ordination, and strategic decision-making, increase in number and scope, now concentrating in major quaternary transactional space (Cohen, 1981; Conti, 1993). On the other hand, organizational flexibility of the corporate system grows through the formation of decentralized internal and external networks (Håkansson, 1989; Johanson and Vahlne, 1990). These changes result in the formation of global nodal points possessing world-wide command and control, information, communication, and financial networks. The emerging global cities, which house MNCs' headquarters coupled with large financial institutions and social and physical infrastructure, are the control points of the global economy.

This chapter focuses on the spatial implications of corporate reorganization in general and the changing system of linkages among multinational corporate headquarters and subsidiary head offices, in particular. Multinational corporate headquarters centres are quaternary places which control world-wide information and capital flows. Research on the spatial impacts of multinational corporate command and control linkages, their concentration or dispersion, and resultant changes in the system of global cities, can shed light on the understanding of the evolution of the global quaternary place system.

Conceptual framework

This section deals with two theoretical concepts. The first is quaternary place theory and deals with the location of decision-making power (Semple, 1985). The second is network theory and deals with the internationalization of business organizations. This section links these two spatial theories by means of multinational corporate control networks.

Multinational corporate command and control centres are the major nodal points of the business world. Corporate decision-making and transactions link global quaternary places together. In the tightly interconnected world economy of the MNCs, national borders almost disappear. Individual nations are more interrelated and mutually dependent. The global web of multinational corporate control linkages connects the spatial units of corporate command and control centres and follows a spatial logic of the corporate internationalization process. This section examines and interprets the spatial behaviour of MNCs.

International quaternary places

Corporate headquarters process, send, and receive information from all parts of their internal and external environment. The major components of the internal organization consist of departments, subsidiaries, and internal agents. Whereas the components of the external environment consist of corporate competitors, government regulators, financial markets and the external providers of business services. Headquarters act as hubs of information flows and business intelligence. These quaternary activities follow a spatial logic that contrasts with that of manufacturing and service functions (Weber, 1929, pp. 219-21). This logic can be summarized in the following manner. Systems of urban centres that house clusters of interconnected corporate offices spatially disperse business power and decision making throughout the system. In other words, headquarters influence their immediate urban area, as well as the system of interconnected urban areas created by their internal and external economic and informational linkages (Green, 1993, p. 67).

Researchers have had success in modeling the spatial evolution of human activities over time (Semple, 1977; Morril, 1979) Alonso (1980) noted that many socioeconomic activities could be described by a bell-shaped curve. Semple and Phipps (1982) and Semple (1985) used this well known curve to conceptualize the evolution of quaternary place systems for continental sized countries partitioned this evolutionary process into a series of stages. This stage model has been examined and verified many times (Semple and Green, 1983; Strickland and Aiken, 1984; Wheeler and Michelson, 1989; Holloway and Wheeler, 1991; Aksoy and Marshall, 1992; Lyons, 1994; Ward, 1994). These previous works examined exclusively the internal evolution of national quaternary place systems. It is the external international quaternary place system that is the focus of the present chapter[1].

Quaternary places in the past have evolved as a system of interlinked command and control centres. The connections, for the most parts, were internal and hierarchical with only moderate contacts externally. Today, in a globalizing world, although internal contacts are still important, external contacts are the focus. This is true, not only for the largest domestic places, but also for those centres considered as secondary or even tertiary in the internal hierarchy. These external contacts, moreover, appear to be flatter in terms of the hierarchy of centres. That is, instead of information going up and down the external system, it appears to be directed across the system at all levels. Also, important domestic quaternary places find most of their activities directed outward to the international community with residual activities directed toward a formerly dominated domestic urban system. In other words, many domestic quaternary places find their external activities and influences more important than their internal contacts. For example, the flows of information, capital, and financial transactions from American quaternary centres to their international subsidiary quaternary places are greater than to their domestic secondary place counterparts.

Growing interest in the command, control and decision-making structure of particular global cities, as well as the general system of centres focuses on corporate headquarters. Located in major centres, they have international subsidiary headquarters dispersed throughout the general international system. (Friedmann, 1986; Meyer, 1991; Castells, 1993; Shachar, 1994). It is the quaternary activities that bring about the cumulative concentration of producer and financial services, social infrastructures, informational linkages, and the associated communication hubs (Friedmann and Wolff, 1982; Moss, 1987; King, 1990). It is important to note that the system of quaternary places can be treated in a theoretical context as a grand international network of hubs and spokes.

Network theory of internationalization

The reorganization of business structure constitutes one of the major changes faced today by all large international firms. These companies tend to disintegrate supply, design, manufacturing, marketing and distribution functions within the overall framework of an integrated flow system. At the same time, merger and acquisition, joint-ventures, and strategic alliances contribute to the concentration of the command and control functions. As Amin and Dietrich (1991, p. 65) argue, the more operational and functional disintegration within the corporation, the greater the degree of integrated management and control.

Independent firms within the network perform these disintegrated functions that were previously conducted within a single firm (Miles and Snow, 1986). The international network is the structure within which a company operates. More specifically, it is this system of spatial relationships among firms that forces them to maintain a close relationship with local markets while taking advantage of global network development (Johanson and Mattsson, 1988). Hakansson (1989) identified three important components of all networks; namely, *actors, resources, and activities*. Actors are groups of companies that co-ordinate and perform complementary and competitive industrial activities. They also control resources directly through an internal hierarchy, and indirectly, through external ties to the network. *Resources* such as input goods, financial capital, technology, personnel, and marketing are necessary conditions for all industrial activities. And finally, *activities* are the processes of production and exchange which internally transform inputs to outputs; externally they provide services and transactions among other linked organizations in the network.

The network is by no means stable over time. It evolves as firms compete with each other and either advance or decline. There is a struggle to gain control over resources. Firms need investments to thrive and acquire control in the network. Investments which require considerable financial capital are often associated with other disinvestments. This dichotomy changes the internal network structure, as well as the external links of individual firms. In general, the evolution of a firm within the network, as a process to gain more power and resource control, results in internal hierachization of the firm along with the associated externalization of linkages.

The network model of internationalization holds that existing theories of MNCs and foreign direct investments cannot relate the internationalization process to the concept of an industrial network. The process of internationalization is an interplay between increasing commitments of resources and developing a knowledge base about foreign operations and markets (Johanson and Mattsson, 1988). Thus, internationalization of a firm means that a firm establishes and develops positions in relation to counterparts in the foreign networks which change over time. The foreign investment behavior of a firm follows, to a large extent, its long-lasting relationships with suppliers, customers, and competitors. These relationships give the firm a certain control over its environment and, at the same time, make it subject to some reciprocal control. In short, the network model of internationalization stresses the importance of relative position in industrial networks[2].

The network model of internationalization aims at explaining the pattern and mode of establishing international operations (Johanson and Vahlne, 1990, p. 16). Executives at headquarters determine the location of foreign subsidiaries and decide the pattern of international operations. Herein lies the spatial implications of the network model. The model postulates that firms first invest by invading physically and culturally close markets; then, as experience grows, they enter more distant markets. As the functional separation between conception and execution of economic processes continues, corporate power and decision-making systems concentrate in the major nodes of world-wide information, communication, trade, and financial networks (Conti, 1993). On the other hand, operating activities disperse by taking advantage of expanding corporate networks and advances in telecommunication technologies (Hepworth, 1986; Gillespie, 1991; Capello, 1994).

In short, multinational foreign subsidiary centres, initially concentrated, disperse over time. As network evolves, more new candidates based on various spatial points enter into the network, they gradually obtain experimental knowledge and reduce uncertainty within the network. The headquarters centres of MNCs diversify and disperse over time. The developing phase of industrial networks and the location of global nodal centres, however, constrains the dispersion pattern of headquarters and subsidiary centres. By the late 1980s and early 1990s, the global pattern of investments can be characterized as a tri-polar or the Triad system consisting of the European Union (EU), North America, and Japan (Ohmae, 1985; UNCTAD, 1993). In 1990, this system accounted for 76.2 per cent of total inward stock in foreign direct investments; a percentage that was up from 66.9 in 1983. Similarly, total outward stock in 1990 amounted to 97.0 per cent, almost identical to the 97.3 per cent of 1983 (Dunning and Cantwell, 1987; UNCTAD, 1993). These patterns suggest that global corporate activity constitutes a concentrated yet dispersing trend. While command and control centres concentrate in the Triad; existing flatform of corporate networks expands and disperses within the Triad. Furthermore, as technological and locational requirements differ among sectors, their dispersion tendency differentiates by sector of the economy. Market-oriented companies, for example, may locate their headquarters and also subsidiary centres in major product or service markets, while companies with great financial needs favour locations in major banking cities.

Premises

The study of the spatial concentration and dispersion of economic activity over time is of great importance to economic geography. The endless pursuit of profit, growth, and technological advances has provoked firms headquartered in established national and international core centres to reassess their locations. They relocate in newer or sometimes more remote areas. The rapid development of global telecommunication networks, with other distance-shrinking technologies, appears to be accelerating this trend. At the same time, a dichotomous process leads international firms to concentrate their headquarters activities into a small number of large metropolitan centres in the leading industrialized countries. The added preference for informational and telecommunication hubs found in these large centres, strengthen the trend (Moss, 1987; Warf, 1989). These simultaneous and opposite tendencies lead to a number of important premises.

This chapter addresses three premises. Firstly, multinational corporate domestic headquarters and foreign subsidiaries tend to be more concentrated in the three trading blocs of the world, namely; North America, European Union, and Japan (Ohmae, 1985; UNCTD, 1993). Secondly, multinational control centres disperse over time within the three major trading blocs. At the same time, capital flows, associated with information and communication flows, spread and diversify across national borders (Wheeler and Mitchelson, 1989). Thirdly, the dominance of the largest cities in the world system lessens as the international economy integrates while the global urban system disperses (Ettlinger and Archer, 1987). The gradual decline of a global political hegemony and the emergence of a multicentric world system contribute to this trend.

Data

This chapter investigates the premises for the top 600 manufacturing, top 100 resource, top 100 service MNCs based on revenues, by location of domestic headquarters and foreign subsidiaries for the period 1974-91. Since there is no standard definition of the term 'multinational corporations[3]. The study employs an operational definition of MNCs adopted from Stopford, Dunning and Haberich (1980) and Stopford (1992):

1 A domestic firm has a minimum of 25 per cent of the voting equity of subsidiary companies in at least three foreign countries.

2 The firm has a minimum of 5 per cent of its consolidated sales or assets attributable to foreign investments.

3 The firm has a minimum value of sales in millions of US dollars generated by foreign operations of 30 (1974), 50 (1980), 80 (1985), and 100 (1991).

The data set consists of the location of the headquarters and subsidiary centres of the MNCs and associated revenues. A number of sources provide data for the investigation of the premises. The primary sources of the headquarters location and corporate size data are the *Directory of Multinationals* (Stopford, Dunning and Haberich, 1980; Dunning and Cantwell, 1987; Stafford and Purkis, 1989; Stopford, 1992) and Business Week's *The Global 1000*. The dataset is supplemented by data from Forbes' *Foreign 500,* Dun and Bradstreet's *Principal International Business* and *Moody's International Manual.* Subsidiary data on location and corporate size varies according to their host countries.

Methodology

This study utilizes a corporate concentration ratio, spatial concentration ratio, and the rank-size distribution to assess the concentration and dispersion trends of multinational corporate headquarters and subsidiaries. The corporate concentration ratio measures the proportion of total revenues controlled by the largest firms with respect to all firms. Similarly, spatial concentration ratio measures the proportion of total revenues controlled by the largest centres with respect to all centres.

To assess the position of each centre in the global city system defined by multinational corporate control network, the study employs a measure of point centrality developed by Bonacich (1987). Constructed to measure the position of each centre in networks of interaction, this measure shows the relative importance of corporate centres in the system of domestic headquarters and foreign subsidiary linkages.

The centrality score for any centre is:[4]

$$C_i(\alpha,\beta)=\sum_j(\alpha+\beta c_j)R_{ij}$$

where C_i is the centrality score of centre i, α is a network specific constant that standardizes centrality scores, β specifies the range of interactions considered, c_j is the centrality score of centre j, and R_{ij} is the magnitude of the control of centre i over centre j. Bonacich (1987) suggests that a differential weight be given to the range of direct and indirect interactions for assessing network position, which can vary between -1 and +1 as determined by β parameter. A β of 0 uses only direct transactions among centres. Since multinational headquarters-subsidiary linkage is considered as a direct transaction, $\beta = 0$ is appropriate for this analysis. The measure produces standardized scores, allowing comparisons of networks of varying sizes and time-scale. An α, determined by $\Sigma_i\ c_i(\alpha, \beta)^2$ = number of units in the network, standardizes the centrality scores for each network (Bonacich, 1987, p. 1173).

This study defines network position as the dominance by a centre of the headquarters- subsidiary network. Domestic headquarters centre's controlling subsidiary revenues indicates the magnitude of flow between the two centres. In other words, domestic headquarters centre is the originating place of flow and foreign subsidiary centre is the destination. It implies that a city controlling a disproportionate share of multinational revenues occupies a more central position in the system of global cities.

The changing multinational corporate control linkages

Changes in regional and national standing

During the period 1974-91, most notable change is the sharp fall of the dominance of American multinational headquarters centres. Over these years, the USA suffers a net loss of almost 20 per cent in the revenues of its multinational headquarters centres (Table 12.1). Aside from the declining competiveness of American MNCs, mergers and acquisitions also contribute to the decreasing US dominance. British holding firm Grand Metropolitan acquired Pillsbury (Burger King, Doughboy, and Green Giant) for US$ 5.8 billions in 1989 and Hanson Trust acquired US Industries (1984), SCM (1986), and Kidde (1987) for more than US$ 2 billions. The Swiss firm Nestlé acquired Carnation for US$ 3 billions in 1985. The merger of SmithKline Beckman with British Beecham produced the pharmaceutical giant SmithKline Beecham headquartered in London.

Three other industrialized countries experienced declines in representation among the top 800 nonfinancial MNCs during the period 1974-91. The United Kingdom declined from 9.2 per cent in 1974 to 7.0 per cent in 1991. Canada's and Italy's shares declined by 0.7 per cent and 0.6 per cent, respectively. The rapid growth of

Japan matches the decline of American corporations. Overall, the share of industrialized countries in the revenues of the 800 nonfinancial multinational headquarters centres was more than 97 per cent of world total, indicating steady concentration of international quaternary places in these areas.

Table 12.1: Regional share of the 800 nonfinancial MNCs' revenues

	1974 HQ(*Sub*)	1980 HQ(*Sub*)	1985 HQ(*Sub*)	1991 HQ(*Sub*)
Industrializing Countries	99.6(*96.6*)	97.2(*95.9*)	97.0(*93.0*)	97.6(*91.1*)
USA	50.1(*9.3*)	45.0(*21.2*)	45.0(*33.2*)	33.9(*37.4*)
Japan	17.3(-)	17.7(-)	20.9(-)	29.4(-)
Germany	7.7(*19.5*)	7.8(*16.0*)	6.8(*11.3*)	9.8(*10.2*)
UK	9.2(*17.7*)	9.3(*14.7*)	7.5(*14.9*)	7.0(*15.7*)
France	3.3(*7.6*)	4.8(*7.4*)	3.8(*5.5*)	5.5(*5.8*)
Netherlands	2.7(*4.0*)	3.5(*3.4*)	3.1(*2.5*)	2.6(*2.6*)
Italy	2.7(*3.9*)	2.6(*4.3*)	2.4(*2.6*)	2.1(*2.1*)
Sweden	1.3(*2.6*)	1.4(*1.9*)	1.3(*1.5*)	1.2(*1.3*)
Canada	1.9(*22.3*)	1.6(*14.1*)	1.5(*10.7*)	1.1(*7.7*)
Others	3.6(*9.7*)	3.5(*10.5*)	4.5(*12.0*)	5.1(*8.3*)
Industrializing Countries	0.4(*3.4*)	2.8(*4.1*)	3.0(*7.0*)	2.4(*8.9*)
Total	100.0(*100.0*)	100.0(*100.0*)	100.0(*100.0*)	100.0(*100.0*)

* The values in the parenthesis indicate the share of subsidiary centres.

Subsidiaries in the USA account for more than one third of the total subsidiary revenues in 1991 risen from only 9.3 per cent of 1974. This sharp increase of US dominance as subsidiary centres stems from aggressive investments by Japanese corporations, accompanied by increasing involvement of European firms in the American market. The US dominance is followed by United Kingdom (15.7 per cent), Germany (10.2 per cent), and Canada (7.7 per cent). The USA is not alone

Table 14.2
The 800 nonfinancial multinational headquarters-subsidiary linkages by region, 1974-91

A. 1974 Subsidiaries	North America	(%)	Europe	(%)	Japan & Oceania	(%)	Others	(%)	Total	(%)
Headquarters										
North America	31,639	(16.1)	69,636	(35.5)	68	(0.1)	300	(0.2)	101,643	(51.8)
Europe	29,447	(15.0)	61,757	(31.5)	692	(0.4)	-	-	91,896	(46.8)
Japan&Oceania	522	(0.3)	2,118	(1.1)	-	-	-	-	2,640	(1.3)
Others	-	-	-	-	-	-	-	-	-	-
Total	61,608	(31.4)	133,511	(68.1)	760	(0.4)	300	(0.2)	196,179	(100.0)

B. 1991 Subsidiaries	North America	(%)	Europe	(%)	Japan & Oceania	(%)	Others	(%)	Total	(%)
Headquarters										
North America	152,695	(8.6)	437,201	(24.5)	2,783	(0.2)	47,194	(2.6)	639,906	(35.9)
Europe	399,623	(22.4)	353,139	(19.8)	18,584	(1.0)	30,383	(1.7)	801,772	(45.0)
Japan & Oceania	241,828	(13.6)	62,087	(3.5)	-	-	15,581	(0.9)	319,513	(17.9)
Others	15,835	(0.9)	5,171	(0.3)	-	-	390	(0.1)	21,397	(1.2)
Total	809,981	(45.4)	857,598	(48.1)	21,367	(1.2)	93,548	(5.3)	1,782,58	(100.0)

in increasing the share of subsidiary revenues. Developing countries also raise their share from 3.4 per cent in 1974 to 8.9 per cent in 1991, as Japanese and American MNCs gradually invest there taking advantage of relatively cheap cost and docile labor (Fröbel et al., 1980; Schoenberger, 1988). Like headquarters, more than 90 per cent of total subsidiary revenues reside in the industrialized countries during the study period. These patterns of domestic headquarters and foreign subsidiary revenues indicate that most of the international capital flows, which usually entail corporate information and control flows, occur among industrialized countries, especially among the Triad countries. Table 12.2 shows the headquarters-subsidiary linkages represented by the revenues of the controlling subsidiaries with reference to headquarters regions. In 1974, European countries were the major recipients of multinational subsidiaries, accounting for almost 70 per cent (133.5 billion dollars). Among them, North American corporations controlled 52 per cent of revenues and European firms controlled 46 per cent. The second largest recipient region, North America, held about one third of total subsidiary revenues. Major controlling flows occurred within North America itself, characterized by cross investment between Canadian and American corporations.

The most notable changes during the 1974-91 period is, firstly, the decline of the 'within region cross-national investments', such as cross-investments between Canada and the USA and intra-continental investments among European countries. The second characteristic is the increase of capital flows among major trading blocs. Within the European region, multinational control linkages declined to 41 per cent in 1991 from 46 per cent of 1974. The decline of corporate linkages within North American region go down to 18 per cent in 1991 from 51 per cent of 1974. On the other hand, European control over North American subsidiaries increases from 47 per cent to 49 per cent. Japanese and Oceanic control over North America rises from 1 per cent to 30 per cent and control over Europe from 0.5 per cent to 7 per cent during the study period. Other regions, especially the East Asian newly industrializing economies (NIEs), are still negligible as multinational headquarters and subsidiary centres both in 1974 and 1991.

The implications of these changes are two-fold. Firstly, multinational corporate industrial networks evolve over time. Foreign subsidiary centres diffuse from physically and culturally close markets within continental border towards more distant and diverse countries across the continents. Secondly, the global industrial networks, represented by multinational headquarters-subsidiary linkages, develop almost within the Triad. Increasing cross-control of subsidiaries among the countries in the Triad reinforces the concentration trend of multinational corporate control linkages. Regional and national figures show only the broad trend of world economic power and control centres. City level statistics can exhibit the precise nature of the linkages and the system of global cities.

The concentration and dispersion dichotomy of multinational quaternary centres

In capitalist societies, the concentration of economic power in a small number of large business organizations is a persisting trend. The locations of corporate power, or domestic headquarters and foreign subsidiary centres of the large firms also tend to concentrate into a large urban places in major developed market economies. Later, the centres of world economic power tend to disperse to rather remote and small areas mainly due to the advances of information and telecommunication technologies as well as to the resultant business reorganizations. The bigger and more powerful that a corporation becomes, the more it tends to connect globally and to reorganize itself to cope with changing international conditions and opportunities (Amin and Thrift, 1992). This section investigates these dichotomous trends, the concentration of corporate power and corporate decision making centres and the dispersion of corporate control centres within the major developed market economies.

Table 12.3 depicts these dichotomous trends for multinational firms and their domestic headquarters centres. Corporate concentration ratios, by companies, indicate the proportion of total value of revenues controlled by the largest firms with respect to all firms. The spatial concentration ratios by headquarters centres represent the proportion of total value of revenues controlled by largest centres with respect to all centres. Over the years from 1974 to 1991, corporate concentration ratio for the 800 nonfinancial MNCs has grown steadily. Corporations in the top 1 per cent, led by Exxon, General Motors, Mitsubishi Corp., Mitsui Co., Texaco Inc., Ford Motor Co., and others accounted for 13.4 per cent of total revenues in 1974. The concentration ratio has increased a little in 1991 (15.1 per cent), but is now produced

Table 12.3: Corporate and spatial concentration ratios* for the 800 nonfinancial MNCs

Top firms (*centres*) by %	Share in all nonfinancial MNCs (*centres*) 1974	1980	1985	1991	Change 74-91
Top 1	13.4(*16.7*)	14.4(*15.5*)	14.6(*18.2*)	15.1(*25.0*)	+1.6(*+8.3*)
Top 5	36.2(*58.2*)	36.2(*58.2*)	36.7(*57.2*)	36.9(*56.0*)	+0.6(*-2.2*)
Top 10	49.2(*71.5*)	49.5(*71.6*)	50.1(*70.4*)	50.6(*67.9*)	+1.4(*-3.6*)
Top 20	65.0(*82.9*)	64.4(*83.1*)	64.9(*81.8*)	65.3(*81.7*)	+0.3(*-1.3*)
Top 50	87.2(*95.9*)	86.5(*95.8*)	86.4(*95.8*)	87.4(*95.6*)	+0.3(*-0.3*)
No. of centres	*158*	*177*	*181*	*168*	
Total revenues (US$ bil)	1606.2	3740.7	4211.0	7425.8	

* Spatial concentration ratios represent the proportion of total revenues controlled by specific headquarters centres by category with respect to all headquarters centres.

by the growth in aggressive Japanese general trading companies (*Sogo Sosha*), such as Itochu, Sumitomo Shoji Kaisa, Mitsubishi Corp., Marubeni Co., and Mitsui & Co.. Corporations in the top 10 per cent hold more than a half of the total revenues of the 800 firms in 1991, a figure up from the 49.2 per cent in 1974. The concentration of global corporate power continues in the 1990s.

Spatial concentration ratios are greater than those for corporate concentration, since multinational headquarters tend to agglomerate in large metropolitan areas possessing financial institutions, producer services, and informational and communicational infrastructure (Langdale, 1989; Meyer, 1991; Conti, 1993). Spatial concentration ratios for the corporations in the top 1 per cent and top 10 per cent are 25.0 per cent and 67.9 per cent in 1991, compared to the corporate concentration ratios of 15.1 per cent and 50.6 per cent in 1991, respectively. During this period, the leading headquarters centres remain essentially the same, only their ranks change. New York ranked number one in 1974, followed by London, Detroit, Tokyo, Chicago, Paris, and Stamford. By 1991, Tokyo ranks first, followed by New York, London, Paris, Detroit, Osaka, and Essen. Note that the spatial concentration ratios decline over time. Though the ratio for the top 1 per has increased by 8.3 per cent, those for the top 5 per cent and the top 10 per cent has decreased by 2.2 and 3.6 per cent,

Table 12.4: Corporate and spatial concentration ratios* for the subsidiaries of the 800 nonfinancial MNCs

Top firms (*centres*) by per cent	Share in all nonfinancial MNCs (*centres*)				Change
	1974	1980	1985	1991	74-91
Top 1	13.3(*16.1*)	16.1(*11.6*)	18.2(*16.6*)	18.2(*18.8*)	+4.9(*+2.7*)
Top 5	36.9(*52.1*)	38.5(*45.8*)	41.7(*42.5*)	43.9(*42.6*)	+6.9(*-9.5*)
Top 10	53.0(*63.2*)	51.4(*61.1*)	54.5(*58.3*)	57.7(*55.7*)	+4.6(*-7.5*)
Top 20	67.8(*77.8*)	66.3(*74.1*)	69.4(*75.6*)	73.1(*73.5*)	+5.2(*-4.3*)
Top 50	88.6(*95.2*)	88.0(*92.8*)	89.3(*93.7*)	92.2(*92.4*)	+3.6(*-2.8*)
Number of centres	125	168	256	297	
Total revenues (US$ bil.)	195.4	620.0	1068.1	1748.3	

*Spatial concentration ratios represent the proportion of total revenues controlled by specific subsidiary centres by category with respect to all subsidiary centres.

respectively. As the network model of internationalization predicts, multinational headquarters centres are dispersed gradually, as the development of industrial networks continues (Johanson and Vahlne, 1990). This trend is even more apparent for multinational foreign subsidiary centres.

Table 12.4 exhibits the concentration ratios for foreign subsidiaries and subsidiary centres. It depicts patterns almost identical with the parent multinational corporations and domestic headquarters centres. Over time, corporate concentration ratios increase while spatial concentration ratios decrease. The top 1 per cent subsidiary centres provide an exception to this rule. By 1991, Tokyo is a dominant headquarters centre which houses the rapidly growing *Sogo Sosha,* whereas New York is a dominant subsidiary centre. Note that the amount of decrease in spatial concentration for the subsidiary centres is greater than that for the headquarters centres. Major headquarters centres remain less dispersed than their subsidiary centres due to a set of complex inertial factors. Major subsidiary centres are more dispersed because subsidiary headquarters must protect their parents from an even more complex and dispersed external environment. Foreign subsidiary centres are relatively easy to move from one place to another. They can travel from one country to the other country in accordance with the changing environments, following the strategic decisions of the parent firms.

The 1974 period was dominated by centres with resource and manufacturing subsidiaries. Foreign subsidiaries of large petroleum and auto corporations, such as Exxon, Shell, General Motors and Ford Motor, were concentrated in a few major centres. By 1991, service corporations, essentially the Japanese *Sogo Sosha,* create a greater diversification.

Changes in the major multinational subsidiary centres reflect the declining position of American cities as headquarters centres, along with sharp growing as subsidiary centres. This is clear for the changes in the top ranking subsidiary centres during the study period. In 1974, Toronto ranked first as a subsidiary centre followed by London, Hamburg, Paris, New York, Madrid, and Stockholm. New York rises to the first rank in 1991, followed by London, Paris, Toronto, Hamburg, Philadelphia, and Cleveland.

Table 12.5 indicates the share of the top 10 per cent nonfinancial multinational headquarters and subsidiary centres with respect to all headquarters and subsidiary centres. The statistics confirm three world regions i.e., North America, Europe, and Japan & other regions. The dispersion and concentration trends for multinational headquarters and subsidiary centres reveal different patterns among regions. In the North America and Europe, the share of the top 10 per cent centres decrease from 1974 to 1991. The gradual evolution of multinational industrial networks and the dispersion of corporate headquarters and producer services in the metropolitan system across the Atlantic, these factors all contribute to the dispersion of multinational control centres (Strickland and Aiken, 1984; Wheeler, 1988; Lyons, 1994).

Table 12.5: Share of top 10 per cent multinational headquarters and subsidiary centres by region, 1974-1991

Region	1974	1980	1985	1991	Change
	HQ (Sub)	HQ (Sub)	HQ (Sub)	HQ (Sub)	HQ (Sub)
North America	61.9(66.2)	66.7(58.4)	61.1(59.9)	59.3(53.8)	-2.6(-12.3)
Europe	71.6(*64.6*)	69.7(*65.4*)	68.4(*60.4*)	63.6(*55.8*)	-8.0(*-8.8*)
Japan & Others	82.2(*60.0*)	83.5(*57.2*)	80.9(*56.0*)	84.1(*56.5*)	+1.9(*-3.5*)
World	71.5(*63.2*)	71.6(*61.1*)	70.4(*58.3*)	67.9(*55.7*)	-3.6(*-7.5*)

Over the years, subsidiary centres are more dispersed than headquarters centres. The top 10 per cent of North American subsidiaries exhibit a 12.3 per cent decline, while the top 10 per cent of headquarters mark a 2.6 per cent decline. In Europe, the top 10 per cent of subsidiaries decline by 8.8 per cent compared to an 8.0 for headquarters centres. Only the corporate headquarters concentration in Japan and other regions increases, mainly due to the rapid growth of Tokyo and Osaka as headquarters centres.

Rank-size distributions

The global system of urban centres analyzed in terms of a rank-size rule considers the relationship between changes in urban population and rank. Population size, however, shows little relationship with the centralization of economic and political power in urban centres. Chase-Dunn (1985, pp. 291-2) also demonstrates that population size fails as a good measure of centrality. Downward convex patterns of rank-size distribution reflect dispersion of economic resources among global command and control centres.

Graphs of the relationships between city size, defined by revenues of multinational headquarters, and city rank in 1974, 1980, 1985, and 1991 (Figure 12.1) show, first, that the world rank-size distribution develops a downward convex pattern for the large headquarters centres over time. Second, the convex pattern varies among regions. In North America and Europe, the overall convex pattern contains minor fluctuations in downward concavity, while in Japan and other regions the convexity appears for the mid-sized centre. Tokyo exhibits primacy for this pattern.

Regression analysis for a mathematical form of the rank-size relationship confirms the overall dispersion trend. The equation is:

$$\ln R_r = \ln R_1 - q \ln r$$

where r is rank of a centre, R_r is total headquarters revenues of the *r*th ranked centre, R_1 is total headquarters revenues of the biggest centre, and -q is the coefficient of dispersion. The coefficient -q indicates the degree of relative concentration and dispersion of economic powers among the centres in the world urban system: the greater -q, the more concentration (Sheppard, 1982; Ettlinger and Archer, 1987). For the top 100 headquarters centres, the slope coefficient -*q* changes from -1.362 in 1974 to -1.305 in 1991, indicating that the system disperses over time.

The rank-size relationship for the multinational subsidiary centres (Figure 12.2) reveals same downward convexity for the mid sized centres with downward concavity for the largest centres. The overall change during the study period exhibits a more convex pattern, i.e., more dispersion over time. This dispersion trend is more salient in Europe and Japan and other regions. Regression coefficient -q for the top 100 subsidiary centres also reveals the dispersion pattern over time, from -1.574 in 1974, through -1.387 in 1980 and -1.290 in 1985, to -1.164 in 1991.

Graphs and regression coefficients indicate that the quaternary places housing the headquarters of the world's largest corporations dispersed moderately from 1974 to 1991 although their overall concentration remains quite high. They also show that subsidiaries of these corporations remain in the largest centres such as New York and London but also disperse to secondary quaternary places.

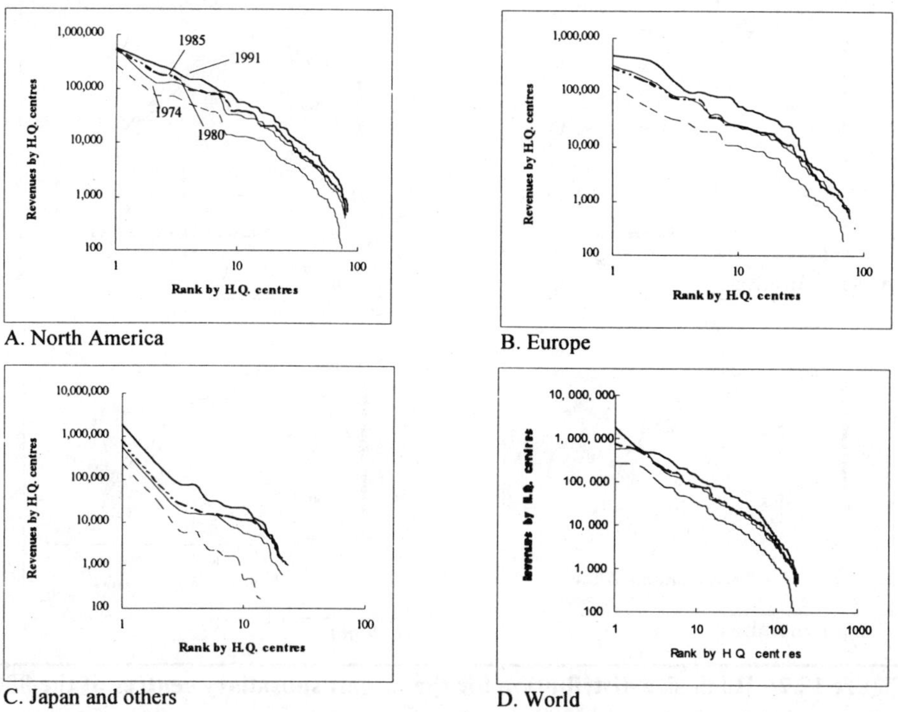

Figure 12.1: Rank-size distribution for the largest headquarters centres of the 800 nonfinancial MNCs by region

System of the global quaternary places

The previous section examines trends in the concentration and dispersion of quaternary places housing the headquarters of the world's largest corporations and their foreign subsidiaries. This section assesses the relative importance of each quaternary place in the international headquarters-subsidiary network by calculating centrality scores by place for years 1974 and 1991.

The scores indicate, in a general way, the level of globalization for a particular centre by measuring the degree of control exerted by a major corporate place over its foreign subsidiary cities. The criteria is the share of total foreign revenues with respect to all other network centres. Table 12.6 shows the centrality scores and sizes of headquarters for the top 50 centres. The size of headquarters doesn't affect directly the centrality score, since it also includes domestic revenues. New York dominates the system in 1974 with a score of 2.902. Also, the revenues of New York-based headquarters exceeded the revenues of second ranked London by a factor

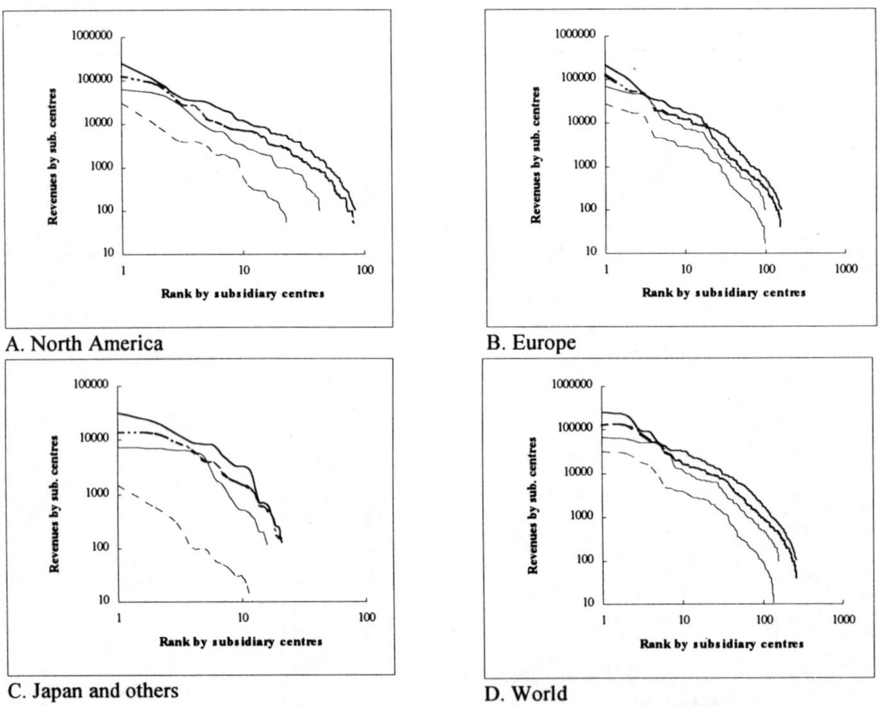

Figure 12.2: Rank size distribution for the largest subsidiary centres of the 800 nonfinancial MNCs by region

Table 12.6: Centrality scores for the top 50 nonfinancial multinational headquarters centres in terms of revenues in controlling subsidiary centres, 1974-91

Rank		HQ centre	Centrality score		Size of headquarters*	
1	(19)**	Tokyo	2.7721	(0.1079)	1,855,132	(239,966)
2	(2)	London	2.2109	(1.6334)	481,577	(132,123)
3	(1)	New York	1.4162	(2.9022)	556,907	(267,823)
4	(5)	Paris	1.2645	(0.7013)	382,235	(49,733)
5	(3)	Detroit	1.2198	(1.4533)	292,915	(78,666)
6	(4)	The Hague	0.7442	(1.0964)	102,697	(19,336)
7	(-)	Dallas	0.6757	(-)	149,845	(-)
8	(24)	Montreal	0.6169	(0.0900)	35,755	(12,174)
9	(6)	Frankfurt	0.4250	(0.5755)	81,749	(18,432)
10	(8)	Eindhoven	0.3176	(0.3005)	32,336	(9,406)
11	(-)	Osaka	0.3038	(-)	200,731	(-)
12	(13)	Brussels	0.2846	(0.1846)	37,926	(8,190)
13	(-)	Zurich	0.2663	(-)	46,964	(-)
14	(46)	Washington	0.2626	(0.0319)	79,081	(3,991)
15	(12)	Vevey	0.2586	(0.2381)	34,112	(6,138)
16	(7)	Chicago	0.2569	(0.4434)	214,755	(72,103)
17	(9)	San Francisco	0.2541	(0.2739)	114,050	(32,654)
18	(18)	Toronto	0.2471	(0.1125)	34,134	(14,492)
19	(-)	Boston	0.2425	(-)	35,158	(-)
20	(10)	Stamford	0.2412	(0.2537)	145,023	(51,208)
21	(16)	Minneapolis	0.1973	(0.1427)	87,999	(10,800)
22	(29)	Basel	0.1836	(0.0682)	31,062	(6,076)
23	(15)	München	0.1774	(0.1428)	90,704	(8,269)
24	(35)	Stuttgart	0.1754	(0.0482)	80,381	(10,852)
25	(33)	Köln	0.1694	(0.0516)	53,872	(11,189)
26	(14)	Stockholm	0.1634	(0.1561)	42,363	(10,504)
27	(21)	Goteborg	0.1413	(0.1058)	18,133	(4,638)
28	(27)	Amsterdam	0.1354	(0.0775)	47,315	(9,573)
29	(49)	Wolfsburg	0.1300	(0.0307)	56,959	(6,556)
30	(28)	Mannheim	0.1262	(0.0704)	34,907	(8,565)
31	(-)	LA	0.1188	(-)	90,167	(-)
32	(36)	Essen	0.1087	(0.0478)	174,184	(31,497)
33	(34)	Sydney	0.1069	(0.0502)	30,969	(1,474)

Table 12.6
(continued)

Rank		HQ centre	Centrality score		Size of headquarters*	
34	(44)	Caracas	0.0988	(0.0338)	21,660	(0,494)
35	(31)	Cincinnati	0.0980	(0.0585)	33,248	(10,719)
36	(-)	Houston	0.0970	(-)	58,655	(-)
37	(23)	Utica	0.0872	(0.0945)	18,807	(4,888)
38	(-)	Milan	0.0864	(-)	16,378	(-)
39	(-)	ToyotaCity	0.0779	(-)	78,402	(-)
40	(-)	Düsseldorf	0.0770	(-)	81,946	(-)
41	(26)	Rochester	0.0736	(0.0823)	19,419	(4,584)
42	(41)	Clermont	0.0714	(0.0386)	24,012	(2,583)
43	(43)	Helsinki	0.0702	(0.0342)	23,497	(4,310)
44	(-)	Oslo	0.0683	(-)	24,258	(-)
45	(-)	Hiroshima	0.0672	(-)	21,658	(-)
46	(20)	Turin	0.0585	(0.1074)	40,888	(6,264)
47	(-)	Seoul	0.0555	(-)	73,027	(-)
48	(38)	Philadelphia	0.0548	(0.0463)	43,096	(13,012)
49	(-)	Melbourne	0.0513	(-)	32,723	(-)
50	(-)	Nagoya	0.0490	(-)	23,367	(-)
-	(11)	Pittsburgh	-	(0.2520)	-	(43,573)
-	(17)	Hannover	-	(0.1361)	-	(1,584)
-	(22)	Baden	-	(0.1043)	-	(2,288)
-	(25)	Akron	-	(0.0836)	-	(12,819)
-	(30)	Rome	-	(0.0670)	-	(27,443)
-	(32)	Danbury	-	(0.0569)	-	(5,320)
-	(37)	St.Louis	-	(0.0465)	-	(14,121)
-	(39)	Luxembourg	-	(0.0426)	-	(1,262)
-	(40)	Harrisburg	-	(0.0390)	-	(0,924)
-	(42)	Findlay	-	(0.0372)	-	(1,277)
-	(45)	Hartford	-	(0.0333)	-	(12,864)
-	(47)	Dayton	-	(0.0318)	-	(3,547)
-	(48)	Columbus,GA	-	(0.0309)	-	(1,000)
-	(50)	Moline	-	(0.0305)	-	(2,495)

* Total revenues of headquarters for each centres.
** The numbers in the parentheses are 1974 value.

of almost two. Detroit and The Hague rank next and round out the members of the second level of the quaternary place hierarchy for 1974. Figure 12.3 depicts the other four levels of the hierarchy and its member places. European and North American

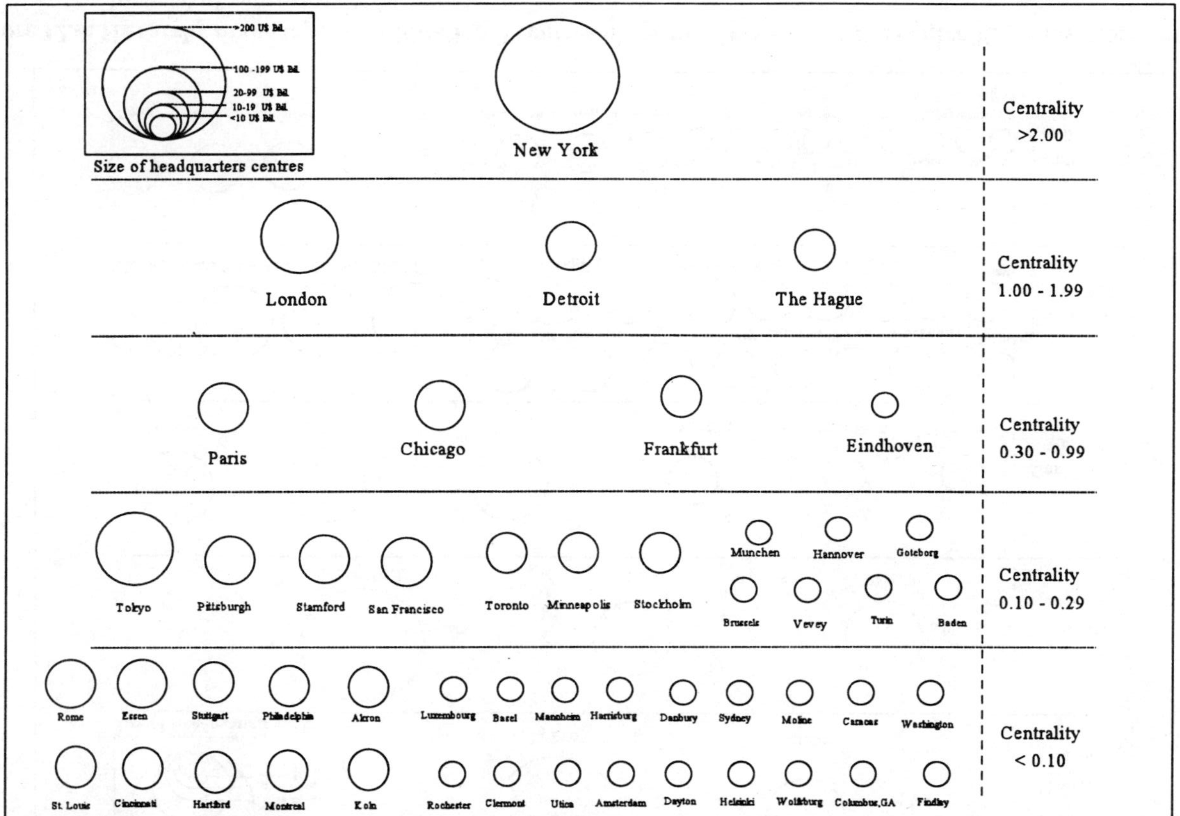

Figure 12.3: Hierarchy of the top 50 multinational centres in terms of revenues in the controlling subsidiary centres by level of centrality 1974

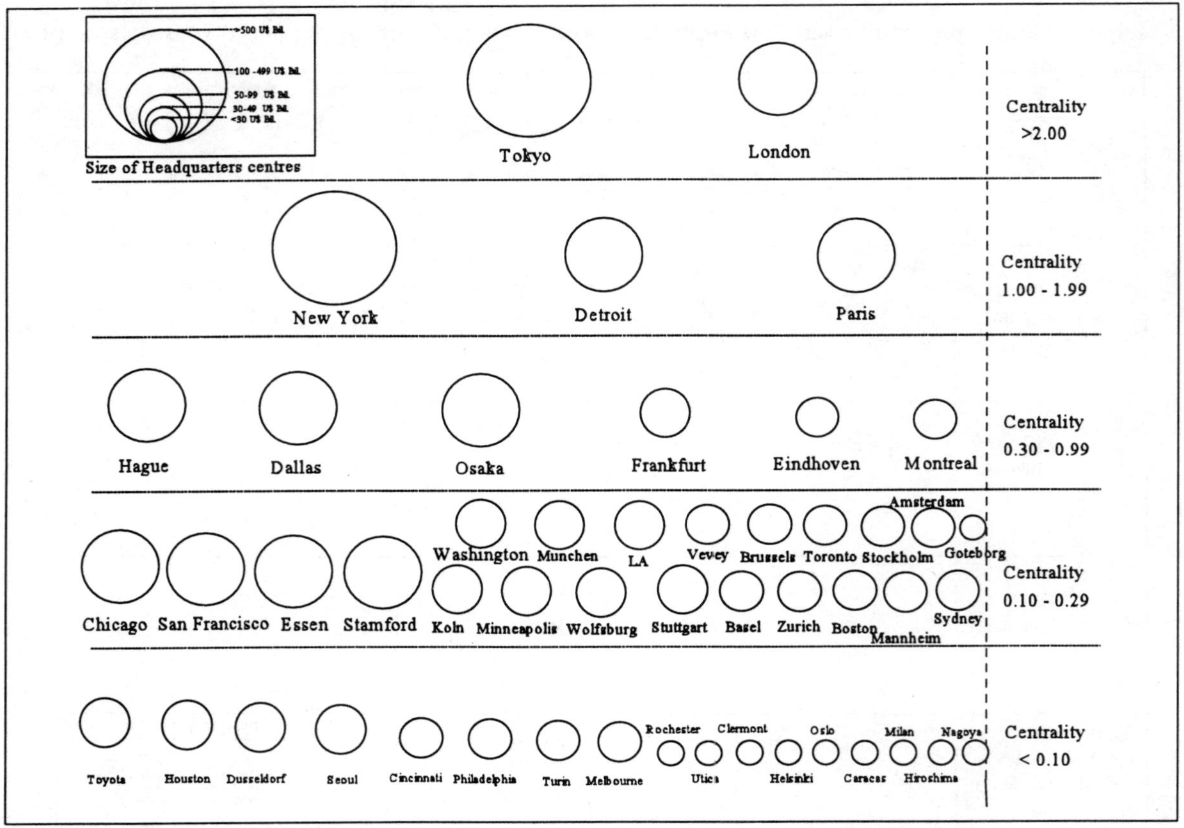

Figure 12.4: Hierarchy of the top 50 multinational centres in terms of revenue in the controlling subsidiary centres by level of centrality, 1991

cities dominate the global system in 1974 with twenty-four and twenty-one centres, respectively. The rest of the world houses only three international class centres, namely; Tokyo, Sydney, and Caracas. It is clear that the global quaternary place system in 1974 reflects the centralizing power of New York and the relatively low scores of the middle-ranked centres.

One comment on The Hague and Eindhoven, that notes relatively higher ranks compared to their small headquarters sizes, is worthwhile. The Hague is the headquarters centre for the Anglo-Dutch Petroleum company, Royal Dutch Shell[5], and Eindhoven is the home of the consumer electronics giant, Philips NV, among other firms. The two corporations are leading forces in resource and manufacturing sectors, respectively and their fast global penetrations contribute to the higher positions of their headquarters cities in centrality score ranking.

Tokyo and London dominate the international quaternary place hierarchy in 1991. Tokyo's rapid rise from a rank of nineteen in 1974 to one in 1991 can be attributed to the increased prominence of its general trading companies; such as Itochu, Mitsui, and Mitsubishi. The decline of New York to a level two centre can be attributed to the relative decline of American MNCs based in New York, along with the exodus of many others to places lower in the hierarchy in 1991 (Figure 12.4). The recent decline of large metropolitan areas in the American urban system due to the corporate movements to the smaller cities, contributes to the diminishing dominance of New York in the global city system (Quante, 1976; Heenan, 1991). The giant resource companies Exxon's move to Dallas in 1991 and Mobil Corp.'s move to Washington in 1987, both from New York, are good examples.

Compared to the dominance of New York in the global quaternary place system in 1974, the pattern in 1991 exhibits a more dispersed trend. During the period, the differences among the centrality scores of the highest ranking cities diminish and scores for middle-ranked cities rise, implying decreasing power for the largest city and thickening layer of mid sized cities. The entrance of Japanese cities, such as Osaka, Toyota City, Hiroshima, and Nagoya into the top 50 global cities at the expense of the falling of American cities is another characteristic of the 1990s. Implications of the dispersion of the global city system are two-fold. Firstly, the degree of the controlling power of the largest global city over other cities weakens. The value of the centrality score shown for the top city falls from 2.902 (New York) in 1974 to 2.772 (Tokyo) in 1991. Secondly, in view of the fact that multinational headquarters centres are also multinational subsidiary centres in most cases, the international net of control and information flows becomes more diversified and balanced. Locations of the top 50 global cities, defined by their controlling revenues of the world-wide multinational subsidiaries, are almost within the Triad (48 cities in 1974 and 47 cities in 1991). The system of global quaternary places is dispersed and diversified with intensified cross-investment and cross-control of world economic resources within the Triad: the concentrated dispersion of global command and control centres emerges.

The same five cities dominate the 1991 quaternary place system. This concentration of power however is more dispersed among group members. Tokyo, for example, is less dominate in the system of 1991 than New York was in 1974. And Detroit is more important in 1991 than Paris was in 1974. The difference in centrality scores for these highest ranking places in the system diminishes from 1974-1991.

The middle ranked cities in 1974 consist of five centres, Frankfurt through Vevey, with a score greater than 2. This number increases to fifteen in 1991 and demonstrates the growing importance of a larger more dispersed system of tier three and four places. Note that in 1974, no Asian centre was included in the top 50 list, only Tokyo, the highest ranked Asian city, had a score of only 0.1079.

Summary and conclusions

The past two decades have witnessed two basic changes in the globalization of the international quaternary place system. Innovations in information technology have permitted the internationalization of resource transfers, the introduction of flexible production techniques, and service provisions, as well as financial transactions. These changes necessitated the reorganization and modernization of the world's largest corporations. The resulting new economic and technological environment have had a profound influence on the location of domestic corporate headquarters and the their international corporate subsidiaries. As a consequence, important changes took place in the global quaternary place system.

This study investigates the nature of the spatial concentration and dispersion of corporate control within an international system of decision-making centres for the period 1974-91. The analysis confirmed the simultaneous concentration and dispersion of certain aspects of multinational control linkages and a concomitant dispersion of the global quaternary place system.

The analysis of quaternary place rank-size distributions and centrality scores reveals a decline in American cities and a rise in the importance of Japanese centres in terms of global linkages. The downward convex pattern of rank-size distributions, the diminishing differences among the centrality scores of the highest ranking centres, and the rise of centrality scores for middle and lower ranked cities all indicate the spatial dispersion of economic power among global centres.

Initially, international control centred on New York and London along with a small set of American and European cities. By 1991, it is apparent that a Triad of quaternary places led by Tokyo, London, and New York as well as increasingly important and diversified set of mid-sized North American, European, and Asian cities dominate global corporate activity. The study also reveals that global cities are almost exclusively associated with the Triad and that these multinational corporate headquarters centres are also the host of foreign subsidiary headquarters as well. It is evident that the absence of substantial representation from nations outside the Triad indicates that a gap might exist among the group of internal post industrial control centres and those industrializing external centres.

This study deals with certain macrogeographical aspects of international quaternary place centres which are both the origins and destinations of much foreign direct investment. Further study could focus on micro geographical analysis which deals with subsectoral characteristics of decision-making centres. Other studies could investigate the actual linkage patterns among headquarters and subsidiary control centres in a who owns whom analysis. Yet other impact studies could examine the changing role of international global centres, their impact on national institutions and their authority. Dicken (1994, p.103) argues that the crux of the interrelationship between global corporations, decision-making centres, and nation-states is control of the production system and the relative distribution of the costs and benefits associated with its operation. For example, the newly found global powers of local control centres may cause distortions in the national quaternary system whereby the support for the local system ceases. The relationship between the city as global quaternary place and national central place should be rigorously investigated to avoid a shallow interpretation of the phenomena of "globalization" and "global cities".

Notes

1. Hoggart (1991) is one exception. He uses Fortune's *Global 500* companies to show the dispersion pattern of corporate control centres with declining dominance of the US firms and the growing strength of secondary centres such as Japan and Germany. His analysis is tentative in nature. He uses the number of corporations as a measuring unit instead of corporate revenues or assets. The economic power of control stems not from the number of corporations *per se*, but from the size of their resources. His spatial unit of analysis is country possessing quaternary activities, not the individual command and control centres. Also, He doesn't differentiate national firms from multinational firms.
2. This is one of the major distinctive characteristics of the network model of internationalization among MNC/FDI theories. Vernon's product life cycle theory (1969) and the new international division of labour thesis (Fröbel, et al., 1981) rest their explanations on the 'market' focusing on the decisions of the firm to trade and invest based on both cost and revenue conditions. They predict that the location of production would ultimately move to less developed countries, which reveals only half the truth (see Schoenberger, 1990). Oligopolistic theory (Caves, 1982) and internalization theory (Rugman, 1987) hold that MNCs possessing monopolistic advantages tend to internalize market transactions within the firm, in other words, as Williamson (1975)puts in, 'hierarchies replace markets'. According to them, MNCs invest abroad when local exploitation is needed and the cost of transactions between independent firms is higher than the administrative costs associated with exploitation within the same hierarchical system. A firm's strength is, however, not only dependent on its capability but also depend on the specific character of its links with suppliers, customers, and competing firms in the industrial network. Furthermore, these existing theories would not be able to explain various forms of foreign involvement such as trade, direct investment, merger and acquisition, and strategic alliances, which are contingent upon a firm's relative position in industrial network.

3. The definition of multinational corporation has changed over time. Probably the first official definition of MNC was given by UN as 'all enterprises which control assets -- factories, mines, sales offices and the like -- in two or more countries (UN, 1973, p. 5). A more recent UN exercise defines a multinational corporation as ' an enterprise (a) comprising entities in two or more countries, regardless of the legal form and fields of activity of those entities, (b) which operates under a system of decision-making permitting coherent policies and a common strategy through one or more decision-making centres, (c) in which the entities are so linked, by ownership or otherwise, that one or more of them may be able to exercise a significant influence over the activities of the others, and, in particular, to share knowledge, resources and responsibilities with others' (UN, 1984, p. 2). Thus, service firms that collect licensing and management-contract revenues from other countries can be considered multinational corporations.
4. Let us consider a hypothetical system consisted of four cities in the multinational corporate headquarters-subsidiary network. If city 1 controls 80 per cent of the subsidiary revenues, city 2 controls 15 per cent, city 3 controls 5 per cent, and city 4 is a subsidiary centre with no controlling revenues, the value of α and centrality score for each city are calculated simultaneously as to $\Sigma_i C_i (\alpha)^2 = 4$ (number of cities in the system). As $\alpha = 2$, centrality score for the city 1 is $.80 \times 2 = 1.6$, city 2 is $.15 \times 2 = .3$, city 3 is $.05 \times 2 = .1$, and lastly, city 4 is $0 \times 2 = 0$.
5. Royal Dutch Shell is a joint-venture corporation between Royal Dutch Petroleum of the Netherlands and Shell Transport and Trading of Britain. The former owns 60 per cent and the latter owns 40 per cent share of the firm. Since the study assigns only one headquarters centre for each firm, The Hague, the headquarters centre of Royal Dutch Petroleum, is assigned as the headquarters centre of the Royal Dutch Shell.

References

Agarwal, J.P. (1980), 'Determinants of foreign investment: a survey', *Weltwirtschaftliche Archiv*, 116(4), pp.739-73.

Aharoni, Y. (1966), *The foreign investment decision process*, Harvard University Press, Cambridge, MA.

Ajami, R.A. and Ricks, D.A. (1981), 'Motives of non-American firms investing in the United States', *Journal of International Business Studies*, 12(Winter), pp. 25-34.

Aliber, R.Z. (1970), 'A theory of direct foreign investment', in Kindleberger, C.P. (ed.), *The international corporation*, MIT Press, Cambridge, pp. 17-34.

Alonso, W. (1980), 'Five bell shapes in development', *Papers of Regional Science Association*, 45, pp. 5-16.

Amin, A. and Dietrich, M. (1991), 'From hierarchy to "hierarchy": the dynamics of contemporary corporate restructuring in Europe', in Amin, A. and Dietrich, M. (eds.), *Towards a new Europe?: structural change in the European economy*, pp. 49-73, Edward Elgar, Hants.

Amin, A. and Thrift, N. (1992), 'Neo-Marshallian nodes in global networks', *International Journal of Urban and Regional Research*, 16(4), pp. 571-87.

Anchordoguy, M. (1990), 'A brief history of Japan's keiretsu', *Harvard Business Review*, 68, pp. 58-59.

Anderson, E. and Gatignon, H. (1986), 'Modes of foreign entry: a transaction cost analysis and propositions', *Journal of International Business Studies*, 17, pp. 1-26.

Ansari, A. and Modarress, B. (1987), 'The potential benefits of just-in-time purchasing for US manufacturing', *Production and Inventory Management Journal*, 28, pp. 30-35.

Aoki, M. (1990), 'Horizontal vs. vertical information structure of the firm', *American Economic Review*, 76(5), pp. 971-983.

Argyris, C. and Schon, D.A. (1978), *Organizational learning: a theory of action perspective*, Addison-Wesley, Reading, MA.

Arnesen, P.J., Cole, R.E., and Krishna, A.R. (1987), *Japanese auto parts companies in the US and Japan: implications for US competitors*, East Asia Business Program, The University of Michigan, Ann Arbor.

Asanuma, B. (1985), 'The organization of parts purchases in the Japanese automotive industry', *Japanese Economic Studies*, 13, pp. 32-53.

Ashcroft, B. and Love, J.H. (1993), *Takeovers, mergers and regional economy*, University of Edinburgh Press, Edinburgh.

Bagchi-sen, S. and Wheeler, J.O. (1989), 'A spatial and temporal model of foreign direct investment in the United States', *Economic Geography*, 65(2), pp. 113-29.

Bagnall, J. (1991), 'If it ain't broke fix it anyway', *Financial Times of Canada*, 21 January, pp. 12-14.

Bain, J. (1956), *Barriers to new competition*, Cambridge, MA, Harvard University Press.

Baranson, J. (1970), 'Technology transfer through the international firms', *The American Economic Review*, 60, pp. 435-40.

Bartlett, C.A. and Ghoshal, S. (1991), 'Global strategic management: impact on the new frontiers of strategy research', *Strategic Management Journal*, 12 (Special Issue), pp. 5-16.

Bartlett, C.A. and Ghoshal, S. (1989), *Managing across borders: the transnational solution*, Harvard Business School Press, Boston.

Baxter, L. and McCalman, J. (1991), 'The shifting locus of control' in Sutherland, E. and Morieux, Y.V.H. (eds.), *Business strategy and information technology*, Routledge, London, pp. 147-159.

Bell, C.G. and McNamara, J.E. (1991), *High-tech ventures; the guide for entrepreneurial success*, Addison-Wesley, Reading, MA.

Bettis, R.A., Bradley, S.P. and Hamel, G. (1992), 'Outsourcing and industrial decline', *Academy of Management Executive*, 6(1), pp. 7-22.

Bhagat, S., Shliefer, A. and Vishny, R.W. (1990), 'Hostile takeovers in the 1980s: the returns to corporate specialization', *Brookings Papers on Economic Activity*, pp. 1-54.

Bhagwati, J.N. (1992), 'Quid pro quo foreign investment', *American Economic Review*, 82, pp. 186-190.

Bhagwati, J.N. (1991), 'Investing abroad', in Irwin, D. (ed.), *J.N. Bhagwati: political economy and international trade,* MIT Press, Cambridge.

Bhide, A. (1989), 'Causes and consequences of hostile takeovers', *Journal of Applied Corporate Finance*, 2(2), pp. 36-59.

Biggadike, E.R. (1979), *Corporate diversification: entry, strategy and performance*, Division of Research, Harvard Business School.

Blackborn, A. (1972), 'The location of foreign-owned manufacturing plants in the Republic of Ireland', *Tijdschrift Voor Econ. en Soc. Geografie*, November/-December, 63, pp. 438-43.

Blain, R. and Norcliffe, G. (1988), 'Japanese investment in Canada and Canadian exports to Japan 1965-1984', *Canadian Geographer*, 32, pp. 141-150.

Blois, K.J. (1972), 'Vertical quasi-integration', *The Journal of Industrial Economics*, 20, pp. 253-272.

Boddewyn, J.J. (1988), 'Political aspects of MNE theory', *Journal of International Business Studies*, 19(3), pp. 341-363.

Boddewyn, J.J. (1985), 'Theories of foreign direct investment and divestment: a classificatory note', *Management International Review*, 25, pp. 57-63.

Bonacich, P. (1987), 'Power and centrality: a family of measures', *American Journal of Sociology*, 92, pp. 1170-82.

Booz, Allen & Hamilton (1979), *The electronics industry in Scotland; a proposed strategy*, Scottish Development Agency, Glasgow.

Bowman, E.H. and Hurry, D. (1993), 'Strategy through the option lens: an integrated view of resource investments and the incremental-choice process', *Academy of Management Review*, 18(4), pp. 760-782.

Bradley, J.W. and Korn, D.H. (1982), *Acquisition and corporate development*, Lexington Books, Lexington, MA.

Bradley, M., Desai, A. and Han Kim, E. (1988), 'Synergistic gains from corporate acquisitions and their divisions between the stockholders of target and acquiring firms', *Journal of Financial Economics*, 21, pp. 3-40.

Bradley, M., Desai, A. and Han Kim, E. (1983), 'The rationale behind interfirm tender offers: information or synergy', *Journal of Finacial Economics*, 11, pp. 183-206.

Breheny, M. and McQuaid, R. (eds.) (1987), *The development of high technology industries*, Croom Helm, London.

Brewer, T.L. (1993), 'Government policies, market imperfections, and foreign direct investment', *Journal of International Business Studies*, 24(1), pp. 101-120.

Britton, J.N.H. (1993), 'A regional industrial perspective on Canada under free trade', *International Journal of Urban and Regional Research*, 17(4), pp. 559-577.

Browne, L.E. and Rosengren, E. (eds.) (1987), *The merger boom*, Federal Reserve Bank of Boston.

Buckley, P.J. (1990), 'Problems and developments in the core theory of international business', *Journal of International Business Studies*, 21(4), pp. 657-665.

Buckley, P.J. (1988), 'The limits of explanation: testing the internalization theory of the multinational enterprise', *Journal of International Business Studies*, 19(2), pp. 181-193.

Buckley, P.J., and Casson, M. (1976), *The future of the multinational enterprise*, Macmillan, London.

Burgelman, R.A. and Sayles, L.R. (1986), *Inside corporate innovation: strategy, structure, and managerial skills*, Free Press, New York.

Burns, T. and Stalker, G.M. (1961), *The management of innovation*, Tavistock, London.

Burton, T.T. (1988), 'JIT/repetitive sourcing strategies: "tying the knot" with your suppliers', *Production and Inventory Management Journal*, 29, pp. 38-40.

Business Week (1990), 'Building cars the Mitsubishi way', *Business Week*, 24 September, p. 103.

Calvet, A.L.(1982), 'Mergers and the theory of foreign direct investment', in Rugman, A.M. (ed.), *New theories of multinational enterprise*, St. Martin's Press, New York, pp. 44-54.

Calvet, A.L. (1981), 'A synthesis of foreign direct investment theories and theories of the multinational firm', *Journal of International Business Studies*, 12(1), pp. 43-59.

Cameron, G.C. and Reid, G.L. (1966), 'Scottish economic planning and the attraction of industry', University of Glasgow Social and Economic Studies, *Occasional Papers* No. 6, Oliver and Boyd, Edinburgh.

Cantwell, J. (1989), *Technological innovations and the multinational corporation*, Basil Blackwell, London.

Capello, R. (1994), 'Towards new industrial and spatial systems: the role of new technologies', *Papers in Regional Science*, 73(2), pp. 189-208.

Carnoy, M. (1993), 'Multinationals in a changing world economy: whither the nation state?', in Carnoy, M., Castells, M., Cohen, S.S. and Cardoso, F.H. (eds.), *The new global economy in the information age: reflections on our changing world*, The Pennsylvania State University Press, University Park, PA, pp. 45-96.

Casson, M. (1987), *The firm and the market: studies on multinational enterprise and the scope of the firm*, MIT Press, Cambridge.

Castells, M. (1993), 'European cities, the informational society, and the global economy', *Tijdschrift voor Economische en Sociale Geografie*, 84(4), pp. 247-57.

Caves, R.E. (1982), *Multinational enterprise and economic analysis*, Cambridge University Press, Cambridge, Mass.

Caves, R.E. (1974a), 'Causes of direct investment: foreign firm's share in Canadian and United Kingdom manufacturing industries', *Review of Economics and Statistics*, 56(3), pp. 279-293.

Caves, R.E. (1974b), 'Multinational firms, competition, and productivity in host-country markets', *Economica*, 41, May, pp. 176-93.

Caves, R.E. (1971), 'International corporations: the industrial economics of foreign investment', *Economica*, 38(3), pp. 1-27.

Caves, R.E. and Jones, R.J. (1985), *World trade and payments*, Cambridge University Press, Cambridge.

Caves, R.E. and Mehra, S. (1986), 'Entry of foreign multinational into US manufacturing industries', in Porter, M. (ed.), *Competition in global industries*, Boston, Ma., Harvard Business School Press, pp. 449-481.

Cebenoyan, S., Papaioannou, G. and Travlos, N. (1989), 'Foreign acquisition of US firms: shareholder wealth effects and reverse foreign direct investment theories', Paper prepared for the presentation at the 25th Annual Meeting of Eastern Finance Association, Philadelphia, April 13-15.

Chambers, J. (1992), 'The back page', *Connexion*, 2.ix, p. 44.

Chandler, A. (1990), *Scale and scope*, Harvard University Press, Cambridge.

Chandler, A.D. (1991), *Scale and scope; the dynamics of industrial capitalism*, Belknap Press, Boston.

Chase-Dunn, C.K. (1985), 'The system of world cities, AD 800-1975', in Timberlake, M. (ed.), *Urbanization in the world economy,* pp. 269-72, Academic Press, Orlando.

Checkland, S. (1981), *The Upas tree; Glasgow 1875-1975 ... and after 1975-1980,* University of Glasgow Press, Glasgow.

Cheng, J.L.C. and Bolon, D.S. (1993), 'The management of multinational R&D: a neglected topic in international business research', *Journal of International Business Studies*, 24(1), pp. 1-18

Child Hill, R., Indergaard, M., and Fujita, K. (1989), 'Flat Rock, home of Mazda: the social impact of a Japanese company on an American community', in Arnesen, P.J. (ed.), *The auto industry ahead: who's driving*, East Asia Business Program, The University of Michigan, Ann Arbor, pp.69-131.

Coase, R.H. (1937), 'The nature of the firm', *Economica*, 4, pp. 386-405.

Cohen, R.B. (1981), 'The new international division of labor. Multinational corporations and urban hierarchy', in Dear, M. and Scott, A.J. (eds.), *Urbanization, and urban planning in capitalist society*, pp. 287-315, Methuen, New York.

Cohen, W.M. and Levinthal, D.A. (1990), 'Absorptive capacity: a new perspective on learning and innovation', *Administrative Science Quarterly*, 35, pp. 128-152.

Cole, R.E. and Deskins, D.R. (1988), 'Racial factors in site location and employment patterns in Japanese auto firms in America', *California Management Review*, 31, pp. 9-22.

Cole, R.E. and Yakushiji, T. (eds.) (1984), *The American and Japanese auto industries in transition*, Center for Japanese Studies, The University of Michigan, Ann Arbor.

Committee of Public Accounts (1990), *Fourth report; locate in Scotland*, HMSO, London. [HC 1989-90 217]

Committee on Scottish Affairs (1980), *Second report from the committee on Scottish affairs; inward investment*, HMSO, London.

Conti, S. (1993), 'The network perspective in industrial geography: towards a model', *Geografiska Annaler*, 75B(4), pp. 115-30.

Contractor, F.J. (1981), 'International technology transfer: major issues and policy responses', *Journal of International Business Studies*, 12(Fall), pp. 113-35.

Contractor, F.J. and Lorange, P. (eds.) (1988), *Cooperative strategies in international business*, Lexington Books, Lexington, MA.

Coughlin, C.C., Terza, J. and Arromdee, V. (1991), 'State characteristics and the location of foreign direct investment within the United States', *The Review of Economics and Statistics*, 73(4), pp. 675-83.

Cox, J.C. and Rubinstein, M. (1985), *Options markets*, Prentice-Hall, Englewood-Cliffs, NJ.

Craig, C.S., Douglas, S.P. and Grein, A. (1992), 'Patterns of convergence and divergence among industrialized nations: 1960-1988', *Journal of International Business Studies*, 23 (Winter), pp. 773-787.

Cunningham, E. (1990), 'Mister Cunningham says goodbye to all that', *Scottish Business Insider*, September, pp. 10-11.

Cusumano, M.A. (1988), 'Manufacturing innovation: lessons from the Japanese auto industry', *Sloan Management Review*, 30, pp. 29-39.

D'Aveni, R.A. (1994), *Hypercompetition*, Free Press, New York.

Davidson, W.H. (1980), 'The allocation of foreign direct investment activity: country characteristics and experience effects', *Journal of International Business Studies*, 11 (Fall), pp. 9-22.

Dicken, P. (1994), 'Global-local tensions: firms and states in the global space-economy', *Economic Geography*, 70(2), pp. 101-28.

Dicken, P. (1992), *Global shift: the internationalization of economic activity*, 2nd ed., The Guilford Press, New York.

Dicken, P. (1988), 'The changing geography of Japanese foreign direct investment in manufacturing: a global perspective', *Environment and Planning A*, 20(5), pp. 633-653.

Dicken, P. (1987), 'Japanese penetration of the European automobile industry: the arrival of Nissan in the United Kingdom', *Tijdschrift voor Economische en Sociale Geographie*, 78, pp. 94-107.

Dicken, P. and Lloyd, P.E. (1976), 'Geographical perspectives on United States investment in the United Kingdom', *Environment and Planning*, 8, pp. 685-705.

Dietrich, J.K. and Sorenson, E. (1984), 'An application of logit analysis to prediction of merger targets', *Journal of Business Research*, 12, pp. 393-402.

Digital Equipment Corporation (1995), *http://www.dec.com*, DEC, Boston, MA, USA.

Digital Equipment Corporation (1977-1994), *Annual reports*, DEC, Maynard, MA, USA.

Doeringer, P.B. and Terkla, D.G. (1992), 'Japanese direct investment and economic development policy', *Economic Development Quarterly*, 6, pp. 255-272.

Dohse, K., Jurgens, U. and Malsch, T. (1985), 'From "Fordism" to "Toyotism"?: the social organization of the labor process in the Japanese automobile industry', *Politics and Society*, 14, pp. 115-146.

Doz, Y. (1986), 'Government policies and global industries', in Porter, M.E. (ed.), Dunning, J.H. (1988), *Multinationals, technology and competitiveness*, Unwin Hyman, London.

Dubin, M. (1976), *Foreign acquisition and the spread of the multinational firm*, D.B.A. thesis, Graduate School of Business Administration, Harvard University.

Dunford, M. (1989), 'Technopoles, politics and markets: the development of electronics in Grenoble and Silicon Glen'. in Sharp, M. and Holmes, P. (eds.), *Strategies for new technologies; case studies from Britain and France*, Philip Allen, London, pp. 80-118.

Dunning, J.H. (1993a), *Globalization of business: the challenge of the 1990s*, Routledge, London.

Dunning, J.H. (1993b), *Multinational enterprises and the global economy*, Addison-Wesley Publishing Company, Wokingham.

Dunning, J.H. (1988), 'The eclectic paradigm of international production: a restatement and some possible extensions', *Journal of International Business Studies*, 19(1), pp. 1-31.

Dunning, J.H. (1981), *International production and the multinational enterprise*, Allen and Unwin, London.

Dunning, J.H. (1980), 'Toward an eclectic theory of international production', *Journal of International Business Studies*, 11, pp. 9-31.

Dunning, J.H. (1977), 'Trade, location of economic activity and the MNE: a search for an eclectic approach', in Ohlin, B., Hesselnorn, P.O. and Wijkman, P.J. (eds.), *The international allocation of economic activity*. Macmillan, London.

Dunning, J.H. (1973), 'The determinants of international production', *Oxford Economic Papers*, 25(3), pp. 289-336.

Dunning, J. and Cantwell, J. (1987), *The IRM directory of statistics of international investment and production*, New York University Press, New York.

Dunning, J.H. and Robson, P. (1987), 'Multinational corporate integration and regional economic integration', *Journal of Common Market Studies*, 26, pp. 103-125.

Dunning, J.H. and Rugman, A.M. (1985), 'The influence of Hymer's dissertation on the theory of foreign direct investment', *American Economic Review*, AEA Papers and Proceedings, May, pp. 228-232.

Dutz, M.A. (1989), 'Horizontal mergers in declining industries: theory and evidence', *International Journal of Industrial Organization*, 7, pp. 11-33.

Edgington, D.W. (1995), 'Japanese direct investment in Canada: patterns and prospects', in Fry, M., Kurosawa, M. and Kirton, J. (eds.), *The North Pacific triangle: United States, Japan and Canada at the end of the century* (forthcoming).

Edgington, D.W. (1994), 'The new wave: patterns of Japanese direct investment in Canada during the 1980s', *Canadian Geographer*, 38, pp. 28-36.

Edgington, D.W. (1993), 'The globalization of Japanese manufacturing corporations', *Growth and Change*, 24, pp. 87-106.

Edgington, D.W. (1992), *Japanese direct investment in Canada: recent trends and prospects*, B.C. Geographical Series, No 49, Department of Geography, University of British Columbia, Vancouver.

Edgington, D.W. (1990), 'Japanese perceptions of the Canada-US free trade agreement', *Canadian Journal of Regional Science*, 23(2/3), pp. 349-366.

Edgington, D.W. and Fruin, M. (1994), 'NAFTA and Japanese investment', in Rugman, A. (ed.) *Foreign investment and NAFTA*, University of South Carolina Press, Columbia, SC., pp. 253-275.

Elhance, A.P. and Chapman, M. (1992), 'Labor market of a US-Japanese automobile joint venture', *Growth and Change*, 23, pp. 160-182.

Employment Committee (1993), *The operation of employment legislation governing industrial disputes; minutes of evidence; Wednesday 18 April 1993*, HMSO, London. [HC 1992-93 638i]

Encarnation, D.J. and Wells, L.T. (1986), 'Competitive strategies in global industries; a view from host governments' in Porter, M.E. (ed.), *Competition in global industries*, Free Press, New York, pp. 267-290.

Ensign, P.C. (1993), 'A system theory of foreign direct investment: advantages of being multinational', *Advances in competitiveness research*, 1(1), pp. 67-77.

Errunza, V.R. and Senbet, L.W. (1981), 'The effects of international operations on the market value of the firm: theory and evidence', *The Journal of Finance*, 36(2), pp. 401-417.

Estall, R.C. (1985), 'Stock control in manufacturing: the just-in-time system and its locational implications', *Area*, 17, pp. 129-133.

Ettlinger, N. And Archer, J.C. (1987), 'City-size distribution and the world urban system in the twentieth century', *Environment and Planning A*, 19, pp. 1161-74.

Financial Times of Canada (1993), 'Mitsubishi: who's afraid of free trade?', January 9, p.10.

Fiol, C.M. and Lyles, M.A. (1985), 'Organizational learning', *Academy of Management Review*, 10(4), pp. 803-813.

Florida, R. and Kenney, M. (1991), 'Japanese foreign investment in the United States: the case of automotive transplants', in Morris, J. (ed.), *Japan and the global economy: issues and trends in the 1990s*, Routledge, London, pp. 91-114.

Florida, R. and Kenney, M. (1990a), *The breakthrough illusion; corporate America's failure to move from innovation to mass production*, Basic Books, New York.

Florida, R. and Kenney, M. (1990b), 'High-technology restructuring in the USA and Japan', *Environment and Planning A*, 22, pp. 233-252.

Forsgren, M. (1989), 'Foreign acquisitions: internalization or network interdependency?', *Advances in International Marketing*, 3, pp. 141-159.

Forsyth, D.J.C. (1972), *US investment in Scotland*, Praeger, New York.

Franko, L.G. (1989), 'Global corporate competition: who's winning, who's losing, and the R&D factor as one reason why', *Strategic Management Journal*, 10, pp. 449-474.

Friedmann, J. (1986), 'The world city hypothesis', *Development and Change*, 17, pp. 69-83.

Friedmann, J. and Wolff, G. (1982), 'World city formation: an agenda for research and action', *International Journal of Urban and Regional Research,* 6(3), pp. 309-44.

Fröbel, F., J. Heinrichs and O. Kreye, (1980), *The new international division of labor*, Cambridge University Press, Cambridge.

Gereffi, G. (1992), 'New realities of industrial development in East Asia and Latin America', in Appelbaum, R. and Henderson, J. (eds.), *States and development in the Asian Pacific Rim*, Sage Publications, Newbury Park, pp. 85-111.

Gerlach, M.L. (1994), *Economic organization and innovation in Japan*, Working paper, University of British Columbia, Vancouver.

Gertler, M.S. (1991), 'Canada in a high-tech world: options for industrial policy', in Drache, D. and Gertler, M.S. (eds.), *The new era of global competition: state*

policy and market power, McGill-Queen's University Press, Montreal, pp. 367-398.
Gillespie, A. (1991), 'Advanced communication networks, territorial integration and local development', in Camagni, R. (ed.), *Innovation network*, pp. 214-44, Frances Pinter, London.
Giunipero, L.C. and O'Neal, C. (1988), 'Obstacles to JIT procurement', *Industrial Marketing Management*, 17, pp. 35-41.
Glasmeier, A.K. and McCluskey, R.E. (1987), 'US auto parts production: an analysis of the organization and location of a changing industry', *Economic Geography*, 63, pp. 142-159.
Glickman, N.J. and Woodward, D.P. (1988), 'The location of foreign direct investment in the United States: patterns and determinants', *International Regional Science Review*, 11(2), pp. 137-54.
Glismann, H.H. and Horn, E.J. (1988), 'Comparative invention performance of major industrial countries: patterns and explanations', *Management Science*, 34(10), pp. 1169-1187.
Goldstein, D.J. (1988), 'Foreign direct investment in the United States and national security policy', *Comparative Strategy*, 7, pp. 143-158.
Gordon, S.L. and Lees, F.A. (1986), *Foreign multinational investment in the United States*, Quorum Books, Connecticut.
Government of Ontario (1992), *Japanese investment profile*, Ontario House, Tokyo.
Graham, E.M. (1974), *Oligopolistic imitation and European direct investment in the United States*, Doctoral Dissertation, Harvard Business School.
Green, M.B. (1993), 'A geography of institutional stock ownership in the United States', *Annals of the Association of American Geographers*, 83(1), pp. 66-89.
Grosse, R. (1981), *The theory of foreign direct investment*, University of South Carolina, College of Business Administration, Center for International Business Studies; Essays in International Business, No. 3, Columbia, SC.
Grubaugh, S.G. (1987), 'Determinants of direct foreign investment', *The Review of Economics and Statistics*, pp. 149-152.
Gruber, W., Mehta, D. and Vernon, R. (1967), 'The research and development factor in investment of US industries', *Journal of Political Economy*, 75, pp. 20-37.
Gupta, A.K. and Govindarajan, V. (1991), 'Knowledge flows and the structure of control within multinational corporations', *Academy of Management Review*, 16(4), pp. 768-792.
Hakansson, H. (1989), *Corporate technological behaviour: co-operation and networks*, Routledge, London.
Hall, P., Breheny, M., McQuaid, R. and Hart, D. (1987), *Western sunrise; the genesis and growth of Britain's major high tech corridor*, Allen and Unwin, London.
Hamel, G. (1991), 'Competition for competence and inter-partner learning within international strategic alliances', *Strategic Management Journal*, 12 (Special Issue), pp. 83-104.

Hamel, G., Doz, Y.L. and Prahalad, C.K. (1989), 'Collaborate with your competitors: and win', *Harvard Business Review*, 65 January-February, pp. 133-139.
Hannah, K.H. (1987), 'Just-in-time: meeting the competitive challenge', *Production and Inventory Management Journal*, 28, pp. 1-3.
Helpman, E. (1984), 'A simple theory of international trade with multinational corporations', *Journal of Political Economy*, 92, pp. 451-471.
Harris, R.S. and Ravenscraft, D. (1989), 'The role of acquisition in foreign direct investment: evidence from the US stock market', Darden School Working Paper, Graduate School of Business Administration, University of Virginia.
Harvie, C. (1992), *No gods and precious few heroes*, University of Edinburgh, Edinburgh.
Harvie, C. (1977), *Scotland and nationalism; Scottish society and politics, 1707-1977*, George Allan and Unwin, London.
Hasbrouck, J. (1985), 'The characteristics of takeover-targets: q and other measures', *Journal of Banking and Finance*, 9, pp. 351-362.
Hedlund, G. (1986), 'The hypermodern MNC: a heterarchy?' *Human Resource Management*, 25, pp. 9-35.
Heenan, D.A. (1991), *The new corporate frontier: the big move to small town, USA*, McGraw Hill, New York.
Hennart, J.-F. (1991), 'The transaction cost theory of the multinational enterprise', in Pitelis, C. and Sugden, R. (eds.), *The nature of the transnational firm*, Routledge, London.
Hennart, J.-F. (1982), *A theory of multinational enterprise*, University of Michigan Press, Ann Arbor.
Hepworth, M. (1986), 'The geography of technological change in the information economy', *Regional Studies*, 20, pp. 407-24.
Hill, C.W.L. and Kim, W.C. (1988), 'Searching for a dynamic theory of the multinational enterprise: a transaction cost model', *Strategic Management Journal*, 9, pp. 93-104.
Hill, C.W.L., Hwang, P. and Kim, W.C. (1990), 'An eclectic theory of the choice of international entry choice', *Strategic Management Journal*, 11, pp. 117-128.
Hill, S. and Munday, M. (1992), 'The UK regional distribution of foreign direct investment: analysis and determinants', *Regional Studies*, 25(6), pp. 535-44.
Hirsch, S. (1976), 'An international trade and investment theory of the firm', *Oxford Economic Papers*, 28, pp. 258-270.
Hitt, M.A., Hoskisson, R.E. and Ireland, R.D. (1990), 'Mergers and acquisitions and managerial commitment to innovation in M-form firms', *Strategic Management Journal*, 11 (Special Issue), pp. 29-47.
Hladik, K. (1985), *International joint ventures*, D.C. Heath, Lexington, MA.
Hoggart, K. (1991), 'The changing world of corporate control centers', *Geography*, 67, pp. 109-20.
Holloway, S.R. and Wheeler, J.O. (1991), 'Corporate headquarters relocation and changes in metropolitan dominance', *Economic Geography*, 67, pp. 54-74.

Holstein, W.J., Treece, J., Crock, S., and Armstrong, L. (1990), 'Hands across America: the rise of Mitsubishi', *Business Week*, 24 September, pp. 102-103, 106-107.

Hood, N. (1991), 'The Scottish development agency in retrospect', *Royal Bank of Scotland Review* Number 171, pp. 3-21.

Hood, N. (1990), 'Scottish enterprise; the basis of a Scottish solution to Scottish problems?', Fraser of Allander, *Quarterly Economic Commentary*, 16(2), pp. 65-75.

Hood, N. and Young, S. (1982a), *Multinationals in retreat; the Scottish experience*, Edinburgh: University of Edinburgh Press.

Hood, N. and Young, S. (1982b), 'US multinational R&D; corporate strategies and policy implications for the UK', *Multinational Business*, 2, pp. 10-23.

Hood, N. and Young, S. (1980), *European development strategies of US-owned manufacturing companies located in Scotland*, HMSO, Edinburgh.

Hood, N. and Young, S. (1979), *The economics of multinational enterprise*, London, Longman.

Hood, N. and Young, S. (1976), 'US investment in Scotland; aspects of branch factory syndrome', *Scottish Journal of Political Economy*, 23, No. 3, pp. 279-294.

Horstmann, I. and Markusen, J.R. (1987), 'Licensing versus direct investment: a model of internationalization by the multinational enterprise', *Canadian Journal of Economics*, 20, pp. 464-481.

Hurry, D. (1993), 'Restructuring the global economy: the consequences of strategic linkages between Japanese and US firms', *Strategic Management Journal*, 14, pp. 69-82.

Hurry, D., Miller, A.T. and Bowman, E.H. (1992), 'Calls on high-technology: Japanese exploration of venture capital investments in the United States', *Strategic Management Journal*, 13, pp. 85-101.

Hymer, S.G. (1976), *The international operations of national firms: a study of direct foreign investment*, MIT Press, Cambridge.

IDS (1991), *Statistical Bulletin C1.4; the electronics industry in Scotland*, Industry Department Scotland, Edinburgh.

IDS (1987), *Review of SDA???* Industry Department Scotland, Edinburgh.

IDS (1987), *Statistical Bulletin C3.1; aspects of employment structure in the electronics industry in Scotland*, Industry Department Scotland, Edinburgh.

Imai, K. (1987-88), 'The corporate network in Japan', *Japanese Economic Studies*, 16, pp. 3-37.

Imai, K. and Itami, H. (1984), 'Interpenetration of organization and market: Japan's firm and market in comparison with the US', *International Journal of Industrial Organization*, 2, pp. 285-310.

Innami, H. (1986), 'There's profit in picture tubes: Mitsubishi shows Midland the secret to success', *BC Business*, Asia Pacific Business Supplement, October, pp. 5-7.

Investment Canada (1993), *Foreign multinationals and Canada's international competitiveness*, Working Paper No. 16, Investment Canada, Ottawa.

Japan Economic Institute (1992), 'Japan's FY 1991 foreign direct investment', *JEI Report*, 23B, pp. 10-11.

Japan External Trade Organization (1993), *1993-94 directory: Japanese-affiliated companies in USA and Canada*, Jetro, Tokyo.

Japan External Trade Organization (1990-93), *Handy facts on US-Japan economic relations*, JETRO, Tokyo.

Japanese Automobile Manufacturers Association of Canada (1993), *JAMA Canada annual report*, Toronto.

Jarrell, G.A., Brickley, J.A. and Netter, J.M. (1988), 'The market for corporate control: the empirical evidence since 1980', *Journal of Economic Perspectives*, 2(1), Winter, pp. 48-68.

Jensen, M.C. (1988), 'Takeovers: their causes and consequences', *Journal of Economic Perspectives*, 2, pp. 21-48.

Jensen, M.C. and Meckling, W. (1976), 'Theory of the firm: managerial behavior, agency costs and ownership structure', *Journal of Financial Economics*, 3, pp. 305-360.

Jensen, M.C. and Ruback, R.S. (1983), 'The market for corporate control: the scientific evidence', *Journal of Financial Economics*, 11, pp. 5-50.

Johanson, J. and Mattsson, L.G. (1988), 'Internationalisation in industrial systems -- a network approach', in Hood, N. and Vahlne, J.E. (eds.), *Strategies in global competition*, pp. 287-314, Croom Helm, London.

Johanson, J. and Vahlne, J.E. (1990), 'The mechanism of internationalisation', *International Marketing Review*, 7, pp. 11-24.

Johanson, J. and Vahlne, J.E. (1977), 'The internationalization process of the firm: a model of knowledge development and increasing foreign market commitments', *Journal of International Business Studies*, 8 (Spring/Summer), pp. 23-32.

Johnson, H.G. (1970), 'The efficiency and welfare implications of the international corporation', in Dunning, J.H. (ed.), *International investment*, Penguin Books Ltd., Middlesex, England, pp. 455-76.

Johnson, H.G. (1970), 'The efficiency and welfare implications of the multinational corporation', in Kindleberger, C.P. (ed.), *The international corporation: a symposium*, MIT Press, Cambridge.

Jones, P.N. and North, J. (1991), 'Japanese motor industry transplants: the west European dimension', *Economic Geography*, 67, pp. 105-123.

Jordan, H.H. (1988), 'Inventory management in the JIT age', *Production and Inventory Management Journal*, 28, pp. 57-59.

Julian, S.D. and Keller, R.T. (1991), 'Multinational R&D siting', *Columbia Journal of World Business*, 26(3), pp. 46-57.

Kamien, M. and Schwartz, N. (1982), *Market structure and innovation*, Cambridge University Press, Cambridge.

Kanter, R.M. (1983), *The change masters: innovation and entrepreneurship in the American corporation*, Simon & Schuster, New York.

Kenney, M. and Florida, R. (1994), 'Japanese Macquiladoras: production organization and global commodity chains', *World Development*, 22, pp. 27-44.

Kenney, M. and Florida, R. (1993), *Beyond mass production: the Japanese system and its transfer to the United States*, Oxford University Press, New York.
Kenney, M. and Florida, R. (1992), 'The Japanese transplants: production organization and regional development', *Journal of the American Planning Association*, 58, pp. 21-38.
Kenney, M. and Florida, R. (1991), 'How Japanese industry is rebuilding the rustbelt', *Technology Review*, 94, pp. 25-33.
Kindleberger, C.P. (1969), *American business abroad: six lectures on direct investment*, Yale University Press, New Haven.
King, A.D. (1990), *Global cities: post-imperialism and the internationalization of London*, Routledge, London.
Kline, S.J. and Rosenburg, N. (1986), 'An overview of innovation', in Laudau, R. and Rosenburg, N. (eds.), *The positive sum strategy: harnessing technology for economic growth*, National Academy Press, Washington, DC.
Knickerbocker, F.T. (1973), *Oligopolistic reaction and the multinational enterprise*, Harvard University Press, Cambridge.
Kobrin, S.J. (1991), 'An empirical analysis of the determinants of global integration', *Strategic Management Journal*, 12 (Special Issue), 17-31.
Koechlin, T. (1992), 'The determinants of the location of USA direct foreign investment', *International Review of Applied Economics*, 6(2), pp. 203-16.
Kogut, B. (ed.) (1992), *Country competitiveness and the organization of work*, Oxford University Press, Oxford.
Kogut, B. (1991a), 'Country capabilities and the permeability of borders', *Strategic Management Journal*, 12 (Special Issue), pp. 33-47.
Kogut, B. (1991b), 'Joint ventures and the option to expand and acquire', *Management Science*, 37, pp. 19-33.
Kogut, B. (1983), 'Foreign direct investment as a sequential process', in Kindleberger, C.P. and Audretsch, D.B. (eds.), *The multinational corporation in the 1980s*, MIT Press, Cambridge, pp. 38-56.
Kogut, B. and Chang, S.J. (1991), 'Technological capabilities and Japanese direct investment in the United States', *Review of Economics and Statistics*, 73, pp. 401-413.
Kogut, B. and Zander, U. (1992), 'Knowledge of the firm, combinative capabilities, and the replication of technology', *Organization Science*, 3(3), pp. 383-397.
Kojima, K. (1976), *Direct foreign investment: a Japanese model of multinational business operations*, Groom Helm, London.
Korbin, S.J. (1976), 'The environmental determinants of foreign direct manufacturing investment: an ex post empirical analysis', *Journal of International Business Studies*, 7(2), pp. 29-42.
Lall, S. (1980), 'Monopolistic advantages and foreign involvement by US manufacturing industry', *Oxford Economic Papers*, 32(1).
Lall, S. (1979), 'The international allocation of research activity by US multinationals', *Oxford Bulletin of Economics and Statistics*, 41(4), pp. 313-30.

Lall, S. (1978), 'Transnationals, domestic enterprises, and industrial structure in host LDCs: a survey', *Oxford Economic Papers*, 30, No. 2.

Langdale, J.V. (1989), 'The geography of international business telecommunications: the role of leased networks', *Annals of Association of American Geographers*, 79, pp. 501-22.

Law, C.M. (1980), 'The foreign company's location investment decision and its role in British regional development', *Tijdschrift voor Econ. en Soc. Geografie*, 71(1), pp. 15-20.

Lecraw, D.L. (1993), 'Outward direct investment by Indonesian firms: motivation and effects', *Journal of International Business Studies*, 24(3), pp. 589-600.

Lessard, D.R. (1979), 'Transfer prices, taxes and financial markets: implications of internal financial transfers within the multinational firm', in Hawkins, R.G. (ed.), *Economic issues of multinational firms*, JAI Press, Greenwich, CT.

Levitt, B. and March, J.G. (1988), 'Organizational learning', *Annual Review of Sociology*, 14, pp. 319-340.

Levitt, T. (1983), 'The globalization of markets', *Harvard Business Review*, 61, May-June, pp. 92-102.

Li, W. and Qu, T. (1989), *Progress and problems in setting up foreign invested industrial enterprise in the PRC*, a paper presented on the Conference on Industrial Change, IGU, Germany.

Lim, D. (1983), 'Fiscal incentives and direct foreign investment in less developed countries', *The Journal of Development Studies*, January, pp. 207-12.

Lindgren, U. (1982), 'Foreign acquisitions: management of the integration process', Stockholm.

Lipsey, F.G. (1981), 'The new international division of labour, multinational corporations and the urban hierarchy', in Dear, M. and Scott, A.J. (eds.), *Urbanization and urban planning in capitalist society*, London, Metheun.

Lipsey, R.E., Karvis, I.B. and O'Connor, L. (1983), *Characteristics of US manufacturing companies investing abroad and their choice of production locations*, Working Paper No. 1104, National Bureau of Economic Research, Cambridge, MA.

Little, B. (1991), 'Firm warms to trade deal', *Globe and Mail*, Toronto, 30 November, p.B1.

Little, J.S. (1988), 'Foreign investment in the United States: a cause for concern?', *New England Economic Review*, July/August, pp. 51-58.

Livesay, H.C. (1976), *Andrew Carnegie and the rise of big business*, Little Brown, Boston.

Lubben, R. (1988), *Just-in-time manufacturing: an aggressive manufacturing strategy*, McGraw-Hill, New York.

Lynn, L. (1982), *How Japan innovates?* Westview, Boulder, CO.

Lyons, D.I. (1994), 'Changing patterns of corporate headquarter influence, 1974-1989', *Environment and Planning A*, 26, pp. 733-47.

MacInnes, J. and Sproull, A. (1987), 'Electronics employment in Scotland', Fraser of Allander, *Quarterly Economic Commentary*, 12(3), pp. 77-82.

MacKnight, S. (1992), *Japan's expanding US manufacturing presence: 1990 update*, Japan Economic Institute, Washington, D.C.

Maddala, G.S. (1987), 'Limited dependent and qualitative variables in econometrics', Cambridge University Press. 1987 edition.

Magee, S.P. (1977), 'Information and the multinational corporation: an appropriability theory of direct foreign investment', in Bhagwati, J.N. (ed.), *The new international economic order: the north-south debate*, MIT Press, Cambridge.

Magee, S.P. (1976), 'Technology and the appropriability theory of the multinational corporation', in Bhagwati, J.N. (ed.), *The new international economic order*, MIT Press, Cambridge.

Mahood, C. (1994), 'Ontario wins $600-million plant', *Globe and Mail*, 4 November, pp. 1-2.

Mair, A., Florida, R. and Kenney, M. (1988), 'The new geography of automobile production: Japanese transplants in North America', *Economic Geography*, 64, pp. 352-373.

Malley, J.C. and Ray, R. (1988), 'Informational and organizational impacts of implementing a JIT system', *Production and Inventory Management Journal*, 29, pp. 60-66.

Mandelker, G. and Nachtmann, R. (1990), *Evidence on the global market for corporate control*, Working Paper, US Securities and Exchange Commission and University of Pittsburgh, March.

Manne, H.G. (1965), 'Mergers and the market for corporate control', *Journal of Political Economy*, 73, pp. 110-120.

Mansfield, E. (1988), 'The speed and cost of industrial innovation in Japan and the United States: external vs. internal technology', *Management Science*, 34(10), pp. 1157-1168.

Mansfield, E. (1985), 'How rapidly does new technology leak out?', *Journal of Industrial Economics*, 54, pp. 217-223.

March, J.G. and Simon, H.A. (1958), *Organizations*, Wiley, New York.

Massey, D., Quintas, P. and Wield, D. (1992), *High tech fantasies; science parks in society, science and space*, Routledge, London.

Matsumoto, M. (1994), 'Politically wary Honda opens Mexico plant: carmaker assures US, Canada it won't export north of the border', *Nikkei Weekly*, 16 May, p. 12.

McCalman, J. (1989), 'Smart technology and smart people; human resource development in the electronics industry', Fraser of Allander, *Quarterly Economic Commentary*, 14(4), pp. 53-59.

McCalman, J. (1987), 'What's wrong with Scottish firms? Local sourcing in electronics', Fraser of Allander, *Quarterly Economic Commentary*, 12(3), pp. 62-64.

McConnell, J.E. (1983), 'The international location of manufacturing investment: recent behaviour of foreign-owned corporations in the United States', in Hamilton, F.E.I. and Linge, G.J.R. (eds.), *Spatial analysis, industry, and the industrial environments*, 3, pp. 337-58.

McConnell, J.E. (1980), 'Foreign direct investment in the United States', *Annals of the Association of American Geographers*, 70(2), pp. 259-70.

McDermott, P.J. (1979), 'Multinational manufacturing firms and regional development; external control in the Scottish electronics industry', *Scottish Journal of Political Economy*, 26(3), pp. 287-306.

McDermott, P.J. (1977), 'Overseas investment and the industrial geography of the United Kingdom', *Area*, 9, pp. 200-7.

Melin, L. (1992), 'Internationalization as a strategy process', *Strategic Management Journal*, 13 (Winter Special Issue), pp. 99-118.

Meyer, D. (1991), 'Change in the world system of metropolises: the role of business intermediaries', *Urban Geography*, 12(5), pp. 393-416.

Miles, R.E. and Snow, C.C. (1986), 'Organizations: new concepts for new forms', *California Management Review*, 28(3), pp. 62-73.

Mintzberg, H. (1990), 'The design school: reconsidering the basic premise of strategic management', *Strategic Management Journal*, 11, 171-195.

Mintzberg, H. and Waters, J.A. (1985), 'Of strategies, deliberate and emergent', *Strategic Management Journal*, 6, pp. 257-272.

Mitchell-Weaver, C. and Bremm, H. (1993), 'Multinational regionalism in Europe and North America', *Built Environment*, 19(1), pp. 5-15.

Morck, R. and Young, B. (1990), *Internalization and managers' interests: an event study test*, Working Paper No. 10-90, Institute for Financial Research, Faculty of Business, University of Alberta, November.

Morck, R. and Young, B. (1989), *Why investors value multinationality*, Working Paper No. 5-89, Institute of Financial Research, Faculty of Business, University of Alberta, Canada.

Morck, R., Shleifer, A. and Vishny, R.W. (1988), 'Characteristics of targets of hostile and friendly takeovers', in Auerbach, A.J. (ed.), *Corporate takeovers: causes and consequences*, The University of Chicago Press, Chicago, pp. 101-134.

Morril, R.L. (1979), 'Stages in patterns of population concentration and dispersion', *Professional Geographer*, 31, pp. 55-65.

Morris, J. (1991a), 'Japanese manufacturing investment in Canada: regional presence and integration strategies', in Morris, J. (ed.), *Japan and the global economy: issues and trends in the 1990s*, Routledge, London, pp. 115-134.

Morris, J. (1991b), 'A Japanization of Canadian industry?', in Drache, D. and Gertler, M.S. (eds.), *The new era of global competition: state policy and market power*, McGill-Queen's University Press, Montreal, pp. 206-228.

Morris, J. (1989), *The changing industrial structure of Canada in the 1980s: the role of Japanese foreign direct investment*, Final Report to Canadian High Commission, Canadian Studies Research Awards, 1988, Cardiff Business School, University of Wales College Cardiff, Cardiff, (mimeo).

Moss, M.L. (1987), 'Telecommunications, world cities, and urban policy', *Urban Studies*, 24, pp. 534-46.

Mueller, W.F. and Rogers, R.T. (1980), 'The role of advertising in changing concentration of manufacturing industries', *Review of Economics and Statistics*, February, 62, pp. 7-13.

Nathans, L. (1987), 'Then came Kawamura (president of Dainippon Ink and Chemicals)', *Business Month*, 130, October, pp. 4-24.

National Audit Office (1989), *Locate in Scotland; report by the Comptroller and Auditor General*, HMSO, London. [HC 1988-89 300]

National Audit Office (1988), *Scottish Development Agency; involvement with the private sector; report by the Comptroller and Auditor General*, HMSO, London. [House of Commons 1987-88 HC 478]

Neff, R. and Holstein, W.J. (1990), 'Mighty Mitsubishi is on the move', *Business Week*, 24 September, pp. 98-101.

Ohmae, K. (1990), *The borderless world*, McKinsey & Company, New York.

Ohmae, K. (1985), *Triad power: the coming shape of global competition*, Free Press, New York.

Ó hUallacháin, B. (1994), 'Foreign banking in the American urban system of financial organization', *Economic Geography*, Vol. 70(3), pp. 206-228.

Ó hUallacháin, B. (1993), 'The restructuring of the US steel industry: changes in the location of production and employment', *Environment and Planning A*, 25, pp. 1339-1359.

Ó hUallacháin, B. (1991), 'Industrial geography', *Progress in Human Geography*, 15, pp. 73-80.

Ó hUallacháin, B. (1985), 'Spatial patterns of foreign direct investment in the United States', *Professional Geographer*, 37(2), pp. 155-63.

Ó hUallacháin, B. (1984), 'Linkages and foreign investment in the United States', *Economic Geography*, 60, pp. 238-53.

Okumura, H. (1982), 'Interfirm relations in an enterprise group: the case of Mitsubishi', *Japanese Economic Studies*, 10, pp. 53-82.

Oliver, N. and Wilkinson, B. (1988), *The Japanization of British industry*, Basil Blackwell Ltd., Oxford.

O'Neal, C.R. (1989), 'The buyer-seller linkage in a just-in-time environment', *Journal of Purchasing and Materials Management*, 25, pp. 34-40.

Osborn, R.N. and Baughn, C.C. (1987), 'New patterns in the formation of US/Japanese cooperative ventures: the role of technology', *Columbia Journal of World Business*, 22, pp. 57-65.

Ostrom, D. (1990), 'Keiretsu and other large corporate groups in Japan', *Japan Economic Institute (JEI) Report*, 2A, pp. 1-17.

Pa (1979), *Labour performance of US-owned plants in Scotland; a research report*, Scottish Development Agency, Glasgow.

Pacific Automotive Co-operation Inc. (1994), *PAC: responding to the needs of Canada's auto part industry*, Pacific Automotive Co-operation Inc., Willowdale, Ontario.

Palepu, K.G. (1986), 'Predicting takeover targets: a methodological and empirical analysis', *Journal of Accounting and Economics*, 8, pp. 3-35.

Pascale, R. and Rohlen, T.P. (1983), 'The Mazda turnaround', *The Journal of Japanese Studies*, 9, pp. 219-263.
Payne, P.L. (1992), *Growth and contraction; Scottish industry c1860-1990*, The Economic and Social History Society of Scotland, Glasgow.
Peng, M.W. (1994), 'The shifting rationale for foreign direct investment: toward a learning option perspective', *The Best in Management Worldwide*, Proceedings of the Second World IFSAM Conference on Management, Dallas, pp. 104-105.
Penrose, E.T. (1956), 'Foreign investment and the growth of the firm', *Economic Journal*, 66 (June), pp. 220-35.
Penrose, E.T. (1959), *The theory of the growth of the firm*, Basil Blackwell, Oxford.
Perrucci, R. (1994), *Japanese auto transplants in the Heartland*, Aldine de Gruyter, New York.
Piore, M.J. and Sabel, C.F. (1984), *The second industrial divide*, Basic Books, New York.
Poniachek, H.A. (1986), *Direct foreign investment in the United States*, Lexington Books, New York.
Porter, M.E. (1991), 'Toward a dynamic theory of strategy', *Strategic Management Journal*, 12, pp. 95-117.
Porter, M.E. (1990), *The competitive advantage of nations*, The Free Press, New York.
Porter, M.E. (1987), 'From competitive advantage to corporate strategy', *Harvard Business Review*, 65 (3), pp. 43-59.
Porter, M.E. (1985), *Competitive advantage: creating and sustaining superior performance*, Free Press, New York.
Pound, J. (1988), 'Proxy contests and the efficiency of shareholder oversight', *Journal of Financial Economics*, 20, pp. 237-265.
Powell, W.W. (1990), 'Neither market nor hierarchy: network forms of organization', *Research in Organizational Behavior*, 12, pp. 295-336.
Prescowitz, C.V. (1987), *Trading places: how we allowed the Japanese to take the lead*, Basic Books, New York.
Price Waterhouse (1993), *Doing business in the United States: information guide*, Price Waterhouse World Firm Ltd., New York.
Ptak, C.A. (1988), 'A comparison of inventory models and carrying costs', *Production and Inventory Management Journal*, 29, pp. 1-2.
Pucik, V. (1988), 'Strategic alliances, organizational learning, and competitive advantage: the HRM agenda', *Human Resource Management*, 27(1), pp. 77-93.
Quante, W. (1976), *The exodus of corporate headquarters from New York City*, Praeger, New York.
Quinn, J.B. (1969), 'Technology transfer by multinational companies', *Harvard Business Review*, 47, November-December, pp. 147-161.
Rankine, S. (1994), 'The last picture show', *Globe and Mail*, 26 July, p. 14.
Rao, A. and Scheraga, D. (1988), 'Moving from manufacturing resource planning to just-in-time manufacturing', *Production and Inventory Management Journal*, 29, pp. 44-49.

Ravenscraft, D.J. (1987), 'The 1980s merger wave: an industrial organization perspective', in Browne, L.E. and Rosengren, E.S. (eds.), *The merger boom*, Federal Reserve Bank of Boston.

Ray, D.M. (1971), 'The location of United States subsidiaries in Southern Ontario', in Gentilcore, R.L. (ed.), *Geographical approaches to Canadian problems*, Prentice-Hall, Scarborough, ON., pp. 69-82.

Reich, R.B. and Mankin, E.R. (1986), 'Joint ventures with Japan give away our future', *Harvard Business Review*, 64, March-April, pp. 78-90.

Reid, N. (1995), 'Just-in-time inventory control and the economic integration of Japanese-owned manufacturing plants with the county, state, and national economies of the United States', *Regional Studies*, 29 (forthcoming).

Reid, N. (1990), 'Spatial patterns of Japanese investment in the US automobile industry', *Industrial Relations Journal*, 21, pp. 49-59.

Reid, S.D. (1981), 'The decision-maker and export entry and expansion', *Journal of International Business Studies*, 12 (Fall), pp. 101-111.

Reuber, G.L. (1973), *Private foreign investment development*, Clarendon Press, Oxford.

Richardson, G.B. (1972), 'The organization of industry', *The Economic Journal*, 82, pp. 883-893.

Richardson, T. (1990), *Perspectives on Japanese direct investment in Canada*, Toronto (mimeo).

Rogers, E.M. (1962), *Diffusion of innovations*, Free Press, New York.

Roll, R. (1986), 'The Hubris hypothesis of corporate takeovers', *Journal of Business*, 59, pp. 197-216.

Root, F.R. (1987), *Entry strategies for international markets*, Lexington Books, Lexington, MA.

Root, F.R. and Ahmed, A.A. (1979), 'Empirical determinants of manufacturing foreign investment in developing countries', *Economic Development and Cultural Change*, 27(4), pp. 751-67.

Rosenberg, N. and Steinmueller, W.E. (1988), 'Why are Americans such poor imitators?', *American Economic Review Proceedings*, 78, pp. 229-234.

Rubenstein, J.M. (1992), *The changing US auto industry: a geographical analysis*, Routledge, New York.

Rubenstein, J.M. (1991), 'The impact of Japanese investment in the United States', in Law, C. (ed,), *Restructuring the global automobile industry*, Routledge, London, pp. 114-142.

Rubenstein, J.M.(1986), 'Changing distribution of the American automobile industry', *Geographical Review*, 76, pp. 288-300.

Rugman, A. (1990), *Multinationals and Canada-United States free trade*, University of South Carolina Press, Columbia, S.C.

Rugman, A.M. (1987), *Inside the multinationals*, Croom Helm, London.

Rugman, A.M. (1982), 'Internalization and non-equity forms of international involvement', in Rugman, A.M. (ed.), *New theories of multinational enterprise*, St. Martin's Press, New York, 1982, pp. 9-23.

Rugman, A.M. (1981), *Inside the multinationals: the economics of internal markets*, Croom Helm, London.

Rugman, A.M. (1980), 'A new theory of the multinational enterprise: internalization versus internationalization', *Columbia Journal of World Business*, 15, pp. 23-29.

Rugman, A.M. and Waverman, L. (1991), 'Foreign ownership and corporate strategy', in Waverman, L. (ed.), *Corporate globalization through mergers and acquisitions*, University of Calgary Press, Investment Canada and Canada Communication Group, Calgary, pp. 59-87.

Rugman, A.M., Lecraw, D.J. and Booth, L.D. (1985), *International business: firm and environment*, McGraw-Hill, Toronto.

Saxonhouse, G.R. (1986), 'Industrial policy and factor markets: biotechnology in Japan and the United States', in Patrick, H. (ed.), *Japan's high technology industries: lessons and limitations of industrial policy*, University of Washington Press, Seattle.

Sayer, A. (1986), 'New developments in manufacturing: the just-in-time system', *Capital and Class*, 30, pp. 43-72.

Scaperlanda, A.E. and Mauer, L.J. (1969), 'The determinants of US direct investment in the E.E.C.', *American Economic Review*, 59, pp. 558-68.

Schieve, C. and Majumdar, B.A. (1990), 'Direct foreign investment and the linkage effects: the experience of Taiwan', *Canadian Journal of Development Studies*, 11 (2), pp. 325-42.

Schneider, F. and Frey, B.S. (1985), 'Economic and political determinants of foreign direct investment', *World Development*, 13(2), pp. 161-75.

Schoenberger, E. (1990), 'US manufacturing investments in Western Europe: markets, corporate strategy, and the competitive environment', *Annals of the Association of American Geographers*, 80(3), pp. 379-93.

Schoenberger, E. (1988), 'Multinational corporations and the new international division of labor: a critical appraisal', *International Regional Science Review*, 11(2), pp. 105-19.

Schoenberger, R.J. (1982), *Japanese manufacturing techniques: nine hidden lessons in simplicity*, The Free Press, New York.

Scott, A.J. (1983), 'Industrial organization and the logic of intra-metropolitan location: I theoretical considerations', *Economic Geography*, 59, pp. 233-250.

Scottish Office (1988), *Scottish enterprise, a new approach to training and enterprise creation*, HMSO, Edinburgh. [Cm 534]

Semple, R.K. (1985), 'Toward a quaternary place theory', *Urban Geography*, 6, pp. 286-96.

Semple, R.K. (1977), 'Regional development theory and sectoral income inequalities', in Odland, J. and Taaffe, R.N. (eds.), *Geographical Horizons*, Dubuque, pp. 45-63, Kendall-Hunt, Iowa.

Semple, R.K. and Green, M. (1983), 'Interurban corporate headquarters relocation in Canada', *Cahiers de Géographie de Québec*, 27, pp. 389-406.

Semple, R.K. and Phipps, A.G. (1982), 'The spatial evolution of corporate headquarters within urban system', *Urban Geography*, 3, pp. 258-79.

Semple, R.K. and Rice, M.D. (1994), 'Canada and the international system of bank headquarters cities, 1968-1989', *Growth and Change*, Vol. 25 (Winter), pp. 25-50.

Semple, R.K. and Rice, M.D. (1993), 'Foreign headquarters centers, changing linkage patterns and the Canadian urban system, 1970-1991', presented at Canadian Association of Geographers Meeting, Ottawa.

Servaes, H. (1988), 'Tobin's Q, agency costs and corporate control: an empirical analysis of firm-specific parameters', Working Paper.

Shachar, A. (1994), 'Randstad Holland: a "world city"?', *Urban Studies*, 31(3), pp. 381-400.

Shan, W. and Hamilton, W. (1991), 'Country-specific advantage and inter-national cooperation', *Strategic Management Journal*, 12, pp. 419-432.

Shapiro, A. (1982), *Multinational finacial management*, Allyn and Bacon Inc.

Sheard, P. (1983), 'Auto-production systems in Japan: organization and locational features', *Australian Geographical Studies*, 21, pp. 49-63.

Sheppard, E. (1982), 'City size distributions and spatial economic change', *International Regional Science Review*, 7, pp. 127-51.

Short, J. (1981), 'The regional distribution of public expenditure in Great Britain, 1967/70-1973/74', *Regional Studies*, 12, pp. 499-510.

SOID (1994), *Statistical Bulletin C1.6; the electronics industry in Scotland*, Scottish Office Industry Department, Edinburgh.

SOID (1993), *Statistical Bulletin A3.5; overseas ownership in Scottish manufacturing industry 1992*, Scottish Office Industry Department, Edinburgh.

Stafford, D.C. and Purkis, R.H.A. (1989), *Directory of multinationals*, Stockton Press, New York.

Stewart, J.C. (1976), 'Linkages and foreign direct investment', *Regional Studies*, 10, pp. 245-258.

Stinson, M. (1991), 'Just-in-time can become downtime', *Globe and Mail*, 20 September, p.B1.

Stopford, J.M. (1992), *Directory of multinational enterprises*, Stockton Press, New York.

Stopford, J.M., Dunning, J.H. and Haberich, K.O. (1980), *The world directory of multinational enterprises*, Facts on File, New York.

Strickland, D. and Aiken, M. (1984), 'Corporate influence and the German urban system: headquarters location of German industrial corporations, 1950-1982', *Economic Geography*, 60(1), pp. 38-54.

Suzuki, K. (1985), 'The application of Japanese competitive methods to US manufacturing', *Journal of Business Strategy*, 5, pp. 10-19.

Taylor, M. and Thrift, N. (1986), 'New theories of multinational corporations', in Taylor, M. and Thrift, N. (eds.), *Multinationals and the restructuring of the world economy*, pp. 1-20, Croom Helm, London.

Taylor, W. (1990), 'Can big owners make a big difference?', *Harvard Business Review*, 68, pp. 70-72, 74-75, 78, 80-82.

Teece, D.J. (1986a), 'Transaction cost economics and the multinational enterprise', *Journal of Economic Behavior and Organization*, 7, pp. 21-45.

Teece, D.J. (1986b), 'Profiting from technological innovation: implications for integration, collaboration, licensing and public policy', *Research Policy*, 15, pp. 285-305.

Teece, D.J. (1985), 'Multinational enterprise, internal governance, and industrial organization', *American Economic Review Papers and Proceedings*, 75, pp. 233-238.

Tejima, S. (1993), 'Future prospects of Japanese foreign direct investment (FDI) in the 1990s, based on the trend and the features of Japanese FDI in the 1980s', *Exim Review*, 13(1), pp. 43-95.

Toothill, J.N. (1961), *Inquiry in the Scottish economy; report of a committee appointed by the Scottish Council (Development and Industry)*, Scottish Council, Edinburgh.

Toyo Keizai Shimpo (1993), *Japanese overseas investments, 1992*, Tokyo Keizai Shimpo, Tokyo, (in Japanese).

Tsurumi, Y. (1976), *The Japanese are coming: a multinational spread of Japanese firms*, Cambridge, Ma., Ballinger.

Turok, I. (1993), 'Inward investment and local linkages; how deeply embedded is Silicon Glen?', *Regional Studies*, 27(5), pp. 401-417.

UNCTD (1994), *World investment directory*, United Nations, New York.

UNCTD (1993), *World investment directory*, United Nations, New York.

UNCTD (1992), *World investment report - 1992*, United Nations, New York.

UNCTD (1991), *World investment report - 1991*, United Nations, New York.

United Nations (1984), *Work related to the definition of transnational corporations*, United Nations, New York.

United Nations (1973), *Multinational corporations in world development*, United Nations, New York.

United States Department of Commerce (1991), *Foreign investment in the United States*, US Department of Commerce, Washington, D.C.

United States General Accounting Office (1988), *Foreign investment: growing Japanese presence in the US auto industry*, US General Accounting Office, Washington, D.C.

US Foreign Investment, Business International Corp.

US News and World Report (1988), 'How Japan is winning Dixie', *US News and World Report*, 9 May, pp. 43-45, 48-51, 54-55, 57.

Van de Ven, A.H. (1992), 'Suggestions for studying strategy process', *Strategic Management Journal*, 13 (Special Issue), pp. 169-188.

Vernon, R. (1974), 'The location of economic activity', in Dunning, J.H. (ed.), *Economic analysis and the multinational enterprise*, Allen and Unwin, London.

Vernon, R. (1971), *Sovereignty at bay: the multinational spread of US enterprises*, New York, Basic Books.

Vernon, R. (1966), 'International investment and international trade in the product cycle', *Quarterly Journal of Economics*, 80, pp. 190-207.

Vernon, R. and Wells, L.T. (1991), *The economic environment of international business*, Prentice-Hall, Englewood Cliffs, NJ.

von Hippel, E. (1988), *The sources of innovation*, Oxford University Press, Oxford.

Wang, A. (1986), *Lessons; an autobiography*, Addison-Wesley, Reading, MA.

Ward, S. (1994), 'Trends in the location of corporate headquarters, 1969-1989', *Urban Affairs Quarterly*, 29, pp. 468-78.

Warf, B. (1989), 'Telecommunications and the globalization of financial services', *Professional Geographer*, 41(3), pp. 257-71.

Watts, H.D. (1980a), *The large industrial enterprise: some spatial perspectives*, London: Croom Helm.

Watts, H.D. (1980b), 'The location of European direct investment in the United Kingdom', *Tijdschrift voor Econ. en Soc. Geografie*, 71(1), pp. 3-14.

Watts, H.D. (1979), 'Large firms, multinationals, and regional development: some new evidence from the United Kingdom', *Environment and Planning A*, 11, pp. 71-81.

Weber, A. (1929), *Alfred Weber's theory of the location of industries*, The University of Chicago Press, Chicago.

Webley, S. (1979), *Foreign direct investment in the United States: opportunities and impediments*, British-North American Committee.

Weston, J.F., Chung, K.S. and Hoag, S.E. (1990), 'Mergers restructuring and corporate control', Prentice Hall, Englewood Cliffs, NJ.

Wheeler, J.O. (1988), 'The corporate role of large metropolitan areas in the United States', *Growth and Change*, 19(2), pp. 75-86.

Wheeler, J.O. and Mitchelson, R.L. (1989), 'Informational flows among major metropolitan areas of the United States', *Annals of the Association of American Geographers*, 79, pp. 523-43.

Williamson, O.E. (1985), *The economic institutions of capitalism*, Free Press, New York.

Williamson, O.E. (1979), 'Transaction-cost economics: the governance of contractual relations', *The Journal of Law and Economics*, 22, pp. 233-261.

Williamson, O.E. (1975), *Markets and hierarchies: analysis and antitrust implications*, Free Press, New York.

Wilson, B.D. (1980), 'The propensity of multinationals to expand through acquisitions', *Journal of International Business Studies*, 11, Spring-Summer, pp. 59-65.

Woodward, D.P. (1992), 'Locational determinants of Japanese manufacturing startups in the United States', *Southern Economic Journal*, 58, pp. 690-708.

Wright, R.W. (1984), *Japanese business in Canada, the elusive alliance*, Institute for Research on Public Policy, Montreal.

Wu, F. (1993), 'Stepping out the door: China's overseas investment', *China Business Review*, 4, November-December, pp. 14-19.

Yamawaki, H. (1991), 'Location decisions of Japanese multinational firms in European manufacturing industries', in Hughes, K. (ed.), *European competitiveness*, Cambridge University Press, Cambridge.

Yeon, Y.D. (1992), 'The determinants of Korean foreign direct investment in manufacturing industries', *Weltwirtschaftliches Archiv*, 128(3), pp. 527-41.

Yip, G.S. (1982), *Barriers to entry: a corporate strategy perspective*, Lexington, Lexington Books.

Young, S. (1984), 'The foreign-owned manufacturing sector', in Hood, N. and Young, S. (eds.), *Industry policy and the Scottish economy*, Edinburgh University Press, Edinburgh, pp. 93-127.

Due to a word processing error the references to chapters 4,9,10 and 11 are incomplete. These missing references may be obtained in several ways. For those readers wanting an electronic copy:

http://www.sparky.sscl.uwo.ca/FDI_ref.html

or FTP site at host:sscl.uwo.ca user:anonymous in directory [.FDI] with the file called FDI_REF_TXT.

If a paper copy is required, please contact the editors at the following address:

Dr M Green
Department of Geography
University of Western Ontario
London, Ontario, CANADA
N6A 5C2

Fax: 519 661 3750
E-mail:GREEN@sscl.uwo.ca

The paper copy matches in size and appearance the pages of the book and can be appended to the back of the text. The editors apologize for any inconvenience caused.